THE QUESTION OF GENDER

The Question of Gender: Joan W. Scott's Critical Feminism
IS VOLUME 4 IN THE SERIES

21ST CENTURY STUDIES
Center for 21st Century Studies
University of Wisconsin–Milwaukee
MERRY WIESNER-HANKS, GENERAL EDITOR

Terror, Culture, Politics: Rethinking 9/11
Edited by Daniel J. Sherman and Terry Nardin

Museums and Difference
Edited by Daniel J. Sherman

The State of Sovereignty: Territories, Laws, Populations
Edited by Douglas Howland and Luise White

THE QUESTION
OF GENDER

Joan W. Scott's Critical Feminism

Edited by Judith Butler and Elizabeth Weed

INDIANA UNIVERSITY PRESS
BLOOMINGTON AND INDIANAPOLIS

This book is a publication of

Indiana University Press
601 North Morton Street
Bloomington, Indiana 47404-3797 USA

iupress.indiana.edu

Telephone orders	800-842-6796
Fax orders	812-855-7931
Orders by e-mail	iuporder@indiana.edu

∞ The paper used in this publication meets the minimum requirements of the American National Standard for Information Sciences—Permanence of Paper for Printed Library Materials, ANSI Z39.48–1992.

Manufactured in the United States of America

Library of Congress Cataloging-in-Publication Data

The question of gender : Joan W. Scott's critical feminism / edited by Judith Butler and Elizabeth Weed.
    p. cm. — (21st century studies ; v. 4)
  Includes bibliographical references and index.
  ISBN 978-0-253-35636-9 (cloth : alk. paper) — ISBN 978-0-253-22324-1 (pbk. : alk. paper) 1. Sex role. 2. Feminist theory. 3. Feminism. 4. Women—History. 5. Scott, Joan Wallach. I. Butler, Judith, [date]- II. Weed, Elizabeth, [date]-
  HQ1075.Q47 2011
  305.4201—dc22

2011004520

1   2   3   4   5   16   15   14   13   12   11

CONTENTS

Introduction

JUDITH BUTLER AND ELIZABETH WEED

In a 2008 essay, Joan W. Scott relays a telling story about the academic discomfort that posing questions can produce.[1] When she first submitted her essay, "Is Gender a Useful Category of Historical Analysis?" to the *American Historical Review (AHR),* the editors asked her to remove the question mark, explaining that question marks were not allowed in the titles of articles. They could not simply drop the question mark without losing the sense of the title. If the question mark were simply missing, the question would still be there, but deflated, deprived of the punctuation mark without which it does not make sense. Of course, the title that was accepted, "Gender: A Useful Category of Historical Analysis," is an assertion and a declaration, however modest. The insertion of the colon makes us think, "Gender, what is gender? What comes after the colon will tell us what it is." What follows is then a kind of understatement: useful. If it is useful, it is not useless, but that makes us wonder who thought it was useless to begin with? If it were to have been declarative and more bold, it could have read "In Praise of Gender as a Useful Category of Analysis." "Useful" is most emphatically not "destructive" or "revolutionary" and not even "critical." One wonders whether "useful" was meant to compensate in an academic forum for all the more raucous ways that gender could be discussed. Indeed, the essay could have been called, "In Praise of Non-Raucous Considerations of Gender in a Presumptively Hostile Academic Context."

More seriously, it turns out that the question mark as well as the reference to "usefulness" proved central to the definition of gender itself. The original question form that Scott wanted to preserve carried a kind of challenge. "Is gender useful or not?" implies a context that one might consult in order to track the effects of gender. So, to ask the question is to presume that there are parameters and contexts that must first be known and analyzed in order to answer the question. When the question mark is dropped, then gender appears simply as "useful" in the abstract, then so too does gender become separated from its specific historical operations and effects as well as its changing contexts. If one declares in a vacuum that gender is "useful," then is one implicitly declaring it always useful, or useful on all occasions? It is a nearly pugnacious claim: "Gender is always useful in all contexts, so don't doubt it!" Scott was precisely *not* trying to advance that polemic—although it seems as if the *AHR* somehow preferred the formulation that implied that she did. If *AHR* did not allow questions in titles, was that because questions are not the same as knowledge—indeed, may be signs of not knowing, or of not yet knowing? How does one, then, write and publish an essay that queries how fields of knowledge are formed, calling into question prevailing paradigms, within such a journal? If the question form is forbidden because of its critical potential, then it seems that only certain kinds of academic inquiries are permissible, and they do not include those that question the paradigms that establish the contours of existing domains of knowledge.

So what is the big deal? It is, after all, a simple punctuation mark that goes missing in favor of another that transforms an interrogative into an assertoric claim. "Gender" is introduced and it is "a" useful category, presumably one among others. We are solicited to imagine a full pantry of useful categories of analysis and to discover gender there, nestled between other such categories, such as class and power. It would be one category among many, useful in the same way as they are. A modest claim, a bid for inclusion in the class of useful things: an understated pluralism of useful categories of historical analysis.

But if we return the title to its question form, then something else happens. First, whoever asks the question (and whoever reads it) *does not know* in advance whether or not it is useful, and this not-knowing proves to be important. The one who poses the question has not settled on the answer in advance only to proceed to explain why it is patently and obviously true that gender is a useful category. In its question form, the title starts with the confession of a certain epistemic uncertainty. One does not know whether gender, as a category, is useful, and one does not even know how one is supposed to go about deciding that question. Some other set of terms has to intervene to help us move the question forward. From the start, however, gender is in an uncertain and unknown quantity in relation to the matter of usefulness. It may or may not be useful, but in order to know, we have to consider how gender works, and to do that, we have to look at specific historical contexts and the dynamics of gender to start to formulate an answer. We also have to know what kinds of uses we are looking for, and so to understand how usefulness will be gauged. Useful for what? We do not yet have grounds for knowing, and we do not yet have a measure for understanding what usefulness might be. But as we read, matters become more clear.

Twenty-four years after the publication of this extraordinarily important essay, Scott now argues, "I want to insist that the term *gender* is useful only as a question."[2] Indeed, she has now reversed the editorial decision of the *AHR* in 1986, showing just how much their decision to change the title rested on a misapprehension of her project. She was trying in the essay not only to ask a question about gender, but also to develop a conception of gender that required asking questions: "It is not a programmatic or methodological treatise."[3] Of course, Joan Scott is credited with having developed *a theory* of gender, but if we mean by "theory" a timeless set of precepts or principles, then we have missed the point of Scott's theoretical explorations. For Scott, theory always proceeds by way of questions, and questions are the means through which taken-for-granted presuppositions are contested and new ways of thinking and analyzing become possible (a point that brings us close to understanding in what "usefulness" consists). This became very clear at the moment within women's history when Scott, along with some other scholars, proposed that it was not enough to look at images of women in certain historical scenes or even how women are treated differentially within certain contexts. Whereas both of these kinds of inquiry have their place and even their urgency, they only make sense once we start to ask how gendered meanings are produced. In other words, we cannot take gender, or gendered meanings, for granted, since gender is precisely that which is being produced and organized over time, differently and differentially, and this ongoing production and mode of differentiation has to be understood as part of the very operation of power or, in Scott's words, "a primary way of signifying power."

This leads to two extremely important conclusions. The first has to do with contextualizing gender; the second, with seeing how gender operates in the production of apparently unrelated domains, such as class, power, politics, and history itself. To understand gender, we cannot pose the question of its ontology. It is not possible to know what gender "is" apart from the way that it is produced and mobilized; and further, it is not possible to know whether gender is a useful category of analysis unless we can first understand the purposes for which it is deployed, the broader politics it supports and helps to produce, and the geopolitical repercussions of its circulation. To say that gender does not have a single meaning or, even, that there is no such thing as "women," is simply to say that we make a mistake if we expect that gender, or the categories of women and men, are either culturally established in fixed form or timeless kinds of beings. If they "are" anything, they are historical. This means that to consider gender or to try and gauge the usefulness of the category is to ask first and foremost, how have such categories been formed, through what means, and with what meanings? Perhaps most importantly, what do they themselves produce? This brings us to the second part of the formulation. Gender is put to use in various historical situations in order to define and promote the public sphere, the principle of universality, or reason, or the body, or citizenship and enfranchisement. In this way, gender cannot be counted as one useful category of historical analysis among others (according to a model of tepid pluralism), since gender is operating to help in the very definition and historical production of major dimensions of social and political life, including labor, class, politics, and rights. It is thus a serious and critical reversal within feminist scholarship to focus not only on when women achieved rights, and through what struggles (important as that is), but how the very notion of rights was gendered from the start, and how women's struggles intervened to reshape the very meaning and range of rights. The first perspective is more or less identitarian, but the second is an example of critique, since it focuses on how gender actively produces and circumscribes a domain of knowledge or a central category of social and political life. Such an approach unleashed a wide range of questions: how is gender to be understood in relation to other prevalent concepts such as universality, equality, freedom, but also rights, civil society, private and public spheres, labor?

In this way, gender as a category never works alone. It will not do to consider it as one pantry item among others, since gender is formed in relation to other social and political modes of social organization and is itself actively producing and reproducing such modes, including the family, labor, class, slavery, imperialism, immigration politics, and the state, to name a few. Thus, to ask about gender and its uses means accepting as a point of departure a historically dynamic and complex field of analysis. Since gender is not an isolated factor or element on such a map, but is itself mobilized in a constitutive and productive relation to those other modes of organizing political life, the only way to gauge its usefulness is by tracking those effects. Gender will be useful, it seems, only under those conditions in which we can see how it works, as a mode of signifying power, to produce and sustain certain ways of organizing social and political life. If this is the task, then gender cannot be known in advance (it "is" nothing in advance), but can only be illuminated as a result of a set of specifically *historical questions that seek to know how it is at once formed in history and formative of history.* In other words, we have to suspend our compulsion to stipulate in advance what gender is in order to begin the task of analyzing gender as a useful category of historical analysis.

That said, the question remains whether this very approach to gender is still possible. Scott's approach operates at a critical distance from those modes of gender mainstreaming and other NGO deployments of "gender" as variable factors in a social analysis. Those projects tend to know in advance what gender is, and even formulate transposable methodologies to secure their object (and their funding). Scott's version of gender is distinguished from these by its critical impetus and effect. The ability to rethink analytic categories, as Wendy Brown makes clear in the epilogue to this volume, is part of the "permanent revolution" in thought that Scott's work performs. Moreover, over and against a sociological definition of gender that would presume the social making of the body without psychic remainder, Scott turns our attention to the question of sexual difference, where that difference seems to persist, even as the various ways of giving that difference meaning seem to vary. This persistent and irresolvable dilemma gives rise to phantasmatic efforts to settle the question of what a man or woman may be, and these take numerous historical forms with powerful effects within social and political life.[4]

The essays in this volume provide no resounding answer as to whether or not the category of gender remains useful.[5] They aim neither to pin down gender nor fix Scott's contribution to critical thinking, but instead address in some way the critical efficacy of "gender" more than two decades after the publication of "Gender: A Useful Category of Historical Analysis." A number of the essays address gender directly; some move quickly through gender to other critical terrain. Some of the essays offer sustained readings of Scott's own work; others take on topics ranging from the historical to the art historical, from film theory to theories of sexuality. The essays are united by a common engagement with Scott's work: throughout them, we can read the question form in action, that form of questioning that has long been the signature of Scott's work.

Judith Butler's opening essay on Joan Scott poses a question that is at once quite personal and illuminating for the volume as a whole—how to think *about* Joan Scott when she is so used to thinking *with* her as a friend and close interlocutor. Butler observes that the hesitation she feels in writing about Scott's work has a good deal to do with the way Scott herself mobilizes the scene of interlocution, how she actively engages with the critical presumptions of her interlocutors in such a way as to excite and also to consternate. This mode of critical engagement troubles the distinction between the *about* and the *with*. And it is this practice of Scott's of "speaking up and talking back" that is a force that runs through all of her work, uniting her brilliant theoretical and scholarly contributions with her political beliefs and principles. Tracing the major turns in Scott's work—women, gender, sexual difference, through paradox and critique—Butler takes a close look at the ways notions of *difference* and *change* are continuous players in Scott's critical feminism.

"The Case of History" brings together the essays of four historians and a sociologist that explore questions in the neighborhood of Scott's disciplinary home of history. There is no one history, of course, and in that sense no one *case,* as the title might suggest. The case is constituted rather by the very particular connection between historical inquiry and *change,* and by the considerable challenges Scott has brought to the ways historians think about notions of sameness and difference that underpin theories of change. The Spanish historian Miguel Cabrera looks at the ways that Scott questions the very premises of social history in her theorization of the categories of language, experience, and identity. Cabrera argues that Scott's rethinking and reanimation of these "cornerstone notions" of historical research make her one of the most important architects of the new historiography that emerged in the past two decades. Engaging with this new historiography, Mary Louise Roberts looks at the ways Sarah Bernhardt and Rosa Bonheur used eccentricity to produce and manage their celebrity. Roberts argues that since both eccentricity and celebrity were emerging notions in nineteenth-century France, the two were able to challenge restrictive norms of womanhood by creatively exploiting the "hyper-individualism" of the eccentric.

Demonstrating that the category of gender can be useful outside of its Western provenance, Mrinalini Sinha uses it to examine the collective politics of Indian women in colonial India and finds there a surprising genealogy for liberalism. What she reveals is not a footnote to the narrative of Western liberalism, but a particular logic of gender that recasts both the supposed universality of European liberalism and the history of the citizen-subject in colonial India. Elora Shehabuddin turns to a more contemporary imperialist project in her analysis of the ways gender has recently been used to shore up the U.S. "war on terror." At a time when a critical feminism is most urgently needed, a monolithic feminism has helped construct a monolithic Islam in order to once again "save" Muslim women. At the same time, Muslim feminist efforts are effaced. In a discussion of the vicissitudes of "gender" in contemporary France, sociologist Éric Fassin shows the way emancipatory movements for "sexual democracy"—such as for gay marriage—have become racialized in a troubling way, reacting against Muslims and other "others" in the name of sexual modernity. For Fassin, such a turn demonstrates the way sexual democracy, like gender, can be a double-edged sword.

The essays in "Seeing the Question" address in different ways the elusiveness of the category of gender in visual texts, questioning whether or not to see is in any simple way to know. Surveying the state of her discipline, art historian Mary Sheriff is critical of early feminist readings that replaced canonical interpretations of art with, to her mind, similarly inflexible gendered interpretations and proposes instead strategies for rereading texts that preserve the instability of gender. Analyzing an image that joined a female dancer and a printing press, art historian Janis Bergman-Carton reveals how the very instability of gender offered late nineteenth-century artists, printers, and dealers ways to negotiate symbolically the shifting relationships between high artistic creation and commercial reproduction. She argues that far from being a mechanical couple, the image serves to suggest a new and self-generating art form. For film theorist Mary Ann Doane, the problem with "gender" is that however unstable it might be, it always inevitably has a "contract with the notion of identity," and this through the stabilizing process of *recognition*. She examines the ways the device of the female-face-as-screen serves, in both avant-garde and mainstream cinema, to stage and manage the anxieties about knowability and intelligibility that attend the spread of representational technologies in the twentieth century.

The next three essays, grouped under the title "Body and Sexuality in Question," question corporality and sexuality in different ways. Gayle Salamon turns to Maurice Merleau-Ponty's *Phenomenology of Perception* for a generative mode of theorizing trans embodiment. Taking up Merleau-Ponty's notions of bodily potentiality, his understanding of the ambiguity of the sexual schema, and his thoughts on the flesh, Salamon offers a dynamic way of thinking about trans embodiment that displaces all too familiar theoretical impasses. Intervening in the division between queer theory and feminism—a division that figures "queer" as liberatory and feminism as moralizing and limiting—Lynne Huffer engages with Michel Foucault's little-read 1961 book, *Folie et déraison: Histoire de la folie à l'âge classique,* translated in 2006 as *History of Madness.* She argues that this book challenges the foundational assumptions of queer theory and, in doing so, offers possibilities for a postmoral ethics of lived experience that values a generative convergence of feminist and queer approaches to sexuality. Elizabeth Weed looks at the different kinds of rhetorical work done by the category of gender and by the psychoanalytic notion of sexual difference. She argues that in the writing of Joan Scott, the "useful" category of gender figures a plenitude of meaning, while sexual difference figures its impossibility.

In the epilogue, Wendy Brown is struck by two strains that run through a number of the essays: a decided turn to the ethical as distinct from the political, and a frustration with the co-optability of gender and sexual equity projects by nonprogressive groups. In order to sustain the work of the political—in concert with the ethical and against co-optation—she urges us to look at Joan Scott's example, to Scott's "incisive appreciation of paradoxical political discourse" and to her "deep commitment to critique, to 'thinking in time.'"

In asking whether gender is a useful category of analysis, this volume also alerts us to *the ways in which gender is used* as a category of analysis. We see, through these diverse essays, that gender is, by definition, neither emancipatory nor nefarious. Its meaning can only be determined by its usage; hence, it is always bound up with operations of power that demand complex analyses in which we cannot claim to know in advance what we will find. A testimony to the complexity of gender, the volume is also a testament to Joan Scott, whose work continues to offer us a model of how to pay attention to complexity, how to find the questions to ask, and how to persist in asking—especially when the terrain is unknown, and in spite of those who wish the questions were already settled—when, clearly, they are not.

NOTES

1. Joan W. Scott, "AHR Forum: Unanswered Questions," *American Historical Review,* 113 (December 2008): 1422–1430.

2. Ibid., 1422.

3. Ibid., 1423.

4. See Joan W. Scott, "Fantasy Echo: History and the Construct of Identity," *Critical Inquiry* 27 (Winter 2001): 284–304.

5. Most of the essays were written initially for a conference held at the Center for 21st Century Studies at the University of Wisconsin–Milwaukee in May 2007, "In Terms of Gender: Crosscultural and Interdisciplinary Perspectives." The one piece not written for the conference is the essay by Miguel Cabrera.

PART 1
READING JOAN WALLACH SCOTT

CHAPTER ONE

Speaking Up, Talking Back

Joan Scott's Critical Feminism

JUDITH BUTLER

I confess that this is not an easy task—to think *about* Joan W. Scott as a thinker—since it is different from what I usually do, which is thinking *with* Joan. This doesn't mean that we always share each other's view, but it does mean that I always have her in mind. How does one, then, transform one's interlocutor into the topic of an essay? She is the one I write with or to, not about, so I am stumbling as I try to think about Joan Scott's work outside this interlocutory frame. The only way to do this, it seems, is to think about the scene of interlocution itself, and to ask myself not only why I write to Joan, for Joan, but also why I write with Joan, and how the circuit of this conversation has sustained and vexed me for the last twenty years. One reason I write *to* her and *with* her has to do with her own relation to the scene of interlocution. And so I want to begin in a way that might seem odd, might seem initially, at least, to be at a distance from the concerns of social history, the history of feminism, feminist critique and the problem of history, or the politics of equality and difference. Scott is, of course, known not only for her central engagements in all those fields, and I want to consider what we mean when we say she is centrally *engaged*. One way she is centrally engaged is that she speaks to, speaks out, and even speaks or talks back in ways that tend to cause excitement and consternation. My suggestion is that Scott's own mode of address—understood as a way of engaging critically with the presumptions of her audience—actually has everything to do with the questions of social history and left-liberal principles. I even want to suggest that we might trace a certain pattern of address from *The Glassworkers of Carmaux* to her recent work on academic freedom.[1]

Before I attempt to make clear this mode of address, let me recount in a summary way some of the major turns in her publishing career. If one conducts a quick review of her major works, one finds general acclaim for her first book, an effort to understand the glassworkers of Carmaux as a socially constituted group that took up a specific labor struggle. The subsequent move into feminist questions of history, known predominantly through her work with Louise Tilly in *Women, Work, and Family,* surprised some historians who noted that there was but one endnote dedicated to a woman in the first book.[2] The work with Louise Tilly very clearly began her influential argument that the collective subject of history could not be thought as uniform or homogenous, and that the subject in question was riven by inequalities that were essential to its formation. Moreover, if one were to move from a consideration of the formation of the subject to an account of the transformative action of the collective subject, it becomes clear that, for Scott, opportunities for action are not determined, but result from contingent and converging historical effects. In both of these early works, the question that Scott posed is, how does change take place over time? Where causal notions of action and the unity of the subject used to reign, we find that questions of inequality, of difference, and of historically shifting and open-ended chances for action came to the fore. Thus, the monolithic (uniform or homogenous) concept of the collective subject as well as the causal notion of agency suffered some setbacks in the course of those two early works.

Just as the relative absence of women in her first book surprised critics, the subsequent turn to "women" was surprising to others. And yet, the next turn was even more surprising: in *Gender and the Politics of History,* Scott made her strong and provocative case for the linguistic turn within history, a move that scandalized some historians who expected a different version of social history, but clearly incited others to new directions in research. In this landmark text, Scott also formulated a certain paradoxical condition of politics that came to structure her writing from the Sears case through her work on the French feminist struggle for political rights and *parité.* She made this paradoxical condition clear in *Only Paradoxes to Offer:*

> Feminism was a protest against women's political exclusion; its goal was to eliminate "sexual difference" in politics, but it had to make its claims on behalf of "women" (who were discursively produced through "sexual difference"). To the extent that it acted for "women," feminism produced the "sexual difference" it sought to eliminate. This paradox—the need both to accept and to refuse sexual difference—was the constitutive condition of feminism as a political movement throughout its long history.[3]

Let us try to understand how sexual difference is that for which there is a need "both to accept and refuse." Feminism is understood as that movement which had to make its claims on behalf of women and which had to oppose those forms of sexual difference that produced the exclusion of women. If we are to narrow in on what the claim of feminism actually is, it is invariably two-fold: it speaks on behalf of women, it understands and avows that the category of women is produced through sexual difference; and it seems to refuse a version of sexual difference. If we ask which version of sexual differ-ence this is, Scott makes clear that it is produced through historical and cul-tural means, indissociable from power, and so not only or exclusively a bio-logical difference. This is a tricky claim to make, since it difficult to imagine any version of biological sexual difference that is not articulated through one matrix of power or another. So, to the extent that sexual difference is under-stood as biological difference, it is invariably seized upon by cultural and his-torical forces; in other words, biological difference cannot be thought apart from that seizure by forms of power operative in culture and history. This last thought, of course, has consequences for how we understand the biological sciences as well as theories of power, culture, and history. Sexual difference is not a term that belongs over there, with biology, and then gets transformed in the course of a subsequent and separable cultural and historical articulation over here.[4] Rather, sexual difference is precisely that which, whether in the biological or the cultural sciences, occasions a set of shifting articulations. If we conclude further that no one articulation of sexual difference exhausts its meaning, that is because we never find this difference outside of an articula-tion, and yet, no single articulation seizes it for all time. Moreover, sexual difference is as much articulated by forms of power as it is a matrix for ac-tively articulating such modes of power. We are not only talking about sexual difference as a "constructed" difference (though some do that), but in Scott's work, sexual difference is a matrix through which and by which certain kinds of articulation take place. If that seems like a conundrum, it probably is; but it is a conundrum without which we cannot function, and it is even a constitu-tive conundrum of feminist theory. Scott's point, though, goes further than this, since, you will remember, feminism has to do with making a claim.

How do we understand this feminist claim? It speaks on behalf of the category of women; it seems to eliminate established understandings of the category of women according to which women are excluded from the concept of the social subject, or conceived only through a matrix of presumptive ine-quality. At first it seems that feminism seems to have given itself the task to speak on behalf of the category that it simultaneously seeks to eliminate. What first appears to be a contradiction, however, is reformulated in more promising ways when this procedure of representation and negation is understood as a temporal development. If what the claim seeks to oppose, even to eliminate, are certain historically specific modes of sexual difference, that claim does not seek to negate every form of that difference. On the contrary, it seems to show that those versions of difference are historical, subject to change and to alteration. Time, it turns out, is crucial to Scott's understanding of feminism, and to the kind of history she writes, and writes about. To negate the mode of sexual difference that is bound up with inequality, for instance, is not to obliterate sexual difference per se. And even if there is no sexual difference per se, that is no reason to identify sexual difference with its historically established versions. After all, sexual difference is not only made or constructed, but is itself a matrix for articulating domains of life we may not immediately associate with sexual difference, such as culture, history, and power, to give a few of the most salient examples. To seek to negate a mode of sexual difference that reinstitutes inequality, for instance, is not only to expose its historical status, but to try to intervene in the historical process that sexual difference names, forms, and activates. To negate that established and problematic mode of sexual difference is thus at once to try to establish a new mode; at this point, we move from an apparent impasse that requires that we accept and refuse sexual difference to a process of social and historical transformation, a mode of re-articulation that goes by the name of sexual difference as well. Only if we approach the problem statically does it appear that speaking on behalf of the very category of "women" to eliminate that category culminates in the awkward (but not impossible) situation of seeking to eliminate the condition of one's own speaking—the very social designation that makes one's claim intelligible. But this contradiction would follow only if the conditions of one's own speaking were so highly restrictive that to speak from that condition no longer makes sense or had become effectively impossible. At such a limit, one is compelled to *speak back* to the historical conditions articulated by and through sexual difference; in other words, one is compelled to *speak up* for a new way of speaking, to enact that speaking and so to negate one thing and affirm another, in the very same act of speech.

Let's reflect upon this paradox that follows from a consideration of sexual difference in the kind of formulation in Scott's work. In her extremely influential essay on a 1988 sex discrimination suit against Sears, Scott sought to understand whether feminists had to choose between two apparently incompatible sets of arguments.[5] There were those who thought that women ought to be treated the same as men, and that questions of sexual difference should be set aside in order to establish egalitarian work conditions, including compensation scales. And others used a "difference" argument to suggest that the history of women's work produced distinct and differentiated patterns of socialization and employment trajectories, suggesting that women's work is not the same as men's, and ought to be restrictively conceived as a consequence. The argument was waged in court in 1986 with two feminist historians, with Alice Kessler-Harris taking the first position in favor of equality and Rosalind Rosenberg taking the second in favor of difference. Scott arrives on the scene with her trenchant analysis two years later to suggest that the stand-off between equality and difference is unnecessary. Actually, what Scott does is to make a highly nuanced intervention, suggesting that what appears as a necessary stand-off does not have to culminate in a static impasse, but rather in a paradox—a term that will become increasingly central to Scott's subsequent work—that cannot be thought outside the problem of time and the operation of a specific mode of historical transformation.

So one point I am hoping to make here is that what might seem like contradiction or impasse becomes paradox, and paradox itself is a mode or mechanism of historical change. I began by calling attention to another argument in Scott's work, especially in the first two books on social history: there is no monocausal account of social change, and historical conditions do not act in deterministic ways. Indeed, not only are historical conditions multiple, but the modes of their convergence and contestation are precisely what produce the never fully predictable conditions of change. To put it even more precisely, contestation and convergence are *conditions* for change. This admittedly abstract formulation is meant to illuminate the way change happens: the particular situations of speech, speaking out and speaking back, become more important as Scott's work develops—especially in *Only Paradoxes to Offer, Gender and the Politics of History, The Politics of the Veil,* and the recent work on academic freedom.[6] Change also happens by way of paradox, and this seems to have been established in the early work on feminist history in which Scott repeatedly underscored how sexual difference works to institute historical change through the action of paradox. These two dimensions of the work—the transformative situation of speech or expression and the mechanisms of historical change—are related, since they each find a certain promise in a paradoxical situation. The claim to rights, for instance, takes place on the basis of a certain historical condition of women, and yet the claim to rights is itself a disruption, if not an effort to eliminate, those same conditions. One could only take this to be a contradiction if the conditions referred to *as the basis* for the claim are the same as those that would be maintained *as a result* of the claim. But the whole point of the claim is to change the conditions, and so we have to ask how paradox functions as the modus operandi of historical change. Political claims have their own historical specificity and development; in this way, they are not like most philosophical arguments (*pace* Hegel and Marx). This means that the paradoxical formulations that Scott comes to see as essential to feminism are not to be understood as syllogisms, as purely logical conundrums—formal and ahistorical—but as modes of discourse, broadly construed, functioning in the service of social and historical change.

As far back as Scott's graduate work in social history and in her first book, on the glassworkers of Carmaux, Scott was interested in the problem of historical change. In my view, this has never ceased to be her academic interest and goal. Further, ever since that early work, Scott was arguing with those who sought to understand change monocausally. The monocausalists, as we might call them, took at least two forms. There were the historical determinists who thought some inexorable force in history would work its way toward change according to the laws of dialectic. There were, as well, those who believed in heroic narratives, seeking to understand change as the effect of extraordinary exercises of individual will. Scott's problem with both of these views is that they failed to think historically enough about the problem of change, and that a closer scrutiny of how change happens shows that both the idea of deterministic history and the extraordinarily volitional subject were better understood through the complex interplay of various historical forces. If the deterministic explanation contravened the subject entirely, the volitional explanation presumed a subject not only derived from the historical resources of individualism, but emphatically masculinist. The early work sought to show that the revolutionary subject, presumptively masculine, was not singlehandedly responsible for revolutionary change. This was as true of the idealized revolutionary personality as it was for the idealized collective subject. The second and third parts of *Gender and the Politics of History* make this case in a successive way, first through the critique of E. P. Thompson and then through the careful study of women's work in mid–nineteenth-century Paris.[7] The problem with Thompson's account of the agency of the working class was not only that it subordinated or effaced women's work. Scott was not trying to make a claim for the simple inclusion of a consideration of women in the existing framework; rather she made the much stronger argument that the very framework depended upon that exclusion. To show this, Scott asked a different kind of question, one that relied on Thompson's formulation, but also opposed it. Thompson asked after the historical conditions under which the "working class" was discovered and elaborated. The concept of the working class comes into existence at a certain point in history, and that emergence entails certain consequences. We are not to take the working class for granted as a point of departure for thinking about historical change, asking what the working class did, what effects their actions had. We have to ask first: Through what means does the "working class" emerge as a historical category? If the working class is itself a historically specific emergence, and its arrival as a historical category is the consequence of a certain change in our understanding of history, then the emergence of the category (or concept) is itself a historical change worth noting. According to this formulation, the working class is not to be taken for granted merely as an agent of historical change (though it may well become such an agent), but the concept itself is an effect of historical change. If it becomes agentic, as it surely does, we are under a new obligation to regard that agency as the effect of this historical change, the agentic consequence made possible by certain historical effects. This formulation has implications for how we understand agency to emerge within historical processes rather than as a deterministic cause that mobilizes and structures a historical sequence or as a consequence of volitional acts that presuppose an already formed volitional subject with occasionally extraordinary capacities.

Scott's way of insisting on the historical status of such categories has been to pose the question of "how." One of her major criticisms of Thompson was that he managed to historicize class, in the sense that he could show *that* it came into being as a historical concept in certain specific times and places, but he was not able to attend to the mechanisms by and through which the category of class came into being. In drawing attention precisely to these mechanisms, Scott brings us back to the problem of sexual difference, recalling the difficulty of conceptualizing women's work. The exclusion of women's work from the dominant narratives of the working class were, for Scott, clear signs that the conceptualization of the working class both relied upon and restaged this exclusion. In asking how the conceptual field within which the working class became thinkable relied upon a presumptively masculinist conception of agency as well as the marginalization of women's work, Scott showed how the exclusion of women's work and participation in political struggles were essential to the narratives of working class history. Hence, the historical problem is thus larger than the one that Thompson identified. The question is not simply when and where the idea of the working class came into being, but, more specifically, *through what means,* and whether the means through which the dominant ideas of the working class emerged were the same means through which women's work was marginalized and effaced. These conceptual schemes not only come into being historically, but they actively constrain our ideas of what history can and will become. Thus, we cannot seek recourse to a taken-for-granted notion of women's experience to rebut a masculinist narrative; rather, we have to see how a certain kind of conceptual scheme has come to organize that mode of social life we call "experience." This is not only an epistemological problem, but a historical one, since such schemes become contested and changeable, taking and losing form, taking and losing hold, extending and losing their hegemony. And Scott's writing, we might say, not only describes this process, but enacts it; in rewriting history, she enters this historical process precisely to contest and undo that hegemony. In this sense, the writing of women's history *depends upon* the preliminary efforts of Thompson and others to historicize labor and the working class, but it also *speaks back* to such histories, showing how they fail to consider the mechanisms by which certain conceptions of class are installed and, subsequently, how gender difference functions as one of those key mechanisms. These are not timeless mechanisms, but specific historical modalities that produce intelligible historical phenomena through means of marginalization and exclusion. To ask historical questions rigorously and well means asking the question of how gender difference functions in the making not only of the working class, but of what counts as history itself.

Scott's writing asserts that difference, and so makes a difference in the very account of historical change that is at issue for social historians. I want to suggest that she does this by speaking back to established modes of historiography, but often through turning and revising lexicons she has received from those established modes. This speaking back is a way of opening up a new conceptual field for history. It is a kind of paradoxical speech that calls into question the conditions of its own speaking, enacting one mode of historical contestation. Those conditions—in this case, social history—make this speaking subject possible, but also require a restriction and effacement that any speaking, if it is to be speaking, must speak against. And the point of the speaking against is not to become locked in battle, but to expose and undo the exclusionary means through which dominant categories are installed, to instate the new, and to open a different future. This means that paradox is not only a way to account for historical change, but a way of making historical change and opening up a future. This is not a future in which differences are reconciled, but one in which ongoing contestation reveals and enacts the historicity of the terms in question, such as gender, work, and equality.

In *Gender and the Politics of History,* Scott has reviewed the equality/difference debate, and in the course of her critical reflections, has suggested that we have to refuse those ideas of difference that take established social meanings of women's work for granted as well as those ideas of equality that petition for inclusion in a concept of work that fails to take into account how the very concept has been constructed through sexual difference (the ruling out of women's work in the making of the relevant ideas of work). She writes,

In histories of feminism and in feminist political strategies there needs to be at once attention to the operations of difference and an insistence on differences, but not a simple substitution of multiple for binary differences, for it is not a happy pluralism we ought to invoke. The resolution of the "difference dilemma" comes neither from ignoring nor embracing difference as it is normatively constituted.[8]

Scott offers a key distinction here for thinking about difference that effectively differentiates her view from those who represented the "difference" position in the Sears case. There is one idea of difference which takes established meanings of gender as constituting the difference that we call gender difference. This is a normatively constituted notion of difference. Scott is about to give us a different notion of difference, and so is subjecting the term "difference" to a difference, and we are asked to follow precisely here. Notice in what follows how something called a critical feminist position is also differentiated from other forms of feminism:

> It seems to me that the critical feminist position must always involve two moves: the first, systematic criticisms of the operations of categorical difference, exposure of the kinds of exclusions and inclusions—the hierarchies—it constructs, and refusal of their ultimate "truth." A refusal, however, not in the name of an equality that implies sameness or identity but rather (and this is the second move) of an equality that rests on differences—differences that confound, disrupt, and render ambiguous the meaning of any fixed binary opposition.[9]

There is then an idea of feminine difference established through socialization and the accumulated effect of received meanings, a notion of feminine difference that presumes the workings of a unilinear and cumulative history of its making. But then there is another kind of difference, one that is plural without being pluralistic (which is after all, just another notion of unity). This second kind of difference names the difference between settled binary oppositions and those historical forces that contest and undo that binarism; and a difference from the binary, rather than a difference within it—a difference that must be multiple, but which cannot be assembled under a single term without reinstalling the binary logic that Scott seeks to undo. It is important, as you can see, that this second sense of "differences" not be given a single or unifying "content": the second is the difference that gender makes in the course of conducting a critique of binary oppositions, but it can only fulfill this critical operation by not being tied to a single content. If it were, that would be the end of its critical function as difference.

I wrote *Gender Trouble* in the late 1980s in large part at the Institute for Advanced Study in Princeton where, at Scott's invitation, I spent a year in the company of several extremely interesting scholars who were working on the theme of gender.[10] If I remember correctly, the call for fellowship applications stated that the ongoing seminar of the year would be dedicated to "the meanings of male and female." At that time, Scott was in the midst of finishing *Gender and the Politics of History.* It is probably fair to say that the term "gender" was central to both of our thinking at that time, although you can probably see from the quotations I've supplied here today how, for Scott, sexual difference had a critical function, and for me, it tended to be equated with modes of heterosexual presumption that I opposed. In Scott's vernacular, I understood "sexual difference" to be an established, normative framework that one had to oppose. It was always clear that she distinguished between those modes of normatively constituted gender difference (ways of arguing that drew substantial conclusions about what women do, the kind of work that constitutes women's work, on the basis of what they have traditionally done within specific historical and geographical contours) and a critical view on the very construction of those differences. As a result "sexual difference" was, for her, a framework for understanding how historical differences are established and disestablished through time. And in this way, it was only through such a framework that one could criticize those sociological approaches to gender that merely describe what gender is or does and pay no attention to (a) how it is produced differentially, at what cost, and with what implications and (b) what concepts it itself produces. At first, I found in the term "gender" a way of differentiating a mainly culturally constructivist position from an essentialist one, and I identified the essentialist one with "sexual difference." (I see little reason to rehearse those exhausted debates at the present time.) So I was assuming that "sexual difference" was the name for those normatively constituted identities that Joan was subjecting to a critical perspective in the name of sexual difference. Indeed, at the time, if you asked her to define gender, she would seek recourse to sexual difference, certainly not as a naturalistic or metaphysical concept, but as a very specific set of mechanisms for the historical production of socially differentiated relations. Indeed, what tended to be most important were the historical fields that are produced in part through gendered means: the idea of work, the working class, power, culture, history itself. On the one hand, she showed how concepts of class could not be historically understood if we did not understand how sexual difference was functioning in the articulating of the terms of class itself; on the other hand, she was showing that all the terms that we associate with socially critical political analysis—work, politics, universality, equality, to name a few—were themselves also produced in specific ways through the production of sexual difference. Sexual difference was not the cause, but rather, the means for articulation, and the mechanism for historical reproduction and change. As a result, it has no necessary content, but it always carries some historical content or another. It is always in the business of producing one historical reality or another.

I point this out since it probably should be said, especially within the context of a volume called *The Question of Gender,* that both Joan and I have found ourselves in semi-private moments saying, "enough already with gender!"[11] The reason for such exasperation has to do with the way gender has become operationalized in "gender research projects" under the auspices of the European Union, or some ways of defining gender studies in the United States. In many of these instances, gender is taken for granted as the point of departure for a set of descriptions of social practices, understood as an adjective that qualifies established objects of social science: gendered work, gendered performance, gendered play. In fact, there is little inquiry on the *production* of difference, and little inquiry on how difference works in the production of other kinds of categories. When Scott sought to show that sexual difference was both produced and productive, and queried the region that binds those two modalities, she sought to establish a specifically *critical* feminism, that is, one that would *not* take normative renditions of gender for granted and that maintained a historical skepticism with respect to established binary modes of conceptualizing men and women. And though I certainly set out to upset normative accounts of gender, and to question the restriction of binary thinking on our conceptualization of gender, I worried that sexual difference was itself normative within feminism and that it worked to install heterosexuality as the presumptive mode of conceptualizing difference. Although these were, and remain, different approaches, the commitment to coming up with a critical feminism clearly bound us together in a common project, one that we understood at the time to require and to specify poststructuralism.

If there is now some exasperation with the term "gender," it may be that it has lost its purchase on a certain kind of critical thinking. So someone working in pedagogy can say that they are interested in studying young girls, their relation to emergent sexuality, the media, race relations, and more. But they may embark on this project thinking that they already know who "girls" are, that the category is itself taken for granted, without ever asking how gender is established—if and when it is. The very category by which we identify a certain group of subjects is normative—restrictive and enabling—and has to be part of any critical feminist project that does not want to rely on a field of gender meanings already established and taken for granted. To do the latter is, among other things, to ratify the status quo of gender as a consequence of one's "descriptive" procedure.

When Scott turns to the study of revolutionary French feminisms in *Only Paradoxes to Offer,* she does not simply identify her subjects through their gender. She asks how the norms and conventions of gender produce sites for the enunciation and articulation of certain kinds of revolutionary feminisms; moreover, she considers the available lexicons through which political projects are formed, and tries to understand both the constraints and the agentic possibilities that follow from those historically specific discourses (indeed, agency emerges within the field of constraint, paradoxically). When Olympe de Gouges famously speaks in radically paradoxical ways, defying available standards of consistency and coherence, we are asked to understand the convergences and discontinuities in discourse that produce, incite, and limit this speaking subject. We are not exactly invited to return to the heroic revolutionary characters who were the presumptive subjects of Scott's graduate school seminars with Harvey Goldberg at the University of Wisconsin–Madison.[12] Further, the point is not to show that there were women, too, who count as heroic revolutionary characters. In fact, these women, caught up in discourses not fully of their own making, trip and fall, emerge with political anger and rhetorical claims at the same time that they sometimes undo their own efforts by resisting dominant languages of political enfranchisement. They are different; they are the same; in other words, they mobilize discourses of specificity and of egalitarianism without being able to provide a dialectical reconciliation of the two. In this sense, the revolutionary feminists of the eighteenth and nineteenth centuries may well have prefigured the debates of the Sears case, and offered a way around that debate between equality and difference *avant la lettre.* The resistance to dialectical closure marks this radicalism off from those derived from Hegelian or Marxist histories in which the logic of resolution wins out in the end. Although that kind of closure and reconciliation is not an option here, this is less tragic than it is comic, radical, and hopeful.

Paradoxical efforts such as these continue in a different form in the book *Parité!: Sexual Equality and the Crisis of French Universalism,* in which complex and sometimes logically inconsistent strategic positions are occupied in an effort to establish equal representation for women in the *Assemblée Nationale.* In neither book do we find women who simply transcend their circumstances in heroic ways; rather, we find complex and discontinuous political strategies that are enabled by historically specific forms of political rhetoric, and that produce the situation in which those who are disenfranchised criticize the exclusionary and masculinist character of the model of enfranchisement at the

same time that they insist on enfranchisement for women. This dual operation of refusing the terms by which political enfranchisement is offered, and
yet insisting on enfranchisement, produces a powerful resistance to the logic
of non-contradiction. The point is not that one refutes and affirms enfranchisement at the same time. Rather, the form of enfranchisement that is developed and articulated on the basis of the exclusion of women proves to be a
false and insufficient form of enfranchisement. Over and against such a form,
one thus calls to be enfranchised, liberated from "enfranchisement," thus introducing a second conception of enfranchisement that overcomes the exclusion by which the first was defined. Such a paradoxical strategy relies on the
temporality of citation and disputation, and it leads to positions that are at
once whimsical and radical, mischievous and critical, rebellious, insistent,
and hopeful. How does one *break out* of a framework and *break in* at the same
time that one *breaks it up* and still make a legible claim? Whereas we might
expect that political efforts that traffic in paradox will culminate in impasse,
defeat, or self-negation, it turns out that such paradoxical rhetorical strategies
do two things: they allow for a critical perspective that also makes rights
claims; and they mobilize paradox for the production of an open future which
is constrained neither by the inevitable structural reproduction of masculin-
ism nor by the dialectical closures of certain forms of historical materialism.

One can see the term "critique" embedded in Scott's earlier work, and it
seems time and again to lead us to question how sexual difference operates to
produce and maintain notions of class, work, family, and to specify the mechanism for that production. Paradox also comes up when she tries to take account of historical change. I want to suggest that in more recent years, Scott
has written precisely on the concept of critique, on what is critical, as she has
reflected on the university and the claims of academic freedom, but also on
the history of French feminism as a history of paradox.[13] We can see the incipient formulations for this more recent work in the earlier publications on
gender, work, and the family, the Parisian garment workers, and the Sears
case, to be sure. But can we also understand how these concerns have made
their way into her work on Committee A on Academic Freedom and Tenure
of the American Association of University Professors (AAUP), her testimony
regarding academic freedom before the Pennsylvania legislature, and her
struggles to come to terms with the inheritance of certain liberal principles
regarding public speech and religious expression? In the final section of this
essay, I want to trace what I take to be a set of recurrent figures in these
works, returning first to the critique of revolutionary heroism that informs
her early work, and then to the efforts to rethink the revolutionary actor in
Only Paradoxes to Offer. This return to thinking about agency in history is

clearly addressed again in her recent work on the *parité* movement in France, a work that chronicles in great detail the actions and proclamations of a variety of feminist actors in the French political scene. In relation to these more recent works, I want to point out that speech acts, forms of writing, modes of public expression, all become crucial to revolutionary action and to understanding and fomenting social change. It wasn't just that women took up a position in public space, but that public space also became configured in such a way that women could find themselves speaking; and it wasn't just that women found sites from which to speak, but that women, as a category, became established as a site of enunciation. As a result, there is no agency *in* the subject, but we might find the potential for historical change in the sometimes convergent and sometimes divergent sites of enunciation that shifting historical forces make possible. Historical French feminists such as Jeanne Deroin and Olympe de Gouges, or indeed, contemporary French feminist activists Françoise Gaspard and Claude Servan-Schreiber, are no doubt persons, subjects, and we name them as such. But such names also belong to a concatenation of names that precede them as well as a set of discursive conditions that make their name-ability and speaking possible. That in each of these instances they are accused of betraying principles of French republicanism is all the more interesting given that they are also regarded as extending principles of equality that are clearly derived from republicanism. Such radical mischief is not just a play with words or a flirtation with impasse, but a modality of historical change, serious, patient, and outrageous.

Finally, then, it makes sense to turn to Joan Scott herself as a speaking subject, and as a scholar whose political work has been dedicated in the last years to defending and arbitrating questions of academic freedom and academic expression. Should we be surprised that this is the direction in which Scott has moved publicly? Let's consider some of the precepts that we've already established.

The first is that the conditions for efficacious political speech are both constraining and enabling. This seems true about academic freedom as well, and may be important for distinguishing between academic freedom and freedom of speech.[14] The academy not only permits certain kinds of speech, but also distinguishes the speech it protects on campuses from speech more generally protected under First Amendment principles. In her work in social history, Scott considers discursive venues for enacting social change; in her own political work, she defends precisely those safeguards that allow for the academic pursuit of radical inquiry against reactionary efforts at censorship. Interestingly enough, the kind of academic freedom that Scott defends has everything to do with the notion of the kind of work that academics do. Part of that work is not only speaking, but critical speaking, the kind that calls into question political and epistemological paradigms, even if this disturbs the sensibilities of those who would sanctify them. The point is not that academics have the right or prerogative to pursue their ideas as they wish, as if academic freedom were a personal right of expression, but that the academy is a privileged and protected site for critical practice. As the Chair of Committee A, the committee charged with overseeing academic freedom at the AAUP, Scott made plain the implications of this notion of critical practice for policy.[15] She insisted, for instance, that academic work requires "the free and open exchange of opposing ideas," a norm that disputes a single notion of truth at the same time that it disputes specious requirements for balancing political viewpoints. Scott openly opposed the Horowitz Academic Bill of Rights before the state assembly in Pennsylvania. There as elsewhere, she defended a certain idea of conflict, unresolved and irresolvable, at the core of academic work. Note how her view of academic inquiry reanimates the critical potential of paradox and the refusal of easy resolution and reconciliation: "Conflicts of values and ethics, as well as of interpretation, are part of the process of knowledge production; they inform it, drive it, trouble it."[16] One might hear something of the residual Marxist in the idea that conflict drives knowledge, but consider carefully the obligation she articulates to protect institutional conditions of academic inquiry. Scott states: "It seems to me that scholars and teachers have a responsibility not only to produce and transmit knowledge, but also to protect the institutions within which the free and open production of knowledge takes place. My academic activism is devoted to that end."[17] Is it possible to say that from the beginning of her work through the present she has been concerned with protecting the conditions of work, and still is? In her writing on academic freedom, speech is considered part of academic work, and the rights of academic freedom pertain to providing safeguards for protecting the institutional conditions for that work. In some ways this follows from her considerations of historical and contemporary French feminists, in which she situated public speech as part of political struggle—one that had to redefine not only who can speak, but what counts as politically meaningful speech. In all of these contexts, Scott is speaking out for speaking out, and making "speaking back" into part of what drives the struggle for creating something new and extending political claims for equality.

Finally, in this latter context, we can see an interesting and paradoxical relationship between liberalism and radicalism that informs Scott's work, and that has consequences for us today as we try to think through vexed issues such as secularism and academic freedom. In her essay "Academic Freedom as an Ethical Practice," Scott opens by telling the story of her father, a member of the New York Teachers Union, who was fired from his job in 1953 as part of the effort to purge Communists and their sympathizers from the public schools.[18] She explains that her father's rights to his views and to his position (both speech and workplace) were radically abrogated, and that she understood from that time on that the struggle to protect him and other such teachers was a struggle for academic freedom. Such liberal principles did not in any way conflict with her radicalism or, indeed, her father's, who was apparently fond of reading Jefferson to anyone who might care to listen. On the contrary, defending the rights of the left, including members of the Communist Party, to their views involved a strengthening of liberal principles, a consequence that might have proven contradictory for some people. After all, if liberal principles were strengthened through the defense of Communists, then does that give liberalism the edge over communism? Following from Scott's views, we misread this situation as contradictory only if we fail to grasp the process as paradox. There is no sustainable radicalism without its conditions, its protections, its institutional venues, and its recourse to rights. This doesn't make liberalism prior to Marxism, but it does establish a liberalism that must serve to protect those institutional venues in which substantive disagreements, such as those between liberalism and Marxism, can and must take place. There is no debate without a site of debate, and it is protection of that site to which academic freedom is dedicated, even if it means hosting the point of view that would trouble its own philosophical presuppositions.

At the end of Scott's tenure on Committee A at the AAUP, she found herself in an interestingly paradoxical position. She was one of the signatories on the AAUP statement opposing academic boycotts, a position that was prompted by the British Association of University Teachers' vote to support a call by Palestinian activists on an academic boycott of the state of Israel in 2005. Although Scott has publicly criticized Israeli politics, she found herself in a principled position against academic boycotts and the specific terms of the boycott in question. She did, however, agree to help coordinate a conference in which individuals with various views on the matter of the boycott might convene to openly air their differing viewpoints. As a result, she was then charged by various Zionist critics of condoning the boycott as a result of her willingness to coordinate a meeting with those whose views she did not share. What became clear in the course of a campaign against her was that her very willingness to include, acknowledge, listen to, consider, and debate the point of view she opposed was considered to be an illicit way of giving standing to the pro-boycott point of view. Some of those who argued, along with Scott, that the boycott defied principles of academic freedom could not follow Scott when, without backtracking on her earlier position, she maintained that academic freedom also means safeguarding venues for an airing of conflicts over the meaning and implications of academic freedom itself. Such debates, in her view, are part of the process of knowledge production that academic freedom is meant to defend. It was, after all, this last argument that Scott, as a then representative of the AAUP, made against the specious Academic Bill of Rights, and no one at the AAUP objected to the voicing of that principle in that context.

When Scott sought to bring together those with divergent opinions on the academic boycott of Israel, and to do so in the name of academic freedom, was Scott's public speaking paradoxical? Or was she holding out for the kind of critical complexity that makes academic freedom worth fighting for? Could she occupy both positions at once? Is it that her position was irrational, or was it that she delivered too strong a challenge to the regime of rationality within which her liberal colleagues were willing to hear? Scott is surely one of those relentlessly innovative and embattled figures whose transformative acts are worthy of historical explanation. It is no wonder that Edward Said called her "an exemplary engaged public intellectual for our time." I'm reminded of a remark she made in 1989 in an interview for *Radical History Review* when asked, "What is your sense of the place of women's history in post-modern left history?" And she replied: "permanent revolution"—a good daughter, she! But then, Scott went on to make sure her interlocutor knew such a revolution was not interested in uncritical allegiances: "Feminism has been, at least for the last two-hundred years, in an embattled, critical position in relation to liberalism and socialism. There are a lot of worse situations to be in than embattled and critical."[19]

NOTES

1. Joan W. Scott, *The Glassworkers of Carmaux: French Craftsmen and Political Action in a Nineteenth-Century City* (Cambridge, Mass.: Harvard University Press, 1974); "Academic Freedom as an Ethical Practice," *Academe* 81 (July/August 1995): 44–48; "Joan Wallach Scott on Threats to Academic Freedom," interviewed in *Academe* 91 (Sept/Oct 2005): 39–41; "Middle East Studies Under Siege," *The Link* 39 (Jan–Mar 2006): 1–12; and "Knowledge, Power, and Academic Freedom," *Social Research: An International Quarterly* 76, no. 2, (Summer 2009): 451–480.

2. Louise A. Tilly and Joan W. Scott, eds., *Women, Work, and Family* (New York: Holt, Rinehart and Winston, 1978).

3. Joan W. Scott, *Only Paradoxes to Offer: French Feminists and the Rights of Man* (Cambridge, Mass: Harvard University Press, 1996), 3–4.

4. See Charles Shepherdson, "The *Role* of Gender and the *Imperative* of Sex," in *Vital Signs: Nature, Culture, Psychoanalysis* (New York: Routledge, 2000), 85–114.

5. "The Sears Case" was first published as "Deconstructing Equality vs. Difference; or, the Uses of Post-Structuralist Theory for Feminism," *Feminist Studies* 14 (Spring 1988): 33–50. It appeared later as "The Sears Case" in *Gender and the Politics of History* (New York: Columbia University Press, 1988), 167–177.

6. Joan W. Scott, *The Politics of the Veil* (Princeton, N.J.: Princeton University Press, 2007).

7. See Scott, *Gender and the Politics of History* part 2: Gender and Class, chapter 4, "Women in *The Making of the English Working Class,*" 68–92, and part 3: Gender in History, chapter 5, "Work Identities for Men and Women: The Politics of Work and Family in the Parisian Garment Trades in 1848," 93–166.

8. Scott, *Gender and the Politics of History,* 176.

9. Ibid.

10. Judith Butler, *Gender Trouble* (New York: Routledge, 1990).

11. See Judith Butler, Éric Fassin, and Joan W. Scott, "Pour ne pas en finir avec le 'genre' . . . Table ronde," *Sociétés et Représentations* 2, 24 (2007): 285–306.

12. See Elaine Abelson, David Abraham, and Marjorie Murphy, "Interview with Joan Scott," *Radical History Review* 45 (Fall, 1989): 41–59; and Joan W. Scott, "Finding Critical History," in *Becoming Historians*, ed. James M. Banner, Jr., and John R. Gillis (Chicago: University of Chicago Press, 2009), 26–53.

13. Joan W. Scott, "The New University: Beyond Political Correctness," *Boston Review,* (March/April 1992); "The Rhetoric of Crisis in Higher Education," in *Higher Education Under Fire: Politics, Economics, and the Crisis of the Humanities,* ed. Michael Bérubé and Cary Nelson (New York: Routledge, 1995); "Les 'guerres académiques' aux États-Unis" [Academic wars in the United States], in *L'Université en question: Marché des savoirs, nouvelle agora, tour d'ivoire?* [The question of the university: Marketing knowledge, new agora, ivory tower?], ed. Julie Allard, Guy Haarscher, and Maria Puig de la Bellacasa (Brussels: Editions Labor, 2001).

14. On this point, see Matthew W. Finkin and Robert C. Post, *For the Common Good: Principles of American Academic Freedom* (New Haven, Conn.: Yale University Press, 2009).

15. Scott served on the committee of the American Association of University Professors Committee on Academic Freedom and Tenure between 1993 and 2005, and served as chair from 1999–2005.

16. Scott, "Threats to Academic Freedom," also available online at http://www.aaup.org/AAUP/pubsres/academe/2005/SO/Feat/scot.htm (accessed May 23, 2010).

17. Ibid.

18. Scott, "Academic Freedom," 44–48.

19. "Interview with Joan Scott," 57.

PART 2
THE CASE OF HISTORY

CHAPTER TWO

Language, Experience, and Identity

Joan W. Scott's Theoretical Challenge to Historical Studies

MIGUEL A. CABRERA

Translated by María Constanza Guzmán and Joshua Martin Price

This article highlights some of Joan W. Scott's theoretical challenges to historical studies over the past two decades. This period has seen not only a theoretical and conceptual renovation of historical research, but also the increasing visibility of a new movement in historiography. Scott has been one of its most important architects because of her challenge to the way we approach such basic concepts as experience, objectivity, causality, and the subject of history.

The paradigm of social history used to be based on the assumption that reality is an objective entity and that therefore the consciousness, identity, and actions of historical subjects are determined by the material conditions of their existence. From that point of view, the subjectivity and behavior of people are the expression and effect of their experience of reality, which means that the subject is conscious of meanings already embedded in reality. According to this view, the language people use to refer to the world they inhabit and even to their place in that world—indeed, the language by which they define their identities and interests and give expressive form to their beliefs—is a means of recognizing and enunciating an objective reality. Affirming the objective nature of social reality, considering consciousness and culture as representations and reflections of an objective world, and explaining the signifying practice of historical subjects as the result of a causal determination of that reality, have served as fundamental theoretical assumptions of social history.

Nevertheless, in recent years each one of these theoretical assumptions, so rooted in the common sense of historiography, has been subject to ongoing discussion and critical revision; as a result, an alternative explanatory model, based on new theoretical premises, has begun to take shape.[1] This new *post-social history* questions the notion that social and material reality is an objective entity on the model outlined above and can, therefore, causally determine the conduct of historical actors. In this account, language is not merely a means of representing reality, but also operates as a system of signification that intervenes actively in the production of meanings attributed to the real world and through which practice is organized and its meanings established. Language is not merely a repertoire or set of resources from which a subject draws, but it is also discourse, that is, a series of culturally bound conceptual means of perceiving, apprehending, and making intelligible the very notion of historical context. Consequently, linguistic concepts not only designate reality in a way that is presumptively referential, but also contribute to constructing our image of that reality, making that image inseparable from the reality itself. Therefore, they influence the way in which we experience the world and the place we have in it.

Joan Scott's work has been seminal in compelling a critical revision of the objectivist paradigm and in reconstructing theoretically the field of history. Her main contribution lies in particular in problematizing and reformulating three cornerstone notions of historical research: language, experience, and identity. Regarding the first notion, Scott argues that language is not simply a means for the transmission and representation of reality, but that it is an effective system of signification. In her view, it is crucial to avoid any confusion between "language" and "words," because language is not to be understood as mere vocabulary or as a codifiable set of grammatical rules; rather, language is a system that constitutes meanings.[2] It is a system "through which meaning is constructed and cultural practices organized and by which, accordingly, people represent and understand their world, including who they are and how they relate to others."[3] Such a notion of language, Scott underscores, cannot be grasped through the conventional opposition between idealism, concerned solely with ideas we may have about social relations, and materialism, understood as the relations themselves, for it refers to the way in which social relations themselves are maintained and conceived. Given that to understand how these relations are conceived entails a comprehension of how they work, language becomes a starting point to understand "how institutions are organized, how relations of production are experienced, and how collective identity is established."[4] For this reason, argues Scott, if in historical inquiry we consider words as mere literary embellishments, we lose the chance to understand how meaning is constructed; such an inquiry may use language to ornament or facilitate the augmentation of new knowledge but would not lead to a transformation of "the way in which we think about the history we write" ("OL," 1).

This theoretical position in Scott's work is the basis of her groundbreaking critique of Gareth Stedman Jones's interpretation of Chartism, for example. For Stedman Jones, Chartism was not a result or an expression of the socioeconomic situation of the members of the Chartist movement, but a phenomenon that was developed within the political sphere and was, therefore, causally independent of the socioeconomic situation. What Scott criticizes in Stedman Jones is his use of a conventional understanding of politics as consisting of a set of ideas; as a result, he conceives of language at face value, simply as texts that reflect the world transparently, without attending to the way in which the meaning of those texts, and of reality itself, has been constructed. Stedman Jones limits himself to rendering a version of the subject of class who is wholly independent of its socioeconomic context, without examining the way in which the Chartists' consciousness and identity were built up through a particular system of historical meaning. As Scott puts it, "by reading language only thematically," Stedman Jones arrives at the conclusion that Chartism is a political movement, because it was interested in expanding formal political representation as a solution to social problems. The key to Chartism, he says, was its use of a radical "vocabulary," the importation of older words and ideas into an early nineteenth-century context. Ultimately, says Scott, what Stedman Jones claims is that historians of Chartism have not understood causal relations properly when they argue that it was "state policies" and not the "relations of production" that determined "the composition and the goals of the movement." In sum, Scott believes that what Jones does is transfer causality from the economic sphere to the political one. Although vocabulary plays a role in the attribution of historical efficacy to the political sphere, the role of language remains underestimated and misunderstood. Scott objects that this is not a novel assertion, nor a major transformation of how we think about history, because it is still centered on the specific words people used, rather than on the "materiality of language itself." That is, it continues to treat "language simply as a vehicle for communicating ideas rather than as a system of meaning or process of signification" ("OL," 4–6).

To arrive at a significant reorientation of historical studies, argues Scott, it is necessary instead to adopt the notion that language reveals entire systems of meaning. According to this notion, language not only refers to how people think about concrete subjects, but to the way people conceive the very differentiating relations that organize the human world—either in terms of hierarchy or interdependence, or as a binary structure "built on oppositions between, say, good and evil, or wet and dry, or dependent and independent, or male and female. It is particularly important to adopt the understanding that language intervenes in the construction of social identities, in this case, of class identity" ("OL," 4–6).

Thus, to reiterate, Scott asserts that language operates not as a transparent means of communication but as *discourse,* understood not as words or phrases but as entire forms of thought, as ways of understanding how the world works, and one's place in that world. According to Scott, discourse "is not a language or a text but a historically, socially, and institutionally specific structure of statements, terms, categories, and beliefs."[5] This definition has two implications: First, it is not possible to separate language from "real life," or from the meaning of our experience, because language in this sense is inextricably bound to both; second, every meaning *is built* through a process of differentiation (not of referentiality); words acquire their meanings through contrasts with other words, and the relevant contrasts are, in turn, established within specific discursive fields.[6] As Scott puts it, "positive definitions depend on negatives, indeed imply their existence in order to rule them out." We are faced with a "kind of interdependence [that] has ramifications well beyond literal definitions for it involves other concepts, other relationships in any particular usage" ("OL," 6).

Thus, language constitutes a system of meaning and, consequently, the meanings that belong to reality depend upon the particular discursive categories we use. This has profound implications for further specifying the other two notions at stake: experience and identity. Before addressing the question of experience, I shall indicate briefly that, for Scott, identity, like any other meaningful notion, emerges through the mediation of its established categories. This is so, Scott argues, because for people to identify themselves in a particular way, that concept of identity must have *already* existed. Concepts like class "are required before individuals can identify themselves as members of such a group, before they can act collectively as such" ("RC," 41). Therefore, concepts and categories such as class, worker, citizen, man, and woman, should be the starting point for any historical research aimed at explaining the formation of subjects and their practices.[7]

This view of language presupposes the elimination of any notion of objective reality, the cornerstone of social history. If language is understood as a system of meaning and not a transparent label reflecting real phenomena, then the phenomena do not carry intrinsic meaning that language simply registers and conveys and upon which consciousness merely reflects. Rather, the meanings emerge when a set of discursive conceptions of the world forms those phenomena. On this basis, Scott poses her critique of the notion of *experience.* Her critique begins with the premise that we do not have direct access to the reality we perceive, observe, or intend but that knowledge occurs through a series of prior categorical assumptions about the workings of reality. This is the case even when the observer makes use of a kind of language, such as numerical signs, that is intended to be totally neutral and transparent. Scott has, for example, focused on statistics and criticized the assumption that statistical data is the objective representation of social reality. From the nineteenth century on, she argues, statistical studies, with their numeric presentation of social data, became the foundation for the analysis of social reality and were used to justify the objectivity of such analysis. Facts and figures served as a kind of self-evident truth widely accepted by historians. As a result, historians have evaded the question of the relationship between reality and representation posed by the numerical sign system.[8]

Statistics do not merely reproduce reality; they organize its meaning. Statistical reports, Scott says, "are neither totally neutral collections of facts nor simply ideological impositions. Rather they are ways of establishing the authority of certain visions of social order, of organizing perceptions of 'experience.' At least since the eighteenth century, numbers have been used to establish the authenticity of interpretive or organizational categories" (*GPH,* 115). For instance, in reference to the case Scott studies that involves industrial statistics in Paris in the years 1847–1848, a number of established assumptions about human reality determine the way that data are collected, analyzed, and presented. These assumptions lead to taking certain phenomena as natural or objective, and thus presumed uncritically as the units of analysis. This clearly happens with the notion of "family." Population statistics are collected according to "households"—rather than, say, villages or workplaces. According to Scott, this procedure "reveals and constructs a certain vision of social organization based on a particular idea of the family that is 'naturalized' in the course of presenting the data" (*GPH,* 115). Consequently, what makes these statistical reports interesting and fascinating is not the data they yield about social reality, but the categories and assumptions on which they are based and which form a particular image of reality. These statistics, in sum, are more revealing about the way their authors and users perceive reality than they are about reality itself. And this is why, insists Scott, when historians use statistics without questioning their underlying categories and interpretations, they end up perpetuating and naturalizing that same version of reality. Instead, a critical approach ought to situate each document in its "discursive context" and read it "not as a reflection of some external reality but as an integral part of that reality, as a contribution to the definition or elaboration of meaning, to the creation of social relationships, economic institutions, and political structures" (*GPH,* 137–138). That is, historians must begin to unearth the terms by which these documents build up a version of reality and contribute "to constructing the 'reality' of the past" (*GPH,* 138).

Questioning the objective character of reality and its representations leads Scott to criticize the concept of *experience,* given that it presupposes an objective reality directly experienced by subjects. Contrary to conventional belief, people do not experience reality as bearing objective properties subsequently registered in their consciousness. Rather, people confer a particular meaning on reality according to the discursive categories at their disposal. In her reply to Bryan Palmer, for whom "the meaning of an event is inherent in the event itself," Scott writes that "experience may be a problematic concept." Contrary to Palmer's view that experience is the basis of our perception of reality, Scott disputes the notion that anything exists as an unmediated experience of reality. This critique has direct bearing on how historians describe the experience of class struggle. Every experience of the world—inasmuch as it is a way of apprehending meaning—is mediated by a specific discourse (or discourses) and thus cannot exist outside that discursive mediation. Moreover, such mediation not only shapes one's perception of reality, but is projected into people's conduct, into their practices, and into institutions, materializing itself in ways of living ("RC," 39).

Thus in her critique of the concept of experience, Scott starts out from two premises. The first is that reality does not consist of transparently available objects on the basis of which consciousness forms representations. The second premise is that language and experience are so inextricably tied together that we cannot separate the object from its linguistic representation. No experience exists outside language. Consequently, neither experience nor language can be analyzed separately from one another. This is why, for Scott, it is absurd to establish an antithesis between "rhetorical text" and "social experience," as Christine Stansell proposes. Doing so reduces language to words or to written documents and effaces its shaping power; this leads to an impoverished theoretical framework for the study of history ("RC," 40).

An inadequate conception of experience can be found, according to Scott, in the work of historians who, in dealing with questions of gender and homosexuality, restrict themselves to rescuing subjects from the silence to which dominant history has condemned them. Often these historians fail to question the conceptual foundations of history; they intend to complete the historical picture by giving visibility to those who were formerly excluded and effaced. But they continue to base their work "on the authority of experience" and to conceive of experience as an expression of reality.[9] This is why this kind of historical study yields such contradictory results. On the one hand, it provides good data about the lives of people otherwise omitted or forgotten.

But in so doing, it leads to a crisis of orthodox ways of writing history, not only by multiplying histories and subjects, but also by revealing that history can be written from various perspectives, all of which are partial and none of which, taken separately, is entirely "true." On the other hand, this challenge to normative history is performed within the framework of a conventional understanding of experience—what Scott calls "positivism"—according to which reality imposes itself on consciousness. This leads her to conclude that this way of writing a history of difference, aimed at documenting the experience of the other, has been both successful and limiting. "It has been successful because it remains so comfortably within the disciplinary framework of history, working according to rules that permit calling old narratives into question when new evidence is discovered." It has been limiting because it continues to depend on "a referential notion of evidence which denies it is anything but a reflection of the real" ("EE," 776).

It is precisely this referential claim to reality, "this kind of appeal to experience as incontestable evidence and as an originary point of explanation—as a foundation on which analysis is based—that seriously weakens the critical thrust of histories of difference." Staying within the epistemological framework of "orthodox history, these studies lose the possibility of examining those assumptions and practices that excluded considerations of difference in the first place" ("EE," 777). That is, these studies miss the opportunity to examine critically the theoretical assumptions that led to the exclusion of those subjects and, hence, they miss the opportunity to theoretically reorient the study of history. In this way, the histories of the "hidden" world of homosexuality, for example, show the impact of silence and repression on the lives of those affected and shed light on the history of their suppression, but the project of rendering the experience visible impedes the critical examination of the operation of the very categories of representation—homosexual/heterosexual, man/woman—as well as of notions of subject, origin, and cause ("EE," 778). In fact, argues Scott, the main limitation of those histories is that they take as self-evident the identities of those whose experience they try to document and rescue, contributing to the naturalization of difference. Situating the subjects and their resistance independently of their discursive construction and taking experience as the ground of knowledge eliminates the possibility of questioning the constructed character of experience and the constitution of subjects themselves. The consequence is that "the evidence of experience then becomes evidence for the fact of difference, rather than a way of exploring how difference is established, how it operates, how and in what ways it constitutes subjects who see and act in the world." Consequently, this "evidence of experience, whether conceived through a metaphor of visibility or in any other way that takes meaning as transparent," presupposes that historical facts speak for themselves and that oppositions such as homosexuality vs. heterosexuality are naturally given ("EE," 777, 778).

According to this way of doing history, homosexuality is presented as an expression of naturally given desire, a desire that is denied or repressed by a society that only recognizes heterosexuality. Nonetheless, the argument continues, homosexual desire cannot be repressed once and for all, "because experience is there," and therefore it will be recognized sooner or later. According to this vision, emancipation is a teleological history in which desire finally wins over social control and becomes visible. History is thereby reduced to a chronology that makes experience visible. In this version the categories—desire, homosexuality, heterosexuality, femininity, masculinity, or sex—name realities that are considered ahistorical, natural, and objective. As a result, concludes Scott, this type of historical inquiry seeks to render experience visible, allows an appreciation of alternative forms of conduct and repressive actions, but accounts neither for the framework of—historically contingent—patterns of sexuality from which that experience emerged, nor for the conduct and action in which they are inscribed, nor for the logic they follow ("EE," 778, 779).

A similar conception of experience, and a similar connection between reality and consciousness, can frequently be found in women's history, according to Scott. When the relationship between thought and experience is conceived as if it were transparent, the life experience of women is seen as directly conducive to resisting oppression, that is, conducive to feminism. In other words, the identity of women and their political action is cast as the natural result of "a pre-existing women's experience" ("EE," 786–7). This is Scott's criticism of Laura Lee Downs. Downs limits herself to applying the categories of difference as if they were a transparent expression of reality and experience, without analyzing the process through which such categories are constituted and how they actively take part in the construction of women's identity.[10]

Thus, whether in the case of homosexuality, of gender, or of class, the above-mentioned historians, according to Scott, mask the "necessarily discursive character" of experience. That is, they fail to see that experience is not the result of reality's direct impact on people's subjectivity, but rather is the result of a discursive apprehension of reality. Experience, writes Scott, "is a linguistic event (it doesn't happen outside established meanings)" ("EE," 793). Therefore, it does not follow, from the fact that every consciousness is tied to a particular historical context, that consciousness originates in experience and that, therefore, experience should be taken as a basis for the historical explanation. Rather, it is experience itself that *ought to be explained by historians.*

What has to be explained is why people have experienced themselves and their position in the world in a particular way. For Scott, it is crucial "to attend to the historical processes that, through discourse, position subjects and produce their experiences," because "it is not individuals who have experiences, but subjects who are constituted through experience" ("EE," 779). Thus—as I have already indicated—for the explanation of identity and the conduct of historical actors, we should look to the historical constitution of categories such as class, worker, citizen, man or woman, homosexual or heterosexual, as well as the way those categories enter into social practice—and not in the allegedly foundational experience (*GPH*, 3–4).

The critical reformulation of the concept of experience leads to a new notion of *identity*. The most important aspect of this reformulation is that Scott rebels against any essentialist, static, ahistorical, or objectivist account of identities. As a consequence, she also resists explaining identity as something achieved through the process of coming to consciousness. As she puts it, experience is not a set of objective circumstances that condition identity, and identity is not a sense of the self objectively determined or defined by needs and interests. Consequently, "politics is not the collective coming to consciousness of similarly situated individual subjects." Rather politics is "the process by which plays of power and knowledge constitute identity and experience" (*GPH*, 5). According to this view, identities and experiences are variable phenomena discursively organized in particular contexts or configurations.

This theoretical premise has consequences for Scott's studies of the subject of feminism. Scott denies that "woman" is a natural subject and thus universal and ahistorical. As a corollary, she rejects the notion that women, as women, and because of their natural condition as women, have a particular experience of the world and of their position in it. In fact, when operating within a notion of *women's experience,* women's contemporary experience gets naturalized and projected transhistorically, that is, beyond any one historical period. On these grounds, Scott criticizes the idea that women acquire an identity for themselves through an experience that is unmediated by cultural concepts, because that view will "always . . . end up in essentialism" by turning the body into the common element of shared womanhood ("RC," 42). Even though this new conception of identity is entirely applicable to the case of women, the historicization of women's identity faces greater difficulties compared to other identities, since it seems to be based on an incontrovertible natural reality. It is more difficult, states Scott, "to historicize the category of women, based as it seems to be in biology," than, for instance, "to historicize the category of worker, always understood to be a social phenomenon, produced not by nature, but by economic and political arrangements." That explains exactly why an essentialist and naturalist notion of women is at work in a large part of women's history and that, as a consequence, such historical inquiries tend to be guided by the goal of showing that women are capable (e.g., of participating in political life), instead of analyzing the changing character of women's identity, the process through which that identity is constituted, and what possibilities for change open up within that process. That is, the difficulty of historicizing the category of woman explains the tendency "to pile up counter examples as demonstrations of women's political capacity," while not attending to "the changing, and often radically different, historical contexts within which women as subjects came into being."[11]

In fact, for a long time the history of women was driven by the goal of rescuing women from their historical invisibility, highlighting their abilities and the major roles played by women as writers, artists, politicians, and so on. In this way, feminist historians contributed to establishing "women's presence" and participation in historical events, contrary to the exclusively masculinist history that prevailed at the time and was held responsible for making women invisible. According to Scott, however, this kind of history tends to operate on the basis of an essentialist notion of women—that is, to treat women as fixed and atemporal subjects. In the past, says Scott, there was a tendency to designate women as "us," as if there were a solidaristic women's identity that existed over time. This happened despite the fact that this *recuperation* of past women inevitably revealed numerous differences among women that called for recognition and explanation. Thus, the "specificity and diversity" of historical evidence came into contradiction with the uniform and ahistorical notion of woman.[12] As a result, as Scott argues, "the desire to legitimize feminist claims about women in order to consolidate an effective feminist political movement treats 'women' uniformly, and therefore, ahistorically. But the creation of women as subjects of history places them temporally in the contexts of their action, and explains the possibilities for such action in terms of those contexts." Thus, "history contains examples of fundamental differences, in experience and self-understanding, among women, potentially undermining the political task of creating an enduring common identity."

Consequently, the question of whether the category of "women" is singular or diverse, preexisting, or historical, is at the heart of both feminist history and the history of feminism. It is a tension between an essentialist and a historical notion of "woman" that generates a contradiction between a feminism that tends to establish a stable and permanent female subject and a feminist history that seeks to account for the historical diversity of identities by means of studying the different contexts in which women have lived. This latter history shows that the identities attributed to and manifested by women change over time and from one society to another. Thus, except for the similarity of their sexual organs, it is hard to find a common identity between, for instance, aristocratic *salonières* in the Parisian eighteenth century and nineteenth-century middle-class housewives.[13]

Scott does not limit herself to criticizing an essentialist notion of woman or calling for a historicization of feminine identity. She also formulates *a theory of identity formation*. Her theorization conflicts with the view that the formation of women as subjects results from a process of coming into consciousness on the basis of a common experience of reality and position in society. In fact, the essentialist notion of woman not only presupposes the existence of a fixed and atemporal feminine subject, but also naturalizes the differentiating categories at work in forming the subject. As Scott states, "by assuming that women have inherent characteristics and objective identities consistently and predictably different from men's, and that these generate definably female needs and interests, historians imply that sexual difference is a natural rather than a social phenomenon. The search for an analysis of discrimination gets caught by a circular logic in which 'experience' explains gender difference and gender difference explains the asymmetries of male and female 'experience.'" As a result, "typically the visions of what constitutes male and female experience appeal to or incorporate existing normative definitions"; therefore, "women's history written from this position, and the politics that follow from it, end up endorsing the ideas of unalterable sexual difference that are used to justify discrimination." To challenge this kind of history, Scott proposes another sort of historical practice which does not merely study "the things that have happened to women and men" and the ways "they have reacted to them." Rather, this new kind of history focuses on how "the subjective and collective meanings of women and men as categories of identity have been constructed" (*GPH,* 4, 6).

The second theoretical premise of Scott's concept of identity is that subjects do not preexist the categories that define their identities. These categories constitute people as historical subjects and actors, classifying them according to a particular conception of the world. Identities are not the sum total of the personal attributes that belong to subjects; rather, attributes are defining and constituting elements of the identities of those who are said to have or bear those attributes. As Scott affirms, identities "don't pre-exist" their "political invocations" and "categories of identity we take for granted as rooted in our physical bodies (gender and race) or in our cultural (ethnic, religious) heritages are, in fact, retrospectively linked to those roots" ("FE," 285). Therefore, it is not that sex, class, or race determines a person's identity, but that sex, class, or race have already been discursively established as criteria or recognizable markers of identity. Thus just as Scott affirms that there is no universal human nature that can be attributed to women in any and all historical times, she denies that women's identity is the expression of a preexisting female identity that can be invoked at any given historical moment. She believes that such a view can neither account for the changing character of women's identity, nor for the very fact that at some point "women" became a form of identity. It cannot account "either for the subjectively different perceptions women have of themselves as women or for the ways in which at certain moments 'women' become consolidated as an identity group." In this way Scott maintains that the community of women does not preexist its invocation, but is generated by signifying operations, including "fantasies," which posit women as transcending both history and difference. That is, such signifying operations wield the category of women in order to give coherence to confusion and reduce multiplicity to unity and, in so doing, to congeal the category as an identity ("FE," 288, 290).

Certainly, the process of the discursive constitution of any identity is masked when that identity appears as something natural and stable. But this appearance should not lead us to forget the operation of the process itself and the need for historians to proceed to its analysis, especially if we want to understand and explain the formation of the identity in question. As Scott indicates, the presumption of a categorical and universal subject (whether worker, peasant, woman, black) obscures the operations of difference that underlie and inform the organization of social life. Each one of these categories, once taken as something fixed, solidifies the subject's constituting process and makes the process less visible; in turn, this leads to naturalizing the effects of the process rather than analyzing its operation ("EE," 791–792). From this argument it follows that what changes through time is not simply the perception about a certain identity, but the identity itself. As Scott argues, "there's an illusory sameness established by referring to a category of person (women, workers, African Americans, homosexuals) as if it never changed, as if not the category, but only its historical circumstances varied over time." Thus, historians of women have wondered, for instance, in what way the changes in the legal, social, economic, and medical status of women affected their possibilities of liberation and equality. However, the question of how these changes altered the meaning of the term women itself has been asked less frequently, even though the category is uncritically presupposed in these sorts of analysis ("FE," 285).

For Scott, identity is not the mere expression of a set of physical or social attributes that serve as its referents. Identity emerges from the mediation of classificatory and differentiated categories of identity at work in each particular case. This is what makes identities differential and relational entities. That is, identities are formed in contrast with other identities and by means of operations of differentiation and exclusion. As Scott puts it, the "relational nature of difference" implies that identities are not inherent in subjects, but rather produced "discursively by contrast with others." A person is "something" not because she or he is that something intrinsically, but because she or he is not something else. So, for instance, "part of being white" meant "not being black"; Englishness was established in contrast to Indianness.[14]

The notion of language as a system of signification and the vision of identity as a historical entity that is differential and discursively constructed crystallize in Scott's concept of "gender." Scott begins with the distinction between sex and gender; she defines gender as "the social organization of sexual difference." Gender, she writes, does not reflect "fixed and natural physical differences between women and men," because the meanings of those differences "vary across cultures, social groups, and time," since "nothing about the body, including women's reproductive organs, determines univocally how social divisions will be shaped" (GPH, 2).[15] However, Scott does not restrict her critique to distinguishing between sex and gender, between the physical fact and the social relations based on it. She goes one step further in her theorization. For her, the concept of gender does not designate merely men's and women's social roles, but refers to modes of knowledge—integrally related to linguistic patterns—that organize the perception of nature and its relation to those social roles. Gender is not just a social phenomenon that changes with time, but the effect of a discursive articulation of sex as well as of the relations between the sexes. As she puts it, "we cannot see sexual difference except as a function of our knowledge about the body and that knowledge is not 'pure,' cannot be isolated from its implication in a broad range of discursive contexts." Consequently, sexual difference is not "the originary cause from which social organization ultimately can be derived. It is instead a variable social organization that itself must be explained" (GPH, 2).

From this point of view, the concept of gender leads us to investigate "the specific forms taken by the social organization of sexual difference," although it would be wrong to presume these forms "as variations on an unchanging theme of patriarchal domination." The concept of gender does not refer merely to the changing relations between men and women or between sexes, but rather to the way in which such relations have been conceived and categorized. This concept demands a careful analysis of the "concrete manifestations" and the "different meanings the same words might have." Even as the term gender refers "to the ways in which relationships between men and women were conceived," neither the relationships nor the men and women are to be taken as the same in all cases. For that reason, it is not enough to apply the notion of gender to these relations; it is more fundamentally a question of interrogating and historicizing the terms with which these relations are conceptualized.[16]

It is precisely this definition of gender that leads Scott both to make a clear distinction between the history of women and the history of gender, and to affirm that a significant number of the works that are published in the area belong to the first category and not to the second. In her view, the object of historical study should not be simply to document the difference between men and women, but to inquire into the operation generating that difference as significant and meaningful; she describes this operation as having a discursive character. According to Scott, a considerable number of studies that purport to offer a "gender analysis" are often "quite predictable studies of women," or studies of differences in the status, experience, and possibilities open to women and men. Those studies "rarely examine how the meanings of 'women' and 'men' are discursively established." In fact, she concludes, many feminist scholars who use the term "gender" explicitly reject the premise that "men" and "women" are historically variable categories. As a result, the concept of "gender" has been losing its critical edge in recent scholarly and political discourse (GPHR, xii). In fact, according to Scott, it is ever more common to find gender equated with the enumeration or explication of the social roles that belong to the sexes. Since the nineties, the concept "seems to have lost its ability to startle and provoke us." In the United States it has become a term of ordinary use that routinely appears offered as "a synonym for women, for the differences between the sexes, for sex." At times, Scott adds, the term "denotes the social rules imposed on men and women," but it rarely refers "to the knowledge that organizes our perceptions of 'nature.'" As a result, the concept of gender is in the process of losing its groundbreaking character along with its analytic potential. Scott confesses that for this reason that she uses it less and less frequently in her work (GPHR, xii).

Despite these problems with "gender," Scott's historical work continues to demonstrate how such categories might be used to alter academic work and reveal the political stakes in such work. For instance, Scott makes use of the notion of women's identity—understood as a historical and discursively constructed entity—as an analytical tool in her historical study of French feminism.[17] The main thesis of her study is that the feminist identity characteristic of the modern age was an effect of the signifying articulation of women's social situation by means of categories of a modern universalizing discourse of individual, equality, and human rights. In concrete terms, it was the perception—through such discourses and their categories—of women's subordination and of their exclusion from the public sphere that led women to start conceiving of themselves as subjects with rights. In so doing, they acquired their historical and political identity as women. Whether claiming their condition as equals—equality-based feminism—or the importance of their differences—difference feminism—feminists defined themselves using a normative pattern of identity, and employing the category of the abstract individual introduced by universalizing discourse.

But the universalizing discourse not only engendered a new women's identity, allowing women to define themselves as subjects with rights, but also gave rise to feminism itself, for feminism emerged as a result of the contradiction between the declaration of equality of all human beings and the exclusion of a portion of them—women—from the public sphere and from political participation. Feminism and the conflicts it generated must be considered "as symptoms of contradictions in the political discourses that produced feminism" and that it appealed to and challenged at the same time. These were the discourses of individualism, individual rights, and social obligation, as used by republicans and socialists to organize the institutions of democratic citizenship (*OP*, 3).

Feminism and feminist practice are caught in a paradox, according to Scott, precisely because contemporary women's identity originates through the mediation of a universalizing discourse. The paradox lies in that to fight difference and exclusion of women, women have to begin and support their claims on the same discursive categories—particularly that of the abstract individual—that have produced that difference and that exclusion. Women's calls for equality are paradoxical because they are based on the same categories or principles that define them as unequal and that, consequently, expel them from the public sphere. Feminists, writes Scott, challenged "the practice of excluding women from citizenship." In order to do so, they based their position on the argument that there was "neither a logical nor an empirical connection between the sex of one's body and one's ability to engage in politics, that sexual difference was not an indicator of social, intellectual, or political capacity." However, Scott continues, even though those arguments are powerful and compelling, they were also paradoxical, because in order "to protest women's exclusion," feminists had to act "on behalf of women and so invoked the very difference they sought to deny" (*OP*, x). Similarly, when exclusion was legitimated "by reference to the different biologies of women and men," sexual difference was established as a natural fact and an ontological basis for social and political differentiation. Thus, in the age of democratic revolutions, "women" came into being as political outsiders through the discourse of sexual difference. Feminism was a protest against the political exclusion of women. Its objective was to eliminate sexual difference from politics. However, feminism had to make its claims on behalf of "women," who were discursively produced, precisely, through sexual difference. As a result, as much as it acted for "women," "feminism produced the 'sexual difference' it sought to eliminate." "This paradox—the need both to accept *and* to refuse 'sexual difference'—was the constitutive condition of feminism" (*OP*, 3–4).

Nevertheless, when women took up their classification as a separate group, a classification made possible within modern discourse itself, it was that discourse that granted authority and effectiveness to their demands. Only then did they articulate their political claims in a discourse shared by their opponents (*OP*, x). This implies that the universalizing discourse not only generated feminism, but also established the conditions for the possibility of its practice, its struggle, and its demands.

In this regard we can also say that the practice is also a "discursive effect."[18] As such, it bears on Scott's theory of human action. In response to individualist and rationalist arguments for human behavior, she argues that, for feminists, action cannot be explained in terms of individual characteristics or will, since subjects are not autonomous entities; rather, action must be explained in terms of the effect of the discursive conditions and contexts which themselves form the conditions of possibility for action. Thus, she states, "instead of assuming that agency follows from an innate human will, I want to understand feminism in terms of the discursive processes . . . that produce political subjects, that make agency . . . possible even when it is forbidden or denied" (*OP*, 16).

This implies, in turn, that discursive contexts establish the rules of domination as well as the terms and possibility for resistance, granting as well its meaning and effectiveness. The universalizing definition of human nature and of equality generates women's identity and establishes a horizon of political expectations for women: achieving equality. Moreover, this discourse makes feminist struggles effective, for they are based on principles, categories, and arguments, especially universality, largely shared with their opponents, who cannot, then, fail to consider them without abrogating their own principles. The claim to rights appeals both to difference and to equality, invoking universalization, but asking also what it means in light of sexual difference. Therefore, argues Scott, the task is not just to focus on the opposition between domination and resistance, or between control and action, but to discern those complex processes that enable and set limits to the possibilities of action by people or groups.[19] From this point of view, feminism's use of universalizing principles, categories, and arguments is not simply a rhetorical appeal, a merely instrumental use of the available language and cultural values; rather, it is a consequence of the fact that feminism itself is constituted by these same principles and categories and seeks to make its intervention there. We might say that feminism was not only born within such language but also depends on that language for its continuing operation. As Scott writes, "[T]he history of feminism is not simply a history of contrary women uttering dissenting opinions. Nor can it be captured by the oxymoronic description of 'women claiming the rights of Man.' *The paradoxes I refer to are not strategies of opposition, but the constitutive elements of feminism itself*" (*OP*, 5, emphasis added). Feminism has offered so many paradoxes because it was articulated on a discourse that equated individuality with masculinity.

Changes in the discursive context affected the shape of feminist identity and practice. This is because modern feminist identity, feminism, and its practice arose from the historical deployment of established political discourses. According to Scott, we should acknowledge that feminists have formulated their claims for rights "in terms of very different epistemologies" and that their arguments "must be read that way," and not as evidence of "a transcendent or continuous woman's consciousness or women's experience." That is, even though the repeated pattern of the paradox grants the claims an "aura of timelessness," the feminist concepts used "were rooted in their times and can finally be understood only in their specificity." History accounts not only for the feminists' "variety of positions," but also for the different ways in which the identity of "woman" was conceived (*OP*, 13).[20]

The theoretical challenge that Scott has posed to historians does not entail, as Scott has carefully noted, a mere idealist *inversion* of the materialist or objectivist model of explanation. On the contrary, it affirms the premise that language, inasmuch as it is discourse, is an active element in the formation of subjects as well as their practices. As a result, the discursive categories underlying these subjects and their practices, and whose mediating effect has made them possible, should not only serve as a point of departure for every historical study, but also be taken as a basic explanatory variable. If this challenge is accepted, Scott argues, we will pay attention to language and to the processes through which categories and meanings have been articulated; otherwise, we will continue to impose models on the world that perpetuate conventional understandings rather than open up new interpretive possibilities.[21] In sum, historians should respond to questions such as: "How have categories of representation and analysis—such as class, race, gender, relations of production, biology, identity, subjectivity, agency, experience, even culture—achieved their foundational status? What have been the effects of their articulations? What does it mean for historians to study the past in terms of these categories and for individuals to think of themselves in these terms?" ("EE," 796). On the basis of this theoretical challenge that Scott has posed, a new practice of history has taken form.

NOTES

1. I have discussed this new historiographic model in greater detail in Miguel A. Cabrera, *Postsocial History: An Introduction* (Lanham, Md.: Lexington Books, 2004).

2. Joan W. Scott, "On Language, Gender, and Working-Class History," *International Labor and Working-Class History* 31 (1987): 3. Hereafter cited as "OL" in parenthetical references.

3. Joan W. Scott, "Deconstructing Equality vs. Difference: or, the Uses of Post-Structuralist Theory for Feminism," *Feminist Studies* 14 (Spring 1988): 34.

4. Ibid.

5. Ibid., 35.

6. Joan W. Scott, "A Reply to Criticism," *International Labor and Working-Class History,* 32 (1987): 40. Hereafter cited as "RC" in parenthetical references.

7. Joan W. Scott, *Gender and the Politics of History* (New York: Columbia University Press, 1988): 3–4. Hereafter cited as *GPH* in parenthetical references.

8. Joan W. Scott, "A Statistical Representation of Work: *La Statistique de l'industrie à Paris, 1847–1848,"* in *Gender and the Politics of History,* 113–138.

9. Joan W. Scott, "The Evidence of Experience," *Critical Inquiry* 17 (1991): 776. Hereafter cited as "EE" in parenthetical references.

10. Joan W. Scott, " 'The Tip of the Volcano'," *Comparative Studies in Society and History* 35, no. 3 (1993): 439 and 442.

11. Joan W. Scott, "Fantasy Echo: History and the Construction of Identity," *Critical Inquiry* 27 (2001): 286. Hereafter cited as "FE" in parenthetical references.

12. Joan W. Scott, "Introduction," in *Feminism and History,* ed. Joan W. Scott (New York: Oxford University Press, 1996), 2–4.

13. Ibid., 4–5.

14. Ibid., 8.

15. This notion of gender as a historical phenomenon is presented in her famous article "Gender: A Useful Category of Historical Analysis," *American Historical Review* 91 (1986): 1053–1075.

16. Joan W. Scott, "Preface to the Revised Edition," in *Gender and the Politics of History,* rev. ed. (New York: Columbia University Press, 1999), xii. Hereafter cited as *GPHR* in parenthetical references.

17. Joan W. Scott, *Only Paradoxes to Offer: French Feminists and the Rights of Man,* (Cambridge, Mass.: Harvard University Press, 1996). Hereafter cited as *OP* in parenthetical references.

18. Joan W. Scott, review of *Heroes of Their Own Lives,* by Linda Gordon, *Signs* 16 (1990): 851.

19. Ibid., 852.

20. As Scott commented about this work, "Feminist identity was an effect of a rhetorical political strategy invoked differently by different feminists at different times" ("Fantasy Echo," 286).

21. Scott, "Deconstructing Equality," 35.

CHAPTER THREE

Out of Their Orbit

Celebrities and Eccentrics in Nineteenth-Century France

MARY LOUISE ROBERTS

What do you call a woman who sleeps in a coffin and keeps a pet alligator? Or a woman who harbors two lions in her backyard? In the nineteenth century, such a woman was called an "eccentric." Two such French eccentrics were Rosa Bonheur (1822–1899) (fig. 3.1) and Sarah Bernhardt (1844–1923) (fig. 3.2). Rosa Bonheur enjoyed international renown as a painter of animals, most famously *The Horse Fair* in 1853. She was the most recognized woman painter of her day, and the first French woman to receive the *Légion d'honneur*.[1] Like Bonheur, Sarah Bernhardt was an international celebrity. Besides bringing Paris to its feet in such plays as *Cleopatra* and *Hamlet,* the actress opened her own Parisian theater, where she acted and produced when she was not touring. By the 1890s, Bernhardt had become far more than an actress: she was also "the Bernhardt," *la Divine,* arguably the most famous woman in the world.

These two women distinguished themselves by establishing reputations as eccentrics as well as celebrities. Bonheur attracted attention as an *excentrique* in the 1850s by jaunting about Paris astride a horse in trousers and a jacket. Men of position scheduled to rendezvous with her in the Bois de Boulogne took one look and galloped off in the opposite direction.[2] Bonheur also attracted gossip by keeping an entire menagerie of animals in her back yard, including lions, almost forty sheep, goats, horses, oxen, mules, and a wild boar. Similarly, a wide range of contemporaries saw Bernhardt "as always in love with eccentricity."[3] "Scour the annals of the theatrical arts," dared the drama critic Francisque Sarcey, "you will never again see as strange a spectacle as this turbulent, treacherous life."[4] Like Bonheur, Bernhardt was fond of large beasts such as pumas and alligators, and gave them the free run of her

FIGURE 3.1. Rosa Bonheur and her lion Fatma

home on the Boulevard Péreire in Paris. The actress was also known to es-
chew a bed as her sleeping place in favor of a coffin (fig. 3.3).[5]

Bonheur and Bernhardt were among the most celebrated of women in
nineteenth-century European society. It was no coincidence, I will argue, that
both women established reputations for being eccentric. To do so, both built
upon their professional status as artists, and exploited the new media technologies of their era. Their embrace of eccentricity as a personal style helped
them to manage their fame; it represented some acknowledgement on their
part that as female celebrities, they had become culturally unintelligible to
their public. Celebrity in the nineteenth century assumed the recognition of
individual self-achievement, and necessitated unprecedented levels of visibility, publicity, and exposure.[6] According to Lenard Berlanstein, because the
female role was to dwell in the private realm and to be barely seen, let alone
heard, "constructing celebrity status for men" was "infinitely easier than for
women." In other words, celebrity challenged the notion of female self-
abnegation inscribed in the dominant bourgeois domestic ideal.[7] As we shall
see, Bonheur and Bernhardt dealt with this "problem" of female celebrity by
playing with their cultural illegibility. Embracing precisely their strangeness

FIGURE 3.2. Sarah
Bernhardt in *L'Aiglon*

as women, they became eccentric, transforming their unconventionality into something amusing and idiosyncratic.

As eccentrics, Bonheur and Bernhardt could not be held responsible for their actions, a fact that was key to the success of their image. Both women presented themselves as "victims" of the celebrity surrounding them. Bernhardt, in particular, made herself out to be the hapless prey of the reporter, whom she condemned as "a veritable dung-beetle."[8] "Since the very creation of reporters," she wrote with her usual flair for understatement, "there is no person on this earth who has suffered as much from them as I did on my first tour."[9] By portraying herself as a casualty of the press, Bernhardt disavowed authorship of her own eccentric image. Such a denial was crucial to the credibility of the eccentric *qua* eccentric, since the behavior was not supposed to be intentional. Bonheur and Bernhardt had to appear to do weird things out of whim or instinct

FIGURE 3.3. Sarah
Bernhardt in her coffin

rather than conscious intent. In this way, they could not be held accountable for
their actions. As creative artists, both women sought lives that were inventive
and unscripted. The particular brand of blamelessness they gained through eccentric behavior made their lives more livable precisely in these terms.

Bernhardt led a scandalous life, which hardly needs rehearsing here: she
engaged in prostitution as a young child, bore an illegitimate child, had one
brief, disastrous marriage, and counted lovers by the dozen. And yet, with the
exception of her anti-Semitic enemies, she was prized by the vast majority
of French people, who viewed her as maddeningly fickle, but ultimately
adorable—an artist who led her life "up so high" that she could not be judged
by normal standards. Bonheur enjoyed the same blamelessness of the eccentric. Like Bernhardt, she was hardly a model of the domestic feminine. Women
artists were dismissed as "unnatural" besides entirely lacking in talent. In addition, Bonheur shunned marriage and lived openly with two women—the
first, an inventor, and the second, an American from San Francisco who was

half her age. In an era when no woman dared put a cigarette to her mouth, she was a chain-smoker. And yet Bonheur was "forgiven" because of her eccentricity. While some critics singled out Bonheur's so-called masculine face as a warning to women seeking an art career, there were many more who, as Tamar Garb has put it, "indulged her personal whims by dwelling on their eccentricity, their very oddness."[10] Again, tolerance sprang from the general view that an eccentric could not be blamed for her behavior, which was beyond individual intent or will.

By using the technologies of celebrity (newsprint, photography, magazine copy) to market themselves as eccentrics, these two women not only managed their fame, but also, notably, got away with mortal sins against true womanhood. How can we understand this immunity in a society notorious for its restrictions on female behavior? Because eccentric behavior was not taken seriously in the nineteenth century, historians have largely disregarded it as well.[11] My aim in this essay is to question the putative innocence of eccentricity. What were the politics of eccentricity? How did eccentricity figure in the efforts of women to sustain an imaginative relation to gender norms in the nineteenth century? Historians have devoted enormous attention to nineteenth-century gender norms, regarding them as a contested but relatively stable set of ideals and practices controlling the terms "male" and "female" during this period. Such norms, historians have argued, were either enacted or rejected by women in their social behavior. The eccentricity of Bonheur and Bernhardt reveals the overly mechanistic way in which we have understood "resistance" to gender norms. Not only did individual women maintain infinitely variable relations to such norms, thus defying the notion of the "normal," but they also produced these norms even as they challenged them.[12] On one level, Bonheur and Bernhardt appear to have used their eccentricity to escape preexisting normative "rules." But such an argument overlooks the fact that eccentricity could not be understood without reference to convention or normality. As such, eccentricity reinforced as well as challenged the stability of norms. The purpose of this article, then, is not only to examine how Bonheur and Bernhardt as "rebel" eccentrics managed to trip up the nineteenth-century gender system, but more importantly, to complicate our understanding of how individual women sustained a creative relation to gender norms.

In being dubbed eccentrics, Bonheur and Bernhardt represented a new breed. For although human beings have exhibited strange behavior since the beginning of time, the very notion of the eccentric individual did not exist in Western societies before the modern era. Up until the eighteenth century, there were eccentric stars but not yet eccentric persons. In fact, "eccentric" had no figurative meaning at all until 1685, when an English poet, in comparing a human to a star, used the metaphor of "the brightest, yet the most excentrick Soul."[13] Originally "eccentric" was an astronomical term which referred to a planet whose axis was other than centrally placed. Stars in eccentric orbit felt the pull of gravity from other stars as well as the one they were orbiting. As a result, their paths diverged from a normal ellipse or circle; an eccentric orbit followed an arc that was remote from where it was supposed to be. Eccentricity was about location, measured precisely by its aberration from a normal orbit. It was produced by and served as an index of normality.

The figurative meaning of eccentric as "odd and whimsical" gained strength in England during the eighteenth century, crossed the Channel to France in 1817, and from there traveled to Germany in the 1830s. Even then, one could still not be an *excentrique* as a type until the 1840s.[14] In the 1850s, however, the word became fabulously *chic*. French writers flocked to variants of the word *excentrique,* including some of the most rebellious French women of the early nineteenth century.[15] It was Germaine de Staël, for example, who introduced the figurative term "eccentric" to French readers in 1817. In addition, the novelist George Sand used it in record numbers in her 1855 autobiography, *Journal de ma vie,* in order to describe her penchant for "walking away from every convention in the world," including her habit of wearing a male suit.[16] From its very invention, eccentricity bore a special relationship to the female gender. In the earliest English usages of the term, eccentric behavior in women became synonymous with the transgression of gender norms. In the *Common Sense* of 1737, for example, women were described as "confined within the narrow limits of Domestic Offices, and when they stray beyond them, they move excentrically, and consequently without Grace."[17]

Eccentricity as a mode of behavior was thus "invented" in the late eighteenth and early nineteenth centuries. It coincides, then, with the emergence of a bourgeois democratic state in France. This chronology makes sense if we consider that eccentricity is grounded in individualism—the central value of liberal society—and can be defined as a kind of hyper-individualism. To use the astronomical idiom, the eccentric feels the gravitational pull of some contrary, singular force moving her into another orbit. An eccentric person, like an eccentric orbit, was located somewhere other than where she was supposed to be, and thus indexed normative behavior. Still another figurative meaning of eccentric was "regulated by no central control."[18] Clearly, eccentricity was a product of the normative society that distinguished modern liberal culture. In recent years, historians have closely linked the consolidation of liberal society with the emergence of such "disciplinary regimes" as medicine, psychology, sexology, and criminology. Through such "disciplines," they argue, professionals began to regulate a variety of human behaviors—sexual activity, personal and public hygiene, workplace conduct, familial relations.

Such disciplining was necessary, they contend, to maintain social order in a state where freedom was considered an innate right.[19]

But the very imposition of homogenous norms on human behavior also created the possibility of differentiation at the level of the individual. The new emphasis on conventional behavior gave rise to the eccentric, who materialized the limits of normative behavior, appearing to resist them but, in fact, reinforcing them. Eccentrics such as Bonheur and Bernhardt engaged precisely these tensions between the norm and the exception, the same and the different, which lay at the heart of nineteenth-century liberal society. They expertly navigated the reverse gravitational forces of convention and individualism. As artists, they inhabited socially marginal spaces where, according to Jerrold Seigel, they helped to act out and resolve the contradictions of bourgeois society.[20] As stars, they steered their lives into eccentric orbits. Like eccentricity, "stardom" was a recent import from the astronomical lexicon, and also an invention of the nineteenth century. Again, England was in the forefront, using the word "star" in 1824 to describe an actress who, by name alone, could pack a theater. The French noted this English usage as early as 1844, and welcomed the new meaning of *étoile* into the French lexicon during the late 1870s, precisely the heyday of Bonheur and Bernhardt's careers. Although the word is not included in the *Littré* of 1875, Zola referred to "La Blonde Géraldine, une étoile d'opérettes" in his 1880 novel *Nana*.[21] Actresses were much more likely to be crowned "stars" than actors. By 1902, *La Vie en Rose* could observe that it was now female *étoiles,* not theatrical pieces, which determined the size of an audience, particularly those "veritable suns, around which revolves all of Paris theater."[22]

Bernhardt was such a sun. When she married in 1882, her husband was dubbed "a satellite of a star."[23] When she left state-sponsored theater in the 1880s to begin her international tours, one journalist wanted to know "why she left the Comédie-Française to become a wandering star?"[24] "I am the morning star; I am the evening star, I am the star of the day, . . . I am she who shines," was how still another contemporary described Bernhardt in 1898.[25] To say that Sarah Bernhardt also knew how to stage a star image would be an understatement. As is well known, the actress pioneered marketing and publicity in the star system, becoming notorious for her manipulation of the press and advertising industries. Quite apart from her profession as an actress (but obviously building upon it), Bernhardt crafted a self that was all illusion and artifice, a surface play of images behind which the "real" Bernhardt became impossible to locate. "A vagabond comet," as one admirer described her in 1896, Bernhardt created and recreated herself according to her own whims and those of her managers and publicists.[26] She became the model of subjectivity as pure performance, a star constantly in orbit.[27]

And so it was with Rosa Bonheur. Although "stardom" was mostly confined to the theatrical world, Bonheur nevertheless became, according to Daniele Digne, "the artistic star" who "knew the tedium of the star system," and was indisposed for her autograph, her photograph, and even the locks of her hair.[28] Bonheur became an international star artist, whose work was commercially successful in the United States and England as well as France. At the heart of this international success story was Bonheur's shrewdness as a self-promoter of a particular image. As Gabriel Weisberg has observed, "she well understood that in order to market her paintings successfully, her dress, demeanor and public image—in addition to her paintings—were crucial to shaping perceptions of her accomplishments as an artist. Bonheur was one of the earliest painters to use modern methods of self-promotion to establish herself as an international personality."[29] Such methods included interviews and biographical portraits in the new mass press, replete with photographs of her "at home" in her studio at Fontainebleau. British and American magazines lavished attention on the artist's clothes, her animals, and her chateau. The press copy generated often exceeded attention to her paintings, but it increased their value in the process. Bonheur also used other media stars to stage her celebrity. When the Universal Exposition of 1889 brought Buffalo Bill and his Wild West Show to Paris, Bonheur recognized a kindred spirit. She smothered the famous cowboy with attention, and famously painted his portrait.[30]

It became impossible to fathom the star power of either Bonheur or Bernhardt without reckoning with their bizarre habits. Building on already culturally embedded links between the artist and capricious behavior, both women flaunted their oddness. For much of her career, Bonheur played up her unconventional appearance and mannerisms in the media. As the critic Judith Grainger has put it, she "knew the advantage of public image and used her eccentricities to build a controversial and somewhat mysterious persona to enhance her reputation."[31] Her paintings became hot commodities on the art market. Like Bonheur, Bernhardt considered herself first and foremost an artist; the fantastic whims of the artist were her only master.[32] Her fans ate it up. "In an era when the marvelous seems to have vanished from sight," wrote the journalist Claude-Roger Marx, "she has also known to remain far-away, to preserve a mystery not exhausted by the years."[33] Marx evoked a common view of Bernhardt as somehow outside the normal order of things. As another critic put it, "Sarah's fantasy and her pride have carried her up so high that her life is no longer visible; nor can we communicate with her. Everything up there is superb but unreal, made only for the charm of the imagination."[34]

Bernhardt hovered on the peripheries of Parisian society, pulled away by the force of her own unpredictable desires. Indeed, an older meaning of eccentric was "out of the way." The word "eccentric" derived from the Greek *ek* meaning "out of" and *kentron* meaning "circle." "Deviation from a centre, in fact, is the very thing which constitutes eccentricity," wrote a British cleric in 1859.[35] As deviations from the center, eccentric orbits were linked to the peripheral. Both Bonheur and Bernhardt were already identified with the social margins as artists. Bonheur's decision to live just outside Paris in By was a common choice for an artist. Many of Bernhardt's closest friends had their roots in the theatrical and literary underworld of Parisian life, among them Jean Lorrain, René Vivien, and Oscar Wilde.[36] In addition, because of her Jewishness, critics tied Bernhardt to an exotic Orient on the peripheries of Europe. According to anti-Semites, her half-Jewish origins "gave her face the troublesome grace of the bohemian or gypsy," and "link[ed] her to the Orient and to the primitive world."[37] Because of its geographical remoteness to Europe, the Orient itself was considered eccentric. As the figurative meaning of eccentricity took root, Europeans linked the eccentric location of Northern Africa and the Middle East to its culture, which they deemed lacking in normative disciplining. As a result, the Orient became to them a "reservoir of infinite peculiarity," to use Edward Said's phrase.[38]

Even as eccentricity became associated with liminality, it took shape in the mass culture developing in urban centers. Through the new technologies of mass newsprint and photography, eccentrics emerged as a new modern "type" or social being. Europeans hardly had to wait until the nineteenth century to witness humans behaving outlandishly. Nevertheless, eccentricity was novel in two ways. First, it served a new purpose, which was to materialize the limits of normative behavior in a bourgeois liberal society marked by disciplining and regulatory controls. Second, eccentrics were now produced as *images* in a mass press particularly preoccupied with the curiosities of the everyday. As Vanessa Schwartz has shown, the daily newspaper, as well as serial novels and guidebooks, "incessantly conjured a never-ending festival of modern life."[39] This set of images produced a new social being—the eccentric—who came to symbolize not only modern "spectacle" but also the modern response to the legislation of identity.

Eccentricity can be defined as an inability to fit easily into any reproducible norm. The eccentric eludes the limits of what we consider to be "normal" categories of identity reproducible through socialization and disciplining. If we take the example of the late Michael Jackson, for instance, we note that Jackson's eccentricity derived precisely from his visual failure to meet normative expectations of race and gender. Jackson's eccentricity originates in the fluid visual space he occupies between black and white, male and female, human and animal. His eccentricity results in a certain lack of intelligibility or legibility—or an inability to be recognized according to prevailing social norms.[40] As we shall see, both Bonheur and Bernhardt became unintelligible in this way, failing to match normative expectations. Visually, they could also be located in the peripheries between male and female, human and animal, just recognizable enough to be "odd" without being "normal." Eccentricity was largely generated through visuality. While we can easily envision an eccentric outfit, we have more difficulty conjuring up an eccentric novel, poem, or comment.[41] To be eccentric was to present a queer spectacle of oneself. More specifically, the illegibility of Bonheur's and Bernhardt's images rested in their *androgynous* and *therianthropic* qualities, that is, their ability to visually merge male and female, human and animal forms.[42]

Critics have often attributed Bonheur's androgyny to her childhood. Her mother died when little Rosa was quite young. As a result, Eugène de Mirecourt noted, "The little girl escaped the surveillance" of her father, and could be seen in Paris "running like a goat along the streets while her maid thought she was at school." With "her brusque manners, her cropped hair and her round face, she could be mistaken for a boy playing hooky."[43] To make matters worse, Bonheur's father was an ardent disciple of St. Simonianism. As a child, the future artist fell under the spell of a social movement itself considered highly eccentric, not least because of its attitude toward gender roles. St. Simonians frowned on marriage, championed free love, and at one point set out for Egypt to find a female messiah who could save the human race. They also adopted androgynous forms of dress, including wide culottes.[44] Bonheur more or less followed this style most of her life. Bonheur's eccentric garb can also be attributed to her early identity as an artist, specifically her association with Parisian bohemian artists who purposely donned clothes that would affront the bourgeoisie in the 1830s and 1840s.[45]

Bonheur's famous excuse for her *travesti* was that she needed to dress like a man in order to visit the slaughterhouses and sketch animals without being harassed.[46] But Bonheur by no means limited her male costume to the slaughterhouse; she consistently wore a male style of dress at her chateau in Fontainebleau. Her friend Joseph Verdier recalled a female neighbor's chagrin when his fiancée took a stroll with the artist one day. She soon dropped by to scold Monsieur Verdier for letting his fiancée walk unchaperoned with a man, and a handsome one at that.[47] But to describe Bonheur's clothes as "male" or to say that she simply "cross-dressed" is not quite right, for her costume was neither really feminine nor masculine. In 1853, an observer described her dress as "a compromise between that of a woman and a man."[48] "Impossible to guess her sex," declared Eugène de Mirecourt in 1856.[49] For her part, Bonheur enjoyed her ability to keep everyone guessing. "They wonder to which sex I belong!" she once wrote gleefully to her sister.[50] The key, as Bonheur's companion Nathalie Micas brilliantly figured out, was to create a costume that was unique to the artist alone. She instructed Bonheur to wear something as "distinctively yours" as Napoleon's cap was to his image. In response, Bonheur created a uniform consisting of a Breton-style smock, a vest, simple pants, and a little cap (fig. 3.1). Contemporaries deemed it "queer" and "odd" but also amusing.[51] Bonheur's costume became eccentric rather than scandalous because it was recognizable as hers alone, and thus inhabited a unique site on the peripheries of gender norms. In her paintings as well, Bonheur positioned herself on the peripheries. Art historians have traditionally viewed Bonheur's art (in contrast to her lifestyle) as conservative and conventional.[52] More recently, however, the art historian James Saslow has argued that Bonheur portrayed herself in drag as a clean-shaven male in her most famous painting, *The Horse Fair.* Saslow describes this painting "as a male space, from which Bonheur was excluded by law and custom, and to which she gained admission by subterfuge."[53] According to her biographer Theodore Stanton, it was while painting *The Horse Fair* that Bonheur first experimented with *travesti:* as a result, she was delighted to be "taken everywhere for a young man and no attention was paid to her comings and goings."[54] If Saslow's interpretation can be believed, Bonheur simply extended the private joke by appearing in drag in her most famous painting.

Bernhardt also trumped normative expectations concerning gender and dress. The artist sometimes wore men's clothes offstage, notably when she explored her talents as a sculptor (fig. 3.4). In a famous portrait of the artist in her studio, she sported a smart white suit softened by ruffles at the collar. Hardly practical for carving stone, the suit was nothing but another costume donned to display her talents for the press. Like Bonheur, Bernhardt claimed that her cross-dressing was a professional hazard—she found male characters to be richer and more complex than female ones.[55] Indeed, some of the most successful moments of Bernhardt's career were her male roles.[56] She had her first big break in 1869 as the troubadour Zanetto in François Coppée's *Le Passant.* At the peak of her career, she played Hamlet as well as the Duc de Reichstadt in Rostand's *L'Aiglon,* both to high, if not unanimous, acclaim (fig. 3.2).[57] While rehearsing for *L'Aiglon,* Bernhardt played with gender roles in her press appearances. For example, when someone asked her about her ability to rehearse until 3:00 or 4:00 A.M. as the Duc, she responded "Bah! Don't be surprised. Now that I've cut my hair short, I feel like I have the strength of a man."[58] As the Duc, she drew this response from a reporter concerning her short hair and male costume: "She wears it with such ease that the 'real' men beside her have the air of being disguised."[59] The effect of Bernhardt's *travesti*

FIGURE 3.4. Sarah
Bernhardt in her studio

was to render masculinity as queer and strange as herself. This denaturalizing
effect explains why Bernhardt was one of the most caricatured personalities
of her day. As a mode of representation that admits to its own mimicry
through parody, caricature perfectly captured Bernhardt's tendency to parody rather than inhabit any normative identity. Her eccentricity signaled a
tendency to *stage* the culturally inscribed limits of gender identity rather than
"naturally" reproduce them.

Androgyny was an important signifier of eccentricity in the nineteenth
century, and firmly established both Bonheur and Bernhardt as "strange" in

the public eye. But it was the two women's relationship with animals that marked them as truly, verifiably eccentric. Eccentricity was certainly not the sole province of females in the late nineteenth century. Oscar Wilde is but one example of the many male eccentrics inhabiting Paris during this time. At the same time, there were arguably specific female traits of eccentricity. One of them was a peculiar relationship with animals, particularly cats. The association of women and cats dates back to medieval times, when black cats were burned as witches.[60] As the early modern icon of the marginal woman famed to live on the edge of town, the witch is probably the closest precursor we have to the female eccentric. Witches were believed not only to harbor cats in large numbers, but to transform themselves into cats in order to better cast spells on their victims. Lonely old women were said to keep black cats as familiars or lesser devils given by Satan at the time of their initiation into witchcraft. Historians have noted how many of these prejudices survived into the nineteenth century.[61] Even in the twentieth century, according to a recent popular study on eccentrics, "the stereotype of the eccentric woman is an old lady in a big house with a hundred cats."[62]

Interestingly enough, Bonheur was often compared to a witch. In an 1856 portrait of Bonheur, for example, Eugène de Mirecourt claimed that the artist "also rides every morning on a broomstick, flying off up the chimney like a witch, especially going out on Saturday night, which is the hobgoblins' frightful hour of orgies."[63] While Bonheur did not live with countless cats, she favored extremely large ones, including several full-grown lions.[64] According to one art critic, she had an "obsessive interest in lions."[65] In 1873, the director of a small zoo near Melun invited Bonheur to make studies of a lioness in their possession. Bonheur sketched "Pierette" again and again, but because she tired of traveling to the zoo, she went on to "rent" a lion named Brutus, and then have two shipped up from Marseilles. She kept these for about two months, then donated them to the Paris zoo. In 1884, Bonheur again took in two lion cubs, one of which, Fatma, lived with her three years.[66] She frequently gave them the run of the yard and house. Bonheur delighted in the trouble Fatma got into when she chose to wander around and make a shambles of her bedroom.

Like Bonheur, Bernhardt had a special place in her heart for cats. On a theatrical tour in London in 1879, she set off to Liverpool to acquire a lion. Instead she returned with a cheetah. Much to everyone's chagrin, she let it loose in the backyard of her neighborhood in Chester Square. Her biographer Cornelia Otis Skinner describes the response of her entourage of friends: "Madame Guérard screamed and crossed herself, the butler dropped a tea tray, de Nittis kept flailing the air with his cane, Doré walked with stately alacrity into the house and everyone else, including Sarah, burst into maniacal gales of laughter. Passers-by peered in amazement over the garden wall and scores of faces appeared at windows in the dignified houses surrounding Chester Square."[67] The scene was summed up in the next day's London papers as a "witches' Sabbath." Returning to France across the channel also posed a challenge, as the cheetah inspired a near mutiny on the boat.[68]

Both women eventually developed a full-fledged menagerie of unconventional pets. Besides her lions, Bonheur kept hundreds of birds as well as an otter, brought back from the Pyrénées, who would sometimes escape his tank and crawl between her companion Nathalie Micas's bedsheets.[69] If we are to believe all reports, Bernhardt's pets included over her lifetime: two Russian greyhounds, a poodle, a bull mastiff, a terrier, an Italian greyhound, a parrot, a monkey (named Darwin), three cats, several birds including a hawk, two horses (Vermouth and Cassis), a boa, a lynx, a tigress, a wildcat, a wolfhound, a lion, a cheetah, six chameleons, and two pet alligators from Louisiana, one that Bernhardt killed by feeding it too much champagne, the other that she shot dead after it swallowed her beloved Manchester terrier. Bernhardt procured many of these animals while touring. Getting them back to France was not easy. A London hotel initially refused to house a tigress on the vicious rumor that she had eaten two waiters.[70] Even in Paris, Bernhardt's menagerie became a problem when she allowed the cats to have the run of her house. Alexandre Dumas, fils once lost his straw boater to a puma while waiting five minutes for Bernhardt in her studio. In 1894, one terrified reporter told the tale of finally gaining entry to the actress's house, only to be introduced to her two jaguars, Antony and Cleopatra.[71]

To keep big cats as pets was a performative gesture. When Bonheur and Bernhardt brought a large wild cat into a domesticated space, they expressed a sheer desire not only to cause trouble, but also to attract attention. Keeping wild animals was dangerous as well as strange; it demonstrated the kind of death-defying behavior already associated with bohemian artists, with their abuse of drugs and alcohol.[72] In domesticating such animals, the two women also displayed a bravura akin to circus performers. The lion was known in the nineteenth century as he is today: "the terror of the forest," in La Fontaine's phrase, who could make animals tremble at his mere smell.[73] Bonheur bragged that, unlike many of her male visitors, she felt no fear whatsoever approaching a four-hundred-pound predator. In order to avoid fights with dogs and visitors, she once had a night cage built for one of her lions. "But," she qualified, "she was so tame that I let her put her paws around my neck, I took her head and embraced her. She was a model of obedience and docility."[74] Fatma was similarly slavish. She followed Bonheur around "like a poodle," she once observed.[75]

When she and her companion Micas went to the train station to pick up the cubs from Marseilles, they did not tell the male train workers that they had been guarding the lions. This was because, explained Bonheur, "they would have died of fright retrospectively."[76] Bonheur's fondness for predators helped to stage her androgyny: she used them to launch herself in the public eye as more manly than men.

Besides being dangerous, wild animals were exuberant in famously unpredictable ways. They engaged in such "uncivilized" behaviors as chasing, attacking, biting, and relieving themselves indoors. Such behaviors were funny, inasmuch as they disrupted the "normal" course of life—causing screams, grasps for high furniture, repellent smells, and agonizing embarrassment. In short, feline behavior launched an all-out assault on the orderly disposition of nineteenth-century bourgeois liberal society. At the same time, such animal behavior—like eccentricity itself—was blameless; one could not blame an animal for behaving like an animal. The Romantics believed that the animal escaped the pull of normative disciplining altogether: its center of gravity was located elsewhere—in instinct and survival. What was considered "undisciplined" behavior among humans was "normal" or "natural" for animals. Animals, in other words, were born eccentrics.

Through their menageries, then, these women used animals not only to thumb their noses at bourgeois probity, but more fundamentally, to call into question the very logic of the cultural norm. What was normal and what was uncivilized? The two artists also turned upside down the nineteenth century domestic imperative: that women maintain the home as a private oasis of comfort and tranquility. Home could hardly serve as a haven in a heartless world if you had a dangerous predator stalking your living room. Both Bonheur and Bernhardt insisted on keeping undomesticated animals uncaged in their houses. Guests and neighbors were troubled by the fact that the lions *should* be restrained and yet *weren't*.[77] Both women, then, allowed normally confined creatures to do as they please, even at the risk of being dangerous. Could not the same be said for them? Out of orbit, out of cages—the two women's delight in large cats was nothing other than vicarious gender trouble once-removed. In leaving wild animals only partially "domesticated," they created a living model of their own rebellious relationship to the French domestic ideal.

Bonheur and Bernhardt situated themselves in the public eye on the peripheries between the animal and human worlds. Besides being overrun with animals, Bernhardt's mansion in Paris was decorated with animal furs from the far reaches of the globe. The gadfly Jean Lorrain recalled beaver from Brazil, buffalo from Canada, and bear from South America; he described Bernhardt's studio as "an accumulation of hair in every shade and from every provenance."[78] According to Skinner, Bernhardt's motivation for buying the lion while in London consisted in the fact that "she was fed up with meeting so many people. She had always found animals more interesting."[79] As Skinner says of Bernhardt: "She could handle a supposedly savage beast such as a lynx or a cheetah with fearless ease. Even reptiles held a fascination for her. When she played Cleopatra, she more than once insisted upon using a real snake for the final scene.[80] Bernhardt once even schemed to graft a tiger tail onto her own spine. Hoping to lash it about when she was angry, she nevertheless allowed her friends to talk her out of it at the last minute.[81]

Similarly, Bonheur presented herself to the mass press as a romantic figure living amid her animals on the edge of the Fontainebleau forest (the periphery again). Her letters were full of animal similes in which she compared herself to a rat, a dog, a tortoise, a mule, a boar, and a bear.[82] Speaking of Bonheur's love of animals at the time of her death, Arsène Alexandre remarked: "The animal is an enigma; he offers the beauty of life in movement, of instinct unspoiled by what makes men so insufferable, that is, education."[83] As a hermit living on the edge of the forest, Bonheur relished her animals' lack of "education." "Since I've been in By, living constantly in the midst of my animals," she once told her companion Anna Klumpke, "I scarcely have time to play the grand lady; so my visitors will have to take me as I am."[84] To live among her animals was the truth of her identity; to be *une grande dame* was to play an imposed role.[85] "I need the society of no one," she wrote in 1886; "What can the world do for me? A portrait painter has need of these things, but not I, who find all that is wanted in my dogs, my horses, my hinds, and my stags of the forest."[86] Through her choice of artistic subject, Bonheur also positioned herself on the social peripheries. A popular genre of painting at this time was to portray domesticated pets or interactions between animals and humans as a way of mediating between the natural and the social.[87] By contrast, Bonheur's art focused almost completely on a natural world cut off from human society. As John Ruskin famously noted, Bonheur focused almost exclusively on animals, and could not, or cared not, to articulate human faces.[88] Biographers personalize this element of Bonheur's art, arguing that, as one critic put it, "a deep psychological need insistently forced her to establish close relationships with her pets, whose fond gazes compensated her for her apparent sense of failure with human relationships."[89] Such an analysis tends to portray Bonheur in stereotypical terms—as a failed spinster clinging desperately to her animals as surrogate children.

In fact, Bonheur understood her closeness to her animals in a much more humorous, ironic and clever way. For example, Bonheur had Micas photograph her snuggling up to Fatma, sometimes called *la favorite de Mademoiselle* (fig. 3.1). The photograph—again very much part of the artist's self-promotion *qua* artist—suggests the productive ways in which Bonheur's eccentricity could operate in relation to her life-long love for women. The artist met Micas when the two were adolescents. Inseparable for fifty-three years, they lived together first in Paris, then at Bonheur's chateau until Micas' death in 1889. That year, Bonheur met Anna Klumpke, an American painter from San Francisco. Klumpke came to stay at By for a few months to paint Bonheur's portrait. When Bonheur asked the young artist to stay on, she did, becoming Bonheur's companion until the latter's death in 1899. These relationships were not without a distinct erotic charge, although it would be anachronistic to call them "lesbian." As Sharon Marcus has argued recently, Micas and Bonheur "had higher levels of involvement and intimacy than even the closest of female friends." Besides living together and being referred to by friends as a "couple," they cared for each others' bodies in illness, they combined their wealth, and they planned to be buried together. At the same time, as Marcus notes, such "friendships" could be highly naturalized so that they did not necessarily "threaten" anyone.[90]

Bonheur's photograph with Fatma suggests one such way in which female "friendships" were assimilated into mid–nineteenth-century culture. Bonheur's eccentric relationship with Fatma came to both symbolize and to disguise her "friendship" with Micas. As a member of the cat family, the lion also symbolized sex. In medieval times, cats were thought to be witches who altered themselves in order to copulate wildly under the direction of a huge devil–Tom Cat. Buffon vividly described the cat's sexual desire: "she invites it, she calls for it, she announces her desires by her piercing cries." When the male refuses her, "she pursues him, bites him and forces him, as it were, to satisfy her."[91] "*Le chat, la chatte*" means in French the same as the English "pussy"; such words had been obscenities for centuries. A woman who allowed herself to be taken sexually was said to have "let the cat go to the cheese."[92] French artists insisted on the cat's association with prostitution, itself once again linked to social marginality. Edouard Manet famously explored these connections in his painting "Olympia" featuring a black cat on a courtesan's bed.[93]

If we return to Micas' photograph with these meanings of the cat in mind, the photograph begs a new, more erotic interpretation. In a pose not unlike Manet's prostitute, Bonheur embraces Fatma in a kittenish manner, and casts her eyes up in a seductive gaze at the photographer, who (significantly) was Micas, her female companion. In her pose and facial expression, Bonheur could very well have been manipulating the sexual meanings of the cat already established in the French imagination. As a painter intimately familiar with French art, she no doubt knew about this sexual symbolism.

Animals in such French paintings as *Obedience Rewarded*, by François Boucher, frequently represented lovers, male sexual excitement, and even sexual intercourse.[94] We are also reminded of the fable by La Fontaine in which a cat, loved "obsessively" by its male owner, turns into a female lover.[95] The same element of eroticism seemed to color all Bonheur's relations with her lions. After her lion Néro had been unhappily consigned to the zoo, the critic Jules Claretie described him as "reveling no longer in the caresses of his mistress, while his mane looked dirty and uncombed."[96] Given the wealth of sexual connotation surrounding cats, it is tempting to see Bonheur using Fatma to express her own erotic feelings for Micas, the photographer. According to the art historian James Saslow, during this period Bonheur staged various other "lesbian genre scenes" (Saslow's term is, again, anachronistic) defined as a complex coding of homosexual love through photography. For example, Bonheur had herself photographed by Klumpke painting at her canvas, and featuring, in Saslow's words, an "exchange of gazes between sitter and subject, with all that suggests about power, autonomy, and eroticism."[97]

Fatma would also play a leading role in Bonheur's liaison with Klumpke. The San Francisco artist first ventured to Bonheur's chateau as a translator for a wealthy horse breeder from Wyoming. John Arbuckle had given Bonheur a very expensive horse, and on a visit to France in 1887, he decided to visit both artist and horse. Years later, Klumpke began her memoir of Bonheur with the story of this visit. Greeting them, a maid gave them the disappointing news that Bonheur was away in Nice, but nevertheless offered to show Arbuckle his gift. At the barn, the guests were treated first to the horse, and then to an animal the maid referred to as "la favorite de Mademoiselle": none other than Fatma. "A young lion, whose gaze became obstinately fixed on the two unknown visitors," Fatma appeared alert, powerful, and self-contained, evoking the presence of the artist herself. When the maid released Fatma from her cage and suggested they all go for a walk, Arbuckle looked, in Klumpke's words, distinctly "uncomfortable." As the two Americans bid a hasty retreat for their carriage, Klumpke noticed "on the lips of the obliging maid a little smile which was not without malice." From the start, Klumpke was in on the joke: the lion was there to make even big old cowboys feel just a wee bit nervous. When Klumpke finally did meet Bonheur two years later, she described her future companion's face as sensuously leonine: "Her face was framed by a mane of magnificent silvery gray hair whose silky, abundant curls fell to the nape of her neck and circled that venerable head like a halo."[98] And when Klumpke settled in at the chateau, becoming herself now "*la favorite de Mademoiselle*," Bonheur's first two gifts to her were a sketch and an engraving of a lion.[99]

At the level of the visual, where eccentricity almost always operated, Bonheur's homoerotic desires remained barely exteriorized, again, on the *peripheries* of consciousness. As long as desire took its distance in this way, barely recognizable, it was considered vaguely peculiar rather than alarming. Bonheur's eccentric mannerisms located her in a safely illegible zone between reassuringly "normal" and plainly transgressive behaviors. If Bonheur's lions served as symbols of her libido, the oddness of her affection for them shifted attention away from her homoerotic desires. After all, the photograph was much more likely to raise the question: "Why is this woman hugging a lion?" than "Why is this woman posing seductively for her female companion?" If Bonheur's therianthropic tendencies helped to stage her androgyny, they did the opposite in the case of her passion for women, which was to divert attention away from it. Bonheur's photo with Fatma also provides a clue as to why eccentricity, as a particularly *visual* strategy of the new print media, worked so well for Bonheur. As an artist, Bonheur was, above all, a clever manipulator of images. Bonheur knew how to express in visual, coded form what often could not be openly said or challenged.

In sum, both Bonheur and Bernhardt's eccentricity consisted in their failure to fit easily into any reproducible norm, whether it be male or female, animal or human. A famous cartoon by André Gill represents Bernhardt precisely in this way—as an androgynous, therianthropic, fantasy creature, dressed in her sculpting suit, with the torso of a human and the legs of a mule (fig. 3.5). Bernhardt's much publicized habit of sleeping in a coffin, it could be argued, also located her on another periphery—that between life and death. By showcasing these miscellaneous identities (in the sense of sundry or unclassifiable), Bonheur and Bernhardt produced media images of themselves that remained just outside the gravitational force of normative cultural systems. Precisely as miscellaneous—recognizable but not categorizable—the two women eluded expectations that they would follow the usual female orbits of marriage and motherhood. They were eccentric stars whose orbits were predictable only in their unpredictability. In this way, their provocative, unconventional celebrity images became intelligible on their own terms. Eccentric stardom enabled Bonheur and Bernhardt to pursue their own orbits—to lead inventive, creative lives even in a universe where female movement was radically proscribed. In this sense, there was nothing innocent about eccentricity at all. Its most clever disguise was its apparent unimportance.

At the same time, however, eccentricity was its own worst enemy. As a behavior, it was an incitement but also a means of normalization. The mere classification of female eccentricity was a normalizing judgment of hyperindividualization: to say that such-and-such was an eccentric was to reaffirm

FIGURE 3.5. Caricature
of Sarah Bernhardt by
André Gill

conventional behavior. Furthermore, eccentricity was by definition individual,
idiosyncratic, and thus of little political importance. Unlike a social movement, for example, it could not gather collective force as an instrument of
resistance. Bonheur and Bernhardt may have gotten away with murder, but
they didn't create an enormous threat to nineteenth-century gender norms, at
least as eccentrics. Furthermore, by the end of the century, stardom under-
went a fundamental change of style, which elided the contradiction between
celebrity achievement and female self-renunciation, thus rendering eccentricity an obsolete strategy. The media focus on stars increasingly emphasized the
ordinariness of actresses' lives. Journalists began to domesticate celebrities by
sanitizing their lives and making them models of proper domesticity. Readers
of such magazines as *Fémina* were treated to photos of pristine actresses in their
immaculate bourgeois foyers, holding forth on their love for their children.[100]

Eccentricity was no longer necessary among female stars; they could just pretend to be ordinary in order to overcome celebrity's challenge to the ideal of female self-denigration.

Finally, through repetition, the eccentric gesture became ordinary. By the turn of the century, harboring large felines had become a cliché of the wealthy. When the art collector Isabella Stewart Gardner took a Sunday walk in the Boston Commons with a lion "borrowed" from the zoo, American journalists christened her an eccentric (fig. 3.6).[101] But when the Italian Marchesa Casati promenaded with her cheetahs outside the Paris Ritz, the more jaded European press largely wrote off her antics as a trendy gesture of wealthy bohemia.[102] As a much-repeated practice, predator-love became a self-consciously fashionable act. This eccentric gesture, at least, had lost its singularity and its innocence. When in 1913 the feminist Marguerite Durand had herself photographed with a lioness named "Tiger" in order to draw notice to the cause of suffrage, she managed to land on the cover of several prominent French journals (fig. 3.7). But the gesture absolutely did not earn Durand the label of eccentric.[103] Her highly political aim, which was to garner publicity for her run for municipal office, demonstrated how far the predator craze had strayed from its seemingly whimsical origins.

FIGURE 3.6. Isabella Stewart Gardner taking a lion for a walk in Boston

FIGURE 3.7. Marguerite
Durand and her lion. *Femina*,
*April 1, 1910, Bibliothèque
Marguerite Durand*

In astronomy, eccentric stars are damned because their orbits end in collision and extinction. In mass cultural society, eccentric stars were also doomed because their orbits were destined for mimicry and, ultimately, a collapse into cliché. From the very beginning, their fates were sealed by the fact that neither celebrity nor eccentricity inhered in the individual. Rather it was the readers and fans who decided who was odd and who was an odds-on favorite. While eccentrics such as Bonheur and Bernhardt may have paraded themselves as singular individuals accountable to no one, they were very much accountable to the masses who, in the last analysis, chose to view them this way. Eccentricity may have been the distinction of the singular few, but in the nineteenth century, it was increasingly grounded in the democratization of culture. In this sense, eccentricity elegantly illustrates the transition from elite to mass democratic society.

NOTES

1. Bonheur received the *Légion d'honneur* in 1865. According to Linda Nochlin, she also won a first medal in the Paris Salon, the Commander of the Order of Isabella the Catholic, and the Order of Leopold of Belgium. See Linda Nochlin, "Why Have

There Been No Great Women Artists?" in *Women, Art, and Power: and Other Essays,* ed. Linda Nochlin (New York: Harper and Row, 1971), 174.

2. See Theodore Stanton, *Reminiscences of Rosa Bonheur* (New York: D. Appleton and Co., 1910), 24. Bonheur complained that such men never showed up, but Stanton conjectures that they galloped off for fear of being seen with her. Stanton was the son of Elizabeth Cady Stanton and a lifelong feminist. His *Reminiscences* of Bonheur is rich in primary documents, and forms a sharp and refreshing contrast to other early twentieth-century biographies of the artist.

3. No title, place unclear: *Le Gaulois?* April 11, 1882, Caricatures, Opuscules, Presse Satirique, Illustrée, Sarah Bernhardt, (hereafter COPSI), Séries 30, Bibliothèque Historique de la ville de Paris (hereafter BHVP).

4. Sarcey is quoted in Henry Lapauze, "Sarah Bernhardt," *La Revue Littéraire, Beaux Arts, Sciences,* December 15, 1893, Boîte Sarah Bernhardt (hereafter BSB), Collection de l'Association des Régisseurs de Théâtres (hereafter CART), BHVP.

5. For other references that mention Bernhardt's "eccentricities," see Marie Colombier, *Le voyage de Sarah Bernhardt en Amérique* (Paris: Maurice Dreyfous, 1881), 315–316; Albert Wolff, "Courrier de Paris: Sarah Bernhardt," *Le Figaro,* February 7, 1883, and "Chronique d'un Indifférent," *Événement,* June 29, 1887, both in vol. 1, Recueil Factice de Coupures de Presse Sarah Bernhardt (hereafter RFCPSB), Collection Rondel (hereafter CR), Bibliothèque National, Département des Arts du Spectacle (hereafter BNDAS); "Le Lion de Sarah Bernhardt," no place, July 15, 1895, Coupures de Presse jusqu'à 1900 sur Sarah Bernhardt (hereafter CPSB), Séries 30, BHVP; no title, *La Vie Parisienne,* November 25, 1893, vol. 3, RFCPSB, CR, BNDAS; Mario Bertaux, "Sarah Bernhardt," no place or date, Dossier Sarah Bernhardt (hereafter DSB), Bibliothèque Marguerite Durand, (hereafter BMD).

6. See Leo Braudy, *The Frenzy of Renown: Fame and its History* (New York: Oxford University Press, 1986). Despite the massive size of *The Frenzy of Renown,* Emily Dickinson does a female solo on Braudy's stage, aptly enough, in his discussion of fame and "aloneness."

7. Lenard Berlanstein, "Historicizing and Gendering Celebrity Culture: Famous Women in Nineteenth-Century France," *Journal of Women's History* 16, no. 4 (2004): 66.

8. "Lettre de Mme. Sarah Bernhardt," *La France,* November 14, 1890, vol. 2, RFCPSB, CR, BNDAS; and see also Jules Huret, *Sarah Bernhardt* (Paris: F. Juven, 1899), 42; Fernand Goupillé, "Sarah à New York," *La Presse,* March 18, 1891, vol. 2, RFCPSB, CR, BNDAS.

9. Sarah Bernhardt, *Ma double vie: Mémoires de Sarah Bernhardt* (Paris: Fasquelle, 1907), 210.

10. Tamar Garb, *Sisters of the Brush: Women's Artistic Culture in Late Nineteenth-Century Paris* (New Haven, Conn.: Yale University Press, 1994), 120. Elsewhere, Garb put it very well: "At best she was seen as an admirable artist and an eccentric, sometimes a lovable caricature, at worst the butt of malicious humor, a woman 'unsexed.'" See Tamar Garb, "L'Art Féminin: The Formation of a Critical Category in Late Nineteenth-

Century France," in *The Expanding Discourse: Feminism and Art History,* ed. Norma Broude and Mary D. Garrard (New York: Harper Collins Publishers, 1992), 192.

11. Historians have paid attention to various eccentrics, but not much to the phenomenon itself. Wanda Corn, "Art Matronage in Post-Victorian America," in *Cultural Leadership in America: Art Matronage and Patronage* (Boston, Mass.: Trustees of the Isabella Stewart Gardner Museum, 1997), 9–24, deals in passing with Isabella Stewart Gardner as an eccentric. Brian Cowlishaw, "A Genealogy of Eccentricity" (Ph.D. thesis, University of Oklahoma, 1998) is a more systematic study of eccentricity in the nineteenth century, but his focus is primarily on literature such as *Don Quixote.*

12. Particularly helpful to me in thinking through the norm here was Georges Canguilhem, *The Normal and the Pathological* (New York: Zone Books, 1989), particularly 51, 178.

13. *Oxford English Dictionary,* second edition (hereafter *OED*), s.v. "Eccentric."

14. *Trésor de la langue française, Dictionnaire de la langue du XIXe et du XXe siècle, Dictionnaire de la langue française; Dictionnaire historique de la langue française, Deutsches Wörterbuch.*

15. This statement is based on word counts collected in the ARTFL (American and French Research on the Treasury of the French Language) database, a cooperative project undertaken by the Centre National de la recherche scientifique and the University of Chicago. According to the ARTFL website (http://humanities.uchicago.edu/orgs/ARTFL/artl.flyer.html), the database contains nearly 2,000 texts, "ranging from classic works of French literature to various kinds of non-fiction prose and technical writing. The eighteenth, nineteenth and twentieth centuries are about equally represented." According to ARTFL, the use of the words *excentrique, excentriques, excentricité,* and *excentriquement* for the modern period are as follows: 1810: 1; 1820: 5; 1830: 7; 1840: 17; 1850: 26; 1860: 17; 1870: 20; 1880: 10, 1890: 12; 1900: 11, 1910: 6; 1920: 12; 1930: 23; 1940: 14; 1950: 5; 1960: 1.

16. See Germaine de Staël, *Considérations sur la révolution française,* 371; citation 51 under ARTFL search "excentricité." For George Sand, see ARTFL, search for "excentriques," #30; "excentricité," #62–64; "excentrique," #44–46.

17. *OED.*

18. *OED.*

19. Michel Foucault, *Surveiller et punir: Naissance de la prison* (Paris: Éditions Gallimard, 1975); Jan Goldstein, ed., *Foucault and the Writing of History* (Oxford: Blackwell Press, 1994).

20. Jerrold Seigel, *Bohemian Paris: Culture, Politics and the Boundaries of Bourgeois Life, 1830–1930* (New York: Penguin Books, 1986). On bohemia, see also Elizabeth Wilson, *Bohemians: The Glamorous Outcasts* (New Brunswick, N.J.: Rutgers University Press, 2000), and Mary Gluck, *Popular Bohemia: Modernism and Urban Culture in Nineteenth-Century Paris* (Cambridge, Mass.: Harvard University Press, 2005).

21. *OED*; *Trésor de la langue française.* Neither *étoile* nor *star* has this metaphorical meaning in the *Dictionnaire de l'Académie française,* 1832–1835.

22. "Soleils couchants," *La Vie en Rose,* October 26, 1902, RFCPSB, CR, BNDAS.

23. Sartorys, "Le roman comique," no place given, April 1882, COPSI, Séries 30, BHVP.

24. See J. M., "Sarah Bernhardt," in *Les Contemporains Célèbres,* 1890, vol. 2, RF-CPSB, CR, BNDAS. See also Charles Landry, "Elle," *Le Petit Parisien,* May 16 ,1892, vol. 2, RFCPSB, BNDAS.

25. Mince, "Les Étoiles des théâtres de Paris: Sarah Bernhardt," no place given, May 14, 1898, fol. SW 208, RFCPSB, CR, BNDAS; for the "fairy of stars," see also Gavroche, "Le théâtre libre," *Echo de Paris,* March 24, 1889; "Imprévoyance," no place or date given (1902?), fol. SW 252, RFCPSB, CR, BNDAS.

26. "Sarah Bernhardt," December 1896, vol. 6, RCPSB, CR, BNDAS.

27. See Mary Louise Roberts, *Disruptive Acts: The New Woman in Fin-de-Siècle France* (Chicago: University of Chicago Press, 2002), chapters 6–7.

28. Danielle Digne, *Rosa Bonheur ou l'insolence: L'histoire d'une vie, 1822–1899* (Paris: Denoël/Gonthier, 1980), 102.

29. Gabriel Weisberg, "Rosa Bonheur's Reception in England and America: The Popularization of a Legend and the Celebration of a Myth," in *Rosa Bonheur: All Nature's Children,* ed. Dahesh Museum (New York: Dahesh Museum, 1998), 3–5.

30. Weisberg, "Rosa Bonheur's Reception," 19–20. See also Joy S. Kasson, *Buffalo Bill's Wild West: Celebrity, Memory and Popular History* (New York: Hill and Wang, 2001), 85–88.

31. Judy Greaves Rainger, "Buffalo Bill, Boulanger and Bonheur: Trans-Atlantic Cultural Exchanges in the Fin-de-Siècle," *Proceedings of the Western Society for French History,* 26 (1999): 248.

32. For Bernhardt as a whimsical artist, see "Sarah Bernhardt: Artiste dramatique," *L'Éclair,* October 25, 1890, vol. 2, RFCPSB, CR, BNDAS; Enrico Ferri, "Physionomie nerveuse des femmes artistes," *La Revue,* December 15, 1896, especially the reference to Bernhardt, 513.

33. Claude-Roger Marx, "Sarah Bernhardt," *Comoedia Illustrée,* no date, RT 5943, CR, BNDAS.

34. Bertaux, "Sarah Bernhardt."

35. Rev. James Kendall, *Eccentricity; or a Check to Censoriousness with Chapters on Other Subjects* (London: Simpkin, Marshall, 1859), 27.

36. For Bonheur's relationship to the lesbian Parisian underworld, see Martha Vicinus, "Fin-de-Siècle Theatrics: Male Impersonation and Lesbian Desire," in *Borderlines: Genders and Identities in War and Peace, 1870–1930,* ed. Billie Melman (New York: Routledge, 1998), 172.

37. Ernest Lys, "Sarah Bernhardt dans Jeanne d'Arc," *Gil Blas,* December 6, 1889, vol. 1, RFCPSB, CR, BNDAS; article without title, date or bibliographical information, fol. SW 251, Recueil de coupures de presse, illustrations et caricatures, Sarah Bernhardt, 1896–1905, 11, CR, BNDAS. See also Marie Colombier, *Mémoires de Sarah Barnum* (Paris: Chez tous les librairies, 1883), 195–196, 209.

38. Edward Said, *Orientalism* (New York: Random House, 1978), 102–104. Said examines the French novelist Gustave Flaubert in his travels to Egypt in the 1840s and

1850s. Flaubert never failed to note sexually eccentric behavior, argues Said, including a couple copulating in public, a man buggered by a monkey, a marabout masturbated by women until he died of exhaustion, or women rubbing themselves with male urine to make themselves fertile. Even Europeans became eccentric in the colonies. In 1881, the British *Spectator* had this to say about the Orient: "The wonder about millionaires is not that they should be sometimes eccentric but that they are usually so ordinary. Power turns all heads more or less, and the absence of resistance develops willfulness, til, as we often see in the East, it becomes monstrous caprice." See "The Eccentricities of the Rich" excerpted in *Littell's Living Age* series 5, vol. 151, December 24, 1881: 758.

39. Vanessa Schwartz, *Spectacular Realities: Early Mass Culture in Fin-de-Siècle Paris* (Berkeley: University of California Press, 1998), 16.

40. This is the definition of *intelligibility* given by Judith Butler, *Undoing Gender* (New York: Routledge, 2004), 3.

41. Lewis Carroll and Edward Lear are two of the few who come to mind.

42. See *OED*, s.v. "Therianthropy": "combining the form of a beast with that of a man; of or pertaining to deities represented in the combined forms of man and beast, as dog- or eagle-headed divinities."

43. Eugène de Mirecourt, *Les contemporains: Rosa Bonheur* (Paris: G. Havard, 1856), 7–8, 14–15.

44. For the Saint-Simonian construction of gender, see Claire Goldberg Moses, " 'Difference' in Historical Perspective: Saint-Simonian Feminism," in *Feminism, Socialism and French Romanticism*, ed. Claire Goldberg Moses and Leslie Wahl Rabine (Bloomington: Indiana University Press, 1993); Claire Goldberg Moses, *French Feminism in the Nineteenth Century* (Albany, N.Y.: SUNY Press, 1984), chapter 3. On Bonheur and the Saint-Simonians, see Stanton, *Reminiscences,* 58–63; Gretchen Van Slyke, "The Sexual and Textual Politics of Dress: Rosa Bonheur and Her Cross-dressing Permits," *Nineteenth-Century French Studies* (Spring-Summer, 1998): 329; Albert Boime, "The Case of Rosa Bonheur," *Art History* 4 (1981): 387.

45. Gluck, *Popular Bohemia,* 28–29.

46. George Sand also claimed to have cross-dressed for practical reasons, namely, to get cheap theater tickets. See Van Slyke, "Sexual and Textual Politics of Dress."

47. Stanton, *Reminiscences,* 365–366.

48. Dore Ashton with Denise Browne Hare, *Rosa Bonheur: A Life and a Legend* (New York: Viking Press, 1981), 109–110.

49. Mirecourt, *Les contemporains: Rosa Bonheur,* 54. Mirecourt also tells a story (55–57) of how Bonheur's "masculine disguise" caused her to have many adventures. Once when she was coming back from the country and had her male clothes on, she found out that a woman friend was sick, and rushed to her side without bothering to put a dress on. The doctor arrived, and seeing Bonheur embracing her friend, he thought to be discreet, not wanting to interrupt the lovers. "Trouvant mademoiselle Bonheur, qu'il prend naturellement pour un homme, assise au bord du lit de sa camarade, et les voyant en train de s'embrasser avec tendresse, il se retire au plus vite."

Bonheur and her friend realized what had happened, and the former rushed after the doctor to explain her true identity. See still other stories, 59–66.

50. Ashton with Hare, *Rosa Bonheur,* 163. For Bonheur's gender ambivalence, see also "L'oeuvre de Rosa Bonheur," *La Fronde,* n.d. [May 1899], Dossier Rosa Bonheur, BMD.

51. See the words of Robert David d'Angers in Stanton, *Reminiscences,* 24. Bonheur's clothing was deemed important enough to talk about even in her obituaries. See for example, "La Vie à Paris: Rosa Bonheur," *Le Petit Niçois,* May 30, 1899; "Rosa Bonheur," *La Fronde,* May 27, 1899; untitled article, *Événement,* May 30, 1899, all Dossier Rosa Bonheur, BMD.

52. See for example, Boime, "The Case of Rosa Bonheur," 386.

53. James M. Saslow, " 'Disagreeably Hidden': Construction and Constriction of the Lesbian Body in Rosa Bonheur's *Horse Fair,*" in Broude and Garrand, eds., *Expanding Discourse,* 192.

54. Stanton, *Reminiscences,* 363.

55. "Les Travestis de Sarah," *Illustré Théâtral,* December 12, 1895, fol. SW 252. Recueil de coupures de presse, 1896–1905, Sarah Bernhardt, CR, BNDAS.

56. Lenard Berlanstein, "Breeches and Breaches: Cross-Dress Theater and the Culture of Gender Ambiguity in Modern France," *Comparative Studies in Society and History* 38 (1996): 338–369, provides an excellent brief history of the stage practice of cross-dressing in modern France. According to Berlanstein, cross-dressing reached its apogee in the second third of the nineteenth century, then began to decline, mostly because of changing views of the body and sexuality.

57. See Ashton with Hare, *Sarah Bernhardt,* 123–124, 126.

58. Related in August Germain, "L'Aiglon," *Echo de Paris,* March 15, 1900. For other reviews of Bernhardt's performance, see *Le Gaulois,* March 16, 1900; *Echo de Paris,* March 17, 1900; *La Fronde,* March 16, 1900.

59. A. Fabrèque, "Chez Edmond Rostand," *Le Journal,* March 7, 1900, vol. 5, RF-CPSB, CR, BNDAS. For other discussions of Bernhardt's cross-dressing, see Ruth Brandon, *Being Divine* (London: Secker and Warburg, 1991), 339–343; Jill Edmonds, "Princess Hamlet," in *The New Woman and Her Sisters: Feminism and Theatre, 1850–1914,* ed. Viv Gardner and Susan Rutherford (New York: Harvester Wheatsheaf, 1992), 59–76. For Bernhardt's own views on cross-dressing, see her *Art du théâtre,* 139–146; "Les travestis de Sarah," *Illustré Théâtral,* December 12, 1895, fol. SW 252. RFCPSB, CR, BNDAS; René d'Armand, "Les travestis de Sarah," *La Rampe,* June 16, 1899; Paul Perret, "Les travestis de S B," *La Rampe,* April 8, 1923, CART, BHVP; G. I. Geller, *Sarah Bernhardt* (Paris: Gallimard, 1931), 221; "Life As I See It: A Few Fancies and Some Stories," *Pearson's Magazine,* November 1912, in CART, BHVP.

60. Robert Darnton, *The Great Cat Massacre and Other Episodes in French Cultural History* (New York: Basic Books, 1984), 92–94; Kathleen Kete, *The Beast in the Boudoir: Petkeeping in Nineteenth-Century Paris* (Berkeley: University of California Press, 1994), 115.

61. Katharine Briggs, *Nine Lives: The Folklore of Cats* (New York: Dorset Press, 1980), 83.

62. Dr. David Weeks and Jamie James, *Eccentrics: A Study of Sanity and Strangeness* (New York: Villard, 1995). In 2003 the *New York Times* reported on a reclusive old Welsh woman forced to leave her twelfth-century castle in order to enter into a nursing home. There she had lived "with countless cats but without electricity, heat or running water, which she apparently could no longer afford." See Nick Madigan, "The Poor Woman is Gone and Her Castle's Besieged," *New York Times,* January 4, 2003.

63. Quoted by Stanton, *Reminiscences,* 40.

64. According to the French *Littré,* a cat can refer to "tout animal du même genre que le chat," including the lion, tiger, lynx, etc.

65. Boime, "The Case of Rosa Bonheur," 399.

66. Ashton with Hare, *Rosa Bonheur,* 135; Anna Klumpke, *Rosa Bonheur, sa vie, son oeuvre* (Paris: Flammarion, 1908), 278–280.

67. Cornelia Otis Skinner, *Madame Sarah* (Boston: Houghton-Mifflin, 1967), 136.

68. G. G. Geller, *Sarah Bernhardt: Divine Eccentric* (New York: Frederick A. Stokes Company, 1933), 151.

69. Ashton with Hare, *Rosa Bonheur,* 97. Bonheur's menagerie was also a constant topic of discussion in her obituaries. See "Rosa Bonheur," *Petit Bleu,* May 27, 1899. Dossier Rosa Bonheur, BMD.

70. Joanna Richardson, *Sarah Bernhardt* (London: M. Reinhardt, 1959), 113–114.

71. "Le lion de Sarah Bernhardt"; Jules Huret, *Sarah Bernhardt* (Paris: F. Juven, 1899), 41; Colombier, *Le voyage de Sarah Bernhardt en Amérique,* 243–244, 134, 189–190, 239; Alberty, "Sarah Bernhardt: La veille d'une première," *Le Figaro,* October 1894, RT 5881, Recueil factice de diverses interviews de Sarah Bernhardt, 1890–1920, CR, BNDAS.

72. I am grateful to Vanessa Schwartz for this insight about wild animals, danger, and bohemia. See her comment to the panel, "Celebrity and Performance," Conference on Charisma, Fame, and Celebrity During the Long Nineteenth Century in Europe, New York University, April 13–14, 2007, unpublished ms.

73. Norman B. Spector, ed. and trans., *The Complete Fables of Jean de la Fontaine* (Evanston, Ill.: Northwestern University Press, 1988), 130.

74. Klumpke, *Rosa Bonheur,* 282.

75. Ibid.

76. Ibid.

77. Jules Claretie, "Rosa Bonheur—An Appreciation with Some Hitherto Unpublished Studies," *Harper's Magazine,* December 1901, 139.

78. Jean Lorrain, "Une visite chez Sarah," *Événement,* November 3, 1887, vol. 1, RFCPSB, CR, BNDAS.

79. Skinner, *Madame Sarah,* 135.

80. Ibid., 16–17.

81. Ibid., xviii, 93–94.

82. Ashton with Hare, *Rosa Bonheur,* 139. See the letters by Bonheur quoted in Stanton, *Reminiscences,* 166–168, 179, 252–254, 279.

83. Arsène Alexandre, "Rosa Bonheur," *Le Figaro,* May 27, 1899.

84. Klumpke, *Rosa Bonheur,* 310.

85. Ibid., 311; Mirecourt, *Rosa Bonheur,* 53.

86. Quoted in Stanton, *Reminiscences,* 338.

87. See Alex Potts, "Natural Order and the Call of the Wild: The Politics of Animal Picturing," *Oxford Art Journal* 13, no. 1 (1990), 20.

88. In *Academy Notes of the French Exhibition of 1857,* John Ruskin said of Bonheur's work: "In *The Horse Fair* the human faces were nearly all dexterously, but disagreeably, hidden, and the one chiefly shown had not the slightest character. Mlle. Bonheur may rely upon this, that if she cannot paint a man's face, she can neither paint a horse's or a dog's nor a bull's. There is in every animal's eye a dim image and gleam of humanity, a flash of strange light through which their life looks out and up to our great mystery of command over them, and claims the fellowship of the creature, if not the soul." Quoted in Ashton with Hare, *Rosa Bonheur,* 112. See also Boime, "The Case of Rosa Bonheur," 397. Saslow revises this view by arguing that Bonheur skillfully hid the faces in such paintings as *The Horse Fair* in order to present her own image there. See Saslow, "Disagreeably Hidden," 189.

89. Ashton with Hare, *Rosa Bonheur,* 143.

90. Sharon Marcus, *Between Women: Friendship, Desire and Marriage in Victorian England* (Princeton, N.J.: Princeton University Press, 2007), 50–51. For Bonheur's relationships with women, see also Gretchen Van Slyke, "Gynocentric Matrimony: The Fin-de-Siècle Alliance of Rosa Bonheur and Anna Klumpke," *Nineteenth-Century Contexts* 20 (1999): 489–502; Alex Potts, "Natural Order and the Call of the Wild"; Britta Dwyer, "Rosa Bonheur and Her Companion-Artist: What Made Anne Klumpke Special?" in *Rosa Bonheur: All Nature's Children,* ed. Dahesh Museum. When she died, Bonheur gave Klumpke the bulk of her very considerable estate, a gift that caused enormous controversy and scandal.

91. Georges Buffon, *Histoire naturelle, générale et particulière* (Paris: L'imprimerie Royal, 1763), vol. 11: 5.

92. Kete, *The Beast in the Boudoir,* 115–118; Darnton, *The Great Cat Massacre,* 95–96. Thanks to Céline Grasser for her clarification on "laisser le chat aller au fromage."

93. Kete, *The Beast in the Boudoir,* 122. Kete argues that the presence of the cat was one of the chief reasons why critics deemed the painting obscene. On the Olympia, see also T. J. Clark, *The Painting of Modern Life: Paris in the Art of Manet and His Followers* (New York: Alfred A. Knopf, 1985), chapter 2.

94. See Mary D. Sheriff, *Fragonard: Art and Eroticism* (Chicago: University of Chicago Press, 1990), 105.

95. See "La Chatte métamorphosée en Femme," in Spector, *Complete,* 88.

96. Claretie, "Rosa Bonheur," 139.

97. Saslow, "Disagreeably Hidden," 194–195. For examples of lesbian genre scenes among the early twentieth-century Parisian lesbian community, see the photos of Renée Vivien and Natalie Barney in Martha Vicinus, *Intimate Friends: Women Who Loved Women, 1778–1928* (Chicago: University of Chicago Press, 2004), 179,185; and Tirza Latimer, *Women Together/Women Apart: Portraits of Lesbian Paris* (New Brunswick,

N.J.: Rutgers University Press, 2005), particularly chapter 3 on Claude Cahun and Marcel Moore.

98. Anna Klumpke, *Rosa Bonheur: The Artist's (Auto)biography* [Translation of *Rosa Bonheur, sa vie, son oeuvre*], trans. Gretchen van Slyke (Ann Arbor: The University of Michigan Press, 1997), 8.

99. Ibid., 3–5, 16.

100. Berlanstein, "Historicizing and Gendering Celebrity Culture," 80–81.

101. Several unidentified newspaper clippings concerning Gardner's romance with the lions are housed in the Gardner Museum Archives in Boston. In the secondary literature, see Wanda Corn, "Art Matronage in Post-Victorian America," 13; Douglass Shand-Tucci, *The Art of Scandal: The Life and Times of Isabella Stewart Gardner* (New York: Harper Collins Publishers, 1997), 26–29. I am grateful to Wanda Corn for bringing the case of Gardner to my attention.

102. For Casati, see Scot D. Ryersson and Michael Orlando Yaccarino, *Infinite Variety: The Life and Legend of the Marchesa Casati* (New York: Viridian Books, 1999), 3, 7, 12–13, 81–82. The association between the eccentric and the witch surfaces again with Casati: long rumored as a sorceress, she posed for a portrait in 1942 while seated with a black cat.

103. For the media blitz surrounding "Tiger," see "Rapide: Agence internationale de reportage photographique," February 14, 1910, Folder "Divers," Box 3, Dossier Marguerite Durand, BMD. The two biographies of Durand are Jean Rabaut, *Marguerite Durand (1864–1936): "La Fronde" féministe ou "Le Temps" en jupons* (Paris: L'Harmattan, 1996) and Sue Helder Goliber, "The Life and Times of Marguerite Durand: A Study in French Feminism," Ph.D. diss., Kent State University, 1975. See also Roberts, *Disruptive Acts,* particularly chapter 2. Annie Dizier-Metz, *La Bibliothèque Marguerite Durand, Histoire d'une femme, mémoire des femmes* (Paris: Mairie de Paris-Agence Culturelle de Paris, 1992), 77–80, also contains a brief but illuminating account of Durand's life, as well as a superb bibliography.

CHAPTER FOUR

Historically Speaking

Gender and Citizenship in Colonial India

MRINALINI SINHA

What, in terms of gender, has the colonial Indian past to offer?[1] Or to put it differently: does gender as an object of inquiry or a tool of analysis in India merely play out a European story with a bit of local color?[2] These are some of the provocations for Third World histories posed by a historiographical project aimed at "provincializing Europe": that is, putting Europe in its parochial place instead of allowing it to masquerade falsely as the universal. Yet to seek out "pure" or "autonomous" non-European alternatives, in the wake of the history of European imperialism, would clearly be disingenuous at best. The categories of European political thought, as Dipesh Chakrabarty reminds us, are both "indispensable" and, ultimately, also "inadequate" for writing Third World histories.[3] How, then, might *gender*—arguably, a concept that arises out of a particular European context—contribute to the project of such a recasting of Eurocentric historiography? And, in turn, what might a study of the colonial Indian past add to the "usefulness" of gender as a tool of analysis? I will attempt to address these questions by way of locating the genealogy of the concept of liberal citizenship—and, indeed, of the language of individual rights—in the agonistic liberal universalism of early Indian feminism.[4] My argument rests on the potential of the discipline of history to contribute both substantively *and* theoretically to the project of fully grasping the provinciality of Europe. It depends on working through and beyond the erroneous assumption that the history of Europe is exceptional—and exceptional, above all, in its supposed universality.

The concept of the individual citizen as we know it—with its decidedly European provenance and its normative constitution as implicitly male—

might seem an unlikely candidate as the subject for a feminist project of provincializing Europe.[5] By now, indeed, several generations of both feminist and postcolonial critiques have amply demonstrated the limitations of the putative universality of the liberal language of individual rights and of citizenship. Feminist scholars, for example, have long demonstrated the implicitly gendered construction that has underpinned the supposedly universal subject of political rights in liberal democracies.[6] Even when women acquire formal political rights in the public domain, therefore, their political equality continues to be undermined by women's subordination in the private sphere. Furthermore, as postcolonial critics have argued, the universal political subject of liberal thought was marked by specific cultural attributes that issued in their own "liberal strategies of exclusion."[7] By this logic, then, the withholding of political rights under colonialism seems not so much exceptional as intrinsic to the universalistic doctrines of liberalism. In the wake of such formidable critiques of the liberal conception of citizenship, any attempt to reclaim the concept via its historical translation in colonial India might seem misguided or foolhardy.

The particular history of the liberal conception of civil rights in Europe, whose origins have been traced typically to the challenges to the arbitrary power of an absolutist state, have provided the basis for feminist critiques of universal individual citizenship.[8] The concept of the civic "individual" in the emerging new European polities, as various scholars have argued, was underwritten both by an older civic republican tradition of the virtuous male citizen as well as by a newer fraternal politics based on sexual difference.[9] By now almost too familiar, the argument as regards the implications of this new civic ideal in the constitution of gendered domains of the "public" and "private" has provided the grist for feminist critiques of its inherent—and not just accidental—exclusion of women.[10] The feminist critique of the seeming gender-neutrality of the concept of liberal citizenship has proven enormously productive well beyond Europe as well as, in Alfred W. Crosby's apt term for European settler-societies, the various "neo-Europes."[11] For example, scholars of South Asia have productively extended feminist critiques of the liberal concept of citizenship to the Indian context in order to illustrate how the generic Indian citizen was, indeed, implicitly constituted not only as male, but also as Hindu, upper-caste, and elite.[12] Yet there was nothing necessary or inevitable about this outcome, nothing "inherent" to the gestation of the Indian state: to assume otherwise is to ignore the very particular histories of gender and of citizenship in the subcontinent. It is not, after all, merely a matter of variations on a European theme—the local details that, in the end, confirm the centrality of a European narrative refracted in this or that local color.

There are in fact still further implications of taking on board the implications of feminist scholarship that "men" and "women," no less than masculinity and femininity, are relational categories: that is, they are historically and discursively constructed not just in relation to one another, but also in relation to a variety of other categories, including dominant formulations of the political and social spheres, which are themselves subject to change.[13] How do the particular histories, and meanings, of gender and citizenship in colonial India reveal the contingency of the currently received meaning of Indian citizenship? In other words, the need to account more fully for the "difference" of Indian history creates an opening for alternative feminist engagements with the liberal discourse of citizenship in colonial India.

The "rule of colonial difference," of course, has figured prominently in both feminist and non-feminist versions of postcolonial scholarship.[14] This scholarship has shown that the liberal conception of society had a limited political relevance, at best, in colonial India. The imperatives of colonial rule, as Gyan Prakash has argued, gave rise to a peculiar constitution of the state and society, and of the relationship between the two, in India.[15] The colonial state, despite its ability to penetrate deep into indigenous society by the nineteenth century, was marked by a constant reminder of its "externality": that is, the self-conscious view of the state as a graft from outside rather than a political instance of indigenous society. To be sure, the ideal of a liberal state that related to all its subjects as individuals was seldom more than a normative vision of state–society relationship even in imperial-metropolitan societies; but the limits of this vision become especially evident under colonial conditions. The concept of bourgeois civil society, an association of sovereign individual subjects based on laws and contracts, had a precarious existence in colonial India. In colonial India, therefore, there emerged an alternative framework for the constitution of society.

Its building block was not so much the sovereign individual subject of civil society, but "communities" constituted by castes, tribes, races, and religious groups. These were defined by "notions of collective interest and affiliation" and invoked "collective bonds and rights based on imagined ties of kinship, religion, culture, past, and sentiments."[16] These supposedly primordial communities of ascription, while building on a precolonial past, were largely newly homogenized modern constructs. Indeed, as various scholars have demonstrated, these community formations were the products of the complex negotiation between indigenous processes of class formation and the bureaucratic categorizations of the colonial state that together produced a politics of community-based claims. For example, several caste and denominational communities were formed and reformed as colonial administrative categorizations became the preferred avenues for class mobility as well as for the retention of status and class power.[17] Furthermore, this vision of colonial India as a society constituted by supposedly timeless and particularistic communities was further fueled by the imperatives of a cultural-nationalist politics. These supposedly organic and ancient communities, in turn, provided early nationalists with the basis for demands of cultural autonomy and self-governance.

The peculiar constitution of state–society relations in India produced their own logic of gender. While there were many different types of communities as well as diverse modes for the constitution of collective communal identities in India, at the level of "high politics" and public debates both colonial initiatives and nationalist apprehensions coalesced around certain dominant modes for the constitution of community-based identities. The community, in Partha Chatterjee's important formulation, was constituted typically through the symbolic identification of women with the "inner" essence of the community.[18] In other words, communities constructed seemingly non-gendered public and collective identities by asserting the right to define "their" own women—a process that implicitly marked the default identity of the community as male.[19] Especially from the second half of the nineteenth century, cultural nationalists in India rejected the intervention of the state in matters that were constructed as "internal" to the community; these were to be left ideally to the self-regulation of the community itself. The extent to which the colonial state, for the sake of its own political expediency, was content to leave "domestic" issues to the self-regulation of communities further underwrote a powerful colonial-national consensus about the relationship between the state, communities, and the women of the communities.[20] This, rather than any straightforward antagonism between the state and society, provided the background against which a liberal discourse of individual rights gained public legitimacy in late colonial India. The ontology of liberalism, in the former case, sought typically to empower individuals at the expense of unchecked state authority.[21] In the Indian case, however, a liberal ontology sought to erode, or at least cut across, colonially constituted sectarian communities, the existence of which impeded political integration on a "national" level.

The postcolonial emphasis on "difference," however, has tended to neglect the complex histories of the translation of European categories of political thought in India: in the zigzagging appropriation of concepts such as citizenship, one begins to glimpse the contours of historical agency that is not reducible to mere repetition and variation. Too often, however, contemporary scholarship has posed the issue of indigenous "difference" in terms of artificially separated domains—severely reified, in effect—such as the claim, for example, that the real "difference" of colonial India was located in the inner/spiritual/private world instead of in the outer/material/public world, or in small "fragmentary histories" instead of in big universal history. The result is that the arena of public politics and such concepts as citizenship are too readily conceded as "European" and as merely derivative in their trajectories in India. From within this logic, then, the collective struggles of groups such as women and *dalits* (so-called "untouchables"), which often mobilized the state and the language of individual rights, initially appear less creative and less strikingly original than, say, more community-based struggles.[22] Yet, as Sugata Bose has suggested, "difference" was a viable category no less in the "outer/public" sphere than in the "inner/spiritual" sphere.[23] Indeed, attention to the historical conditions that created a different trajectory for the concept of liberal citizenship in India allows one to reclaim the possibility of a more radical reframing of Europe as one site of historical initiative among others.

These overlapping lacunae in feminist and postcolonial engagements with the concept of citizenship create an opening for an alternative genealogy of the universal citizen-subject in colonial India. The possibility of such an alternative genealogy becomes visible precisely through an emphasis on the specifically *historical:* both the *conjuncture* that enabled the politics of early Indian feminism to become the basis for the elaboration of the universal citizen-subject in India, that is, and the *contingency* of this development. I intend the invocation of history and its vocabulary in its full disciplinary force, and to suggest that disciplinary "difference" itself is sometimes a resource rather than a mere impediment to the dream of a common language.

The European provenance of the citizen-subject is only one part of the history of this concept in India. The other part of this history is its alternative genealogy in the mobilization of "women" as a collective political identity in the historical conjuncture of the interwar period in India. The conditions for this possibility lay in the particular translation of the liberal language of rights in colonial India. What looks like "dead-letter liberalism" in the public and political realm of colonial India, as Tanika Sarkar has argued, had hidden histories and possibilities in the lives of middle-class women.[24] Here liberal claims for protection and rights arose not over and against the arbitrary power of the state, but, rather, precisely as a challenge to the arbitrary power of this or that community that wanted to fly the flag of its reified womanhood as the inner essence of its cultural identity and thus subject actual women to the internal self-regulation of the community. The language of social reform in nineteenth-century India, despite its many limitations, provided a means for mitigating the arbitrary mastery claimed by men, who had been denied rights in the political sphere, over women in the domestic sphere. This was the context in which new political values—a "fledgling notion of something like rights," as Sarkar puts it—emerged in women's private lives long before they came to be articulated in the public and political realms. In other words, the public debates about the reform of the intimate domain of women's lives laid the foundations for an agonistic or truly adversarial liberalism: a language of rights that developed both alongside of and against classical European liberalism.

This hidden history of liberalism in India entered the public realm dramatically and unexpectedly in the 1920s to provide the constitutive condition for the nationalist conception of the individual citizen-subject. The historical conjuncture of the interwar period, for a variety of reasons, was a critical moment in the emergence of new forms of political community and of political subjectivity in colonial India.[25] The impact of world-historical developments—World War I, the emergence of the United States as an international player, the collapse of the erstwhile Ottoman, Austro-Hungarian, German, and Russian empires, the Bolshevik revolution, and the Great Depression—brought important changes in the structure of metropolitan-colonial relations in India. The political economy of colonialism was radically transformed as the older economic relations between Britain and India had to be reconstituted for Britain to continue to draw economic advantage of its control over India. The economic concessions forced by post-war realities had shaken the foundation of India's earlier economic importance to Britain.[26] Likewise, the logic of political devolution—the need to expand the circle of indigenous collaboration—produced a vastly expanded arena of Indian political participation, which was reflected in important constitutional changes in the structure of colonial administration.

At the same time, equally far-reaching changes were taking place in the political landscape in India. The mainstream nationalist movement, under the leadership of the umbrella organization the Indian National Congress, was undergoing important changes as two new political groups—the capitalists and the masses—were drawn increasingly into a hitherto largely middle-class movement.[27] The advent of Gandhian leadership of the Congress in the 1920s was decisive for both these changes. Beyond the realm of colonial versus nationalist politics, this was also a decisive period for the consolidation of a number of other political movements: collective struggles on behalf of peasants as such, of workers as such, of women as such, and of "tribals" as such. Non-Brahmin and *dalit* political movements mounted a challenge to Brahmin hegemony.[28] At the other end of the political spectrum, right-wing religious communalisms (a term that emerged in this period to signify its difference—as a disunifying mode of political mobilization—from a more mainstream nationalist movement) were also being consolidated: aggressive Hindu political organizations emerged with corresponding Muslim counterparts.[29] These changing political imperatives—fraught with implications for the Indian National Congress' claims to speak for the "people" as a whole—inaugurated important changes in the nature of Indian nationalism.

By the 1920s, as Gyanendra Pandey reminds us, the cultural-nationalist vision of Indian society "as already formed into discrete communities, each with its own priorities and interests and each with the right to determine its own ('social') future" was already under challenge. The hitherto dominant nationalist view of India as a quilt-like mosaic—that is, the view that " 'India' was 'Hindu' + 'Muslim' + 'Sikh' + 'Christian,' etc."—became vulnerable to the dangers posed by aggressive community-based mobilizations. The Hindu–Muslim riots that erupted with some frequency in the 1920s, after the collapse of the Non-Cooperation-Khilafat movement, was a symptom of the dangers of community-based political mobilizations in an era of mass politics. The project of mainstream nationalism, therefore, had begun to take seriously the search for a "pure" or political nationalism: that is, "a nationalism that stood *above* (or *outside*) the different religious communities and took as its unit the individual Indian citizen, a 'pure' nationalism unsullied, in theory, by the 'primordial' pulls of caste, religious community, etc."[30] The result was a gradual rethinking of the salient colonial category of the subnational community as the fundamental unit of the national polity.

The associational politics of women, articulated as an agonistic liberalism, did crucial ideological work in this moment.[31] It offered a new political subjectivity of women that potentially bridged the collective identities of discrete communities as the model for the individual citizen of a reformulated national polity. If hitherto the dominant understanding of society had rested on a construction of women as the symbols of the essential identity of a community, then the redefinition of society was likewise mediated by a rival construction of women as themselves the subjects of the state. A new political identity of "women," which was an alternative to the collective constitution of the community, provided the basis for the conception of the individual, as opposed to the collective, political subject at a crucially transitional moment in late colonial India. This moment of transition—before the revised contours of the new political settlement had been established and set in concrete—created the rhetorical openings for a novel political vocabulary: the agonistic liberal universalism of women *qua* women as the paradigmatic Indian citizen.

This development came to a head in October 1929 with the passage of the Child Marriage Restraint Act, or the Sarda Act as it was called.[32] The Act represented a challenge, however briefly, to the autonomy of separate religious communities, the most dominant form of community identity in India.

The gendered norms that underwrote the construction of collective communal identities in India were especially institutionalized in the case of the religious community. This had been given institutional shape by a dual colonial legal system that consisted of a uniform civil and criminal law, on the one hand, and, on the other, separate religious (Hindu, Muslim, Christian, and so on) personal laws that governed such things as marriage, inheritance, caste, and religious institutions).[33] The latter, while themselves the product of the colonial state's attempts at the codification and homogenization of religious laws and customary practices, were delegated as the site of the autonomy of discrete religious communities and, as such, subject to internal self-regulation—a product of that colonial-national consensus whereby religious communities asserted their collective identity through the right to define "their" women.

The Sarda Act became the first, and since then also the only, law on marriage in India that was universally applicable across different religious communities each with their own separate laws.[34] The Act, which was conceived as a penal measure, was able to bypass the separate religious personal laws that governed marriage practices in India to be applicable universally, irrespective of community. By extricating women, at least in this instance, from the internal self-regulation exercised by the religious personal laws of communities, the Act was a significant moment of rupture in the hitherto dominant colonial-nationalist consensus of the relationship between women, community, and the state in colonial India. Indeed, it was a challenge to the colonial constitution of communities, because it created an opening for the recognition of women as individuals—apart from the collective identity of communities—in the political and public realm. Hence its significance in laying the foundations for a revised nationalist political project based on the concept of the individual citizen-subject.

To be sure, as numerous scholars have pointed out, the Act itself was wholly inadequate as a measure against the practice of child marriage in India, the ostensible reason for its passage. Yet an emphasis on the legislative efficacy of the Act alone misses its more momentous political significance: as a rupture in the community-based understanding of Indian society, with far-reaching implications for a radically transformed national polity. No wonder, then, that both nationalists and feminists in India, despite the fact that the latter had no illusions about the practical effectiveness of the measure, hailed the Sarda Act in portentous terms as the most significant step in India's claim to take its place among the modern nation-states of the world. It is no coincidence, perhaps, that soon after the Sarda Act, in December 1929, the Indian National Congress announced a major shift in its official demands: from Dominion Status for India within the British Empire to complete political independence.

And, following not long after the Sarda Act, the Congress at its annual session in Karachi in 1931 passed the Fundamental Rights and Economic Program, the first official statement of demands for a political vision of an independent India premised on the basis of universal individual rights.

The contribution of the Sarda Act to this new political configuration derived precisely from the spectacular emergence of a novel political collectivity, "women," in the domain of Indian public politics. The Act, indeed, was widely recognized as the "personal triumph" of the women's movement in India. In the campaign, women's organizations and a nascent all-India women's movement constituted a gender identity for women *qua* women as a legitimate political constituency in India. This was, in fact, the first national campaign in which women were constituted as both the subjects *and* the objects of reform, thereby substituting women for the community as the proper constituency for the reform. The implications of this novel development were felt in the emergence of a revised rhetoric to justify the reform: a justification that was based not merely on scriptures or on a "golden age" in the past, but on modern inalienable rights of women as individuals.[35] The bill, as Sarda argued in the Legislative Assembly in India, was a "very modest attempt" to recognize that female children have "inalienable rights" and that any state with pretensions to civilization had a duty to protect them "without heeding the vagaries that masquerade in the guise of social customs."[36] The women of India, he went on to assert, were no longer content to rely on the Shastras (religious scriptures) and on rewards in the afterlife: they had come out decisively in favor of rights in the present.

The rhetorical invention of women as a collective gender identity in India, unlike what Denise Riley has shown for Victorian Britain, could not occur in the domesticated domain of the "social," safely circumscribed from the domain of "high politics."[37] Rather it was precisely in the domain of high politics—the legitimation of intervention by the state in the internal affairs of the community—that a universalist language of individual rights arose, one that constituted women themselves as right-bearing subjects, *independently* of the mediation of the community. To be sure, this development was given a specifically nationalist dimension as women activists invoked the examples of Turkey, Japan, and many of the "progressive" princely states in India against a colonial state that had conceded the welfare of women to the internal self-regulation of separate religious communities.[38] The nationalist rhetoric notwithstanding, there was much more at stake than a refurbished or modernized community-based collectivity in the campaign of women. Something new had emerged: a language of individual rights alongside the hitherto familiar language of the collective rights of the community. Or, rather, the communities, plural: for these communities were of course often in rivalrous and competitive relations with one another.

Not surprisingly, therefore, arguments made on behalf of women in the campaign were framed increasingly in this new political language of rights. S. Bhagirathi Ammal, responding to criticism of the bill from orthodox Hindus, argued, "It is a most important question vitally concerning the women and children of this country who should have self-determination in this matter"; and "they alone," she wrote, "have the moral right to say whether they want the bill or not and the men should have no voice in passing it however much they protest."[39] She thus summarily dismissed the argument of men as "protecting angels" for uneducated and unfit women. "Education is not needed to form an opinion in this matter," she argued, "for which women's experience is sufficient." Similarly, in a provocatively titled article, "Dominion Status in Matrimony," Mrs. Munshi likened the relationship between husbands and wives to that of the Dominion colonies within the British Empire, acknowledging the "right to secede" alone ensured the stability of both.[40] The "secession" metaphor was carried further in the welcome address of Lakshmi Ammal at the first women's conference in May 1930 organized under the auspices of the Self-Respect Movement in Erode. "If men were to persist thus in not giving into women's demands for freedom and if they were to persist in the belief that women were their playthings," she argued, "women will have no choice but to practice a policy of Non-Cooperation with respect to the men in their lives."[41] The language of autonomy and sovereignty, as encapsulated in references to secession and Non-Cooperation, had arrived in a domain hitherto insulated from such political language. The self-consciousness of this rhetoric, indeed, made clear that a new space had emerged to provide public agency for women.

When the viceroy began to weaken on the question of granting Muslims as a community exemption from the operation of the Sarda Act because it allegedly interfered with Muslim personal law, a deputation of Muslim women activists laid out their objections unambiguously. They denied the right of self-proclaimed spokesmen of the community to declare on a matter whose effect was to be felt most on women and children who were not consulted in the defense of the supposedly collective interests of the community.[42] The Sarda Act, as the Muslim women's deputation insisted, was far more important in its significance than the famous 1829 act abolishing *sati* (*satidaha*), the immolation of widows at their husband's funeral pyres: whereas the latter had affected only a section of Hindu women, the Sarda Act had implications for women of every caste, class, and creed in India. The novel alliance of women's organizations with radical anti-caste organizations, especially in a province like Madras with a strong non-Brahmin movement, signaled further the kind of broad cross-community alliance that became possible in the campaign for the Sarda Act. At stake in the campaign was precisely what Étienne Balibar has called the "ambiguous universality" of women.[43]

In colonial India, against the background of the particular gendering of collective communal identities, the masculine political subject of classical liberal thought could not serve as the model for the liberal language of a citizenry of equivalent subjects. Rather, this task was left to be performed by the rhetorical invention of a gender identity for women *qua* women.[44] I use both "rhetorical" and "invention" here in a largely positive sense to underscore the sense of political agency and the inventive rupture with the status quo. By "rhetorical" I do not mean "false" relative to something supposedly natural or true. By the same token, I do not mean "invention" as counterfeit. The attempt to develop the Indian woman as the generic citizen was constructed, as all such ideals are. In this capacity, it resolved certain contradictions and exacerbated others. Above all, it was the particular outcome of a particular historical conjuncture, and will never become intelligible through an attempt to read it through the lens of "culture."

The actual struggle for constituting women as a cross-community identity, against the symbolic identification of women as the bearers of separate community identities, was a hard-won *political* achievement; as such, it was necessarily transient and even evanescent. The category *women,* of course, was always open potentially to a variety of alternative combinations and recombinations along other possible axes of political identifications.[45] The fraught nature of this political achievement notwithstanding, it had profound implications. The very act of imagining a collective identity for women on the basis of a shared political agenda bridging sectional and communal differences was an achievement worthy of note in the public realm in colonial India. The collective political identity of women was mobilized self-consciously during the campaign for the Sarda Act as both above, and separate from, allegiances to other collectively constituted identities.

This gave the moment a political significance that was twofold. Above all, it provided the precarious construction of the universality of women constituted by a shared political agenda as the basis for a critical reimagining of the national polity. In addition—and this point is widely neglected—the alignment of the "social" with the "political," prizing women apart from the tight embrace of communities, introduced a national language of rights for individuals (beyond simply the collective rights of communities). The moment of the Sarda Act thus briefly—but importantly—provided the basis for the alternative genealogy of the modern citizen-subject in India. The unexpected politicization of the "social" domain of Indian gender relations provided public legitimacy (albeit not uncontested) for a feminist history of the concept: the gender identity of "women" as the basis for the paradigmatic Indian citizen-subject.

Yet for the women's movement in India this ultimately proved to be a Pyrrhic victory. The possibilities that emerged at this particular conjuncture were soon foreclosed. The colonial state, partly in recognition of the constituency-building experiment of women's organizations in the campaign for the Sarda Act, conceded for the first time that women constituted a political group to be recognized as such in any proposed new constitutional framework for colonial India. Ironically, the altered conditions for the political recognition of women in the 1930s, leading up to the proposed colonial constitutional reform in the Government of India Act of 1935, provoked an agonizing crisis for Indian feminism, articulated in the language of an agonist liberal universal politics, with negative consequences for the citizenship of women and of minorities.

The agonistic liberal universalism in the claims for women's political recognition in colonial India went back at least to the first suffrage campaign of women that had been launched in anticipation of the previous Government of India Act of 1919. To be sure, the case for the involvement of women in the political sphere had been articulated largely within a familiar framework of "social feminism": that is, political and civil rights for women were typically justified on the grounds of promoting social reforms for women and children.[46] Yet already the demand for women's civil rights, registering the particular colonial Indian conditions under which women could be constituted as a gender-based collectivity, also carried a specifically political burden: the impact of the cross-communal solidarity of women on communal or sectarian divisions. When Sarojini Naidu made her case for the women's vote before the British Parliament in 1919, for example, she presented the "solidarity of women" as the best guarantee for Hindu–Muslim unity in India.[47] Herein lay the background to the agonistic liberal framing of the mobilization of women as paradigmatic citizen-subjects in the campaign for the Sarda Act: both the articulation of the "social" with the "political" *and* the exemplary political lesson of the cross-communal solidarity of women.

The second suffrage campaign, which was launched in anticipation of the Government of India Act of 1935 and on the heels of the unprecedented triumph of the Sarda Act, tore asunder precisely this unique double burden of Indian feminism. The proposed terms for the expansion of women's franchise and political representation in the new political reforms posed impossible choices that created a fissure in the ranks of women activists. However, the terms of this debate were only superficially rooted in the classical liberal paradox of feminism: that is, the simultaneous denial and assertion of sexual difference in women's claims of equality with, and difference from, men.[48] To be sure, the opposing factions in India articulated their arguments in the familiar perspectives of "equal rights" and "women's uplift."[49] The official position of the Indian women's movement, for example, was expressed in such popular slogans as "equality and no privilege" and "a fair field and no favor." It rejected special franchise qualifications and reserved seats for women in favor of universal adult suffrage. By the same token, the dissenting position that favored preferential franchise and reserved seats for women was justified in the parallel terms of the need for a distinctly women's point of view in the political sphere. On the surface, at least, the Indian debate overlapped with the division between "equality" and "difference" feminists in Britain who, in turn, forged alliances with the respective sides in India. However, this was not the central issue at play in the Indian debate. The generic European map, indeed, makes a poor template for describing the course of events in India as regards women and citizenship.

Sarojini Naidu's presidential speech to the annual meeting of the All-India Women's Conference in 1930 foreshadowed the charged issues at stake in merely transplanting the terms of British women's suffrage experience onto the agonistic liberal politics of women in India. Before this ambitious gathering of organized women in Bombay, Naidu made her by now most controversial declaration: "I am," she stated bluntly, "not a feminist."[50] Even though many prominent Indian contemporaries of Naidu's did not share her repudiation of feminism, her interpretation of feminism bears on the debate that would soon bedevil the women's movement over the competing terms of women's franchise and representation in India. Feminism, according to Naidu, had developed in response to the denial of political rights to women in the West in relation to men; as such, it had necessitated a special pleading on behalf of the rights of women in the political sphere. Indian women had not been excluded similarly from political and civil rights. This, to be sure, was based on a highly selective interpretation of the history of feminism in the West as well as on an overestimation of the relative ease with which women had got the right to vote in India. Yet Naidu's concern was never with a parochial assertion of national cultural difference. She went on in her speech to celebrate the women's movement as the "greatest international gathering" and to embrace the "indivisible fellowship of women" as the privileged grounds for asserting the "common rights of humanity." By the same token, therefore, she even declared herself a "bad nationalist."

The gist of Naidu's speech, indeed, was that the political solidarity of women was an example of the universality of all humanity. For Naidu, the construction of the collective political agency of women provided a self-conscious alternative to the colonial constitution of sectional political identities in India. Hence the ambivalence of her stand toward a feminism that she identified with the assertion of a sectional identity for women in the political sphere. Hers was an alternative vision of "women" as constitutive of a universal political identity and, as such, as the exemplary citizens of a reconstituted political community in India. This agonistic liberal universalist option had still seemed open and worth fighting for in 1930 on the eve of the political wrangling that would culminate in the political reforms of 1935.

The trajectory of this second suffrage debate, which would end with the foreclosing of the brief moment of the construction of women as paradigmatic citizen-subjects, reveals a set of contradictions peculiar to the emergence of the collective politics of women in India. Initially, all factions within the women's movement in India were united on a crucial principle: the recognition of women as a unified and cross-communal political bloc in the reform constitution. The precise terms for women's political representation, however, became inevitably embroiled in the vexed overall question of communal or proportional representation (representation on the basis of communities in proportion to population) in colonial India. In the absence of a satisfactory political resolution on the question of proportional representation, the unique political burden of women's demands became especially fraught. The majority position within women's organizations favored a joint electorate: an electorate constituted territorially that combined men and women of all communities. This put it in conflict potentially with the demands for separate consideration by religious minorities and by non-Brahmins and *dalits* in India. Soon a section of disaffected Muslim women activists broke from the majority position of women's organizations to support reserved seats for women and separate electorates on a communal basis. They sided on this issue with the major Muslim political parties, who favored typically a composite, rather than a unitary, constitution for the revised national polity. The insistence under these circumstances on the representation of women as a unified political bloc became identified with the interests of Hindus, as the majority community, and with that of dominant upper castes, all of whom had most to gain from a unitary conception of the new national polity. These competing conceptions of the nature of the revised polity asserted their priority with negative consequences for the type of liberalism that hitherto was represented in women's collective politics in India.

The unresolved conflict over minority political representation created excruciating choices that beset the articulation of the demands of Indian women during the making of the 1935 reform constitution. The lead-up to the passage of the 1935 Reform Act saw women activists concerned with preventing the representation of women from being drawn into the political deadlock over the terms of representation for India's minorities. The response of the dominant women's organizations was to adopt an official joint position in 1931 in favor of universal franchise with no reservations or special privileges for women. This created an imbalance in which the hitherto dual burden of women's suffrage demands in India—that of women as the model of the universal Indian citizen versus that of women as agents of social reform for women—now pulled in opposite directions. The special need for social reforms for women now rubbed against a construction of the universality of women as citizens. This contradictory new framing of the suffrage demand of Indian women was a crucial turning point for the politics of an agonistic liberal universalism.

The agonizing choices this produced harnessed women's collective agency in a contrarian shift that contributed toward making the Hindu, male, and upper-caste affiliations of the new Indian citizen-subject both invisible and normative. The potential infirmity of its foundations had marked a subtle shift in the articulation of a collective politics of women: that is, from a *political* individualism that acknowledged the multiple claims on the political identification of women who were enmeshed in a web of social relations to a new *abstract* individualism that was invested in a rigid view of women as naturally "separate" and "unencumbered" to serve as the prototype for the generic Indian citizen.[51] The co-optation of women's political demands for consolidating a unitary vision of the national polity that by default was a reconstituted Hindu, male, and upper-caste vision was not inevitable; it was the *contingent* outcome of the particular set of historical conditions that had laid the groundwork for the opportunity, and deflection, of the collective political agency of women as women.

The extent to which women's political demands were implicated in the political wrangling over the nature of the revised polity in India is revealed in the following exchange on the eve of the 1935 Reform Act between British Prime Minister Ramsay MacDonald and Gandhi. The Prime Minister reminded Gandhi, during one of the interminable conferences meant to produce the Government of India Act of 1935, that the minorities, who represented the views of some 46 percent of the Indian population, through their support for separate or proportional representation undermined the Congress' claims to speak for the Indian people. To which Gandhi angrily retorted, "You have had on behalf of the women of India, a complete repudiation of special representation, and as they happen to be one half of the population of India, this forty-six per cent is somewhat reduced."[52] The conference ended in failure with the humiliating admission of the inability of Indians to resolve the thorny issue of the political representation of minorities in the proposed new constitution for colonial India. Prime Minister MacDonald, as Chair of the Minorities Committee, was left to devise a solution for the representation of minorities.

The "solution" offered in MacDonald's Communal Award (August 1932) came at the price of assigning women once again to the "inside" of communities. Hence the Communal Award made the reserved seats for women, unlike the reserved seats for such other special interest groups as labor, subject to the arrangements for separate religious communities. MacDonald would see women only as a plurality of collectivities nestled safely within various discrete bodies politic. His plan was to confirm these supposedly discrete political units as naturally separate communal electorates, asserting once again that women belonged only to "their" communities. Conversely, Gandhi identified women with the imperatives of a unitary political community by invoking an artificial transcendence of women from other social relations and identities. This in effect merely prioritized the collective contours of a reconstituted community—a unitary national polity—over other possible imaginings of a national political collectivity. Thus was the citizenship of women held hostage to competing conceptions of community. Women as a group, however, did not lose in any simple way to men as a group. Sexual difference did not substitute for equality. Because the campaign for the Sarda Act had created the possibility of individual rights and autonomy for women, that earlier achievement now inflected the nature of the conflict over women's citizenship. The context of reinstated communal patriarchies, rather than sexual difference per se, trumped the recognition of women's autonomy.

The dismal outcome for women's citizenship in the making of the reform constitution of 1935 highlights a crucial point. The paradox of Indian feminism did *not* consist in the contradictory denial and assertion of women's sexual difference from men: the contradiction, that is, that Joan W. Scott has identified for a French feminism arising out of the universalistic rhetoric of republicanism.[53] Rather, it consisted in another set of contradictory assumptions shaped by the constitution of society in colonial India: the simultaneous disavowal and constitution of communities in the claims made by and for women. The political zigs and zags that ushered a new political consolidation in India on the eve of World War II effectively nipped in the bud the potential of a moment in which a collective mobilization of women had succeeded in constituting women as individuals in their own rights. Collective communal identities now returned, refurbished; and women were folded in once again as the essence of supposedly gender-neutral collective group identities.

Our story thus reveals a discontinuity in the ideological construction of citizenship in India, a significant and serious one, but for reasons that are only poorly understood. Just as the serendipitous convergence of several social forces in the historical conjuncture of the 1920s created the conditions for a new construction of women as ideal citizens, so also the particular context of the political wrangling over a reform constitution for colonial India in the 1930s forced open its contradictory foundations. The mobilization of women during the campaign for the Sarda Act had disclosed a collective consciousness constructed around a new political identity for women: that is, a cross-communal identification constituted apart from women's symbolic identification as the "inside" of discrete community identities. The central tension of this political formation, therefore, was between women *qua* women versus women *insofar* as they belonged to, and "symbolized," competing communities. The constitutional debates over a revised national polity in the 1930s once again asserted the collective rights of communities at the cost of individual rights of women—an outcome with which the collective agency of women was itself complicit.

This alternative history of the citizen-subject in colonial India, notwithstanding its discontinuity, challenges the inevitability of its present understanding as merely one more victory of a male-centered nationalism. The recognition of a marked contingency to this outcome leaves open the possibility of reclaiming that which was nipped in the bud, but, in fact, could have played out differently. This recognition provides an opening for reclaiming the language of individual rights for women for a progressive politics. The implications of this history also suggest that the language of citizenship-based individual rights in modern Europe, no less than its unfolding in India, was contextually shaped, and hence equally partial and parochial, in both places. By the same token, moreover, the entangled but differently inflected history in both places also suggests the potential universality of the rights of individuals. This is the double move that is enabled by an adequate engagement with the historicity both of gender and of citizenship in colonial India: *both* the demonstration of generic European concepts as partial or parochial, *and* their simultaneous remaking as potentially universal.

NOTES

1. The material for this essay is drawn from my book *Specters of Mother India: The Global Restructuring of an Empire* (Durham, N.C.: Duke University Press, 2006; New Delhi: Zubaan Press, 2006). I have reworked some of the material in the book to make the broader argument about disciplinary history in this essay, which was originally

written as a paper for the conference "In Terms of Gender: Crosscultural and Interdisciplinary Perspectives," a Center for 21st Centuries Studies Conference at the University of Wisconsin–Milwaukee, May 4–5, 2007. I am grateful to the organizers for the opportunity to distill the arguments from my book; and I thank the participants at the conference and the anonymous readers of the volume for their insightful comments. The words and works of Joan W. Scott, as I hope will be obvious from this essay, have provided me the inspiration and the resource with which to think.

2. See Joan Wallach Scott, "Gender: A Useful Category of Analysis," *American Historical Review* 91 (1986): 1053–1075.

3. See Dipesh Chakrabarty, *Provincializing Europe: Postcolonial Thought and Historical Difference* (Princeton, N.J.: Princeton University Press, 2000).

4. I borrow the phrase from Homi Bhabha, but the responsibility for its elaboration is my own; see Bhabha, "Liberalism's Sacred Cow," in *Is Multiculturalism Bad for Women? Susan Moller Okin with Respondents,* ed. Joshua Cohen, Matthew Howard, and Martha C. Nussbaum (Princeton, N.J.: Princeton University Press, 1999), 79–84. The origins of the phrase, of course, may be traced to John Gray, *Isaiah Berlin* (Princeton, N.J.: Princeton University Press, 1995).

5. Yet see early arguments about the extra-European origins of the universalism of the modern concept of citizenship: C. L. R. James, *The Black Jacobins: Touissant L'Ouverture and the San Domingo Revolution* (New York: Vintage Books, 1963) and Laurent Dubois, *A Colony of Citizens: Revolution and Slave Emancipation in the French Caribbean, 1787–1804* (Chapel Hill: University of North Carolina Press, 2004).

6. The classic text here is Carole Pateman, *The Sexual Contract* (Stanford, Calif.: Stanford University Press, 1988). But for a different argument, see Anne Phillips, *Engendering Democracy* (Cambridge, UK: Polity Press, 1991).

7. See Uday Mehta, *Liberalism and Empire: A Study in Nineteenth-Century British Liberal Thought* (Chicago: University of Chicago Press, 1999).

8. Typically the origins of individual rights are traced to sixteenth- and seventeenth-century England in the outcome of the struggle against royal absolutism. See Alan Macfarlane, "The Group and the Individual in History," in *Space, Hierarchy and Society: Interdisciplinary Studies in Social Area Analysis,* ed. Barry C. Burnham and John Kingsbury (Oxford: BAR International Series 59, 1979), 17–22; and his *The Origins of English Individualism: The Family, Property and Social Transition* (New York: Cambridge University Press, 1978). To be sure, seventeenth-century England—often regarded as the seedbed for the concept of individual rights in "Western" (European and North American) political thought—was anticipated by developments in the United Provinces and followed by those in various eighteenth-century European monarchies and states where state-power could not be characterized strictly as "absolutist." Furthermore, the debate over collective versus individual rights was never entirely settled in European political history; consider, for example, Karl Marx's classic disquisition on "the Jewish Question," which is increasingly being seen as a critique of the regime of liberal rights; see Marx, *Zur Judenfrage,* first published in *Deutsch-Französische Jahrbücher* in 1844; and for the English translation, see "On the Jewish Question,"

http://www.marxists.org/archive/marx/works/1844/jewish-question/ (accessed August 10, 2008). My point, however, is not to suggest that concerns about collective rights did not haunt European political thought and practice; rather it is to suggest a different genealogy for a seemingly parallel discourse about individual and collective rights in colonial India. I am grateful to an anonymous reader's report for pushing me to acknowledge and clarify this point.

9. See Anna Clark, Stefan Dudink, and Karen Hagemann, eds., *Representing Masculinity: Male Citizenship in Modern Western Culture* (London: Palgrave Macmillan, 2007).

10. The classic text here is Joan B. Landes, *Women in the Public Sphere in the Age of the French Revolution* (Ithaca, N.Y.: Cornell University Press, 1988).

11. See Alfred W. Crosby, *Ecological Imperialism: The Biological Expansion of Europe, 900–1900* (Cambridge, UK: Cambridge University Press, 2004).

12. See Susie Tharu and Tejaswini Niranjana, "Problems for a Contemporary Theory of Gender," in S. Amin and D. Chakrabarty, *Subaltern Studies* IX (Delhi: Oxford University Press, 1996), 232–260; also Nivedita Menon, *Recovering Subversion: Feminist Politics Beyond the Law* (Urbana: University of Illinois Press, 2004).

13. See Denise Riley, *"Am I That Name?" Feminism and the Category of "Women" in History* (Minneapolis: University of Minnesota Press, 1988).

14. The phrase is from Partha Chatterjee, *The Nation and its Fragments: Colonial and Postcolonial Histories* (Princeton, N.J.: Princeton University Press, 1993), esp. 10.

15. The discussion below is from Gyan Prakash, "The Colonial Genealogy of Society: Community and Political Modernity in India," in *The Social in Question: New Bearings in History and the Social Sciences,* ed. Patrick Joyce (New York: Routledge, 2002), 81–96.

16. Ibid., 84. For a somewhat different argument about the nature and implications of colonial communities in India, see Sandria B. Freitag, *Collective Action and Community: Public Arenas and the Emergence of Communalism in North India* (Delhi: Oxford University Press, 1990).

17. There is a vast body of scholarship on the classificatory regime of the colonial state; for an early pioneering study, see Bernard Cohn, "The Census, Social Structure, and Objectification in South Asia," in *An Anthropologist Among Historians and Other Essays* (Delhi: Oxford University Press, 1990), 224–254. I owe the point of the colonial and indigenous collaboration in the constitution of community identities to Kumkum Sangari, "Politics of Diversity: Religious Communities and Multiple Patriarchies," parts 1 and 2, *Economic and Political Weekly,* Dec. 23, 1995, 3287–3310, and Dec. 30, 1995, 3381–3389; also see on this point Ayesha Jalal, *Self and Sovereignty: Individual and Community in South Asian Islam* (New York: Routledge, 2000).

18. The argument has been variously elaborated in Partha Chatterjee, "Colonialism, Nationalism, and Colonized Women: The Contest in India," *American Ethnologist* 16 (Nov. 1989): 622–633; "The Nationalist Resolution of the Women's Question," in *Recasting Women: Essays in Indian Colonial History,* ed. K. Sangari and S. Vaid (New Brunswick, N.J.: Rutgers University Press, 1990), 233–253; and Chatterjee, *The Nation and its Fragments.*

19. I owe this formulation to Nivedita Menon, "Women and Citizenship," in *Wages of Freedom: Fifty Years of the Indian Nation-State,* ed. Partha Chatterjee (Delhi: Oxford University Press, 1999), 241–266.

20. For the reverberations of this equation in post-Independent India, see Maitrayee Mukhopadhyay, "Between Community and State: The Question of Women's Rights and Personal Laws," in *Forging Identities: Gender, Communities and the State in India,* ed. Zoya Hasan (New Delhi: Kali for Women, 1994), 108–129; and Rajeswari Sunder Rajan, "Women Between Community and State: Some Implications of the Uniform Civil Code Debates in India," *Social Text* 18 (Winter 2000): 55–82.

21. However, the story of liberalism in Europe may itself need to be modified to consider the extent to which the community—apart from the state, absolutist or otherwise—may have shaped the discourse (and not just the practice) of individual rights even here. I am grateful to Wendy Brown for urging me to consider this possibility, even though I am unable to pursue this point here.

22. For a nuanced attempt to rethink the role of the state in India, see Rajeswari Sunder Rajan, *The Scandal of the State: Women, Law, and Citizenship in Postcolonial India* (Durham, N.C.: Duke University Press, 2003).

23. This point has been variously made in Sugata Bose, "Nation as Mother: Representations and Contestations of 'India' in Bengali Literature and Culture," in *Nationalism, Democracy, and Development: State and Politics in India,* ed. Sugata Bose and Ayesha Jalal (New York: Oxford University Press, 1997), 50–75; Bose and Jalal, *Modern South Asia: History, Culture, Political Economy* (Delhi: Oxford University Press, 1998), 122–125; and Bose, "Post-Colonial Histories of South Asia: Some Reflections," *Journal of Contemporary History* 38 (2003): 133–146.

24. I am drawing here on Sarkar's important argument; see Tanika Sarkar, "Enfranchised Selves: Women, Culture, and Rights in Nineteenth-Century Bengal," *Gender and History* 13 (Nov. 2001): 546–565; "A Prehistory of Rights: The Age of Consent Debate in Colonial Bengal," *Feminist Studies* 26 (Fall 2000), 601–622; and *Hindu Wife, Hindu Nation: Community, Religion and Cultural Nationalism* (New Delhi: Permanent Black, 2001).

25. I have elaborated the details of this particular conjuncture in *Specters of Mother India.*

26. For one argument about the changing economic potential of India as a British colony in the period, see B. R. Tomlinson, *The Political Economy of the Raj, 1919–1947: The Economics of Decolonization in India* (London: Macmillan, 1979).

27. For an overview, see Sumit Sarkar, *Modern India, 1885–1947* (Madras: Macmillan, 1990); and Bose and Jalal, *Modern South Asia.*

28. See Gail Omvedt, *Dalits and the Democratic Revolution: Dr. Ambedkar and the Dalit Movement in Colonial India* (New Delhi: Sage, 1994); and V. Geetha and S. V. Rajadurai, *Towards a Non-Brahmin Millennium: From Iyothee Thass to Periyar* (Calcutta: Samya, 1998).

29. For a discussion of how "communalism" became the "other" of nationalism in colonial India, see Gyanendra Pandey, *The Construction of Communalism in Colonial North India* (Delhi: Oxford University Press, 1992).

30. Ibid., 231, 234, 235.

31. For an overview of women's organizations in colonial India, see Geraldine H. Forbes, *Women in Modern India,* vol. 4.2 of *The New Cambridge History of India* (Cambridge, UK: Cambridge University Press, 1996).

32. The Sarda Act penalized the marriage of girls below fourteen and of boys below sixteen, but the provisions of the Act were so toothless, as both proponents and opponents quickly recognized, as to have little practical effect. In fact, the immediate result of the passage of the Act was a spate of child-marriages before the Act could come into effect in order to avoid persecution under the Act. The Sarda Act, moreover, required reinforcement from an amending legislation in 1938 before it could be anything more than a "dead letter" in the statute book. While criticisms of the Act are well known, my focus here is not on its legislative efficacy. I am drawing attention instead to the symbolic and rhetorical implication of its passage. For an overview of colonial law in its relation to women, see Janaki Nair, *Women and Law in Colonial India: A Social History* (New Delhi: Kali for Women, 1996).

33. For a discussion of the process of the codification of personal, especially Hindu, law, see Marc Gallanter, *Competing Equalities: Law and the Backward Classes in India* (Berkeley: University of California Press, 1984).

34. For some recent, albeit belated, acknowledgements of the signal role of the Sarda Act as a uniform law cutting across communities, see my *Specters of Mother India;* and Lakshmi Arya, "The Uniform Civil Code: The Politics of the Universal in Postcolonial India," *Feminist Legal Studies* 14 (2006): 293–328.

35. For a critique of this "golden age" argument, see especially Uma Chakravarti, "Whatever Happened to the Vedic Dasi? Orientalism, Nationalism, and a Script for the Past," in Sangari and Vaid, *Recasting Women,* 27–87.

36. Quoted in Sinha, *Specters of Mother India,* 183.

37. See Riley, *"Am I that Name?"*

38. See Sinha, *Specters of Mother India,* 168–169.

39. Quoted in Sinha, *Specters of Mother India,* 170.

40. Ibid.

41. Ibid.

42. Ibid., 187–188.

43. Étienne Balibar, "Ambiguous Universality," *differences: A Journal of Feminist Cultural Studies* 7, no. 1 (1995): 165–187. For an argument about the universality of women in a historical context quite different from late colonial India, see Joan W. Scott, *Parité! Sexual Equality and the Crisis of French Universalism* (Chicago: University of Chicago Press, 2005).

44. Cf. Joan W. Scott's discussion about the "maleness" of the abstract individual in the republican tradition, in her *Only Paradoxes to Offer: French Feminists and the Rights of Man* (Cambridge, Mass.: Harvard University Press, 1996).

45. I have learned here from Rajnarayan Chandavarkar's study of the construction of a cross-community class consciousness in Bombay in the same period; see his *Imperial Power and Popular Politics: Class Resistance and the State in India, c. 1850–1950* (Cambridge, UK: Cambridge University Press, 1998).

46. See Geraldine H. Forbes, "Votes for Women: The Demand for Women's Franchise in India, 1917–1937," in *Symbols of Power: Studies in the Political Status of Women in India,* ed. Vina Majumdar (Bombay: Allied Press, 1979), 3–23.

47. Quoted in Jana Matson Everett, *Women and Social Change in India* (New Delhi: Heritage Publishers, 1979), 105.

48. See Scott, *Only Paradoxes to Offer.*

49. See Everett, *Women and Social Change in India.*

50. Quoted in Sinha, *Specters of Mother India,* 204–205.

51. I owe this clarification about abstract versus political individualism to Nanette Funk, "Feminist Critiques of Liberalism: Can They Travel East? Their Relevance in Eastern and Central Europe and the Former Soviet Union," *Signs* 29 (Spring 2004): 695–726.

52. Quoted in B. R. Nanda, *Mahatma Gandhi: A Biography,* 2nd ed. (Delhi: Oxford University Press, 1998), 315.

53. Scott, *Only Paradoxes to Offer.*

CHAPTER FIVE

Gender and the Figure of the "Moderate Muslim"

Feminism in the Twenty-First Century

ELORA SHEHABUDDIN

For more than thirty years, much of the Muslim world has been sliding backward, away from modernity. Maybe the West and Israel, defeat and humiliation, dictators, emirs or mullahs are to blame. Or maybe it's one of those cycles of fanatic religiosity that afflicts every society from time to time. Some voices of reason, however, have to stand up and say "Enough! There is a modern world and Muslims should be part of it." Some apostles of progress have to do more than bemoan their fate, bow to the diktats of intolerance, make excuses for willful ignorance or turn their backs on the faith altogether.

Well, at long last that chorus is growing among Muslims, and if you listen to the most strident voices, damned if they don't sound like an all-woman band. They're way out there on the edge of the faith; their message and their lifestyles are so far from the torpid Muslim mainstream they're almost in the desert.[1]

What is needed is a move beyond tradition—nothing less than a reform movement to bring the core concepts of Islam into the modern age, a Muslim Reformation to combat not only the jihadist ideologues but also the dusty, stifling seminaries of the traditionalists, throwing open the windows to let in much-needed fresh air.[2]

Irshad Manji sees herself as moving Islam into the 16th century; Ayaan Hirsi Ali wants to move it into the 18th. It's as if Luther and Voltaire were living at the same time.[3]

The moderate Muslim is almost a Western invention. Since 9/11, she has been eagerly sought out as an ally in various causes and adventures that ultimately hurt Muslims more than help them. As the first quotation above shows, the "moderate," "reform"-minded, "good" Muslims most celebrated in the West today also happen to be female. Strike that. They are female precisely because certain Western political entities and cultural outlets insist that Muslim women are severely and uniquely oppressed even in "the torpid Muslim mainstream" and need to be saved. Perhaps aware of the rich scholarship criticizing the long tradition of what Leila Ahmed has called "colonial feminism," many journalists, scholars, and bloggers are now relieved to have found women who are Muslim, ex-Muslim, or non-Muslim (but from the Muslim world) to further their rescue missions into the Muslim world. What is striking about the recent refrains about "moderate Muslims" and calls for an Islamic Reformation are their basic underlying assumptions: that Islam must follow a path similar to Western Christianity, that modernity and freedom must be understood the same way for and by everyone everywhere, and that the issues of women and gender are central to this much-needed overhaul of Islam. These assumptions ignore the violent and complex history of the European Reformation itself, as well as the long history of critique and reform within Muslim societies, and ultimately reveal more about the interests of those issuing the calls than the priorities and concerns of Muslims themselves.

Gender analysis has played an invaluable role in the scholarly study of what is broadly referred to as the Muslim world, transforming our understanding of colonialism and imperialism, political participation, representations of Muslims, and, indeed, Islam itself. There has been an outpouring of insightful new work in recent years, from feminist interpretations of religious texts to deeply contextualized studies of Muslim women's lives, faith, and everyday practices. Today, however, this nuanced, sophisticated work risks being overshadowed and undermined by the more imperial use and abuse of gender to serve U.S. foreign policy objectives. Gender has become crucial in the fabrication of the category of "moderate Islam" and the figure of the "moderate Muslim." Perhaps as in no other field, gender has long been and continues to be extraordinarily politicized on the subject of Islam and Muslims, at both intellectual and policy levels. Gender issues and feminism have become closely linked to American projects of domination, exploitation, and self-representation in ways that are reminiscent of the nineteenth-century colonial and missionary enterprises, but are, of course, also quite distinct. As Saba Mahmood reminds us, it would be naïve to argue that "the discourses of feminism and democracy have been hijacked to serve an imperial project. Such an argument would assume that democracy and feminism are strangers to the project of empire building and that aspects of liberal thought and practice have little to do with the neoconservative imaginary that informs the policies of the Bush White House."[4]

Today's imperial feminists, much like the "radical," "misogynist" Muslim men they lambaste, assume an immutable "Islamic" gender ideology, as though the categories Islam and the West, "Muslim man" and Muslim woman," and the roles and the status of Muslim women, arise, exist, and persist apart from and above societal, economic, and political developments in specific geographical contexts. Indeed, their very mission and personal survival depend on their ignoring Joan W. Scott's important call to "disrupt the notion of fixity, to discover the nature of the debate or repression that leads to the appearance of timeless permanence in binary gender representation."[5]

What is startling about these recent avowals of feminist concern for Muslim women and the insistence on the necessity of a war on terror to "save" Muslim women is the disingenuous blending of facts and misstatements about the very real problems in the lives of Muslim women, as well as a blatant disregard for the clearly gendered consequences of the war, not only on women in Iraq and Afghanistan but also on women in the United States. There is no apparent awareness of what one commentator has called the "hypocrisy" explicit in the concern evinced by these "newly minted feminists" for women elsewhere while they actively support measures that would reduce "freedom" for women in the United States, nor of the well-documented historical precedents for such a stance.[6] While some scholars have recently remarked on the parallels in the use of the plight of women as a justification for the colonial enterprise in the nineteenth century (the "civilizing mission") and for the wars in Iraq and Afghanistan today, I believe the truly stark congruity—and significant differences—between the two instances merit greater elaboration.[7] The incongruities arise not only from differences in the formal structures of the former British and French empires and the U.S. empire today. Also important is the very nature of the relations between the imperial power and the Muslim world, a relationship that today is mediated through oil and, crucially for the purposes of my argument in this essay, Israel. Moreover, Muslims, whether converts or immigrants, are now present in the West in numbers that could not have been foreseen at the height of colonialism. It is from this population that the most vehement and best-publicized attacks against the "Islamic oppression of women" have been launched, with grave implications for the scholarly and gendered study of Muslim women, for the Muslim women in the "real world" whom they purport to support, for U.S. women, and for feminism today.

Colonial Feminism Then

There is a long history of Western interest in Muslim women. As Mohja Kahf shows, until the eighteenth century, the abiding image was that of "a queen or noblewoman wielding power of harm or succor over the hero. . . . The figures are loquacious and transgress the bounds of traditional femininity, reflecting the failure of their parent religion to inculcate proper gender roles."[8] By the eighteenth and nineteenth centuries, with growing Western presence in the Muslim world in the form of missionaries, travelers, and colonial administrators, there emerges a near consensus that Muslim women are oppressed, and by Islam specifically, and that they can be saved only by outside intervention. This axiom is then used to different ends by different groups and individuals. While Mary Wollstonecraft, writing *A Vindication of the Rights of Woman* in 1792, used the image of the extreme subjugation of women in an Eastern harem to demand more rights for Western women, colonial administrators sought to justify their presence in India, Egypt, Algeria, and elsewhere by pointing to the need to save local women from such traditions as *sati* or widow-immolation (in the case of Hindu women), child marriage, and the veil. Men and women in the West also used the image of the oppressed women of the East generally as a foil against which to view themselves as *not* oppressed but free. Missionaries, for their part, were affiliated with the imperial project but were also motivated by a sincere, religiously informed desire to help those they felt were in need. Thus, while it is commonplace to acknowledge that "East" and "West" are largely constructed categories rather than territorial givens, it is important to remember the very gendered nature of the construction of the East—not simply as feminized relative to the powerful, rational, civilized West, but also criticized for the inability of its native men to protect and respect their women properly. I focus here on American missionaries, who were present throughout the Muslim world, but most famously in the Ottoman Empire, and were in a somewhat different situation vis-à-vis the local population than their English colleagues since the United States, at the time, had no imperial presence in that part of the world.

In his classic 1873 text, *The Women of the Arabs,* Rev. Henry Harris Jessup (1832–1910) notes that the "remarkable uprising of Christian women in Christian lands to a new interest in the welfare of woman in heathen and Mohammedan countries is one of the great events of the present century" and in fact dedicates the book to "the Christian women in America." The book is itself intended "as a record of the work done for women and girls of the Arab race; to show some of the great results which have been reached and to stimulate to new zeal and effort on their behalf." He concludes the preface to the volume by expressing hope that the work will draw others to the missionary cause and thereby hasten "the time when every Arab woman shall enjoy the honor, and be worthy of the elevation which come with faith in Him who was first foretold as the seed of the woman."[9] As late as 1906, at the first major conference bringing together Christian missionaries from different parts of the Muslim world, Jessup continued to warn against the peculiar oppression of women under Islam:

> Many in the Christian Church have been led to think of Islam as a mild Oriental Unitarianism . . . and have been satisfied to let the Moslems alone. . . . The evils of polygamy, the harem seclusion of women, facility of divorce, exclusiveness and hatred of other sects—these and other features have been ignored or defended. Much may be said in approval of Islamic doctrines which are borrowed from Christianity, but vital doctrinal errors, and corrupting social and moral teachings, especially in the degradation of woman, are too great to allow any thoughtful Christian to be satisfied with Islam.[10]

To improve the lives of Muslim women, in the hope of "saving" them through conversion, missionaries established schools for girls throughout the Muslim world, and reported great success in educating ever-growing numbers of Muslim girls—though less so in converting them to Christianity.

The other great Western presence in Muslim societies at this time was of course that of colonial administrators. Among the best-documented nineteenth-century colonial feminists is Evelyn Baring, Lord Cromer, who had the opportunity to serve the British empire in both India and Egypt. In his two-volume book *Modern Egypt,* which he published in March 1908, upon returning to England after twenty-four long years in Egypt, he noted that the "first and foremost" reason why "Islam as a social system has been a complete failure" was that "Islam keeps women in a position of marked inferiority."[11] He emphasized the vast chasm separating the practices and principles of Muslims and Christians (or, as he also referred to them, Europeans), particularly regarding women.[12] He discussed at length "the consequences which result from the degradation of women in Mohammedan countries," in particular seclusion and polygamy. The arguments about the "baneful effect on Eastern society" of seclusion are "so commonplace that it is unnecessary to dwell on them," but suffice it to say that, he continues, seclusion "cramps the intellect and withers the mental development" of half the population of Muslim countries, women, and subsequently, their husbands and sons too.[13] Polygamy, he pointed out, was even worse than seclusion in terms of its impact on women and was indicative of the alien mindset of Muslims:

> The monogamous Christian respects women; the teachings of his religion and the incidents of his religious worship tend to elevate them. He sees in the Virgin Mary an ideal of womanhood, which would be incomprehensible in a Moslem country. The Moslem, on the other hand, despises women; both his religion and the example of his Prophet, the history of whose private life has been handed down to him, tend to lower them in his eyes.[14]

The only way out of the dire situation in which Egyptians found themselves was for "the new generation of Egyptians . . . to be persuaded or forced into imbibing the true spirit of Western civilization."[15] Cromer identified the "position of women in Egypt, and in Mohammedan countries generally, . . . [as] a fatal obstacle to the attainment of that elevation of thought and character which should accompany the introduction of European thought and civilization, if that civilization is to produce its full measure of beneficial effect."[16] In the end, although he pointed to women's education as "the obvious remedy" and, in *Modern Egypt,* claimed that the British were supportive of the Egyptian women's movement, both Robert Tignor and Leila Ahmed have shown that the policies he pursued were actually "detrimental to Egyptian women."[17] For instance, he raised school fees and discouraged the training of women doctors on the grounds that, the wishes of local women notwithstanding, "throughout the civilized world, attendance by medical men is still the rule."[18]

Despite the different reasons for their interest in Muslim girls and women, missionaries and colonial administrators shared a conceit that that it was only through their intervention that "blighted," "degraded" females could be saved. Thus they ignored a vigorous debate within those societies about the need to improve women's lives and the presence of "native" reform movements concerned with the very same issues—education, veiling, polygamy, etc. At first, these movements were led by men from the local community—such as Syed Ahmed Khan and Syed Mumtaz Ali in India, Muhammad Abdu and Qassim Amin in Egypt, and Butrus al-Bustani in Syria—and often their primary concern was to respond to Western discourses about their societies by projecting an image of their societies as modern. By the late nineteenth and early twentieth century, however, Muslim women themselves were making passionate pleas for change.

One such exemplary character was the Bengali Muslim woman Rokeya Sakhawat Hossain (1880–1932).[19] Maleka Begum, a veteran of the late–twentieth-century women's movement in Bangladesh, described Rokeya

Hossain as "the trailblazer in the cause of the awakening of Muslim women."[20] Indeed, as early as 1905, Rokeya asserted that the common Bengali word for husband, *swami* (meaning master), should be replaced with *ardhanga* (meaning the other half of the same body). For historian Bharati Ray, this is clearly "a manifesto of early feminist thought."[21] In 1905 Begum Rokeya published a short story in English titled "Sultana's Dream," about a utopian society called Ladyland where all the men lived in seclusion and women ran society. This predated the American Charlotte Perkins Gilman's own utopic story *Herland* by a full decade. An eloquent and vehement critic of the practice of purdah, her far greater concern was girls' need for education, so that they could become better mothers and wives, as well as develop their own faculties and attain economic independence.[22] She recognized that purdah, along with early marriage, posed a major obstacle to Muslim women's education. In a collection of short stories called *Avarodhbasini* (*The Secluded Ones*), she narrated a series of true-life vignettes about both Hindu and Muslim women's lives in purdah. She herself, however, never gave up purdah and did not equate unveiling with emancipation. Recognizing the superficiality of the liberation bestowed on women by male reformers eager to impress Western powers with their women's modernity, she commented on the situation within the Parsi community in India, among the first to take up Western education and permit their women to wear Western dress:

> Recently we see the Parsi women moving about unveiled, but are they truly free from mental slavery? Certainly not! Their unveiling is not a result of their own decision. The Parsi men have dragged their women out of purdah in a blind imitation of the Europeans. It does not show any initiative of their women. They are as lifeless as they were before. When their men kept them in seclusion they stayed there. When the men dragged them out by their "nose-rings" they came out. That cannot be called an achievement by women.[23]

In this passage, marked perhaps also by some degree of communal prejudice, Rokeya presages current associations of women in purdah with backwardness and dependence, despite evidence of activist, educated, feminist, veiled women throughout the Muslim world. When she opened a school for girls in Calcutta in 1911, she provided transportation to and from the school in buses that would shield the girls from public view.

Another Muslim feminist pioneer known by many in the West today is the Egyptian Huda Shaarawi (1879–1947).[24] A contemporary of Rokeya Hossain, she led a far more public life, serving in a variety of official positions including (founder and) president of the Egyptian Feminist Union from 1923–1947.[25] She is perhaps most famous *in the West* for having removed her face veil on a Cairo railway platform, along with her young friend Saiza Nabarawi, upon their return from an international feminist meeting in Rome in 1923. Margot Badran, who translated part of her memoirs, thus notes the significance of that action: "At that moment, Huda stood between two halves of her life—one conducted within the conventions of the harem system and the one she would lead at the head of a women's movement."[26]

The manner in which Shaarawi was introduced to many in the West, through her edited and translated memoirs, *Harem Years,* anticipates the astute packaging and marketing of today's moderate Muslim women celebrities like Irshad Manji, Ayaan Hirsi Ali, and others. According to Mohja Kahf, the "pressures of the United States reception environment" had very significant consequences for the ultimate shape of Margot Badran's translation of Shaarawi's memoirs, *Mudhakkirati.* She identifies four ways in which the translation transformed the original text:

> Sha'rawi's engagement with Arab men in relationships she saw as satisfying and enriching is minimized; her orientation toward Europe is exaggerated; and her command of class privilege is camouflaged. Finally, her story, which, in *Mudhakkirati,* is the story of a public figure, is recentered in *Harem Years* around private life and the "harem." In these ways, Sha'rawi can be accommodated within the United States reading environment as a victim and an escapee and shielded from the negative category of pawn.[27]

Writing these words before 9/11 and the explosion of popular interest in Islam and in the alleged Islamic support for violence and misogyny, Kahf—and journalist Barbara Nimri Aziz, whom Kahf credits for the concept of Arab woman as escapee—could not, of course, have foreseen the boom in the bestselling memoirs of ever-growing numbers of "escapees," Muslim, non-Muslim, and ex-Muslim, from Muslim societies. I turn to these more recent memoirs later in the essay.

Like Rokeya Hossain, whose education and writing benefited from the support of her brother when she was young and her husband later, Huda Shaarawi's commitment and passion for women's rights emerged out of a nurturing family environment rather than brute oppression. Kahf notes, "*Mudhakkirati* evinces a woman who, far from desiring escape from her people, saw women's liberation as something nourished by love for her family and rooted in her culture." However, "given the poverty of a reception environment that wants to imagine Arab women only as victims, escapees, or pawns," warm and positive relationships of "an Arab feminist with her own culture" are hard to sell.[28]

Also, as with Hossain, Shaarawi's critique of women's position in her society was not accompanied by a belief that all European women were, by contrast, liberated. Shaarawi is equally critical of acts of injustice against women in Egypt and France though, again, her condemnations of European treatment of women and of Western stereotypes about Egyptian women do not find a place in the English translation. Kahf recounts a telling incident from the Arabic memoir (one that was omitted from the English translation). Shaarawi describes how, in the course of an audience with Mussolini during the famous Rome conference of 1923, "I repeated my personal appeal that the Italian woman be granted political rights."[29] From her close reading of the Arabic memoir, Kahf insists that Shaarawi did not see herself "on inferior ground with European women."[30]

The translation is also reticent about Shaarawi's deep interest in the unfolding situation in Palestine. Toward the end of her life, Shaarawi severed links with the international women's movement over the question of Palestine and channeled her energies into a pan-Arab feminist movement. At the 1939 meeting of the International Alliance of Women for Suffrage and Equal Citizenship (IAW), Shaarawi called on the IAW to protest against the continued Jewish immigration to Palestine and also insisted that a Palestinian delegation comprising just three Jewish women was not acceptable. The IAW did not support Shaarawi's resolution on immigration to Palestine because they saw it as "an intervention into local politics."[31] Interestingly, despite the clear importance of Palestine to Shaarawi and her activism in the last decade of her life, there is only one mention of Palestine in the English translation, on the penultimate page, and that to mention that Shaarawi simply collected some money to send to Palestine.[32]

Talented visionaries and reformers who were very much rooted in their respective cultures, both Rokeya Hossain and Huda Shaarawi articulated important critiques of gender inequality in their own societies without necessarily "falling into collusion with European and American colonialists and Orientalists," without calling for blind imitation of Western society, and with a clear awareness of the role of colonialism in perpetuating these injustices.[33] Rather than assume unchanging, timeless, fourteen-hundred-year-old misogyny in an intangible entity such as "Islam," they were cognizant of the role of the greater global context, of structures and institutions beyond "religion," and of actual historical developments.

With the onset of decolonization in much of the world after World War II, women's rights advocates assumed that the new sovereign states that came into existence would ensure equality for women on all fronts. However, as is now well known, despite their crucial participation in nationalist movements, women found their interests often marginalized in these newly independent states.[34] As national feminist movements continued their battles for women's rights within the new nation-states, the United States was preoccupied with its own new wave of feminism, the strengthening of the women's liberation movement in the United States, and the establishment of the first academic programs in women's studies, but also attacks on the feminist movement as imperialist toward non-bourgeois, non-white women even within the United States. The late 1970s saw a renewed interest in Muslim women's oppression and the ubiquitous "veil" on the part of U.S. feminists following the Iranian revolution, as well as the publication of Edward Said's *Orientalism,* which transformed the way most scholars studied not only the Arab and Muslim worlds, but many other societies. In the years that followed, increasingly sophisticated scholarship on Islam and Muslims flourished alongside the stereotypical portrayal of Muslims and Arabs in popular culture through books and films such as *Not Without My Daughter* (1991) and *True Lies* (1994). With the defeat of the Soviets in Afghanistan and the fall of the Soviet Bloc, the severing of U.S. ties with the mujahideen, and the war with Iraq over Kuwait, Islam emerged as the "green peril" to replace the "red menace." Despite the strenuous efforts of the Feminist Majority Foundation, however, to draw attention to the Taliban's horrific treatment of women, Muslim women did not explode onto the public consciousness in the United States until just after 9/11, when scenes of Taliban executions of women were repeatedly broadcast to make the case for attacks on Afghanistan. Imperial feminism was thus reborn—and it was as strident as ever. Whereas in the nineteenth century, concern for Muslim women had been expressed to justify a prior colonial presence and colonial policies, in 2001 the U.S. government used feminist concerns to justify the planned invasion of a foreign nation. Thus, in November 2001, First Lady Laura Bush delivered a radio address to the nation, the first time a first lady had done so, in order to

> kick off a world-wide effort to focus on the brutality against women and children by the al-Qaida terrorist network and the regime it supports in Afghanistan, the Taliban. . . . Because of our recent military gains in much of Afghanistan, women are no longer imprisoned in their homes. They can listen to music and teach their daughters without fear of punishment. Yet the terrorists who helped rule that country now plot and plan in many countries. And they must be stopped. The fight against terrorism is also a fight for the rights and dignity of women.[35]

From Cromer to Coulter: Imperial Feminism Redux

A century after he penned *Modern Egypt,* we find echoes of Lord Cromer in the United States today, perhaps most pithily represented by the conservative American author Ann Coulter.[36] Infamous for declaring on September 12, 2001, that "we should invade their countries, kill their leaders, and covert them to Christianity," she has more recently bemoaned the nineteenth amendment which granted women suffrage: "If we took away women's right to vote, we'd never have to worry about another Democrat president. It's kind of a pipe dream, it's a personal fantasy of mine, but I don't think it's going to happen."[37] This is an eerie reminder of Cromer's own opposition to women's suffrage in the early twentieth century, a cause he championed with great enthusiasm upon his return from Egypt.

It is tempting for scholars to dismiss speakers and writers like Coulter, but I believe it is important to recognize their crucial role in openly supporting the current wars, with direct consequences for gender roles within the United States as well as overseas. While few others have publicly called for a repeal of American women's right to vote, it is clear that many who so support imposing Western notions of feminism and freedom on Muslim women are opposed to women's right to choose and in favor of a return to traditional gender roles in society within the United States.[38] The trump card that Coulter and her likes enjoy today—and that was not available to Cromer—is the presence of what Hamid Dabashi has called "comprador intellectuals," Muslims who will lead the fight against Islam for them, thereby, they hope, sparing them from charges of orientalism and imperial feminism.[39]

In October 2007, Ann Coulter was a featured speaker at Tulane University and the University of Southern California as part of Islamo-Fascism Awareness Week (IFAW).[40] According to David Horowitz, head of the David Horowitz Freedom Center, editor of FrontPageMagazine.com, and one of the main organizers of the IFAW, 114 campuses organized speeches and events in observation of the week.[41] The IFAW events "highlighted the threat from the Islamic jihad, and the oppression of Muslim women." According to *A Student's Guide to Hosting Islamo-Fascism Awareness Week,* among the activities planned for the week were a "teach-in on the oppression of women in Islam" and "sit-ins in Women's Studies Departments and campus Women's Centers to protest their silence about the oppression of women in Islam."[42] An article on *FrontPageMagazine.com* in early October 2007 had thus expressed surprise at this "silence":

> Despite their vigilance in behalf of women's rights in America and other Western nations, Women's Studies Departments across the nation have

been strangely passive in the face of the barbaric treatment of women in Islamic regimes. Numerous hours are spent in the classroom, dissecting the reasons for the "wage gap" in America, violence against women and the "privileges" accorded Caucasian males. But courses on the plight of women in Islamic regimes are strangely absent. Where there are a few courses that touch on Islamic women in Women's Studies programs, the focus is often cultural and literary, while the abuses go unmentioned.[43]

The flyers for the event that were created by the organizers for use on the various campuses also revolved around the oppression of Muslim women. The first, a still from a film dramatizing the stoning of a young Iranian woman charged with adultery, was discarded following complaints that this was a reconstruction of a stoning rather than an actual stoning. The second showed a public execution of a burqa-clad woman under the Taliban.[44] Robert Spencer and Phyllis Chesler co-authored a pamphlet for distribution on campus during IFAW titled *The Violent Oppression of Women in Islam* and the David Horowitz Freedom Center produced a short film of the same title, also for distribution and screening that week. The film begins with a warning from Robert Spencer: "The war we are fighting against Islamic jihad is not just about bombs and hijacked airliners. It's also about the oppression of women."[45] The same warning appears in the pamphlet, worded slightly differently.[46] Like the other organizers of IFAW quoted earlier, Spencer and Chesler go on to argue that feminists in the United States are preoccupied with trivial matters when they should be focusing on Muslim women. They contend that there is nothing for feminists to complain about in the United States, where gender equality is taken for granted: "For Americans living in a world committed to equality between the sexes, it may seem hard to imagine that such systematic violence against women, sanctioned by religious belief, still exists."[47] Chesler, Horowitz, Spencer, and others not only call for increased condemnation of the atrocities inflicted upon Muslim women but also see war on Muslim countries as the only solution. Thus they fully support the war on terror in Afghanistan and Iraq; the focus on Iran in the book and video is also understandable given the Bush regime's own interest in Iran.

As the student's guide to IFAW shows, according to the new champions of Muslim women's rights, U.S. feminists have rendered themselves irrelevant by failing to join this cause. In her book, *The Death of Feminism: What's Next in the Struggle for Women's Freedom,* longtime activist, self-avowed veteran of feminism, and professor emerita of psychology Phyllis Chesler criticizes women's studies programs on American campuses for not linking the known atrocities against Muslim women to a "feminist foreign policy."[48] She points out that today women in the Islamic world are still pressured into arranged marriages; forced to veil themselves; not allowed to vote or travel without a male escort; not allowed to work at all or to work in mixed-gender settings. Worse, many are mutilated in childhood and routinely beaten as daughters, sisters, and wives; some are murdered by their male relatives in honor killings and stoned to death for alleged sexual improprieties or for asserting the slightest independence.[49]

As she announced in an earlier piece she co-wrote with Donna M. Hughes for the *Washington Post,*

there is a need now, in the opening years of the 21st century, to rethink feminism. There are new challenges and new potential allies that didn't exist in the mid-20th century. Islamic fundamentalism threatens women all over the world. Wherever they have gained power, Islamists have denied women their essential humanity and dignity. Islamic fundamentalism is not conservative religion but a fascist political movement that aims for world domination. Many feminists are out of touch with the realities of the war that has been declared against the secular, Judeo-Christian, modern West.[50]

Chesler and Hughes are not the sole purveyors of such views. Canadian commentator Robert Fulford echoes these views in a piece of his own titled "Feminists Fall Silent":

Surely honour killing is the ultimate male oppression, being uniquely permanent and committed by close relatives in the name of an abstraction. It's among many anti-woman atrocities in the Arab world that should enrage feminists of the West and rouse them to urgent action. . . . But no action of this kind ever materializes, which amounts to a grave abdication of responsibility. Feminism, after all, embodies the principle that women deserve the same rights and dignity as men. In the original discussion nobody said "except for Muslims."[51]

Similarly, San Francisco-based writer Cinnamon Stillwell notes, "The oppression of women in Muslim culture and the threat it poses to women's rights all over the world is clearly the next frontier for the feminist movement. Either feminists will rise to the occasion or be rendered meaningless by their hypocrisy."[52] Christina Hoff Sommers also laments that "The condition of Muslim women may be the most pressing women's issue of our age, but for many contemporary American feminists it is not a high priority."[53]

Chesler attributes the feminist movement's attitude partly to ignorance about the real threat of radical Islam, the "exceptionally bloody jihad that Islam has long declared against women," but also to its greater interest in "actively propagandizing students against America and against Israel—which means that in reality they are choosing tyranny and gender apartheid over democracy and human rights for women."[54] She traces this shift in the movement's concerns with real women's real problems to the publication of Edward Said's *Orientalism* in the late 1970s. "Professor Said stole our feminist thunder when it was at its academic height," she writes. "Ultimately, even feminists came to believe that the 'occupation of Palestine' was far more important than the worldwide occupation of women's bodies."[55] Indeed, as she later elaborates, this attitude plagues much of academia, not just feminists: "The reaction and non-reaction of Western academics and intellectuals to the 2000 Intifada against Israel—and to 9/11—finally persuaded me that this group had become suicidally intolerant."[56] Chesler's views are by no means unique. Canadian legal scholar Sherene Razack recounts an email campaign to which she was subjected in 2002. In these messages, the miserable plight of women in Muslim-Arab countries were pitted against Israel as a " 'free country, with tolerance of all religions and equality for women.' To criticize Israel, my correspondents insisted, was not only to be anti-Semitic and anti-American, but also to be on the side of patriarchy."[57]

It is blatantly untrue, of course, that U.S. feminists were all and always opposed to the war on terror. The Feminist Majority Foundation had drawn attention to the plight of Afghan women long before 9/11 and was initially supportive of the war for women's rights.[58] As Sarah Wildman notes in an article in the *New Republic* in November 2001, women's rights activists "garnered praise from across the political spectrum—even from quarters where 'feminist' is normally a dirty word." However, Wildman continues, "at the very moment feminists should be finishing the battle they began, they are nowhere to be found. . . . [W]hat they aren't vigorously supporting—or even vigorously debating—is the one thing that might bring on a post-Taliban Afghanistan into being: America's war."[59] According to Susan Faludi, it was the Bush administration that shut out the feminists once it had received the support needed to launch the strikes: "Bush Administration officials were making it clear they had 'other priorities,' as one put it, than women's rights and didn't want to 'impose our values' on that country."[60]

There was a range of perspectives on the war even within the feminist community, but it was clear to many that war could not be a viable solution. Veteran French feminist Christine Delphy noted, "To say that war is beneficial for Afghan women is to decide that it is better for them to die from bombs, from hunger, from cold, than to live under the Taliban. Death rather than servitude: that is what Western public opinion has decided for Afghan women."[61] Writing in 2002 about the then-imminent invasion of Iraq, historian Afsaneh Najmabadi, for her part, draws attention to the racism and arrogance implicit in the American dissident community's anti-intervention attitude that it knows better than

> the people who have lived and suffered under these regimes and who . . . welcomed (and at times begged for) outside, including American and including military, interventions. . . . What here may seem the honorable position of opposing the war machine and military adventurism of one's own government, in this configuration, came as the price of other people continuing to suffer with no end in sight. . . . Why shouldn't dissident energies in this country be focused on *the kind* of American intervention rather than on a policy of non-intervention?"[62]

In the end, there was little scope to influence the nature of U.S. intervention. Saddam Hussein is indeed gone, but the Taliban is still flourishing. By most accounts, in many ways, women in both Afghanistan and Iraq are worse off than before the U.S. invasions of those countries, and women's rights advocates in both countries are tainted as "Western."[63]

The New Saviors of Muslim Women

For Stillwell, the U.S. military is today at the helm of the noble effort to rescue Muslim women from their oppressed existence:

> While some merely talk the talk, it is the women warriors of the U.S. Military who are on the front line bringing justice to the Muslim world. They face challenges in Afghanistan, Iraq and beyond, but this does not diminish their accomplishments. If just one girls' school is reopened, one woman goes back to work, one burka is discarded or one stoning is prevented, we have made a concrete difference in the lives of Muslim women. Restoring freedoms and providing medical care, humanitarian aid and protection, women in the military are the true feminists. So are the valiant men who work and fight alongside them.[64]

To quote writer Arundhati Roy, "It's being made out that the whole point of the war was to topple the Taliban regime and liberate Afghan women from their burqas. We're being asked to believe that the U.S. marines are actually on a feminist mission."[65] Fortunately, for supporters of these rescue missions, there are also many women from the Muslim world who can guide these efforts and lend them credibility. Indeed, as Saba Mahmood points out, some of these "authentic voices" earn the support and admiration even of feminists who are opposed to the Bush agenda.[66] To paraphrase Spivak, then, what we have this time is an attempt to have "moderate" Muslims work with "democratic" and "feminist" Western men and women to save Muslim women from Muslim men.[67] (And to borrow from Marx, what we have in this most recent round of imperialism is a tragic farce.)

Nonie Darwish, whom Chesler describes as "heroic" and "a beautiful and passionate speaker . . . an expressive, emotional orator, dramatically thrilling (as so many Arabs can be)," is the author of *Now They Call Me Infidel: Why I Renounced Jihad for America, Israel, and the War on Terror*.[68] She is also the narrator for the film *The Violent Oppression of Women in Islam*, mentioned earlier. The daughter of an Egyptian army officer, she spent some years in Gaza while her father was stationed there. He was assassinated by the Israelis, but her brother more recently received lifesaving treatment at Hadassah Hospital in Jerusalem, leading Darwish to discard the hatred of Jews she said she had been raised with and eventually found a website, www.ArabsforIsrael.com. She left Egypt for Los Angeles and now lives there with her husband and children. Somewhat predictably, in her book, she refers to her plans to migrate to the United States with her then-boyfriend as their "'escape' dreams," while Canadian journalist Robert Fulford describes how "America provided an escape from the pathology of jihad."[69]

Unlike Darwish, Brigitte Gabriel was born into an Arab Christian family in southern Lebanon. In her book, *Because They Hate: A Survivor of Islamic Terror Warns America*, Gabriel chides Americans for failing "to recognize the nature of the extent of the threat presented by radical Islam," for their refusal "to accept that in the Muslim world, extreme is mainstream."[70] Gabriel had the opportunity to experience life in Israel firsthand when she accompanied her mother to a hospital in Israel, just across the border from her hometown. She remembers the women soldiers she saw:

> I was amazed at how assertive and self-confident they were. I did not yet understand the language that they spoke, but I could tell from their tone of voice and the way that they carried themselves that they felt accepted and respected the men. Some of them were even officers! This was such a stark contrast to the Arab world in which I had grown up. No Arab soldier would take an order from a woman. In the Arab

world, women were property. We were owned by our parents, and then we were reowned by our husbands. Israel was truly a different world.[71]

By contrast, according to Gabriel:

> Women have no rights in Islamic societies. Women are not permitted to get an education. They are not allowed to leave the house or work without a male guardian's written approval. The Koran gives the husband the right to beat his wife. . . . A girl born in the Middle East is doomed to a life of misery, especially if she is a Muslim. Many girls commit suicide as the only way out of a miserable situation, be it a forced marriage, soiled honor because of rape, or just rumored sexual promiscuity.[72]

Gabriel admits that the trip to Israel had "not only saved my mother's life, but had changed mine."[73] Over time, she grew increasingly "disgusted with my culture. I began to compare my place as a female in Lebanese society to that of females in Israeli society." The final straw was when a male relative insisted she change out of a pair of shorts an Israeli nurse had given her and put on something more modest and conservative in order to accompany her mother to the local hospital. She "swore that I would leave Lebanon as soon as I could. . . . I did not belong in Lebanon, I had no fond feelings toward the country. The more I thought about it, the more I realized I felt more at home in Israel, the place that has given me a glimpse of Western civilization."[74] Gabriel eventually got a job as news anchor, working under the assumed name of "Nour Saman" for World News, broadcast by Middle East Television, "a TV station backed by the Israelis, located in the Israeli security zone."[75] Now based in the United States, she is founder and president of American Congress for Truth, a regular commentator in the media, and author of a second book, titled *They Must be Stopped: Why We Must Defeat Radical Islam and How We Can Do It*.[76]

Wafa Sultan, an Arab American psychologist, became a highly valued speaker on Islamic extremism following a heated exchange with an Egyptian professor, Dr. Ibrahim al-Khouli, on al-Jazeera in February 2006 that was quickly broadcast by Middle East Media Research Institute (MEMRI). It is worth noting that the co-founder and president of MEMRI is Col. Yigal Carmon, a veteran of Israeli intelligence, as are several other members of the named staff.[77] She promised shortly thereafter that she was working on a book that was "going to turn the Islamic world upside down." For her favorable comments about Jews, she received an invitation from the American Jewish Congress to speak at a conference in Israel in May 2006. The *New York Times* promptly described her as "an international sensation," while *Time* magazine named her one of the world's 100 most influential people.[78] During the debate, Sultan referred to the war on terror as "a clash between civilization and backwardness . . . between barbarity and rationality . . . between human rights on the one hand and the violation of these rights on the other, between those who treat women like beasts and those who treat them like human beings."[79] In the *New York Times* interview conducted a few weeks later, she grandly stated, "Knowledge has released me from this backward thinking. Somebody has to help free the Muslim people from these wrong beliefs."[80]

Sultan, who has been described by a rabbi in the *Los Angeles Times* as "Islam's Ann Coulter," considers the subject of Muslim women one of her "top priorities."[81] She is concerned that women in the Middle East "are slaves, but they believe they are free." During a meeting with *Women's eNews,* she announces that she hopes to become the "savior" of Muslim women. She plans to establish a nonprofit foundation to educate Middle Eastern women and to have a TV program called "The True America," which would seek to shatter stereotypes of American women held by people in the Arab and Muslim world. "They believe American women are just naked waiting to make sex with anyone who asks them, just prostitutes on the street. I'm dreaming to go to every factory, to every university, videotape American women and show them how strong they are and how positive they are."[82] While her plan to highlight the diversity of American women is laudable, it is difficult to understand how she does not discern a similar diversity among Muslim women and in fact sees herself as a lone voice for reform. Sultan's views on Islam and on Muslim women specifically earned her star billing during Islamo-Fascism Awareness Week as a speaker on the Oppression of Women in Islam, along with Nonie Darwish and Ayaan Hirsi Ali. Sultan's book eventually appeared in 2009 with the title *A God Who Hates: The Courageous Woman Who Inflamed the Muslim World Speaks Out Against the Evils of Islam.*[83]

Irshad Manji and Ayaan Hirsi Ali are the best known of these authors, with regular appearances in such widely circulated outlets as the *New York Times* (including the Sunday *Book Review*), *USA Today, Newsweek,* and *Time.* Much has been written about them both, so I only wish to note here the significant points of congruence between them and the other authors mentioned above, in particular their "escapee" experiences and their celebration of Israel and the West as exemplars of feminist and progressive havens in contrast to Islamic societies. Manji fled an Islamic school in a Vancouver suburb that suppressed her ability to ask critical questions, and Hirsi Ali, while the details are in dispute, fled a forced marriage to the freedom of the Netherlands. Like Darwish, Gabriel, and Sultan, Manji recalls how, as a child, she "regularly imbibed two major messages—that women are inferior and that Jews are treacherous, not to be trusted."[84]

Hirsi Ali, for her part, remembers very clearly what "Sister Aziza told us about the Jews. She described them in such a way that I imagined them as physically monstrous: they had horns on their heads, and noses so large they stuck right out of their faces like great beaks."[85] Aglow from her visit to Israel in 2002, Manji discusses "Muslim complicity in the Holocaust" in her book, and praises Israel for being the only democracy in the Middle East and for hosting "the only annual gay pride parade" in the region.[86] Following a visit to the Temple Mount, she concludes that she "feels at home," and "more viscerally than ever, I know who my family is."[87] Several of these women describe the moment they first met a Jew and, to quote Hirsi Ali, how she was "astonished that he was an ordinary human of flesh and blood." For having "condemned the virtual enslavement of Muslim women in the name of Islam," Hirsi Ali was awarded the American Jewish Congress's 2006 Moral Courage Award.[88] Manji, for her part, now heads the Moral Courage Project at New York University.[89]

By ignoring history in both the Muslim world and in the West, all these authors deftly manage to displace the charge of anti-Semitism from its historical European origins onto Arabs and Muslims. In this worldview, where the West treats its women correctly and cherishes and protects Israel, this newly constructed Arab/Muslim East not only continues to oppress its women, but it is now also guilty of anti-Semitism. Israel is seen to be part of the West, a bastion of democracy and Western ideals, an outpost of "Judeo-Christian" heritage in the midst of the despotic, misogynist Arab world. As historian Richard Bulliet points out in a book provocatively titled *The Case for Islamo-Christian Civilization*:

> The unquestioned acceptance of "Judeo-Christian civilization" as a synonym for "Western civilization" makes it clear that history is not destiny. No one with the least knowledge of the past two thousand years of relations between Christians and Jews can possibly miss the irony of linking in a single term two faith communities that did not get along during most of that period.[90]

He concedes that the term is warranted today for various reasons, but argues for a recognition of the role of Islamic thinkers in the very creation of Western civilization and of the close doctrinal and scriptural linkages between all three religions, rather than the "current insistence on seeing profound differences between Islam and the West."[91] The omission of history and politics from their analyses of both Western and Islamic cultures affects the conclusions Hirsi Ali, Manji, and the others draw about both the Israel/Palestine question and women's rights.

A 2008 *New York Times* article comparing Hirsi Ali and Manji concludes that despite their important differences—Hirsi Ali seeks to change Islam from outside, Manji from within—both women are staunch feminists:

> No element more thoroughly informs the work of both women than feminism; its influence on their thinking can hardly be overstated, and in this sense they might be considered crown jewels in the history of the modern women's movement. . . . As feminists, Ms. Hirsi Ali and Ms. Manji are demanding more than equality; they are very self-consciously challenging the foundations of an entire way of life.[92]

Hirsi Ali traces the problems facing Muslims today to "the sexual morality that we were force-fed from birth" while Manji sees the empowerment of women as "the way to awaken the Muslim world."[93] Hirsi Ali's first book was titled *The Caged Virgin: An Emancipation Proclamation for Women and Islam* (2006). In her second book, *Infidel* (2007), she declares that honor killings are "the largest, most important issue that our society and our planet will face in this century," a claim reviewer Ian Buruma dismisses as "perhaps a trifle overblown."[94] The title of her most recent book, *Nomad: From Islam to America—A Personal Journey Through the Clash of Civilizations* (2010), simply reinforces popular notions about the incompatibility of the monolithic entities called "Islam" and "America."

In presenting change in the Muslim world as possible only with intervention from the United States—either by force through the violent eradication of oppressive Muslim men or the less dramatic support of "moderate" Muslim groups and individuals—these writers foreclose the possibility of change from within Muslim societies. They can do so only by studiously ignoring or dismissing longstanding local efforts to confront the injustices, notably the Revolutionary Association of the Women of Afghanistan (RAWA); Chesler, for example, describes RAWA as "a marginal group whose political influence would have no future other than as dancing dogs among the American left," while Irshad Manji makes no mention of the organization at all in her discussion of the Taliban in her bestselling book *The Trouble with Islam Today.*[95] Nonie Darwish, for her part, asserts that polygamy is directly responsible for the lack of women's groups seeking change in women's lives in the Muslim world:

> The end result is an environment that sets women up as adversaries against one another, causing much unnecessary distrust and caution. Competitive relationships among women also deprive them of forming support groups to stand up to the many injustices they are suffering

under. Thus relationships among women in Muslim countries become haphazard, strained, and even hostile. Few Muslim women venture to form relationships outside the family or clan, and very often husbands discourage it. Western-style women's groups and organizations working for a common cause and to influence change are almost nonexistent in the clanlike Muslim culture.[96]

What becomes clear fairly quickly is that there are reform-oriented groups in Muslim societies that merit generous funding from American government-affiliated sources and groups that do not. RAWA, for example, was openly critical of the U.S. plan to bomb Afghanistan, predicting correctly that Afghan women's suffering would only increase. In late March 2007, the Rand Corporation released the latest in a series of reports on U.S. strategies vis-à-vis the Muslim world since 9/11, this one titled "Building Moderate Muslim Networks." The report argues that it is incumbent upon the United States to help develop and support networks of moderate Muslims in order to fight the "ideologically driven global jihadist movement," just as the United States fought the spread of communism during the Cold War by supporting democratic networks and institutions in the Soviet bloc.[97] One of the first steps in this process, the report points out, is to separate true moderates from those who may appear to be moderate.

According to the report, the characteristics of true moderate Muslims are the following: they support democracy, gender equality, and freedom of worship; they respect diversity; they accept nonsectarian sources of law; and they oppose "terrorism." It calls these "marker issues" and suggests that "the position of groups or individuals on them allows for a more precise classification of these groups in terms of their affinity for democracy and pluralism."[98] The report recommends that the United States work closely with five groups in particular: liberal and secular Muslim academics and intellectuals; young moderate religious scholars; community activists; moderate journalists and scholars; and, finally, women's groups engaged in gender equality campaigns. To quote from the report: "The issue of women's rights is a major battleground in the war of ideas within Islam, and women's rights advocates operate in very adverse environments. Promotion of gender equality is a critical component of any project to empower moderate Muslims."[99] However, as it turns out, support for neoliberal and neoconservative agendas are taken to be far more reliable indicators of one's moderation.

The authors discussed here are indeed the perfect "apostles of progress" sought by *Newsweek*. They are also precisely the kind of Muslim Rev. Henry H. Jessup had in mind when, at the first missionary conference on the Muslim world in 1906, he conceded that the most effective means of bringing enlightenment to the Muslims would be a through a recent convert from Islam:

> They need an apostle from their own ranks; a Mohammedan scholar, enlightened, renewed by God's Spirit, thoroughly converted to faith in Jesus the Son of Mary, as the only Redeemer, who will proclaim that the set time to favour Islam has come and that they are all called to accept Christ. Foreigners cannot do it: "a tree must be cut down by one of its own branches." The *Babi* (*Behai*) movement in Persia shows what a tremendous influence one man can exert in breaking up the solidarity of Islam. Let us pray that God will raise up such leaders in Egypt and Arabia, in Syria and India.[100]

To appreciate why these women are so celebrated, it is worth turning our attention briefly to another female, ex-Muslim critic, one who often appears on the same lists as Manji and Hirsi Ali—but significantly, not always.[101] Taslima Nasrin's rise to international fame precedes that of the others by a full decade: in 1993, an Islamic group in Sylhet, Bangladesh, offered a bounty of $1,250 for the death of this physician and writer, arguing that she deserved to be executed for "blasphemy and conspiracy against Islam."[102] Meredith Tax was chair of PEN's Women Writers' Committee when details of Taslima Nasrin's plight first went out on the news wires. She established fax correspondence with Taslima and would become one of her closest friends in the West. In a review of Nasrin's memoir of her "girlhood" in *The Nation,* Tax describes how, in 1994, Nasrin became "an international press sensation, the 'female Rushdie,' a poster child for the oppression of Muslim women."[103] Tax recalls being surprised at the "unprecedented" media interest in "a writer who had not even been translated into one of the 'power languages'" and soon came to see the press coverage as a "double-edged sword," given the reporters' eagerness to "use the story as a stick with which to beat Islam. . . . The Western press tended to portray her solely as a victim and symbol of the oppression of Muslim women, downplaying her courage and ignoring the work of the Bangladeshi women's movement."[104] Bangladeshi anthropologist Dina Siddiqi observed at the time:

> Nasreen was not only a "female Rushdie" but was better than Rushdie; she could expose the patriarchal as well as the authoritarian aspects of Islam. For in the arsenal of orientalist imagery, the fear of the abrogation of women's civil liberties under Islamic law is elementary. Moreover, Western feminists who championed Nasreen's rights as a woman

and a writer could lionize her as a heroic individual in an oppressive society and at the same time reaffirm their positional superiority.[105]

Like the more recent group of women writers discussed in this essay, she "is disliked by many progressive social activists as well as by religious extremists"; she has consistently failed to acknowledge the efforts of others, ignoring Bangladesh's "vibrant feminist movement," and presenting herself "as the lone voice of dissent."[106]

There are a number of possible explanations for why Nasrin has not achieved the level of acclaim and popularity that Manji, Hirsi Ali, and the other have. She writes her major works in Bengali and they are then translated into English. The latest cohort of Muslim escapees has been easier to see as brave heroes because they have written their own stories of overcoming the Islamic strictures on their lives, while Nasrin did not write her personal story until several years after she appeared on the global stage. The Bengali title *Amar Meyebela* was translated in English as *Meyebela, My Bengali Childhood: A Memoir of Growing up Female in a Muslim World.*[107] The second part, about her adolescence, is called *Utol Hawa,* translated as *The Wild Wind.* She does not live in the United States, though she has spent brief stints here, and lacks both the Westernized fashion flair of Hirsi Ali (which led to the *Vogue* profile cited earlier) and the media-savvy eloquence and presence of Manji. What I believe is most significant, however, is that she has been critical of *all* religions, while admitting that she has most experience with Islam. In an interview with the Indian English daily *The Statesman* on May 9, 1994, Nasrin had supposedly said that she supported a total revision of the Quran. Two days later, on May 11, 1994, she issued a rejoinder to clarify her position:

> I hold the Koran, the Vedas, the Bible and all such religious texts determining the lives of their followers as "out of place and out of time." We have crossed that historical context in which these were written and therefore we should not be guided by their precepts; the question of revising thoroughly or otherwise is irrelevant. We have to move beyond these ancient texts if we want to progress. In order to respond to our spiritual needs let humanism be our new faith.[108]

A few weeks later, a government-owned newspaper in Bangladesh reprinted the interview without the rejoinder, setting into motion a series of events that culminated in her departure from Bangladesh.[109] Second, she has been critical of the recent U.S.-led wars. In an interview published in 2002, Nasrin criticized the war on terror, thereby distinguishing herself as the wrong kind of Muslim dissident:

> There are three kinds of terrorism in the world. Private, group, and state. Among these, state terrorism is the most dangerous terrorism. The Bush administration is involved in state terrorism; you cannot eradicate terrorists by dropping bombs. In South Asia, religious terrorists have become much more active since the war on terrorism began, and it's because of the inhuman activities of Bush. In the Middle East, the hatred against the United States is increasing, too. More and more people are joining the fundamentalist organizations, and will continue to.[110]

Finally, and this is related to the first explanation, she has not identified Christianity or Judaism as better for women, and the West or Israel as havens of refuge for women. She cannot therefore be as easily promoted as a "reasonable" or moderate Muslim who openly recognizes the obvious virtues of the Israel and the West. And certainly there is no need to when there are others who are far more vocal on the subject.

What Muslim Women Need, What Muslim Women Want: "Muslim" Women Speak

In a piece published shortly after September 11, 2001, and the first American attacks on Afghanistan, anthropologist Lila Abu-Lughod bluntly lays bare the arrogance implicit in claims to save Afghan or Muslim women.

> When you save someone, you imply that you are saving her from something. You are also saving her *to* something. What violences are entailed in this transformation, and what presumptions are being made about the superiority of that to which you are saving her? Projects of saving other women depend on and reinforce a sense of superiority by Westerners, a form of arrogance that deserves to be challenged. All one needs to do to appreciate the patronizing quality of the rhetoric of saving women is to imagine using it today in the United States about disadvantaged groups such as African American women or working-class women. We now understand them as suffering from structural violence. We have become politicized about race and class, but not culture.[111]

According to the memoirs mentioned above, all published in the last five years, Muslim women need to be saved *to* Western and Israeli/Jewish culture, seen as synonymous and equally respectful of gender equality. Again, a notable exception is Nasrin's writing, which does not single out Western or Israeli culture as the ultimate goal. As though working from the same manual, each of the women mentioned above attacks the treatment of women in Islamic countries, celebrates gender equality in Israel and the West, and generally ignores recent serious scholarship on the subject. What is most pernicious of course is that it is these books rather than the painstaking labor of scholars that is eagerly consumed by the media and the public, reinforcing misconceptions and lending support to destructive government policies.[112]

In the acknowledgments in her book, Darwish thanks her husband for being the first to tell her, " 'You have a story to tell' at a time when I wanted to block out my past."[113] And indeed, she, Gabriel, Sultan, Manji, and Nasrin all have fascinating and often painful personal stories to share with a wider readership. The problem with all these books, however, is that these personal stories are seen as representative of all Muslims or Arabs; these individuals are taken to be exemplary victims of an Islam that is opposed to women and feminism; they are then feted as authorities on "Islam," "Muslim women," and "feminism" at all times and in all places. This failure, on the part of these women as well as their audience, to understand the internal complexity of these categories has profound political consequences.

Thus, by discussing "Islam" and "Muslim women" as an undifferentiated category (though the latter is over half a billion strong and spread over the entire globe), these authors are able to deliberately disregard important differences in domestic and global political, legal, and economic contexts, individual women's relationship to class and religion, and changes over time. Acknowledging the role of context and, to borrow from Uma Narayan, the importance of history and politics in understanding Islamic "traditions" would reveal the contingent nature of many of their own experiences and diminish their exemplary status, their "authentic" voices.[114] Given their lack of interest in the diversity of Muslim experiences, their prescriptions for reform are of little value. Indeed, their proposals for change have little value precisely because they are not really designed to help Muslims as much as to pander to a particular Western audience that simply wants "authentic" Muslim voices to confirm its preconceived ideas about Islam and Muslim women. The books and statements of Manji and others appear in a global context that already holds dear certain notions about Islam and Muslim women. For example, commentator Brenda Walker describes, in stark Orientalist fashion, the treatment of women by Muslim immigrants in the West:

> The newcomer Muslims bring an ancient social structure that is authoritarian and misogynist, where knowledge is an inherited commod-

ity rather than derived through rational inquiry. Western culture, on the other hand, has built upon its Greek, Roman and Renaissance traditions to value democracy, gender equality, individual rights and rational thought.[115]

More recently, in 2006, Australian Prime Minister John Howard said of immigrants:

> Fully integrating means accepting Australian values, it means learning as rapidly as you can the English language if you don't already speak it. And it means understanding that in certain areas, such as the equality of men and women . . . people who come from societies where women are treated in an inferior fashion have got to learn very quickly that that is not the case in Australia.[116]

Like the pronouncements of Hirsi Ali and Manji, these statements are, in time-honored Orientalist manner, as much celebrations of the West as expressions of concern for Muslim women. The best evidence of these authors' successful "Westernization" is, of course, their enthusiastic espousal of feminism. Sam Harris and Salman Rushdie have described Ayaan Hirsi Ali as "the world's most visible and imperiled spokeswoman for the rights of Muslim women," the *Economist* as "the world's most famous critic of Islam," and *Vogue* "a controversial freedom fighter."[117] The eleven-minute film *Submission,* which shot Hirsi Ali and Theo van Gogh to international prominence, was, according to Ali, intended for a female Muslim audience. It was narrated in English precisely because she wanted to "show it to women who live under the sharia and also to other women, smart women."[118] Yet, as Marc de Leeuw and Sonja van Wichelen remark, when given the opportunity to show the film and discuss it with four Muslim women in a shelter home, with "real abused persons," Hirsi Ali evinced little interest in their perspectives, especially when they disagreed with her:

> During the conversation, Hirsi Ali found herself confronted with anger, outrage, and disgust of the Muslim women who reacted to her film. This culminated in a woman running out on the discussion for "since Hirsi Ali did not want a genuine dialogue there was no reason for her to stay." At this moment Hirsi Ali made a dismissive gesture waving her hand to the woman and saying, "okay, goodbye then." More than just uncovering an elitist or a defensive attitude, this gesture shows to what extent Hirsi Ali cannot account, or be accountable, for the stories of these

women. As explicated in the televised discussion, in the eyes of these real abused women, Hirsi Ali is clearly not "one of them."[119]

As a former "victim" who has "chosen to be liberated"—by her own admission, along a path initially strewn with Danielle Steel and Barbara Cartland romance novels—Hirsi Ali has no time for other views: any Muslim woman who disagrees must simply be suffering from false consciousness.[120] Indeed, on another show, *Meetingpoint,* broadcast in January 2005, Hirsi Ali tells a young Muslim woman to "Please go wake up."[121]

It should go without saying that Muslim men and women have been far from asleep for the last fourteen hundred years, but unfortunately it does not. In fact, the image is reinforced in other examples of the "popular eyewitness literature."[122] Thus, in her book, Manji refers to Muslims as "an army of automatons" and urges them to "wake up" and reject the false consciousness from which they suffer.[123] Just as the authors discussed here—and their supporters—view Islam and Muslim women as monolithic and immutable categories, so too do they assume feminism to come in a singular, familiar (read Euro-American) package. They write therefore with a lack of understanding of the history and diversity not only of Islam, but also global feminism.

Muslim Women Speak Back

Responding to the interference of hegemonic white feminists in Asian family practices a quarter-century ago, Valerie Amos and Pratibha Parmar wrote:

> Many white feminists have argued that as feminists they find it very difficult to accept arranged marriages which they see as reactionary. Our argument is that it is not for them to accept or reject arranged marriages but up to us to challenge, accept, or reform, depending on our various perspectives, on or own terms and in our own culturally specific ways.[124]

Today, as Abu-Lughod points out in the excerpt cited earlier, any talk of "saving" African American or working-class women would be challenged as patronizing. Yet, there is much agreement that Muslim women need outside help, that they cannot bring about the needed change—in fact, that most are not even aware of the need for change. Moreover, the only change possible is to discard "traditional" Islam, but better yet, to embrace Western, Judeo-Christian, modernity.

In reality, of course, large numbers of Muslim women throughout the world are struggling for change. Their diagnosis of the problem, however, is different. It is not "Islam" that is the problem, and thus changing or doing away with Islam is not the solution. Of course, injustices should be publicized, but in an accurate, responsible, and constructive manner. Today, at the dawn of the twenty-first century, Muslim women are fighting unjust laws and male-biased interpretations of the Quran, and they have little patience for the self-aggrandizing revelations of the "native informant" authors. Novelist Laila Lalami writes about Muslim women today being "saddled with what can only be referred to as the 'burden of pity.' "[125] Fareena Alam, editor of the British Muslim magazine *Q-News,* states in her review of *The Caged Virgin:*

> It's obviously what I've been waiting for all my life: a secular crusader—armed with Enlightenment philosophy, the stamp of the liberal establishment and the promise of sexual freedom—swooping into my harem and liberating me from my "ignorant," "uncritical," "dishonest," and "oppressed" Muslim existence. . . .
>
> Long before Hirsi Ali arrived in Europe, Muslim women were fighting against ignorance, religious prejudice and cultural misunderstanding. They are still pushing the boundaries, laying an increasingly important public role and advocating real long-term change—slowly but surely. . . . Many Muslim women want to maintain a strong, spiritual connection with their faith, a choice Hirsi Ali seeks to deny them. These brave women sadly do not have the luxuries of monetary resources, bodyguards, spin-doctors and PR agencies that she takes for granted.[126]

Sarah Husain, editor of an anthology of writing, fiction and non-fiction, by "Muslim" women titled *Voices of Resistance,* thus explains why "Muslim" is within quotation marks throughout her introduction to the volume:

> As our lives become targets of manufactured "truths," and the real questions are hidden behind corporate media sound bites, "Islam" becomes the new demon to be exorcized. The reason why "Muslim" is in quotes throughout this introduction is *not* to just move away from those tendencies that seek to reduce us to monological stereotypes and to define us in one homogeneous way. Our work subverts stereotypes, claims them, often with humor, moves beyond them, or simply ignores them, but, in doing so, troubles the dominant generalizations. Writing our selves into quotes does not mean that we are not a legitimate or a "real"

force in our communities. What it means is that we are not one fixed homogenous body that is always ready to be written by, and in, someone else's language. We seek to move sometimes as whole and sometimes unholy, perhaps as shadows, but like water, always fluid, constructing our myriad selves.[127]

In response to Salman Rushdie's longing "for the voices of Muslim women to be heard!" in a *New York Times* op-ed piece in November 2001, scholar, poet, and playwright Fawzia Afzal-Khan writes:

> Well, I have news for Mr. Rushdie. Muslim women *have* been speaking out against the obscurantist Islam he decries in his essay, for years and years and years, although clearly Mr. Rushdie, and many others, have not paid them much heed. There are Muslim women who are feminists, theologians, writers, lawyers, activists, scholars both in the "Islamist" societies he paints with a broad brush, as well as in the "west," who have been engaged in a two-pronged struggle against *both* Islamic extremism as well as—and this is where their difference from Mr. Rushdie arises—the unjust foreign policies of the United States that have contributed, and continue to contribute, to the "hijacking" of Islam for terrorist ends.[128]

It is with this implicit distinction made by pundits, the media, and policymakers, between the right kind of Muslim woman and the wrong one, that I conclude this essay.

Defining the Good Muslim Feminist

In an article in the *Washington Post* in December 2002, Robert Satloff, director for policy and strategic planning at the Washington Institute for Near East Policy, criticizes the State Department's decision to use scholar Asma Barlas as an official government speaker in a program meant to help the United States win the hearts and minds of Muslims. He does this on the grounds that her website is "a collection of blame-America-first tirades" and cites such excerpts from her articles as "When we ask, 'Why do they hate us' I believe it is because we don't want to ask the question we should be asking: 'Why do we hate and oppress them.'" Although he concedes that speakers in this program "should be independent, not government surrogates, and constructive critiques of U.S. policy should be tolerated," he points out that using someone like her is "self-defeating" and ultimately only "lends succor to our enemies."[129] Barlas, the author of an egalitarian interpretation of the Quran, responds:

The irony of this has never escaped me. For criticizing Muslim interpretive violence, I am courted as a moderate Muslim but, for criticizing the U.S.'s political violence, I am denounced as a militant anti-American. Where then is the space for Muslim-Americans like me to live in accordance with our religious and political principles and beliefs?[130]

Barlas's statement pinpoints perfectly the strategic nature of the current search for and celebration of moderate Muslims, and in particular, moderate Muslim women, by the U.S. government, think tanks, the media, and sections of the public. The figure of the moderate Muslim is fabricated in direct opposition to the figure of the terrorist or fundamentalist. Since the latter is generally a bearded man who is religious, lives in the past, and hates America, Israel, and their culture and policies, the moderate Muslim must be a woman, who is not visibly religious but rather modern and Western (read: she doesn't veil), thinks critically about Islamic texts and traditions, or better still, has renounced Islam, and loves America, Israel, and their culture and policies. Any attempt to situate one's understanding of Muslim women's oppression under religion-based law or government in the broader context of war, occupation, colonialism, or globalization is dismissed as unnecessarily nuanced and complicated and certainly suspicious. To borrow from Mahmood Mamdani, then, there are good and bad Muslim feminists.[131]

These recent "exposés" of Muslim women's oppression stand to make increasingly difficult the production of the nuanced sophisticated work that can best challenge them at the level of substance. Even well-intentioned feminism or interest in women, whether on the part of researchers or activists or both, risks being seen as suspect. As a high-ranking Islamist woman in Bangladesh told me in July 2007, "If I had the money, I would send people to America to study *their* women and *their* parties." She knew me from my previous fieldwork, and I did not take this to suggest that she saw me as an agent of those providing funds for my new research. However, this time there was a clear sense of unease and weariness with research on "Muslim women." When I sought research clearance from an Islamist party in Lebanon more recently, I was told I was welcome to do research on any subject except women. Colleagues have reported noticing a similar attitude in these as well as other contexts. This is unfortunate, since it is only a richer, contextualized understanding of Muslim's women lives that will necessarily lead to prescriptions for change and empowerment more helpful than discarding Islam or providing microcredit. The former does not take into consideration the millions of Muslim-identified women throughout the world who seek to change certain aspects of their lives while still holding on to their faith and religious practices.[132]

On the face of it, the latter at least betrays a recognition that poverty is an oppressive factor in the lives of Muslim women around the world. It does not follow, however, that the best solution is, as Irshad Manji glibly proposes, "a God-conscious, female-fueled capitalism."[133] In a speech in March 2004, George W. Bush also sang the praises of microloans and described his administration's use of these loans to empower women: "It turns out that the world is learning what we know in America: The best entrepreneurs in the country are women. In America, most new small businesses are started by women. With the right help, that will be case around the world as well."[134] Just as Manji chooses to ignore the vast critical feminist literature on the Islamic world, as well as on Israel and the West, she—and the White House—seem blissfully oblivious to the scholarship produced over the past two decades on the dangers of seeing microcredit as a panacea, Dr. Yunus's and the Grameen Bank's 2006 Nobel Peace Prize notwithstanding.[135]

In the end, the only way to find out "what Muslim women want" is to listen to them, rather than assuming their needs and concerns are self-evident because they identify as Muslims, or taking a small group of vocal, articulate individuals—whose opinions on issues like Israel and the war on terror are more acceptable—as *the* representative and authentic voices. In the uphill battle we face against the media and Washingtonian imperial feminists in what I might call feminist Islamic studies, our best weapons remain close contextualized studies that reveal the complex and artificial nature of the term "moderate." My point is not that there is no such thing as moderation in Islam or among Muslims, certainly not in the sense proposed by those who would have us believe that all Muslims harbor a latent hostility to the West and democratic liberal modernity. Rather, I am emphasizing the need to contextualize Islam and, of course, Muslims—Muslim individuals, men and women, groups, parties, states, and ideologies. We need to move beyond dichotomies like radical and moderate and preconceived notions about such terms and be acutely aware of the variety of—and the constantly changing nature of—local and international contexts within which Muslims, like everyone else, must operate. To ignore the diversity among Muslims and their multiple identities and varied concerns is to have learned nothing from history and to repeat the mistakes of an earlier era of colonialism.

The authors discussed in this essay have had exciting, often tragic and disturbing, experiences, and their memoirs make for good reading. What is forgotten is that they are fascinating precisely because they are unusual, dramatic experiences. (After all, who really wants to read—let alone pay money for—a book about the woman who was born into a Muslim family, was loved and cared for by both male and female relatives, was sent to school, grew up and got a job, and made a happy home with someone she loved?) Yet, their stories are taken to be emblematic of the "authentic" female Muslim experience, both in the basis for their suffering (Islam) and the source of their hope and renewal (the West and, in some cases, Israel). Those who support them can simply point to them in response to charges that the East has not been allowed to represent itself, that the subaltern has not been permitted to speak. Yet, by ignoring the diversity within the Muslim world, these supporters are actually still using Muslims, Arabs, and the East, to define and celebrate themselves, and the West. The Arab and Muslim East is now portrayed as not only oppressive toward women, but also hostile to Jews and Israel. So the only acceptable feminist voice is one that is anti-Islamic, pro–war on terror, pro-West, and pro-Israel. This is the true moderate Muslim voice that the U.S. media and government seek so urgently and that the government hopes to nurture with generous funds, as it did some anti-Soviet groups in what was the Soviet bloc. This is dangerous—not because a handful of women are achieving fame and fortune, but because it diverts attention from the wide variety of very real problems facing women in the Muslim world as elsewhere, takes vital resources from projects that could help them, and suppresses critics of government policy toward the Arab and Muslim worlds by dismissing them as anti-Semitic and Islamo-fascist. Surely, in this global climate, it is not immoderate to point out that what is needed is not an "Islamic reformation" led by those who support the wealthy and well-armed; what this era demands is attention to history and politics, and a feminism that is anti-racist, and critical of unjust policies everywhere, in the West as in the Muslim world.

NOTES

1. Christopher Dickey and Carla Power, "Rocking the Casbah," *Newsweek* (U.S. edition), December 20, 2004: 30.

2. Salman Rushdie, "The Right Time for an Islamic Reformation," *Washington Post,* August 7, 2005, http://www.washingtonpost.com/wp-dyn/content/article/2005/08/05/AR2005080501483.html (accessed May 13, 2010).

3. Barry Gewen, "Muslim Rebel Sisters: At Odds with Islam and Each Other," *New York Times,* April 27, 2008, http://www.nytimes.com/2008/04/27/weekinreview/27gewen.html (accessed May 14, 2010).

4. Saba Mahmood, "Feminism, Democracy, and Empire: Islam and the War of Terror," in *Women's Studies on the Edge,* ed. Joan W. Scott (Durham, N.C.: Duke University Press, 2008), 82.

5. Joan W. Scott, "Gender: A Useful Category of Historical Analysis," in *Gender and the Politics of History,* rev. ed. (New York: Columbia University Press, 1999), 43.

6. T. Redtree, "The Hypocrisy of 'Newly Minted Feminists' . . . and David Horowitz' Dangerous Agenda," *Revolution* 105, October 21, 2007 (reprinted March 9, 2008), http://revcom.us/a/122/new-minted-feminists-en.html (accessed May 14, 2010).

7. See, for example, Sherene H. Razack, "Geopolitics, Culture Clash, and Gender After September 11," *Social Justice* 32, no. 4 (2005): 11–31; Laila Lalami, "The Missionary Position," *The Nation,* June 19, 2006, http://www.thenation.com/article/missionary-position (accessed September 12, 2010); and Mahmood, "Feminism, Democracy, and Empire."

8. Mohja Kahf, *Western Representations of the Muslim Woman: From Termagant to Odalisque* (Austin: University of Texas Press, 1999), 4; Meyda Yegenoglu, *Colonial Fantasies: Towards a Feminist Reading of Orientalism* (Cambridge, UK: Cambridge University Press, 1998).

9. Rev. Henry Harris Jessup, "Preface," *The Women of the Arabs* (New York: Dodd and Mead, 1873), viii.

10. Rev. Henry Harris Jessup, "Introductory Paper," in *The Mohammedan World of To-day (Being papers read at the First Missionary Conference on behalf of the Mohammedan World held at Cairo April 4th–9th, 1906),* ed. S. M. Zwemer, E. M. Wherry, and James L. Barton (New York: Fleming H. Revell, 1906), 18.

11. Evelyn Baring, Earl of Cromer, *Modern Egypt* (New York: Macmillan, 1908), 2:134, quoted in Leila Ahmed, *Women and Gender in Islam: Historical Roots of a Modern Debate* (New Haven, Conn.: Yale University Press, 1992), 152.

12. Cromer would remark on these distinctions between Muslim and European societies again in a later piece, "East and West," published in 1916. In this article, he made a table of what he believed were the eleven most significant differences between European and Oriental cultures. Predictably, among these were "polygamy" in the Orient versus "monogamy" in the West, the "seclusion of women" in the Orient versus the "freedom of women" in the West. Lord Cromer, "East and West," *Quarterly Review* 226 (1916): 21–39, quoted in Robert Tignor, "Lord Cromer on Islam," *Muslim World* 52, no. 3 (1962): 227, n. 22.

13. Cromer, *Modern Egypt,* 2:155–156; see also Ahmed, *Women and Gender,* 153; Tignor, "Lord Cromer on Islam," 223–233; Timothy Mitchell, *Colonising Egypt* (Berkeley: University of California Press, 1991), 111–112; Judith Tucker, *Women in Nineteenth-Century Egypt* (Cambridge, UK: Cambridge University Press, 1985).

14. Cromer, *Modern Egypt,* 2:157.

15. Ibid., 2:538; see also Ahmed, *Women and Gender,* 153.

16. Cromer, *Modern Egypt,* 2:539; see also Ahmed, *Women and Gender,* 153.

17. Ahmed, *Women and Gender,* 153; see also Tignor, "Lord Cromer on Islam," 230–231.

18. Quoted in Ahmed, *Women and Gender,* 153.

19. Other prominent Muslim Bengali women reformers of the early twentieth century include Begum Shamsunnahar Mahmud and Begum Sufia Kamal. See Sharmila Mitra, "The Movement for Women's Emancipation Within the Bengali Muslim Community in India," *Women's History Review* 15, no. 3 (2006): 413–422; Bharati Ray, *Early Feminists of Colonial India: Sarala Devi Chaudhurani and Rokeya Sakhawat Hossain* (Oxford:

Oxford University Press, 2002); Sonia Nishat Amin, *The World of Muslim Women in Colonial Bengal, 1876–1939* (Leiden: E. J. Brill, 1996); Sonia Nishat Amin, "The Changing World of Bengali Muslim Women: The 'Dreams' and Efforts of Rokeya Sakhawat Hossein," in *Understanding the Bengal Muslims: Interpretative Essays,* ed. Rafiuddin Ahmed (Oxford: Oxford University Press, 2001); Geraldine Forbes, *Women in Modern India* (Cambridge, UK: Cambridge University Press, 1996).

20. Maleka Begum, *Banglar Nari Andolon* [Women's movement of Bengal] (Delhi: Dhaka University Press, 1989), 85, quoted in Bharati Ray, *Early Feminists,* 113.

21. Ray, *Early Feminists,* 75.

22. Roushan Jahan, "Rokeya: An Introduction to Her Life," in Rokeya Hossain, *Sultana's Dream* (New York: Feminist Press, 1988), 49; Amin, *World of Muslim Women,* 205.

23. Rokeya Sakhawat Hossain, "Strijatir Abanati" [The degradation of women], in *Rokeya Racanavali* [Collected works of Rokeya] (Dhaka: Bangla Academy, 1973), 27, quoted in Jahan, "Rokeya," 50.

24. Interestingly, the writings of both women were translated, edited, and made available to American college campuses by the Feminist Press of CUNY in the late 1980s.

25. Huda Shaarawi, *Harem Years: The Memoirs of an Egyptian Feminist,* trans. and ed. Margot Badran (New York: Feminist Press, 1986).

26. Margot Badran, "Introduction," in Shaarawi, *Harem Years,* 7.

27. Mohja Kahf, "Packaging 'Huda': Sha'rawi's Memoirs in the United States Reception Environment," in *Going Global: The Transnational Reception of Third World Women Writers,* ed. Amal Amireh and Lisa Suhair Majaj (New York: Garland, 2000), 149. Fatemeh Keshavarz makes a similar point about the absence of "good" Muslim men in the New Orientalist literature today, such as Azar Nafisi's *Reading Lolita in Tehran.* See Fatemeh Keshavarz, *Jasmine and Stars: Reading More than* Lolita *in Tehran* (Durham: University of North Carolina Press, 2007), 61–62.

28. Kahf, "Packaging 'Huda,'" 155–156.

29. Huda Shaarawi, *Mudhakkirati* (Cairo: Dar al-Hilal, 1981), 260; quoted in Kahf, "Packaging 'Huda,'" 159.

30. Kahf, "Packaging 'Huda,'" 159.

31. Ruth Abrams, "'Pioneering Representatives of the Hebrew People': Campaigns of the Palestinian Jewish Women's Equal Rights Association, 1918–1948," in *Women's Suffrage in the British Empire: Citizenship, Nation, and Race,* ed. Ian C. Fletcher, Laura E. N. Mayhall, and Philippa Levine (London: Routledge, 2000), 133.

32. Shaarawi, *Harem Years,* 135.

33. Cynthia Enloe, "Foreword," in *(En)Gendering the War on Terror: War Stories and Camouflaged Politics,* ed. Krista Hunt and Kim Rygiel (Burlington, Vt.: Ashgate, 2006), ix.

34. See, for example, Kumari Jayawardena, *Feminism and Nationalism in the Third World* (London: Zed Books, 1995).

35. Available from *The American Presidency Project* [online], ed. John T. Woolley and Gerhard Peters (University of California, Santa Barbara), http://www.presidency.ucsb.edu/ws/?pid=24992 (accessed May 14, 2010).

36. Nick Marinello, "Coulter Leads Circus at McAlister Auditorium," *New Wave,* October 24, 2007; Radomir Avila, "Ann Coulter Comes to Campus, Criticizes Liberal Politics," *Daily Trojan,* October 25, 2007. A word on terminology: I have chosen to use the familiar phrase imperial (or colonial) feminism to refer to the position of people like Cromer then and the Bush administration more recently; however, I acknowledge Zillah Eisenstein's cautionary reminder that "it does not quite work to name imperial women's rights rhetoric feminist at all. And many of these women in the United States would never identify as feminist. Yet they employ the language of democracy, in neoliberal form, on behalf of women, especially elsewhere. It is therefore imperative to locate their particular manipulations as a decoy form of feminism itself." Zillah Eisenstein, *Sexual Decoys: Gender, Race, and War in Imperial Democracy* (London: Zed Books, 2007), 98.

37. Ann Coulter, "Coulter Culture," *New York Observer,* October 2, 2007, http://www.observer.com/2007/coulter-culture (accessed May 8, 2008).

38. Just months after the first attacks on Afghanistan, the Bush government imposed a "global gag rule" on foreign aid, withdrawing millions from population programs, including UNFPA, that perform abortions: http://www.alternet.org/story/html?StoryID=13656, July 23, 2002, cited in Bronwyn Winter, "Religion, Culture and Women's Human Rights: Some General Political and Theoretical Considerations," *Women's Studies International Forum* 29 (2006): 387. According to Susan Faludi, the U.S. response to the attacks of 9/11 was a call for the "return to Betty Crocker domesticity" and "John Wayne 'manly men.' " Susan Faludi, *The Terror Dream: Fear and Fantasy in Post-9/11 America* (New York: Metropolitan Books, 2007), 199.

39. Hamid Dabashi, "Native Informers and the Making of the American Empire," *al-Ahram Weekly,* June 1, 2006.

40. Marinello, "Coulter Leads Circus"; Avila, "Ann Coulter Comes to Campus."

41. David Horowitz, "What We Did Last Week," *FrontpageMagazine.com,* October 29, 2007, http://www.terrorismawareness.org/islamo-fascism-awareness-week/ (accessed May 7, 2008).

42. *A Student's Guide to Hosting Islamo-Fascism Awareness Week,* http://www.terrorismawareness.org/islamo-fascism-awareness-week/ (accessed May 7, 2008).

43. Sara Dogan, "Women's Studies Departments Ignore the Plight of Women in Islam," *FrontPageMagazine.com,* October 9, 2007, http://97.74.65.51/readArticle.aspx?ARTID=28410 (accessed May 10, 2010); see also Kay S. Hymowitz, "Why Feminism is AWOL on Islam," *City Journal* (Winter 2003), http://www.city-journal.org/html/13_1_why_feminism.html (accessed February 12, 2008); Phyllis Chesler, *The Death of Feminism: What's Next in the Struggle for Women's Freedom* (New York: Palgrave Macmillan, 2005), 7.

44. Flyer, http://www.terrorismawareness.org/islamo-fascism-awareness-week/75/new-islamo-fascism-awareness-week-poster/.

45. The video is available for viewing at http://terrorismawareness.org/videos/108/the-violent-oppression-of-women-in-islam/.

46. Robert Spencer and Phyllis Chesler, *The Violent Oppression of Women in Islam* (Los Angeles: David Horowitz Freedom Center, 2007), 5–6. Frontpagemag.com provides a summary of the pamphlet—see http://www.terrorismawareness.org/islamo-fascism/

81/the-violent-oppression-of-women-in-islam/—though the links to the pdf version don't work. The pamphlet is available at http://www.scribd.com/doc/2526263/The-Violent-Oppression-of-Women-in-Islam (accessed May 14, 2010).

47. Spencer and Chesler, *Violent Oppression,* 6.

48. Chesler, *Death of Feminism,* 100.

49. Ibid., 84.

50. Phyllis Chesler and Donna M. Hughes, "Feminism in the 21st Century," *Washington Post,* February 22, 2004.

51. Robert Fulford, "Feminists Fall Silent," *National Post* (Canada), September 15, 2007.

52. Cinnamon Stillwell, "Today's True Feminists," *San Francisco Chronicle,* March 22, 2006, http://www.sfgate.com/cgi-bin/article.cgi?file=/gate/archive/2006/03/22/cstillwell.DTL (accessed November 2007).

53. Christina Hoff Sommers, "The Subjection of Islamic Women and the Fecklessness of American Feminism," *The Weekly Standard* 12, no. 34, May 21, 2007, http://www.weeklystandard.com/Content/Public/Articles/000/000/013/641szkys.asp (accessed December 8, 2007).

54. Chesler, *Death of Feminism,* 7, 102–103.

55. Ibid., 6. No doubt even more widely read than her Palgrave book is her blog "Chesler Chronicles" (http://pajamasmedia.com/phyllischesler/), where similar statements appear regularly. Also see Sherene Razack, "Geopolitics, Culture Clash, and Gender after September 11," *Social Justice* 32 (October 2005): 11–31; and Sherene Razack, *Casting Out: The Eviction of Muslims from Western Law and Politics* (Toronto: University of Toronto Press, 2008) for a discussion of Chesler's earlier book, *The New Anti-Semitism and What We Must Do About It* (San Francisco, Calif.: Jossey-Bass, 2003), in which Chesler explicitly equates any criticism of Israel with opposition to women's rights.

56. Chesler, *Death of Feminism,* 67.

57. Razack, "Geopolitics, Culture Clash, and Gender after September 11."

58. Krista Hunt, " 'Embedded Feminism' and the War on Terror," in *(En)Gendering the War on Terror,* 51–72.

59. Sarah Wildman, "Arms Length: Why Don't Feminists Support the War?" *New Republic,* November 5, 2001: 23.

60. Rashi Kesarwani, "Susan Faludi: America's Terror Dream," *The Nation,* November 26, 2007.

61. Christine Delphy, "A War for Afghan Women?" in *September 11, 2001: Feminist Perspectives,* ed. Susan Hawthorne and Bronwyn Winter (North Melbourne, Vic.: Spinifex, 2002), 309; see also Charles Hirschkind and Saba Mahmood, "Feminism, the Taliban, and Politics of Counter-Insurgency," *Anthropological Quarterly* 75 (2002): 339–354.

62. Afsaneh Najmabdi, "Must We Always Non-Intervene?" in *Shattering the Stereotypes: Muslim Women Speak Out,* ed. Fawzia Afzal-Khan (Northampton, Mass.: Olive Branch Press, 2005), 84–85.

63. Eisenstein, *Sexual Decoys,* 124–127; Hunt, " 'Embedded Feminism,' " 62–66; Lori J. Marso, "Feminism and the Complications of Freeing the Women of Afghanistan

and Iraq," in *W Stands for Women: How the George W. Bush Presidency Shaped a New Politics of Gender,* ed. Michaele L. Ferguson and Lori Jo Marso (Durham, N.C.: Duke University Press, 2007), 227–229; see also Nadje Al-Ali and Nicola Pratt, *What Kind of Liberation?: Women and the Occupation of Iraq* (Berkeley: University of California Press, 2010), and Cynthia Enloe, *Nimo's War, Emma's War: Making Feminist Sense of the Iraq War* (Berkeley: University of California Press, 2010).

64. Cinnamon Stillwell, "Today's True Feminists," *San Francisco Chronicle,* March 22, 2006.

65. Arundhati Roy, "Not Again," *The Guardian,* September 27, 2002.

66. Mahmood, "Feminism, Democracy, and Empire," 84.

67. Marc de Leeuw and Sonja van Wichelen paraphrase Spivak a little differently: "[A] 'brown' woman [Hirsi Ali] wants to save other 'brown women' from 'brown' men." Marc de Leeuw and Sonja van Wichelen, " 'Please, Go Wake Up!' *Submission,* Hirsi Ali and the 'War on Terror' in the Netherlands," *Feminist Media Studies* 5 (2005): 333. See also Miriam Cooke, "Saving Brown Women," *Signs* 28, no. 1 (2002): 468–470.

68. Phyllis Chesler, "The Heroic Nonie Darwish Faces Muslim 'Mean Girl' Power at Wellesley," *The Chesler Chronicles,* October 22, 2007, http://pajamasmedia.com/ phyllischesler/2007/10/ (accessed February 5, 2008).

69. Nonie Darwish, *Now They Call Me Infidel: Why I Renounced Jihad for America, Israel, and the War on Terror* (New York: Sentinel, 2006), 107; Robert Fulford, "Saving Muslims from Islamists," *National Post* (Canada), February 11, 2006.

70. Brigitte Gabriel, *Because They Hate: A Survivor of Islamic Terror Warns America* (New York: St. Martin's Press, 2006), xi.

71. Ibid., 82.

72. Ibid., 195–196.

73. Ibid., 82.

74. Ibid., 89–90.

75. Ibid., 121.

76. American Congress for Truth, http://www.americancongressfortruth.com/; Brigitte Gabriel, *They Must be Stopped: Why We Must Defeat Radical Islam and How We Can Do It* (New York: St. Martin's Press, 2008). For a recent interview with her, see Deborah Solomon, "Questions for Brigitte Gabriel: The Crusader," *New York Times Magazine,* August 17, 2008.

77. For a discussion of MEMRI's well-documented pro-Israeli slant, see Brian Whitaker, "Selective Memri," *The Guardian,* August 12, 2002: "[T]he stories selected by Memri for translation follow a familiar pattern: either they reflect badly on the character of Arabs or they in some way further the political agenda of Israel."

78. John M. Broder, "For Muslim Who Says Violence Destroys Islam, Violent Threats," *New York Times,* March 11, 2006; Asra Q. Nomani, "Wafa Sultan," *Time,* April 30, 2006.

79. Quoted in Stillwell, "Today's True Feminists."

80. Broder, "For Muslim Who Says Violence Destroys Islam."

81. Rabbi Stephen Julius Stein, "Islam's Ann Coulter," *Los Angeles Times,* June 25, 2006.

82. Brenda Gazzar, "U.S. Muslim Women Weigh Anti-Islam Firebrand," *Women's eNews,* July 16, 2006.

83. Wafa Sultan, *A God Who Hates: The Courageous Woman Who Inflamed the Muslim World Speaks Out Against the Evils of Islam* (New York: St. Martin's Press, 2009)

84. Irshad Manji speech at the 98th Annual Meeting of the American Jewish Committee, May 2004, http://www.ajc.org/site/apps/nl/content3.asp?c=ijITI2PHKoG& b=871779&ct=1124941 (accessed October 25, 2007); see also Irshad Manji, *The Trouble With Islam Today: A Wake-up Call for Honesty and Change,* rev. ed. (Toronto: Vintage Canada, 2005), 69.

85. Hirsi Ali, *Infidel* (New York: Free Press, 2008), 85.

86. Manji, *Trouble With Islam Today,* 102, 74. For piercing analyses of Manji's account of her visit to Israel/Palestine, see Tarek El-Ariss, "The Making of an Expert: The Case of Irshad Manji," *The Muslim World* 97 (January 2007): 93–110, and Podur, "A Multifaceted Fraud," *Z Magazine,* December 5, 2003, http://www.zcommunications.org/a-multifaceted-fraud-by-justin-podur (accessed February 14, 2008).

87. Manji, *Trouble With Islam Today,* 85.

88. "Presentation of Moral Courage Award to Ayaan Hirsi Ali," http://www.ajc .org/site/apps/nlnet/content2.aspx?c=ijITI2PHKoG&b=1591361&ct=2387665 (accessed October 25, 2007).

89. Gewen, "Muslim Rebel Sisters."

90. Richard W. Bulliet, *The Case for Islamo-Christian Civilization* (New York: Columbia University Press, 2004), 6; for a discussion of the recent rise in popularity of the term, see 5–6.

91. Ibid., 7.

92. Gewen, "Muslim Rebel Sisters."

93. Ibid.

94. Ian Buruma, "Against Submission," *New York Times,* March 4, 2007.

95. Chesler, "Wide World Beyond the Left," in "Letters," *The Nation,* July 2, 2007; Podur, "A Multifaceted Fraud"; Manji, *The Trouble with Islam Today.*

96. Darwish, *Now They Call Me Infidel,* 69–70.

97. Angel Rabasa, Cheryl Benard, Lowell H. Schwartz, and Peter Sickle, *Building Moderate Muslim Networks* (Santa Monica, Calif.: Center for Middle East Policy, RAND Corporation, 2007), 35.

98. Ibid., 66.

99. Ibid., 143.

100. Jessup, "Introductory Paper," 17.

101. For example, in the midst of the Danish cartoon crisis, all three women were among the twelve signatories to a much-publicized statement in the French weekly newspaper *Charlie Hebdo* warning against Islamic "totalitarianism"; "Full Text: Writers' Statement on Cartoons," *BBC News,* March 1, 2006, http://news.bbc.co.uk/2/hi/ europe/4764730.stm (accessed January 16, 2008).

102. Meredith Tax, "Taslima's Pilgrimage," *The Nation,* November 18, 2002: 36; for a detailed analysis of the initial furor around Nasrin, see Bishnupriya Ghosh, "An Affair to Remember: Scripted Performances in the 'Nasreen Affair,'" in Amireh and Majaj, *Going Global,* 39–83, and Hanifa Deen, *The Crescent and the Pen: The Strange Journey of Taslima Nasreen* (Westport, Conn.: Praeger, 2006).

103. She received the nickname "the female Rushdie" on the NPR show "All Things Considered" (June 14, 1994); Ghosh, "Affair to Remember," 39.

104. Tax, "Taslima's Pilgrimage," 37.

105. Dina M. Siddiqi, "Taslima Nasreen and Others: The Contest Over Gender in Bangladesh," in *Women in Muslim Societies: Diversity Within Unity,* ed. Herbert L. Bodman and Nayereh Tohidi (Boulder, Colo.: Lynne Rienner Publishers, 1998), 221.

106. Shakira Hussein, "Contrary Dissident," *Weekend Australian,* January 27, 2007.

107. Taslima Nasrin, *Meyebela, My Bengali Childhood: A Memoir of Growing up Female in a Muslim World,* trans. Gopa Majumdar (Hanover, N.H.: Steerforth, 2002). Syed Jamil Ahmed, a practitioner and scholar of theater and music in Bangladesh, clarifies that the book is a novella, "partly based on what she had heard and partly on what she actually saw while she was growing up. . . . Nevertheless, she gives an impression of narrating events that she actually witnessed." Syed Jamil Ahmed, "The 'Non-dit' in the Zenana: Representation of Muslim Women in Islamic Canonical Texts, the Neo-colonial Imagination and a Feminist Response from Bangladesh," *Inter-Asia Cultural Studies* 7 (2006): 448.

108. *The Statesman* does not have online archives from the date of Nasrin's rejoinder, but it can be found at http://www.wworld.org/archive/archive.asp?lastID=152 (accessed May 21, 2010).

109. Ali Riaz, "Taslima Nasreen: Breaking the Structured Silence," *Bulletin of Concerned Asian Scholars* 27 (1995): 23.

110. Hillary Frey and Ruth Baldwin, "An Interview with Taslima Nasrin," in *Nothing Sacred: Women Respond to Religious Fundamentalism and Terror,* ed. Betsy Reed (New York: Thunder's Mouth Press/Nation Books, 2002), 213–214.

111. Lila Abu-Lughod, "Do Muslim Women Really Need Saving? Anthropological Reflections on Cultural Relativism and Its Others," *American Anthropologist* 104 (2002): 789.

112. For a similar analysis of the immensely popular *Reading Lolita in Tehran* (New York: Random House, 2003) by Azar Nafisi, which I do not discuss in this essay, see, for example, Hamid Dabashi, "Native Informers and the Making of the American Empire," *al-Ahram Weekly,* June 1, 2006; Keshavarz, *Jasmine and Stars;* Anne Donadey and Huma Ahmed-Ghosh, "Why Americans Love Azar Nafisi's *Reading Lolita in Tehran,*" *Signs* 33, no. 3 (2008): 623–646; Mahmood, "Feminism, Democracy, and Empire."

113. Darwish, *Now They Call Me Infidel,* vii.

114. Uma Narayan, "Restoring History and Politics to 'Third-World Traditions': Contrasting the Colonialist Stance and Contemporary Contestations of *Sati,*" in *Dislocating Cultures: Identities, Traditions, and Third World Feminism* (London: Routledge, 1997), 43–80.

115. Brenda Walker, "The Canary is Choking," *The Social Contract* (Fall 2002): 60–62, quoted in Christina Ho, "Muslim Women's New Defenders: Women's Rights, Nationalism and Islamophobia in Contemporary Australia," *Women's Studies International Forum* 30, no. 4 (July–August 2007): 292.

116. Richard Kerbaj, "Howard Stands by Muslim Integration," *The Australian,* September 1, 2006, quoted in Ho, "Muslim Women's New Defenders," 291–292.

117. Sam Harris and Salman Rushdie, "Ayaan Hirsi Ali: Abandoned to Fanatics," *Los Angeles Times,* October 9, 2007; "Dark Secrets," *Economist,* February 8, 2007; Rebecca Johnson, "The Unbeliever," *Vogue,* February 2007: 226.

118. *Zomergasten,* August 29, 2004; quoted in de Leeuw, " 'Please, Go Wake Up!'," 328.

119. Ibid., 331; see also the recent analysis of the film in Iveta Jusova, "Hirsi Ali and van Gogh's *Submission:* Reinforcing the Islam vs. Women Binary," *Women's Studies International Forum* 31 (2008): 148–155.

120. de Leeuw, " 'Please, Go Wake Up!'," 331.

121. Ibid., 332.

122. Keshavarz, *Jasmine and Stars,* 17.

123. This is not to say that *no* Muslim women have been supportive of these recent works. Manji, for instance, told her listeners at the American Jewish Committee's 2004 Annual Meeting that she has received a surprising "amount of support and affection, and even love . . . from Muslims around the world, especially Muslim women, and especially young Muslim women" (Manji, speech at 98th Annual Meeting of the American Jewish Committee). Nonetheless, my extensive research shows that the vast majority of laudatory reviews and articles about these authors are written by non-Muslims.

124. Valerie Amos and Pratibha Parmar, "Challenging Imperial Feminism," *Feminist Review* 17 (Autumn 1984): 15.

125. Lalami, "The Missionary Position," 23.

126. Fareena Alam, "Enemy of the Faith," *New Statesman,* July 24, 2006, http://www.newstatesman.com/200607240051 (accessed October 17, 2007).

127. Sarah Husain, "Introduction: Iqra!: A Poetics of Resistance," in *Voices of Resistance: Muslim Women on War, Faith & Sexuality,* ed. Sarah Husain (Emeryville, Calif.: Seal Press, 2006).

128. Fawzia Afzal-Khan, "Here Are the Muslim Feminist Voices, Mr. Rushdie!" *Counterpunch,* November 16, 2001.

129. Robert Satloff, "Voices Who Speak For (And Against) Us," *Washington Post,* December 1, 2002.

130. Asma Barlas, "The Excesses of Moderation," paper presented at colloquium " 'Moderate' Islam," University of Utah, February 21–22, 2004, available at www.asmabarlas.com/TALKS/20040221_Utah.pdf. Her egalitarian interpretation of the Quran can be found in Asma Barlas, *"Believing Women" in Islam: Unreading Patriarchal Interpretations of the Qur'an* (Austin: University of Texas Press, 2002).

131. Mahmood Mamdani, *Good Muslim, Bad Muslim: America, the Cold War and the Roots of Terror* (New York: Pantheon Press, 2004). Jasmin Zine makes a similar point in

"Between Orientalism and Fundamentalism: Muslim Women and Feminist Engagement," in *(En)Gendering the War on Terror*, 37.

132. See, for example, the women discussed in Saba Mahmood, *Politics of Piety: The Islamic Revival and the Feminist Subject* (Princeton, N.J.: Princeton University Press, 2005); Lara Deeb, *An Enchanted Modern: Gender and Public Piety in Shi'i Lebanon* (Princeton, N.J.: Princeton University Press, 2006); Elora Shehabuddin *Reshaping the Holy: Democracy, Development, and Muslim Women in Bangladesh* (New York: Columbia University Press, 2008). On U.S. efforts to institutionalize secularism, see Saba Mahmood, "Secularism, Hermeneutics, and Empire: The Politics of Islamic Reformation," *Public Culture* 18 (2006): 323–347.

133. Manji, *Trouble With Islam Today*, 173.

134. George W. Bush and Laura Bush, "President and Mrs. Bush Mark Progress in Global Women's Human Rights," March 12, 2004. For a discussion of beauty schools as the route to empowerment for Afghan women, see J. Reed, "Extreme Makeover," *Vogue* (November 2003): 465–472, 501.

135. See, for example, Aminur Rahman, *Women and Microcredit in Rural Bangladesh: Anthropological Study of the Rhetoric and Realities of Grameen Bank Lending* (Boulder, Colo.: Westview, 1999), and Lamia Karim, "Demystifying Micro-credit: The Grameen Bank, NGOs, and Neoliberalism in Bangladesh," *Cultural Dynamics* 20 (2008): 5–29.

CHAPTER SIX

A Double-Edged Sword
Sexual Democracy, Gender Norms, and Racialized Rhetoric

ÉRIC FASSIN

Policing the French Language

How does "gender" translate into French? Linguistically, the answer seems simple enough: the word *genre* is a common term, thanks to the central role devoted to grammar in primary education since the Third Republic. Every child schooled in France knows about *genre,* not so much as a binary opposition between male and female, i.e., a polite way to avoid the word *sexe,* but rather as an arbitrary grammatical distinction without natural foundations between, say, sun and moon (*le soleil et la lune*) that includes (in addition to masculine and feminine) a third, unmarked option (*neutre*). However, the state committee in charge of terminology published an official recommendation in the summer of 2005 against what was labelled an "abusive use of the term" (*un usage abusif du mot genre*) in the media, in administrative documents, and specifically in sociological writings.[1]

According to this statement, even in English, "gender" is a neologism, more precisely an extension of the original, grammatical meaning to address issues of equality between men and women, for example in UNESCO's insistence on "gender mainstreaming." In practice, "the term is often used to refer exclusively to women or as a reference to a purely biological difference." Thus, for these wise men (and women, for three out of nineteen members of the commission were women), "replacing 'sex' by 'gender' does not correspond to a linguistic need, nor is the extension of meaning of the word 'gender' justified"—at least in French (no recommendation is issued for the English language). The commission suggests that "the word 'sex' (*sexe*) and derivatives such as 'sexist' (*sexiste*) and 'sexual' (*sexuel*) are perfectly adapted, in most cases, to express the difference between men and women, including in its cultural dimension." *Genre* (the noun), or worse the adjective "gendered" (*et a fortiori l'adjectif genré*), are not advisable (*sont à déconseiller*).

The recommendation is to adopt case by case solutions, depending on the context, based on existing resources in the French vocabulary. Gender equality does translate very well as equality between men and women, or between the sexes (*égalité entre hommes et femmes, égalité entre les sexes*). However, one might ask: if indeed "gender" is *often* used to mean "sex," and if indeed that word is sufficient *in most cases,* what about other occurrences, when "gender" does not mean "sex," and when "sex" just won't do? When is the use of "gender" not abusive? That this short note makes no mention of the term *sexué,* even to translate "gendered," no reference even to "masculinity" or "femininity," but only to men and women, is revealing: by focusing on equality between the sexes, the committee leaves out gender norms, as if these norms were not both the cause and the consequence of such inequalities. The linguistic recommendation not only substitutes one term for another; it replaces one question by another, thus obscuring that they are intricately and intimately related. What the committee performs is the replacement of gender by sex—the concept along with the word: *genre* is left outside of the French language, along with the issues it could raise.

From Gender to *Genre*

The story may sound all too familiar to those of us who have regularly been confronted with the resistance to gender in France, in particular through the conflation of anti-Americanism and anti-feminism in the 1990s. The virulent hostility against American feminism along with the politicization of sexuality expressed at the time of the Clarence Thomas hearings, and thus more broadly the horrified fascination for so-called American "sexual correctness," extended beyond issues of sexuality to include the very notion of gender. Rejecting the concept along with the word made it possible to "nationalize" anti-feminism: this appears clearly in Mona Ozouf's mid-1990s argument about the singularity of the French culture of femininity, which offered an updated version of French exceptionalism.[2] That today's language committee is presided over by conservative literary scholar Marc Fumaroli, whose vindication of Old Regime salon conversation provides historical background for Ozouf's essay, can only confirm the impression that there is nothing new under the French sun. Once again, in 2005 just as in 1995, gender is rejected as alien to French culture. *Plus ça change, plus c'est la même chose* (the more things change, the more they stay the same).

Or is it really déjà vu all over again? In ten years, the intellectual and political landscape has changed considerably. Throughout most of the 1990s, gender was not part of the French vocabulary; in the 2000s, it is. It was then pronounced in English, in order to make clear that it did not belong in the French language; though still perceived as an American import, it has now become common parlance in its French version. This is obvious in intellectual life as well as in the media, as evidenced by the enthusiastic reception of the 2005 translation of Judith Butler's *Gender Trouble,* all the more remarkable if one bears in mind that French publishers had not found it worth the effort until then.[3] Today, gender is fashionable in France, in particular in academia, among students and professors alike, with a whole flurry of book titles and new book series, special issues of journals and conferences, from M.A. programs at the *École des hautes études en sciences sociales* and elsewhere to scholarships from the *Institut Émilie du Châtelet* launched by the *Île-de-France* Region.

As a consequence, the resistance to (allegedly American) gender that could be interpreted in the early 1990s as a preemptive strike against the politicization of sexual issues now appears as a rearguard skirmish. This does not mean that such attacks have lost their importance, but only that their significance is not to be found in some eternal cultural Frenchness: new contexts provide new meanings. How are we to understand such a sudden shift in the intellectual landscape? Broader changes in political context are obviously relevant: starting in the late 1990s with *pacs* (the French civil union, or civil pact of solidarity, and beyond, with same-sex marriage) and *parité* (in politics, and beyond), sexual politics suddenly became politics *par excellence*.[4] After a series of controversies over prostitution and pornography, as well as sexual harassment and violence against women, not to forget the Islamic veil, and at a time when the presidential campaign showed all the major candidates taking stands on gay rights and gender violence, with Ségolène Royal as the first woman to represent a major party having reached the second round of elections while (finally) supporting gay marriage and adoption, who could argue, as many did in the 1990s, that the politicization of gender and sexuality is alien to French culture?

Sex and Gender in Court

In fact, the recommendation of the language committee could be read as a response to this new French political culture, even in its most recent manifestations. In 2004, the example of San Francisco's mayor celebrating same-sex weddings inspired a French manifesto calling for similar initiatives. This is how the mayor of Bègles, Noël Mamère, came to celebrate the first same-sex wedding in France, thus igniting a major uproar in the media. However, not only did most political parties oppose him quite virulently, while the government tried to stop his action, but the courts never recognized the legal value of this ceremony, insisting that, according to French law, marriage is only between a man and a woman. However, a year later, in 2005, another, less publicized case suggested otherwise, and complicated the issue by undermining the ostensibly "natural" logic of sex. Two transgendered women asked to be married. Their case was first a reminder that sex is no more natural than gender: it is indeed a state category. Although one had undergone surgery, the other had not; as a consequence, from the point of view of the state, the former had become a woman, while the latter remained a man.

The argument of sexual difference reiterated a year earlier should logically have opened matrimony to them, but the mayor refused to perform the ceremony. This time, the court supported his decision by providing a new rationale: marriage implies the intention to behave as husband and wife, i.e., as man and woman. In other words, the new case revised the definition of marriage: what was now required, instead of sexual difference, was gender differentiation. Of course, the word "gender" is not used anywhere. And it can safely be assumed that the court did not realize the full implications of this new logic: would the state accept this marriage if Monica (the legal male) agreed to wear a suit and tie, instead of refusing to show up (as she put it when I met her) in "drag"? Conversely, should feminine men and masculine women be denied marriage, or should they be entitled only to marry together? Is the state to organize gender tests in order to deliver marriage certificates? Are sociologists to become the new gender police? Is the gender policing to be extended to private, even intimate, practices?

The language recommendation published just a few weeks later in the *Journal Officiel* can thus be read as an attempt at suppressing such absurd contradictions by a return to "common sense"—hence the idea that gender adds nothing to sex. Ostensibly, the committee does not argue in political terms (there is no suggestion of a danger attached to gender), but in linguistic terms (there is no need for a neologism, as "gender" is a synonym of "sex"). Why use "gender"? "Sex" will do. It is true that, precisely because it has become fashionable, "gender" is often used today interchangeably with "sex"—from sports organizations that categorize men and women by "gender" while rejecting transgender athletes, to scholars who stake a claim in gender studies while simply taking into account that society comprises women as well as men. But as it has no political importance whatsoever, this "abusive use" of "gender" would certainly not have justified issuing such a recommendation. This explains the absence of any reference to gender norms (no masculinity, no femininity, a rejection of *genré,* and no mention of *sexué*); what is left out from the recommendation is also what is at stake in the current debate.

Vatican Theology vs. Gender

Another document, also published in France in 2005, reveals explicitly what is only implicit in the recommendation: a critical dictionary issued by the Vatican's Council for the Family, a "lexicon of ambiguous and controversial terms on family, life, and ethical issues."[5] Central to this critique is the concept of gender, addressed not in just one but in three articles. According to the editors of this volume, during the 1995 U.N. conference on women in Beijing, Vatican representatives came to realize the importance and the dangers of "gender" as a social construction of sexual difference: they understood very well that this notion could imply an "unacceptable program that includes toleration for homosexual orientations and identities." Gender, as illustrated by a quotation from Judith Butler's *Gender Trouble,* whose distance from "common sense" makes the definition of gender sound like "science-fiction," suggests that "there exists no such thing as a natural man or a natural woman," and questions "to what extent there exists any 'natural' form of sexuality": the theologians in this lexicon thus express fears that the denaturalization of sex operated by gender logically leads to the denaturalization of sexuality, as evidenced in claims for opening marriage to same-sex couples.

This critique of gender is not presented as an opposition to feminism, but only to (so-called) "gender feminism," by contrast to a suitable feminism of "equality," or rather "parity," a formulation borrowed from antifeminist Christina Hoff Sommers.[6] This distinction put forward by Vatican theologians restores sex at the expense of gender, just as the language committee appointed by French authorities does. What is at stake is the status of nature— the nature of sexual difference. As then Cardinal Ratzinger had made it clear a year earlier, in a 2004 letter addressed to bishops, the "collaboration of men and women in the Church and in the world" is premised on their "difference." Biblical anthropology defines the roles of men and women based on their complementary natures. As a consequence, according to the 2005 Lexicon, "if we accept the fact that men and women are different, finding a statistical difference between the numbers of men and women in a specific field is not evidence of discrimination, but simply reflects these natural differences existing between man and woman." This is probably why the word "parity" sounds preferable to the more constraining "equality."

The Lexicon proposes in conclusion "a revised definition of gender that is acceptable for the Catholic Church": "Transcendent dimension of human sexuality, compatible with all aspects of the human person, comprising body, thought, spirit, and soul. Gender is thus permeable to influences exerted upon the human person, be they internal or external, but it must conform to the natural order that is already given in the body." This new, Catholic version of gender is in explicit opposition to gender feminism, in which "the reality of nature disturbs, troubles, and thus must go away." In a word, the response of Vatican theologians to the feminist "gender trouble" is a "nature trouble" (*quand la nature dérange*). The social order has a natural foundation in sexual difference, and this anthropology requires that God be identified with Nature: hence the privileged role of sexual politics in the politics of Catholic theology.

Gender and Sexual Democracy

What this theological attack against gender as well as the linguistic recommendation in favor of sex both demonstrate is that today gender, in France and elsewhere, despite (or perhaps also because of) its social success and the fashionable vagueness apparent in much international gender talk, is and remains "a useful category," i.e., a tool, if not a weapon, with a critical edge. It may sometimes lose its heuristic value, but it retains its polemical efficacy. Gender (still) does trouble. What is at stake is the very foundation of the social order in democratic societies, and specifically in what I call "sexual democracy."[7] Instead of starting from (allegedly) democratic institutions, a democratic society can be defined by its claim that laws and norms are not imposed by some transcendent authority (whether it be God, Nature, Tradition, or any other principle that is meant to escape historical change and political critique), but rather by the immanent logic of public deliberation and private negotiations. As a consequence, the order of things is presented explicitly as a social, not a natural, order, steeped in history and thus subject to change, fundamentally political and thus an object of critique: liberty and equality become legitimate claims, whose very definitions are at stake in these political struggles concerning both gender and sexuality.

Sexual democracy can be understood by its proponents as the ultimate frontier of democratization, while sexual difference appears to its opponents as the last refuge of transcendence—a natural reservation immune to history and politics, protected from the turmoil of democratic critique. The importance of sexual politics today throughout the world (from gay marriage to violence against women, from the Islamic veil to prostitution, etc.) is to be interpreted in this context: these are battles about the limits, or on the contrary about the continued extension, of the democratic logic (as defined here). Is everything social, historical, political, or is there still at least one (sexual) domain that is truly, essentially natural, escaping history and politics? This helps understand what theologians mean when they talk of a "transcendent" principle ordering sexual difference, in opposition to gender—and more generally, why they feel the need to devote three whole articles to undermine this notion. This is not just a question of vocabulary: what is at stake is the status of transcendence, if any, in the definition of laws and norms within democratic societies as defined here.

However, this is not just about religion proper. In fact, if the notion of God invoked by theologians merges with Nature, the French debate on *pacs,* gay marriage and families also revealed that the logic of Science could just as well be conflated with the authority of Nature. The symbolic order of psychoanalysts and anthropologists was invoked to prevent a democratic debate about the definition of marriage and family, as they opposed a (capitalized) Law of the psyche and of culture to arbitrary human laws (lower-case).[8] Indeed, at the time, French bishops only relied on this "scientific" dogma to justify their rejection of the *pacs,* not on the Scriptures or the Fathers of the Church—though it is worth noting that their organic intellectual in the late 1990s, a priest and psychoanalyst, was to become the architect of the 2005 theological Lexicon. In fact, one could even argue that *laïcité,* the French version of secularism invoked most forcefully as a founding principle of the recent law against "ostensible religious signs," and in practice against the Islamic veil, has also functioned as a sacred dogma about the nation. Beyond politics, and outside of history, it plays a transcendent role, structurally equivalent, just as the symbolic order was a few years earlier, to the theologians' reference to biblical anthropology.

This does not mean that secularism (any more than science) is in essence "dogmatic," always claiming transcendent value in democratic debates. What these twin examples reveal, rather, is how both can play that role in specific historical contexts. However, it should be remembered that there have also been critics of the sacralization of "*catholaïcité,*" to borrow their term, *in the name of* "*laïcité*" (just as there have been critiques of the sacralization of psychoanalysis or anthropology *in the name of science*). Nor should we conclude, in reaction to such an instrumentalization of secularism, that the Islamic veil ought to be interpreted as the new symbol of sexual democracy. That is what some French commentators proposed, though: they compared the gesture of two young women who defied the new ban on the Islamic veil, and as a consequence were excluded from school, to the dissent of seventeenth-century Puritans. Against those who would only interpret them in terms of alienation, they recast them as the new vanguard of sexual liberty—somewhat paradoxically if we remember their conservative, if not reactionary, views on gender and sexuality. Indeed, Islamic sexual politics, as is the case with the Vatican, is often explicitly defined in opposition to sexual democracy. Evidence of this convergence is to be found in state alliances within international organizations on such issues as abortion or gay rights.

The Racialization of Sexual Democracy

If, to a certain extent, the centrality of sexual politics in today's Islam should be interpreted in part as a reaction against "the West," the reverse is also becoming truer every day: claims for sexual democracy are not always to be taken at face value. More and more, they are to be understood as a reaction against "the rest," that is, against Islam and various Third World "Others." What this means is that we are witnessing a racialization of the rhetoric of sexual democracy, just as there has been a racialization of the rhetoric of secularism. It is used, not as an instrument to question the normative foundations of the sexual order, but rather as a weapon to stigmatize "undemocratic" others in the name of sexual modernity—a disturbing evolution that is of course quite crucial for feminism, as many French feminists, among others, have recently embraced secularism as their fundamental value, to the point that some may sound like born-again *laïques*.

Consider the example of French President Nicolas Sarkozy. His public image has been in large part based on his tough stance on immigration, as he has kept displaying his strength by the dramatic, forcible expulsion of undocumented workers (many of whom have been denied or even deprived of documents as a result of his policies), thus successfully stealing the thunder of the extreme-right National Front of Jean-Marie Le Pen to win the 2007 presidential election. In 2005, while still minister of the interior, he started advocating so-called "chosen immigration" (*immigration choisie*), by contrast to "imposed immigration" (*immigration subie*). In practice, this means, in addition to restrictions on asylum rights, hindering binational marriages and limiting family reunification for immigrants, while allegedly favoring (supposedly single) migrant workers, in the name of economic imperatives. The racist implications of such a policy, which goes against French traditional approaches to the issue, did not go unnoticed. But he tried to defuse criticism by insisting that, appearances notwithstanding, controlling immigration had to do with the defense of universal values: "We are proud of the values of the Republic, equality between men and women, secularism, the French ideal of integration. So, we must dare to speak about these values to those we welcome. Let us make sure that the rights of the French woman also apply to immigrant women."

This is not an isolated remark. It became a central argument in Nicolas Sarkozy's presidential campaign, in particular when he announced that, if elected, he would create a new "Ministry of immigration and national identity," which became one of his first decisions after the election. The proposal created an uproar, as the theme of national identity, framed in opposition to immigration, resonated with the language of today's (as well as yesterday's) extreme right, whose voters Nicolas Sarkozy successfully courted. This is why the candidate chose to hold his ground; he devoted one of his three official campaign ads on television to the issue of national identity. In this short film, the idea is to show that national identity has nothing to do with racism: "I believe in national identity. France is not a race, nor an ethnic group; France is a community of values, an ideal, an idea."

The best way to support this "Republican" contention is to identify national identity with sexual democracy. "So I said: 'We must have identity and immigration.'" (*Il faut identité et immigration.*) But he goes on to explain (with pictures in the background of political meetings with crowds, where he embraces a black woman, apparently in distress, and several white women, ostensibly happy): "In France, women are free, just as men are, free to circulate, free to marry, free to get a divorce. The right to abortion, equality between men and women, that too is part of our identity." Valuing divorce and abortion as essential to French identity clearly shows how much the new racialization of sexual democracy affects political discourse: in order to distinguish "us" (French) from "them" (racialized Others), conservative politicians can be willing to go so far as to jettison traditional moral values. Indeed, one may be surprised to find that Nicolas Sarkozy values feminism so much; but one should be even more disconcerted to learn not only that equality between men and women is part of today's French identity, but that this value shows immigrants, again according to this political ad, how "France comes from a long past, and started before them."

This rhetoric of sexual democracy is also at work in the way the French state deals with immigrants. The "contract to welcome and integrate" immigrants, implicitly aimed mostly at Maghrebian or sub-Saharan African immigrants, confirms this remarkable redefinition of what Frenchness is now supposed to mean.[9] (Ethnographic fieldwork recently presented in several doctoral dissertations confirms that the bureaucracy of naturalization has adopted this new perspective in dealing with applicants.) According to this document introduced in 2006, French democracy is of course classically defined by its Republican motto—"Liberty, Equality, Fraternity." What is remarkable, however, is that equality is understood exclusively as sex equality (rather than in terms of class or race, for example). This point is made before the importance of knowing the French language is even mentioned.

As to "fraternity," there is no reference beyond the motto—no such phrases as "welfare state" or even "social solidarity." Another legacy of French history seems to have replaced the third term of the triptych: secularism. It is not just presented as one principle among many, but as the foundation of the nation: *la France, un pays laïque.* This is of course to be understood in the context of the 2004 law banning the Islamic veil from schools, thus resonating with issues of sexual democracy. According to this "contract" imposed upon immigrants, "in France, religion belongs in the private sphere." Never mind that the French state was then precisely trying to organize Islam after the model of Judaism (the new *Conseil français du culte musulman* as a Muslim equivalent of the old *Consistoire*), thus erecting religion as a legitimate political actor in the public sphere. The implication is that Islam needs to learn (as was the case with Catholicism under the Third Republic) the separation between religion and politics. The democratic values of the French Republic are thus redefined as liberty, equality, and *laïcité.*

What does sexual equality imply, according to the contract that immigrants are required to sign? "The principle of equality between men and women is a founding principle of French society. Parents are jointly responsible for their children. Women have the same rights as well as the same duties as men. This principle applies to all—whether French or foreigners. Women are not subjected to the authority of a husband, nor of a father or brother in order to (for instance) work, go out, or open a bank account." Lest someone misunderstand against whom such rules are emphasized, the next sentence is even more explicit: "Forced marriages are forbidden, while monogamy and the integrity of the body are guaranteed by law." All these elements are in direct reference to recent controversies about immigrant "cultures" (either African or Muslim), from court cases about genital mutilations to a revision of the age of matrimony to combat so-called forced marriages, not to forget the suggestion that polygamy caused the urban riots of late 2005.

Fortress Europe

Although the example of France has been developed at length here, and despite specificities, there is clearly no French exceptionalism in matters of sexual democracy. On the contrary, as evidenced by the echoes in various countries of the debate about the Islamic veil, similar logics are to be found elsewhere in Europe in dealing with immigrants, for example in Germany. Starting in January 2006, in Baden-Württemberg, a *Land* with a population of ten million, new rules have targeted Muslim candidates applying for citizenship with inquiries focusing on sexual politics. Considering that "generally, there is reason to doubt the depth of the attachment of Muslims to the Federal Republic," a new test elaborated by the Interior Ministry includes questions about homosexuality (in addition to others about terrorism and religious freedom), such as: "Should all political functions be allowed for openly gay candidates?" Or, "How would you react if your son came out as a homosexual?"

Not surprisingly, a German deputy of Turkish origin raised the issue for the Green party before the European Commission: why Muslims—and is this not discriminatory, and therefore incompatible with European law? But interestingly, opposition to this measure has also come from the gay and lesbian movement, which has noted that many Germans would fail to qualify for citizenship if they were submitted to the test, starting with Benedict XVI, the first German Pope. Gay activists thus rejected the bait. But in Baden-Württemberg, it is clear that the rhetoric of sexual democracy is being used as a weapon to protect the nation against Muslims—all the more so since this conservative *Land* is known for its anti-immigrant rather than its pro-gay policies.

The Netherlands provide an even more telling example, as the country has only recently renounced its professed multicultural tolerance to embrace a nationalist ideology imbued with racist connotations in the wake of the assassinations of Pim Fortuyn and Theo Van Gogh, and encouraged by recent immigrant from Somalia and former member of Parliament Ayaan Hirsi Ali.[10] In this context, immigrating to the Netherlands for more than three months now requires "integration," including a course in Dutchness preparing for the so-called "civic integration examination abroad." The very description of the pedagogical film *Coming to the Netherlands,* required for the test, is quite revealing.[11] "In the film, a friendly guide tells you about Dutch society. You will be given information about living in the Netherlands and about Dutch politics, work, education and healthcare. You will also be told a bit about the history of the Netherlands."

But there is more to this than friendliness: "Some things that are quite ordinary and acceptable in the Netherlands are forbidden in other countries." And the reference is not to marijuana, whose legal status is a Dutch exception in Europe. "In the Netherlands, women are allowed to sunbathe on the beach with few clothes on, and people have the freedom of expression to show that they are homosexuals or lesbians. The film includes images of this." And indeed, the DVD includes a long shot of a gay couple kissing in a field of spring flowers, and another of a bare-breasted young woman emerging from the waves on the beach, as well as a historical passage on the sexual revolution with bare buttocks and breasts in a Woodstock-like scene. Foreigners need to be educated not just about Dutch politics and history, but also about sexual modernity. If they wish to reside in the Netherlands, Muslims and other immigrants must convert to sexual democracy by voluntarily exposing themselves to images of women's bodies and queers kissing.

The Netherlands cannot be considered as equivalent to Baden-Württemberg: this was the first country to legalize gay marriage, and sexual freedom is protected by law. However, just as in the German case, this test is clearly not about "us," but rather about "them." Indeed, there is a caveat to be found on the government's website: "In some countries, it is against the law to be in possession of films with images of this nature. Because of this, a special film has been made for these countries. In this film, the prohibited images have been deleted. This version of the film is called: 'the edited version.'" One might wonder how Muslims and others from presumably intolerant cultures will be educated if they are to be deprived of the unedited version. Or perhaps ordering one version or the other will help Dutch authorities decide who has proven fit for residence, i.e., who is willing and able to embrace sexual democracy. In fact, the use of sexual democracy for racializing purposes becomes obvious when one realizes that the test is not required if one comes from the European Union of course, or from North America, Australia, New Zealand, Japan—in a word, from the West. Most significantly, the list of countries that are exempt from such a civilizing effort includes the Vatican, thus confirming that claims on behalf of sexual democracy may be the pretext, rather than the real objective, of such a "civic integration" in the Netherlands, as well as throughout Europe.

Sexual Democracy in America

The racialized rhetoric of sexual democracy does not play the same role in the United States as it does in Europe. There is a shift of focus from the restriction of immigration to imperial crusades. But the same instrumentalization can also be found—from Fortress Europe to the so-called "clash of civilizations." This transatlantic difference can be illustrated with an example that touches on both contexts. On February 14, 2006, Zacarias Moussaoui was banned from the courtroom because of his repeated outbursts during jury selection. "These people are Americans. I am al Qaeda. For me, you are enemy." To this, U.S. District Judge Leonie M. Brinkema responded: "Mr. Moussaoui, you are the biggest enemy of yourself." Indeed, as reporters pointed out, the defendant seemed determined to antagonize everyone: he attacked his own attorneys, calling one a "federal lawyer," another (despite his civil rights record) "a KKK [Ku Klux Klan] lawyer," and a third (who is Japanese-American) a "geisha." To make matters worse, he kept attacking the court: "You have been trying to organize my death for four years," Moussaoui told the judge, despite her ruling (overturned on appeal) that Moussaoui was ineligible for the death penalty.

Some of his remarks, "in heavily accented French," though paradoxical, could easily be interpreted in the context: Moussaoui is a French citizen of Moroccan descent, but he declared in court: "I'm not French and never have been French. I stand here as a Muslim only." This is a direct response to French nativism. But he immediately added a more baffling pronouncement: "I do not stand here with a nation of homosexual crusaders." Was it a response to American imperialism? As commentators pointed out, it was not clear whether he was referring to the United States or France: neither country seems to fulfill *both* requirements. In the post-911 context, Bush's America may have been involved in a crusade, but the president is usually not considered a supporter (not to mention an *exporter*) of the gay agenda. Laura Bush did invoke women's rights as justification for the intervention in Afghanistan; however, her concern did not extend to the fate of gays and lesbians. As to France, suffice it to say that President Jacques Chirac proved a famously unreliable ally.

Moussaoui's words apparently make no sense. Journalists have probably been reluctant to speak of insanity, but they clearly suggest as much. The point here is not to proclaim him sound of mind (if only, symmetrically, because of the legal implications). One can still borrow an oft-cited line from *Hamlet*'s Polonius: "Though this be madness, yet there's method in't." There is a logic underlying these otherwise incoherent insults. Moussaoui conflates national, racial, religious, and sexual identifications, thus validating a vision of the world according to which the relevant opposition is that between the West and Islam—a clash of civilizations which is also a conflict between sexual modernity and a traditional sexual order. For Moussaoui, and many crusading on either side, today's wars are sex wars. The so-called war against terror is at the same time a war about the meaning of sexual democracy.

Gendering Sexual Democracy

The racialized rhetoric of sexual democracy has caught feminist as well as gay and lesbian activists and thinkers by surprise. Despite historical precedents (with civilizing projects of immigrants or colonized others among U.S. as well as French feminists in the nineteenth century), it has been difficult to imagine until recently that the critique of the sexual order could be instrumentalized thus, for imperialist or nativistic purposes. But once we come to realize what has happened, the problems only begin, and the solutions are anything but obvious. Are we not required to choose between the interests of sexual and racial minorities, as Susan Moller Okin suggested when she raised the question: "Is multiculturalism bad for women?"[12] In France today, and elsewhere, are we not asked to take sides, either for Muslims or for women—and also, in the Dutch case, which is not limited to heterosexual democracy, for Muslims or *for gays*? Of course, the alternative is not just about religion, as the racialization equally applies to other postcolonial subjects.

Some have convincingly argued, along with Christine Delphy, that this is a "false dilemma," but there remains true tension between sexual and racial issues.[13] This is not mere rhetoric, as this rhetoric often imposes its logic on beliefs, both on Nicolas Sarkozy when he supports abortion rights, and on Zacarias Moussaoui when he attacks "homosexual crusaders." And the risk is that denying the problem—in opposition to those feminists who have all too willingly, in France as elsewhere, joined the democratic crusade of secularism despite its racial context—may result in an implicit choice that only mirrors theirs: focusing on racism, at the expense of sexism. As the rhetoric of sexual democracy becomes racialized, it is all too tempting to downplay sexual democracy itself in order to focus exclusively on its rhetorical instrumentalization by imperialism in the United States, and nativism in Europe.

Perhaps gender can help undermine the dilemma, and alleviate the tension. The instrumentalization of sexual democracy does not include gender itself, except as a synonym of sex. The critical implications of gender are left out of this new rhetoric. Sexual difference is taken for granted, as a natural fact. In the control of immigration developed in France, the Netherlands, or Germany, the implicit definition of sexual democracy is reduced to equality between the sexes, without any critique of gender norms. This is also why, despite their rejection of gender as a feminist concept, equality between the sexes is viewed positively both by the language commission in France and by the Vatican theologians. What is left out from this perspective, however, is what equality does to norms—what gender equality does to the norms of gender, but also of sexuality. On the other hand, that is precisely what theologians worry about when they realize that gender will open the door to same-sex marriage, and that is precisely what is at stake when language experts reject the adjective *genré*.

In itself, the argument about equality does not create "trouble." However, if the normative consequences of equality are taken into account, then there is "gender trouble." Claiming equal rights for men and women has implications for masculinity and femininity, and more broadly, for the logic and mechanic of gender regulations. This normative trouble is not just about gender. It also raises critical questions about race, thus rendering the racial instrumentalization of sexual democracy more difficult. In that sense, in so far as it questions norms, the concept of gender seems less likely to be co-opted thus, unless used as a synonym of sex. And if it is true that the emancipatory promises of sexual democracy can easily be appropriated for the purposes of a civilizing enterprise, perhaps *gender* democracy is less exposed to such an instrumentalization. Or on the contrary, precisely because it can be equated with sex, could gender prove as ambiguous in its definition, open both to normative and critical uses?[14] It may be that no concept is inherently critical. Perhaps they are always, in the end, just like sexual democracy, or even gender: double-edged swords.

NOTES

1. Commission générale de terminologie et de néologie [General Commission on Terminology and Neologisms], "Recommandation sur les équivalents français du mot *gender*" [Recommendation on the French equivalent of the word *gender*], *Journal Officiel de la République française* (July 22, 2005).

2. Mona Ozouf, *Les mots des femmes: Essai sur la singularité française* [Women's words: Essay on French singularity] (Paris: Fayard, 1995). This critique is first formulated by Joan W. Scott, "Vive la différence!" *Le Débat* 87 (Nov.–Dec. 1995): 134–139. See also my essay "The Purloined Gender: American Feminism in a French Mirror," *French Historical Studies* 22 (Winter 1999): 113–138.

3. Judith Butler, *Trouble dans le genre: Le féminisme et la subversion de l'identité* [Gender trouble: Feminism and the subversion of identity], trans. Cynthia Kraus (Paris: La Découverte, 2005; original publication 1990).

4. Clarisse Fabre and Éric Fassin, *Liberté, égalité, sexualité: Actualité politique des questions sexuelles* [Liberty, equality, sexuality: The current politicization of sexual issues], rev. ed. (Paris: 10/18, 2004).

5. Pontifical Council for the Family, *Lexique des termes ambigus et controversés sur la famille, la vie et les questions éthiques* (Paris: Pierre Téqui, 2005), 559–594. English translation available as Pontifical Council for the Family, *Lexicon, Ambiguous and Debatable Terms regarding Family Life and Ethical Questions* (Front Royal, Va.: Human Life International, 2006).

6. Christina Hoff Sommers, *Who Stole Feminism? How Women Have Betrayed Women* (New York: Simon and Schuster, 1995).

7. See Éric Fassin, "Démocratie sexuelle," *Comprendre, revue de philosophie et de sciences sociales* 6 (Fall 2005): 263–276.

8. For a discussion, see Daniel Borrillo, Marcela Iacub, and Éric Fassin, *Au-delà du PACS: l'expertise familiale à l'épreuve de l'homosexualité* [Beyond PACS: Family expertise exposed to homosexuality] (Paris: PUF, 1999); and Éric Fassin, *L'inversion de la question homosexuelle* [The inversion of the homosexual question], rev. ed. (Paris: Amsterdam Publisher, 2008).

9. Agence Nationale de l'Accueil des Étrangers et des Migrations (ANAEM), "Contrat d'accueil et d'intégration" [Contract on welcoming and integration], latest version: http://www.anaem.fr/IMG/pdf/Contrat_2008.pdf.

10. See Éric Fassin, "Going Dutch," *Bidoun: Arts and Culture from the Middle East* 10 (Spring 2007): 62–63.

11. Éric Fassin and Judith Surkis, "National Identities and Transnational Intimacies: Sexual Democracy and the Politics of Immigration in Europe," special section on The Sexual Boundaries of Europe, *Public Culture* 22, no. 3 (fall 2010): 507–529.

12. Susan Moller Okin, et. al., *Is Multiculturalism Bad For Women?* (Princeton, N.J.: Princeton University Press, 1999).

13. Christine Delphy, "Antisexisme *ou* antiracisme? Un faux dilemme" [Sexism or racism? A false dilemma], *Nouvelles Questions Féministes* 25 (2006): 59–83.

14. A question I raise through the history of the concept in my essay, "L'empire du genre: L'histoire politique ambiguë d'un outil conceptuel" [The empire of gender: The political history of an ambiguous conceptual tool], *L'homme* 187–188 (Fall 2008): 375–392.

PART 3
SEEING THE QUESTION

CHAPTER SEVEN

Seeing Beyond the Norm

Interpreting Gender in the Visual Arts

MARY D. SHERIFF

Gender Enters the History of Art

Not so long ago there was much talk of "en-gendering" art. In the 1990s, nearly every session at the College Art Association conference included at least one paper that wrestled with issues of gender. Art historians concerned with those issues had already complicated their work by attending as well to questions of race, ethnicity, and sexual orientation. They had moved beyond an initial focus on Western art, and they had embraced masculinity as an object of study. In short, they had begun to revolutionize the discipline. Yet despite having influenced the practices and assumptions of art history, gender studies today are significantly less visible than they were a decade ago.[1] What factors have led to the current state of gender studies in art history? Are they related to the initial presumptions that spurred and guided the analysis of gender, or to the interpretative strategies of its practitioners? If gender studies in the history of art have reached an impasse, what can be done to reinvigorate and redirect them?

Gender infiltrated art historical writing little by little, in ideas borrowed from here and there and shaped to fit the aims of an art history driven by feminist politics. Those involved in feminist movements during the 1960s opened the way for introducing gender as an analytic category, a situation that likely resonates with the entry of gender analysis into other disciplines.[2] And as in other disciplines, the first feminist art historians were concerned with recovering the work of women and outlining the obstacles to their advancement, a concern they shared with contemporary women artists who addressed similar issues in their practice. Art historians, however, only got fired up in 1971 when Linda Nochlin posed the impertinent question, "Why have there been no great women artists?" in an essay indebted to the work of Simone de Beauvoir and published first in *Art News* (January 1971) and soon after in the interdisciplinary volume *Women in Sexist Society* (1971). With its accessible, irreverent, and trenchant prose, Nochlin's essay remains a powerful statement, and one that I find very readable even today. This first salvo was followed five years later by the catalog of the groundbreaking exhibition Women Artists 1550–1950, held in 1976 at the Los Angeles County Museum, a catalog Nochlin co-authored with Anne Southerland Harris.[3]

Although a pioneer of feminist art history and an effective spokesperson, Nochlin has never undertaken an analysis of gender as a concept. She has consistently defined herself in terms of feminist art history, and what we see in her work is the adaptation of critical and theoretical concepts and terms developed in other disciplines. For example, in the opening essay of *Women Artists 1550–1950*, the exhibition catalog, Nochlin explored the dichotomy that correlated woman with "nature" and man with "culture," drawing not only on Beauvoir's work, but also on Sherry Ortner's 1972 essay in *Feminist Studies*, "Is Female to Male as Nature is to Culture?"[4] My point is not that Linda Nochlin, in particular, or art historians, in general, are derivative thinkers—after all, few of us create our own analytic categories. My observations are rather to suggest that some idea of a sex/gender system took shape early in feminist art history before the term "gender" was in play. When "gender" did enter into art historical analysis, however, it did so in the absence of an intervention on the order of Joan Scott's founding essay. In fact, many art historians read and adopted the concept of gender as articulated by Joan Scott, finding her essay persuasive, lucid, and very useful indeed.[5]

Gender, however, has not necessarily been the main term embraced by feminist art historians in pursuing their work. By 1989, when she published a collection entitled *The Politics of Vision,* Linda Nochlin preferred the term "alterity," proposing that feminism, under its theoretical and political aspects, had brought her to considering the history of art from the perspective of the "other."[6] The "other" included not only "woman," but also peoples of different races, classes, ethnicities, religions, sexualities, and so forth. Nochlin tied her consideration of "othering" to what Griselda Pollock, another influential art historian, would call the "sociological," a term that Pollock associated with "gender" as distinguished from "sexual difference."

Pollock has consistently positioned her work in terms of "difference," as indicated by the title of her best-known work, *Vision and Difference* (1988), and her later work *Differencing the Canon* (1999):

Difference, sociologically defined as gender difference, and *more recently* conceived as a psychic and linguistic position through psychoanalysis as sexual difference, has played a vital role in feminist theory. Difference signifies division between "men" and "women" resulting in a hierarchy in which those placed within the social category of the female gender or assigned the psycho-linguistic position as feminine are negatively valued relative to the masculine or men [emphasis added].[7]

Pollock also uses "difference" in a more generic sense, and it slides from technical to standard usage, pointing to all sorts of divergences between and among people, things, and temporal moments. In contrast to many art historians concerned with gender, Pollock has been increasingly engaged with psychoanalysis, and her definition perhaps implies a hierarchy positioning "sexual difference" located in psychoanalysis as "more recent" than the sociological conception of "gender difference." Her art historical practice, moreover, seems to invoke psychoanalysis as a description of patriarchy, a system of interpretation, and sometimes as a discourse of truth. Her particular attachment to psychoanalysis distinguishes her work from that of art historians like myself who have drawn on psychoanalytic theory and also relied on the critiques of psychoanalysis offered by Luce Irigaray, Michele le Doeuff, Sarah Kofman, Elizabeth Grosz, and Judith Butler.

Although feminist interventions in the history of art have taken many forms and drawn on many different theories, the concept of gender as a culturally constructed counterpart to the assumed division between the sexes has been widely adopted. A 2006 work that takes gender as one of its central terms is Lisa Rosenthal's *Gender, Politics and Allegory in the Art of Rubens:* "Feminist theory's axiom that gender is not natural and fixed but is constantly being constructed within its cultural contexts and that its meanings are fluid, unstable, and difficult to control enables a powerful rereading of both the images and the culture in which they operate."[8] Rosenthal implicitly assumes her readers are both familiar with and accepting of this axiom. I am not, however, convinced that this is the case for all art historians working today. Taking advantage of the fluidity, instability, and uncontrollable nature of meanings is a real strength of Rosenthal's interpretive practice, but such notions have not always guided those in art history who have drawn on the concept of gender. Some analyses of gender have produced meanings that are indeed different from the traditional ones attached to works of art, but at the same time, these analyses sometimes present such meanings as if they were as stable and as unchanging as the interpretations they propose to replace. In other words, not all art historians who undertake the analysis of gender adopt strategies derived from post-structuralism (and, in particular, from deconstruction). Moreover, even from my very brief survey, it should be evident that there is no agreement as to what sort of feminist theory is most pertinent for our discipline, even though gender as an analytic category has been absorbed into our art historical practices.

In the current generation of junior faculty, most practicing art historians have at one time or another used gender as a analytic category, even if only to please an instructor in a graduate seminar. The process of engendering art has led many to criticize or reevaluate canonical and non-canonical works, images that feature the human body and those that don't show it at all, paintings and sculptures, but also architecture, porcelain, and those arts often called "popular," "decorative," or "minor." Those who studied European and North American art introduced gender analysis into art history, and it quickly expanded to the study of all visual cultures.[9] At the same time, certainly not all art historians have been receptive to thinking of art through the concept of gender, and in recent years there has also been attention paid to the "great masters" from Praxiteles to Jackson Pollock, a shoring up that often ignores issues of gender. In trying to locate the current position of gender studies, I can only say that it is neither at the center of the discipline, nor is it at the forefront. Does the current position suggest some broader—although not systematic—effort to displace, or even to silence, gender studies in art history, an effort that could be calculated in projects not funded, practitioners denied desirable positions, manuscripts rejected, and publications denounced, or, even worse, entirely ignored? Is the decline in gender studies attributable to the apparent disappearance of the feminist movement from political life? The birth of gender studies within feminist politics might suggest that one cannot thrive without drawing energy from the other. But are there other factors? For example, have gender studies in art history been "mainstreamed" or "co-opted" to the extent that they have lost their currency and hence their provocative position? Are we, as scholars, only motivated by the newest practices that are deemed on the cutting edge? Do gender studies seem "boring" because no longer fashionable in the discipline? Or might there be other reasons more internal to our practice that we should at least consider?

I raise these questions following a recent experience I had in sitting on an interdisciplinary fellowship committee. A fair number of the project proposals were focused on gender—although not nearly as many as positioned themselves in postcolonial studies. Panel members often judged harshly those projects that were primarily based on gender analysis, especially when the analysis took women as the object of study. Even panel members whom I expected to be most sympathetic to gender analysis criticized these projects not for lack of rigor, but because they did not offer anything "new." Some of the projects may well have deserved this criticism, but nevertheless it gave me pause. I wondered if those who used gender as an analytic category in probing different cultural scenes have come to a sort of impasse—and frankly I wonder about this in my own writing. And I wonder if gender analysis does not seem "new" because the dynamics of oppression under analysis are themselves often so repetitive across time and space. If scholars on the left are finding gender studies unworthy of support because they say nothing new, is their assessment aiding those on the right who would like to efface the analysis of gender (along with that of race, class, sexuality, and so on) from the academic scene? Is the situation in national politics—the splintering of the left and the consolidation of the right—simply replicated in the politics of the academe? I do not advocate supporting unworthy projects simply because I support their politics, but neither do I want to reject worthy projects because they are no longer in academic fashion. The idea that we have heard it all before seems to me particularly pernicious especially when we consider how short a time we have been studying gender, and how long a time we have heard the mantras of traditional art history repeated by noted and not so noted scholars, scholars who again and again talk about the same artists, use the same methods and invoke the same categories of analysis. While there are many external factors that could be cited to account for the current state of gender studies in art history, I am concerned with the internal ones. One that especially interests me is what for lack of a better term I am calling the impasse of critique. What do we do once we have critiqued the entire history of art? Can a new history of art be founded on critique alone?

Critique unveils the prejudices and sins of the past and demonstrates how works of art helped to justify and enforce oppressive ideologies. Critique is important; we cannot do without it. Without critique we cannot understand the interests at play in any work of art. It is nevertheless an end that rarely, if ever, offers a supplementary bonus: a positive reinterpretation of a work for the future. While I appreciate both the necessity for and pleasures of critique, I am concerned that if we recognize only a work's potential for oppression, we silence other historically valid possibilities embedded in the work and limit our own ability to recreate meaning. I am also wary of critiques made only from the position of the present, critiques that ignore the historical contingency of the language and conventions of art making.

Reading in the Past

Feminist studies in art history, whether they adopt concepts of gender or difference or alterity, have since their beginning been rooted in critique. As

Nochlin observed retrospectively in *Women, Art and Power and Other Essays* (1988): "Critique has always been at the heart of my project and remains there today. I do not conceive of a feminist art history as a positive approach to the field, a way of simply adding a token list of women painters and sculptors to the canon."[10] The comments that follow clarify her meaning: when Nochlin says that feminist art history is not a "positive approach to the field," she means that the practice seeks not to add a few women to the canon, but to challenge and change the very premises of the discipline. Still, I find the language odd in labeling feminist art history as not a positive approach. Does such a comment signify merely that the primary goal of feminist art history is critique? Or that as a critique it depends on a negative reading of the discipline's status quo? Do we need an opponent to struggle against—which, of course, means to be dependent on? Have we lost prominence because in using gender as a category of analysis, feminist art history has not offered a positive alternative to the traditional history of art?

The initial tendency in feminist art history was to critique not only the sex-gender systems that oppressed women as subjects, objects, and consumers of representations—but all representations, whether by men or by women, that on the face of it seemed to support that system. While we should applaud these pioneering efforts that opened an entire discipline to new ways of thinking, we can now admit that the first major feminist interventions—sweeping surveys like Nochlin and Harris's *Women Artists 1550–1950* (1976) or Griselda Pollock and Rozsika Parker's *Old Mistresses* (1981)—analyzed many works only superficially. The early, formative texts of gender studies sometimes lacked depth in their interpretations, relying on how a work "appeared" to the critic who in a sweeping survey did not always explore the historical situation, which could include everything from the language of art operative at the time, to the theory of art that governed production, the constraints under which artists worked, and the comments of contemporaries who viewed the art.[11] Of course, these early histories were hindered because there was little basic research on many of these artists, and if there were secondary sources, they were hopelessly out of date.

My first point, therefore, is so basic as to seem obvious, but I think it is worth making: handling images made in the past requires careful historical reconstruction and analysis prior to critique and reinterpretation, and such analyses must go hand in hand with a reading that engages gender and other categories of difference. Without such analysis critique risks devolving into a personal evaluation of political correctness, and gender analysis risks falling into either unvaried repetition or a simple application of "theory" that always arrives at the same conclusion. Without a far-ranging analysis of each work,

we can explore neither the subversive potential of the image within its historical context, nor the historical range of viewing possibilities, nor the rich plurality of meanings that can—and did—attach themselves to art objects.

What first made the problem of critique clear to me was my own work on
the self-portraits of Elisabeth Vigée-Lebrun, images that had been subjected
to superficial critique and quick dismissal in two of Griselda Pollock's works:
in the early survey text, *Old Mistresses*, written with Rozsika Parker, and in her
later *Vision and Difference* (1988). What struck Pollock and Parker in looking at
Vigée-Lebrun's self-portrait (fig. 7.1) was that the artist showed herself as a
beautiful and fashionable lady, and this further suggested to them that Vigée-
Lebrun's work supported the most problematic paradigms of "woman." In *Old
Mistresses,* the analysis is directed toward Vigée-Lebrun's total complicity with
or capture by the prevailing gendered norms for representing "woman," or
the "eternal feminine." Standing before Vigée-Lebrun's painting, these art
historians allowed the spectacle of "woman" to eclipse any possibility of seeing or imagining an artist, concluding "as an image of an eighteenth-century
artist it is wholly unconvincing."[12] But unconvincing to whom?

My investigation of Elisabeth Vigée-Lebrun (*The Exceptional Woman*, 1996)
developed in part from what I saw as the inability of feminist art history to
move beyond a superficial analysis of a painter whose work and history seemed
to me especially complex. My reading of Toril Moi's *Sexual/Textual Politics* (1985)
encouraged me to question the current assessment of the artist. Moi opens
her book with the challenge of rescuing Virginia Woolf, whose work feminist
critics had received negatively, for feminist politics: "It is surely arguable that
if feminist critics cannot produce a positive political and literary assessment of
Woolf's writing, then the fault may lie with their own critical and theoretical
perspectives rather than with Woolf's texts."[13] My work did not claim Vigée-
Lebrun as a feminist, but rather viewed her work from a critical and theoretical perspective that would reclaim it for feminism. That perspective valued
the multiple shifting and fictive identities the artist assumed in representing
herself and other women, as well as her continual questioning of the theoretical divide between woman and artist, between "natural" (re)production and
cultural production. For me, these undercut any attempt to view her art as
essentializing gender, sex, or desire, or to see it as constructing women
as "woman, the eternal feminine." Moreover, in the case of the 1783 self-
portrait, the historical record suggested that contemporary viewers did not
find Vigée-Lebrun's self-portrait unconvincing—they understood the conventions and visual language of the image to represent her as artist. A reading
of the art criticism from 1783 showed, in fact, that contemporary viewers saw
both the artist and the woman quite clearly, and the portrait even provoked

diatribes for its masculine ambitions. Some contemporary critics, in fact, condemned the work for what we might call its discontinuity of sex and gender. In the case of this self-portrayal, the historicized reading—the reading that privileges how viewers of the time understood the work—provided the opportunity for a reinterpretation that stressed the subversive qualities of the self-portrait and broke with a feminist critique that had not investigated the work in its historical context. Even though the historical context proved essential to my analysis, the reading I offered would not have been available in 1783.[14]

My re-reading of Vigée-Lebrun's paintings, and of her self-representations in particular, owe much to the work of Judith Butler, and especially to *Bodies that Matter* (1993), which appeared as I was finishing my final draft of *The Exceptional Woman*. In addition to her re-readings of Lacan, what I found especially inspiring and adaptable to my purposes were Butler's analysis of the practices through which regulatory regimes operate, her conceptualization of performativity and citation, and her handling of the problem of contradiction in relation to identity formation. Drawing on Butler's work, I argued that in the case of Vigée-Lebrun's self-portraits, her imitation of and identification with others (e.g., celebrated artists, the lovers of celebrated artists, aristocratic patrons) occasioned the sort of criss-crossing movement across the sexual divide that produced the complex, layered, and (apparently) contradictory subject we see in Vigée-Lebrun's self-imagings. Very helpful was Butler's emphasis on the subversive potential of citation: although citing (or adhering to) the norms that legislate sexual identity was culturally mandated, citation was inevitably interpretation, and as such it opened gaps between the cultural text and the individual's mimicry of it. I teased out the subversive possibilities of Vigée-Lebrun's citations and self-representations, but only after demonstrating how the artist's interpretation of the cultural text was shaped (but not entirely determined) by the particulars of her historical moment, individual experience, and socioeconomic status. I do not think I could have found a way through this material without drawing on (and bending to my own purposes) *Bodies that Matter*.

As I have argued, the problem with the way feminist scholars had previously read Vigée-Lebrun's self-portrait was that their interpretative performances transformed a highly complicated image into a simple sign for "woman." It is ironic indeed that these interpretations offered fundamentally the same conclusion as those made by traditional art historians who found her work pretty but vacuous, and who quickly dismissed it with just as superficial a reading. This congruence further emphasizes the need to ask several basic questions of our work: What sort of interpretations do we produce when we declare that a work means simply what we, reading it as if its language were transparent, take it to mean? What opportunities do we foreclose in such a practice? I am not arguing that we should only read paintings as we imagine they were read in the past, that we limit ourselves to historicizing. Rather, I am emphasizing that without thoroughly historicizing works, any further subversive or creative or even critical reinterpretation will be either foreclosed or easily put aside. Feminist art history and gender analysis is dangerously vulnerable to dismissal when theoretical, historical, and formal modes of analyses do not support one another; when a concrete and singular—even universal—meaning is ascribed to a work of art; or when the differences between a historicized analysis and one that projects a new meaning for the future are not overtly acknowledged.

Needless to say, many feminist interpretations—and especially those of Griselda Pollock—are much, much more subtle, complex, and satisfying than the examples I have discussed. I certainly do not want to diminish the debt we owe to the pioneering and courageous work of Nochlin and Pollock, and much recent feminist work has engaged the work of art as a site open to multivalent and even contradictory interpretations. And in the current scholarship that engages gender analysis, the tendency to critique images by women artists that appear to affirm gendered stereotypes has been replaced by an attempt to understand not only the constraints that ruled women's (and men's) life and work, but also how people operated within as well as outside of those constraints. In presenting images of themselves, as well as in presenting themselves, women, like men, were not completely free. As Judith Butler has so powerfully argued, there are real social (and psychic) bounds that work to compel obedience to norms for gender and sexuality, and real (as well as imagined) consequences and punishments for transgression.

Reading for the Present and the Future

Since completing my study of "the exceptional woman," my work proposes both implicitly and explicitly that neither historicizing nor critiquing need be the final goal of gender analysis in the visual arts, especially when that analysis is undertaken from a feminist standpoint.[15] A better option in some cases is to conclude with a strategic reinterpretation that not only destabilizes the image, but also reclaims it for different audiences. Many works that we imagine as intended to support prevailing gender norms or regulatory regimes, present opportunities for moving beyond historicized readings and unmodified critique. Whether or not a work's maker intended to subvert or transgress repressive norms is a question often posed. In the case of Vigée-Lebrun, I do believe that she wanted her work to shake things up, to challenge the status quo, if only for herself. Yet whether or not this was truly her intention is a secondary consideration at best. I advocate a process of reinterpretation as one strategy for claiming the right to interpret, a right that throughout history was largely withheld from women and other subaltern groups. Powerful men have often claimed for themselves the power of truth, and with it the right to name, categorize, and produce knowledge—in short, to say what things mean. They have shored up their claims with the authority of science, religion, and history; fixed them with the truth of castration, and sometimes simply insisted on them through brute force. We willingly sacrifice some of our potential for challenging received truth when we tether our interpretations to what we imagine visual images meant only for those who controlled the making, receiving, circulating, and interpreting of images. I do not deny that such readings are valid, nor do I deny the control that those in power had over image making. My claim is that this control has never been total.

In continuing a practice of subversive or oppositional interpretation, I have taken inspiration from many sources—from feminist theory, from literary critics who theorized resistant readers, and from social scientists whose field research has brought to light the resistance of contemporary women.[16] We art historians adopted many practices belatedly and often in the wake of others. Our belatedness is not surprising, given that our work involved translation. To interpret the visual image differently, we not only had to challenge business as usual in art history, we also had to modify strategies developed to analyze language and written texts, and to alter those intended to interrogate narration. Anyone involved in that process began by thinking through the nature of visual images, comprehending their difference from texts, before moving on to adapting models from other disciplines. Certain aspects of painting—and painting is a medium that has figured prominently in my analyses—permit, even invite, subversive reading. A text is semantically dense: a single word, phrase, sentence, paragraph has many meanings depending on context, rhetorical figuring, etymology, and so forth. But a painting is not only semantically dense, it is also syntactically dense; simply put, painting has no code—nothing to compare to the alphabet. In Western painting, there is no standard sequence of marks that forms a specific signifier, no codified way of making a picture that definitely separates one signifier from another.[17] Moreover, in a painting every formal element is potentially a signifier: color, brushstroke, line, chiaroscuro—all the visual elements that have no direct equivalent in language. So no matter how unstable, no matter how open to interpretation, no matter how overdetermined is the text, the visual image is still a little more so.

FIGURE 7.1. Elisabeth Vigée-Lebrun (1755–1842), *Self-Portrait in Straw Hat,* 1783. Oil on canvas. National Gallery of Art, London. *Photo:* © *National Gallery, London / Art Resource, N.Y.*

I cannot go back in time and change the experience of those who viewed a painting in the eighteenth century. But if the painting endures, then the art historian can change how present and future viewers participate in the painting, a possibility the instability of the visual language enables. Of course, one reinterpretation alone cannot alter the prevailing response called forth by a particular work. The "meaning" of paintings becomes *apparently* fixed through repetition—repetition of canonical interpretations, which are interpretations always in someone's interest. No matter how subversive, one single instance of a reinterpretation will not change how a painting is experienced in the future, but a collective effort focused on redirecting the viewer's experience could have important consequences, and might even create a new history of art.

Among those writers I found especially helpful in this practice of reinterpretation was Shoshona Felman, who imagined a woman asking Freud's provocative question: "What does a woman want?" Felman pointed out that for any woman to ask the question of what a woman wants is to displace the question radically, to ask it from a different position in the sociosexual order. Thus

FIGURE 7.2. Auguste Bernard d'Agesci, French (1756–1829), *Lady Reading the Letters of Heloise and Abelard,* c. 1780. Oil on canvas, 32×25½ in. (81.3×64.8 cm). Mrs. Harold T. Martin Fund; Lacy Armour Endowment; Charles H. and Mary F. S. Worcester Collection, 1994.430. The Art Institute of Chicago. *Photography © The Art Institute of Chicago.*

displaced, "What does a woman want?" becomes a question of a woman's desire to interpret. Felman defines an interpretive practice that attends to those aspects of the text that resist dominant cultural assumptions, and I have tried to extend that attention to the visual image. These points of resistance constitute the pictorial or textual dynamic as what she calls a "field of clashing and heterogeneous forces" characterized by a "never quite predictable element of surprise."[18] Once located, resistance and transgression can be amplified by the desire, by the intervention of a particular interpreter. This intervention opens up the field of interpretation, taken as both a unique encounter with the painted image and a pragmatic act, a particular reworking of collective or individual expectations. I respond most fully to Felman's brilliant use of deconstruction and to her subversive readings of psychoanalysis.

I take "the desire to interpret" (or perhaps I should say the desire to reinterpret), neither as one rooted in the unconscious of the individual interpreter, nor, as Griselda Pollock seems to prefer, as one rooted in his or her particular experiences, biography, and psyche.[19] I wonder to what extent can we know and articulate our own desire, in the psychoanalytic sense of the term. If we take psychoanalysis at its word, our access to our unconscious, and thus to our desire, is limited indeed; the unconscious appears in glimpses or under particular conditions of the analytic situation. As I understand and employ it, the desire to reinterpret is a conscious and political desire, one that can be shared across those whose work embraces a like-minded purpose. That desire may be inflected differently in different individuals, and unconscious motivations, along with particular histories, might indeed activate it.

Are there dangers—overt or hidden—in the practice of reinterpretation that I am advocating? I have argued already that without a thoroughgoing historical and formal analysis of the work—of its structures, iconography, language, and so on—we leave our readings open to easy dismissal by those colleagues who would like to see the end of gender analysis and feminist reading. At the same time, a related danger lurks in the background, one that speaks to how a larger public interprets art. Museums are more and more validating the personal, emotional response to works of art, asking their viewers, for example, how does this painting make you feel? Whether official state institutions or private foundations, museums are surrounded by an aura of truth and professional expertise, and thus their encouragement of everyone's personal interpretation carries a particular imprimatur. In the eighteenth century, theorists argued that painting was a "natural language" open to all comers, and many persons today, both lay and learned alike, still cling to that notion even though it has long been proven untenable. I wonder to what extent subversive reading inadvertently supports that claim, suggesting for example that anyone can say anything about any painting and have it be understood as viable critical or interpretive work. While on the one hand I applaud opening the visual arts to everyone's experience, on the other, I believe that we need to insist on the difference between the automatic responses of the uninformed and those readings that come from positions of expertise in the theory, history, and language of the visual arts. This is not to say that art historians alone have purchase on analyzing the visual arts, for their expertise—their visual literacy, if you will—is certainly one that can and should be learned and shared more broadly.

Even if the sort of interpretative practice I advocate risks putting us on the slippery slope to anything goes, a more pressing and immediate question for the present and future is this: Are there images that we should not attempt to reclaim through interpretation? To make the most extreme case, are there images that are so degrading, so violent, and so powerful in their negative effects on the viewer that they are better critiqued and even condemned? Yes, indeed, there are. And it is arguable that the repeated showing of such image, even in a scholarly essay, is problematic when their impact and imprint on senses and brains overrides the interpreter's reasoned discourse. Many countries in Europe out-law hate speech, and violent degrading images can be viewed as a form of hate speech. Of course the question of what we label as violent and degrading is an open one. Works we consider serious art that challenges proscriptive norms—the photographs of Robert Mapplethorpe, for example—have been deemed unacceptable by a sector of the public. I find it difficult—well-nigh impossible—to describe with any exactitude the limits of what can or should be re-interpreted and reclaimed, and the question of limits continues to haunt my work. What I can say, however, is that there are categories of images that can and should be profitably reinterpreted, images of male and female bodies that can be stolen from the canon and returned as subversive facsimiles—images that look the same as before, but that are embedded with them a new and differ-ent meaning.

My practice has attended to several categories of images that I believe are worth our efforts in reclaiming. Images that idealize even as they cir-cumscribe "woman" are often available for reinterpretation, and this cate-gory might include images—whether made by men or women—that seem to reduce women to their reproductive function even as they vaunt mater-nity; those that depict "woman" as a sensitive, sensuous, and vulnerable creature; those that show her as properly modest and subservient to male authority; those that elide "woman" and "beauty," positioning "woman" as object rather than subject of the gaze; and those that use the female body to arouse heterosexual desire.

One of the works that I found most open to my reinterpretation was Au-guste Bernard d'Agesci's *Lady Reading the Letters of Heloise* (fig. 7.2). When I began to study this image, others had already critiqued it as straddling the last two categories—as a work that presented "woman" as object of the gaze and solicited the erotic desires of a male viewer.[20] While these readings provided one possible way to understand the image, there are and were many other possible viewing positions. Indeed, when the image appeared in the Intimate Encounters exhibition, the painting immediately attracted feminists of all stripes, some wanting to categorize the image as fodder for the male gaze, others moved by its beautiful, sensuous surfaces. For me the painting offered the pleasure of subversive reading, especially once I attended to what had aroused the emotion of the pictured reader—the letters of Heloise. Her im-passioned correspondence provided me with the most significant context for viewing Bernard d'Agesci's reader. Subversive readings, in fact, are often fa-cilitated when the central image can be repositioned within a different con-text, or when attention to some iconographic element sets interpretation in a new direction.

Once Heloise entered the picture, the picture changed. The letters of Heloise were wildly popular in France throughout the eighteenth century, and writings about Heloise posed her not only as a learned and impassioned woman, but also as a passionate writer. Her position in eighteenth-century French letters was like that afforded Sappho, a woman who not only suffered from lovesickness, but who also represented it with clarity and enthusiasm. Bernard d'Agesci's reading woman can be seen to celebrate Heloise as an inspired writer, as one who could bring the spectator to experience vicariously the emotions she depicted. Looking only at the female figure and the sensuous surfaces that adorn it, we indeed see Bernard d'Agesci's reading lady in a state of ecstasy that suggests her sexual passions and pleasures, a state perhaps intended to arouse some viewers. But if we pay attention to the book the painted woman holds, we see that the image pictures her ecstasy as a barometer of a woman's—that is Heloise's—poetic enthusiasm. As art's motor force, as the passion that moved the artist to create, enthusiasm was never far from sexual desire. A new reading of the work focuses on Heloise and her creativity, for by inspiring her reader to experience vicariously the passion she depicts, Heloise creates what contemporaneous French theory understood as art of the highest order.[21]

My work with Bernard d'Agesci's *Lady Reading the Letters of Heloise* suggests how crucial it is to look at the whole picture and to locate those elements that can either redirect the historicized reading of the work and/or found a contemporary one. Another class of images allows us to root our re-readings in the past, even as we make them for the future, since they offer evidence of women who in the past reinterpreted images to their own benefit. Works in this category often use the female body allegorically to represent virtues or strengths that actual women were not imagined to have, or to signify professions or undertakings from which they were generally excluded.

Feminist scholar Mary Garrard was the first to identify a strategic use of allegorical imagery in her analysis of a self-portrait made by the seventeenth-century painter, Artemesia Gentileschi, *Self-Portrait as the Allegory of Painting (La Pittura)* (fig. 7.3). In this work Gentileschi merges her portrait with the allegorical figure of Painting, a point that allowed Garrard to offer a compelling interpretation of the work.[22] Historian Londa Schiebinger has shown how women scientists used a similar strategy; Maria Cunitz (1610–1664), for example, juxtaposed the name of Urania, the muse of astronomy, with her own name on the title page of her *Urania propiti.*[23] Especially telling is Schiebinger's argument that a female allegorical figure for Science brought luster to women's scientific heritage, and that women scientists found an attack on the female emblem to be an attack on scientific women. Later, an anonymous portrait (fig. 7.4) of Gabrielle-Émilie Le Tonnelier de Breteuil, Marquise du Châtelet (1706–1749), a well-known scientist and translator of Newton, depicts her seated at her desk along with her compass, celestial globe, and open notebooks. The work presents Châtelet as Urania, Muse of Astronomy, and other aspects of the painting (for example, the pose that recalls the allegory of Study) point to the intellectual nature of the sitter's enterprise.[24] Literalizing allegory, by which I mean substituting the portrait of an actual woman for an idealized female body, reworks allegory, in so far as visual allegory typically uses the idealized figure of woman to stand for man's endeavors, endeavors that like astronomy were gendered masculine and ordinarily closed to women practitioners. Art historian Kathleen Nicholson has also taken up the question of the allegorical portrait's relation to its women patrons. Noting how anxious critics were to demean what they saw as female pretension, she argues that for the women portrayed in allegorical disguise, portraits provided an occasion to question their given place in the social order, to enact a struggle between societal expectations and their own aspirations.[25] Allegorical portraits, as Nicholson so astutely argues, infuse culture into the lives of the women depicted, giving the sitter a dimension beyond the limiting fact of physical beauty.

Another category of images that seems particularly open to re-reading includes those images that show powerful female figures as monstrous, or in a negative light. Medusa, for example, has already been adopted by writers and theorists who have questioned the sociosexual order: Hélène Cixous and Teresa de Lauretis were among the first to recuperate the Gorgon, and the recent *Medusa Reader* (2003), edited by Marjorie Garber and Nancy J. Vickers, includes many examples of writers who regendered and reframed the questions posed by what Garber and Vickers call "this most problematic and elusive of figures."[26] Because the myth always included conflicting elements woven around the gorgon, the figure of Medusa invites interpretation. The *Medusa Reader* is a provocative starting point for any art historian interested in rethinking visual representations of Medusa, especially since it includes many recent reconceptions of the myth proposed by writers and critics, as well as including a small selection of visual images that offer different pictures of Medusa.

If feminist critics undertook rewriting the Medusa story and other myths, visual artists embraced a similar enterprise. Indeed, mythology has proven to be a fertile ground for work on gender as well as for feminist critique and rewriting. Phyllis McGibbon, for example, asked a pertinent question in the subtitle of her 1992 *Panning for Gold: Did Danaë Really Yearn for the Passion of Zeus?* But the practice of remaking myths is not a new one; artists like McGibbon are not so much inventing a genre as restoring a practice that had centuries

FIGURE 7.3. Artemesia
Gentileschi (1593–1652/3),
*Self-Portrait as the Allegory of
Painting (La Pittura),* 1638–
1639. Oil on canvas,
96.5 × 73.7 cm. *The Royal
Collection © 2010 Her Majesty
Queen Elizabeth II*

FIGURE 7.4. Unknown artist,
*Portrait of Gabrielle-Émilie Le
Tonnelier de Breteuil, Marquise du
Châtelet.* The Château de
Breteuil, Choisel, France.

FIGURE 7.5. Angelica Kauffmann (1741–1807), *The Artist Hesitating Between the Arts of Music and Painting* (self-portrait), 1791 or 1794. Oil on canvas, 58 × 85 in. Nostell Priory, West Yorkshire, Great Britain. The St. Oswald Collection (The National Trust, acquired with the help of the Heritage Lottery Fund in 2002). *Photo: National Trust Photo Library / Art Resource, N.Y.*

earlier occupied their predecessors. I understand these visual reworkings of myth as continuous with art historical practices of reinterpretation and suggest that reworkings, whether intended to be disruptive or not, open themselves to reinterpretation. Take, for example, two works by the eighteenth-century painter Angelica Kauffmann: her 1791 self-portrait, *The Artist Hesitating Between the Arts of Music and Painting* (fig. 7.5) and her earlier *Jupiter in the Guise of Diana and the Nymph Callisto* (fig. 7.6)[27] The first is a self-conscious rewriting; the second offers opportunities for further reinterpretation—whether or not it was intended to do so.

The 1791 self-portrait refigures the choice of Hercules, a myth that had become standard fare for visual artists by the eighteenth century. In canonical versions of the story, such as that of Annibale Carracci, Hercules is poised between Virtue and Pleasure presented as allegorical women.[28] One might say they represent the modest virgin and the voluptuous whore. Hercules, of course, will choose duty and thus Virtue, and with it he will follow the rocky

FIGURE 7.6. After Angelica Kauffmann, *Jupiter in the Guise of Diana and the Nymph Callisto,* c. 1781. Oil on canvas, 24 in. diameter. Museum of Fine Arts, St. Petersburg, Fla. Gift of Herbert Weisinger in memory of his late wife, Mildred, 1986.5. *Photo: Thomas U. Gessler and Thaddeus Root.*

road that leads to the temple of immortality. In Kauffmann's self-portrait the allegorical women signify Music and Painting (for Kauffman excelled in both) and they are presented in such a way as to undercut the traditional moral implications associated with the choice of Hercules. Kauffmann, for example, reverses the color opposition of blonde/brunette that had previously marked the allegories of Pleasure repudiated and Virtue chosen in Carracci's *Choice of Hercules* and others that followed from it. And although the artist ultimately casts her lot with blonde-haired Painting, she refuses to associate brunette Music with voluptuousness, presenting her as a modest, even virtuous, alternative. But more significantly, in casting herself as Hercules, as the male hero who chooses, Angelica Kauffmann places herself in the position of a subject who can choose, who can be the subject of her desires—here, the desires to make music or art, to seek her fame and position as great painter by taking the path to glory.[29]

Kauffmann's version of Jupiter and Callisto is one of the few stagings, if not the only one, of Jupiter's amorous exploits by an eighteenth-century woman painter.[30] In drawing on Callisto's story as told in Ovid's *Metamorphoses,* Kauffmann picks a scene that was a standard one. Artists typically represented Callisto in Jupiter's arms just at the moment before the god kisses her and reveals his true maleness. Because at the moment represented Jupiter is still disguised as Diana, what we actually see is one woman about to make love to another. Images of Jupiter and Callisto have been interpreted as offering to the male spectator the erotic charge of lesbian encounter and/or the possibility that he can (albeit imaginatively) enter the scene and take his pleasure with one or both women. But Kaufmann's image can be read quite differently.

Although Kauffman's image stages a traditional moment in the story, it both breaks with visual tradition and includes an unprecedented element. In eighteenth-century painting it was conventional to heighten the contrast between male and female bodies by showing men as having darker flesh tones than women. In *Jupiter in the Guise of Diana and the Nymph Callisto,* the skin tonalities of the two figures are nearly identical, and thus sexual difference is not strongly encoded. Similarly, the traditional role of active male/ passive female is undercut in this love scene. Although Diana/Jupiter seems to take the lead as she leans toward Callisto, the nymph is far from pinned in a passive feminine position, and she returns Diana/Jupiter's gaze in an expression of her own desire. This underplaying of sexual difference suggests visually that Callisto fully believes she is taking her pleasures with another woman. More disruptive to tradition, however, is that the Menacing Cupid is slipped into Kauffmann's composition.[31] Putting his finger to his lips in a gesture that begs our silence, this Cupid asks us not to reveal some secret. The obvious one is that which must be kept from Callisto, who does not yet know it is Jupiter, and not Diana, who pleases her. In some representations of Jupiter and Callisto the cupids are not of the menacing sort, and they have other work to do. They register the god's passion, push the action forward toward his attack, and prepare us for the moment of revelation that is about to come: the moment when the aroused Jupiter, disguised as Diana, will kiss Callisto.[32] Callisto's pleasure will cease precisely when Diana/Jupiter kisses her as a man, for at that moment the nymph realizes she has been deceived, and, as Ovid tells us, she then resists with all her might.

In Kauffmann's painting we see Callisto the moment before Jupiter kisses her, when she still believes he is Diana. We see that Callisto enjoys this love-making, which deceives her because it is (like) that of another woman. Rather than push the action toward the moment of revelation, Kauffmann's Menacing Cupid holds it back. He seeks to stop an action; he tries to prevent the viewer from warning Callisto. His goal is to keep her ignorant of who it is that pleasures her. Cupid's gesture, in fact, has the practical effect of halting *all* imagined action by asking us to help suspend the scene at the moment before Jupiter kisses Callisto. He thus works to extend both Callisto's deception and her pleasure. But this little trickster has another secret, and in soliciting our complicity he implies we know what it is: Callisto enjoys Jupiter's lovemaking as that of a woman, not as that of a man (or male god) disguised as a woman. In reminding us that Callisto is completely deceived, the Menacing Cupid gives away the truth that Jupiter discovers when he performs as woman and then finds himself rebuffed when revealed as male—that female sexuality does not depend on any man's desire, that women, in fact, do know what they want. This conclusion brings me back to Shoshona Felman's work and leads me to think again about what it means for a woman to ask Freud's infamous question. In reviewing my interpretation of Angelica Kauffmann's *Jupiter in the Guise of Diana and the Nymph Callisto,* I cannot determine to what extent I am channeling the artist's desires in repicturing the standard story, and to what extent I am amplifying the resistance that she, deliberately or not, has incorporated into her work. Although some may find such confusion deplorable and condemn it in "respectable" scholarship, I believe that this confusion is endemic to all acts of interpretation. The point for me is to recognize the potential of such confusion and to put it to good use.

The examples I have chosen certainly do not exhaust the possibilities for reinterpreting images: they merely represent those I have found fruitful in my work on eighteenth-century art. I have thought about the practice of reinterpreting images for a long time, and the practice remains a significant aspect of my current work and teaching. I still believe, as I did when I concluded *Moved by Love* (2004), that interpreting images from perspectives other than those urged by the dominant cultural assumptions of a given time and place accomplishes important work. Opening an image to other possibilities takes advantage of the contradictions that are evident in any discourse. It thereby pushes past the impasse of critique, which, while revealing the assumptions that structure a representation, can inadvertently leave those assumptions in place. In the desire to unmask the oppression, injustice, or prejudice justified through cultural representations, a critique can silence other voices that viewed representations differently, or can unintentionally obviate the possibility of different understandings, and hence of resistance. Strategic reinterpretation does not so much rehabilitate an image or text as reclaim it as an object open to interpretation. The representation becomes less an ideal presented, a moral lesson proffered, or a justification for prevailing views, and more a field of potential meanings waiting to be exploited by a savvy viewer.[33] That feminist art historians working on issues of gender can usurp and resignify some of the painted women in art's history is an added bonus.

Coda

The history of art is filled with images that please not through their subject or ideology, but because their formal properties call to us—because they seduce our eyes. When we analyze a work of art, its formal properties can be separated from neither the subject represented nor the ideology proffered. When we stand before the work, we are often strongly affected by the sensory pleasures or displeasures on offer. If the work promises visual pleasure, a prime goal of art throughout much of its history, we might be moved by the balance of form, the pleasing harmony of color, the bold application of paint, the dramatic lighting, or the nervous line. It might be that the handling suggests the work was painted with passion, emotion, conviction, or love. Some works are so downright beautiful they make me cry. Some are dangerously beautiful, promoting an ideology that makes me weep. Many of the art works made in the past—even most of them—overtly or implicitly idealize regimes of sexual differentiation and desire that have historically disadvantaged all women regardless of their race, ethnicity, or sexual orientation, even if these additional factors have made some women more vulnerable than others. So what is an art historian to do with these beautiful, dangerous images? If a striking image puts a woman on display, do I cede that work to the male gaze because I imagine it was made only to give certain men pleasure? Presented with a gorgeous image of smiling maternity, do I imitate Simone de Beauvoir and condemn it for reducing women to their reproductive function?[34] Do I, in essence, cede all the pleasure of these images—maybe of the entire history of art—to the old boys and limit myself to critique, tacitly acquiescing to the notion that these works, being made for their eyes, belong to them? No, not ever, not me. I have cast my lot with those women who have chosen to read things in their own way, who insist on their right to read and interpret differently. It is through those practices that I can imagine a new history of art—one that historicizes responsibly, critiques responsibly, and reinterprets responsibly in ways that speak to the present and future. It is my hope that the analysis of gender will be the driving force of that new art history.

NOTES

1. It is not easy to define what "art history" is today. It is both a truism and a truth that there are many histories of art—many approaches to the material we study and no consensus on which or what sorts of work are within the purview of the discipline. And at many different points, art history overlaps with related disciplines: anthropology, history, archeology, cultural studies, and so forth.

2. For a more comprehensive, albeit by now somewhat dated, look at gender in art history, see my essay, "How Images Got Their Gender: Masculinity and Femininity in the Visual Arts," in *A Companion to Gender History,* ed. Teresa A. Meade and Merry E. Wiesner-Hanks (London: Blackwell Publishing, 2004), 146–169.

3. Linda Nochlin and Anne Southerland Harris, *Women Artists 1550–1950* (Los Angeles: Los Angeles County Museum, 1976), catalog of art exhibition.

4. Ibid., 66; Sherry B. Ortner, "Is Female to Male as Nature is to Culture?," *Feminist Studies* 1 (Autumn, 1972): 5–31.

5. Joan Wallach Scott, "Gender: A Useful Category of Historical Interpretation," in *Gender and the Politics of History* (New York: Columbia University Press, 1988).

6. Linda Nochlin, *The Politics of Vision: Essays on Nineteenth-Century Art and Society* (New York: Harper and Row, 1989).

7. Griselda Pollock, *Differencing the Canon: Feminist Desire and the Writing of Art's Histories* (London: Routledge, 1999), 29; Griselda Pollock, *Vision and Difference: Femininity, Feminism, and Histories of Art* (London: Routledge, 1988).

8. Lisa Rosenthal, *Gender, Politics and Allegory in the Art of Rubens* (New York: Cambridge University Press, 2006), 10.

9. Sheriff, "How Images Got their Gender," 151–152; 157–158; 161–166.

10. Linda Nochlin, *Women, Art and Power and Other Essays* (New York: Harper and Row, 1988), xii.

11. This point is explicated more fully in Sheriff, "How Images Got Their Gender," 147–151.

12. Rozsika Parker and Griselda Pollock, *Old Mistresses: Women, Art, and Ideology* (London: Routledge and Kegan Paul, 1981), 86, quoted in Mary D. Sheriff, *The Exceptional Woman: Elisabeth Vigée-Lebrun and the Cultural Politics of Art* (Chicago: University of Chicago Press, 1996), 200.

13. Toril Moi, *Sexual/Textual Politics: Feminist Literary Theory* (London: Methuen, 1985), 9.

14. This reading can be found in Sheriff, *Exceptional Woman,* 180–220.

15. I developed this reading practice through a number of my essays, including "Letters: Painted/Penned/Purloined," *Studies in Eighteenth-Century Culture* 26 (1996): 29–56; "Reading Jupiter Otherwise, or Ovid's Women in Eighteenth-Century Art," in

Myth, Sexuality and Power: Images of Jupiter in Western Art, ed. Frances Van Keuren, *Archeologia Transatlantica* series (Providence, R.I.: Center for Old World Archeology and Art, Brown University, 1998): 79–98; "A rebours: Le problème de l'histoire dans l'interprétation féministe" [Against the grain: The problem of historicism in feminist interpretation], in *Où en est l'interprétation de l'oeuvre d'art* [What is the current state of interpreting works of art], ed. Régis Michel (Paris: Ecole des Beaux-Arts and Réunion des Musée Nationaux), 2000.

16. Mentioning all the influential work in this area would transform this note into a long bibliographic essay. In addition to those works mentioned in the text, particularly important for me was work by colleagues with whom I had ongoing interchange at the University of North Carolina: E. Jane Burns, *Body Talk: When Women Speak in Old French Literature,* (Philadelphia: University of Pennsylvania Press, 1993) and Jacqueline Bobo, *Black Women as Cultural Readers* (New York: Columbia University Press, 1995). In developing my perspective through essays, I found Nancy Miller's work inspirational, and in particular, "Arachnologies: The Woman, The Text, The Critic," in *The Poetics of Gender,* ed. Nancy K. Miller (New York: Columbia University Press, 1986), 270–296, as well as that of Joan de Jean, whose essay, "Looking Like a Woman: The Female Gaze in Sappho and Lafayette," *L'Esprit Créateur* 28 (Winter 1988), was especially important for my work on Elisabeth Vigée-Lebrun.

17. My discussion here depends on the work of Nelson Goodman, *Languages of Art* (Indianapolis, Ind.: Hackett Publishing, 1976), 127–154.

18. Shoshona Felman, *What Does a Woman Want? Reading and Sexual Difference* (Baltimore, Md.: Johns Hopkins University Press, 1993), 6.

19. In *Old Mistresses,* Pollock viewed the dominant culture as more or less completely dominant in producing, consuming, and co-opting images of women's bodies, and in determining what those images meant. In *Differencing the Canon,* her deepening embrace of psychoanalysis led her to a new position in which she viewed paintings as spaces in which meanings vied with one another and in which none was excluded. The play of meanings depended on the perspective of the viewer, who might be reading in either a dominant or a subcultural formation. In this later work she argues that what motivates reading and interpretation is desire, and that we are responsible for recognizing that which is our own. In Pollock's text, this desire is tied directly to the personal psychic history of the individual viewer, and in *Differencing the Canon,* often to her own psychic history.

20. For readings that privilege the "male gaze," see, for example, Virginia Swain, "Hidden from View: French Women Authors and the Language of Rights, 1727–1792," in *Intimate Encounters: Love and Domesticity in Eighteenth-Century France,* ed. Richard Rand (Hanover, N.H.: Hood Museum of Art, Dartmouth / Princeton, N.J.: Princeton University Press, 1997), 27. Published in conjunction with the exhibition Intimate Encounters: Love and Domesticity in Eighteenth-Century France shown at the Hood Museum of Art, Dartmouth College, Hanover, New Hampshire; the Toledo Museum of Art, Toledo, Ohio; and The Museum of Fine Arts, Houston, Texas.

21. For a full explication of this work, see Mary D. Sheriff, *Moved by Love: Inspired Artists and Deviant Women in Eighteenth-Century France* (Chicago: University of Chicago Press, 2004), 201–245.

22. Mary Garrard, "Artemesia Gentileschi's *Self Portrait as the Allegory of Painting*," *Art Bulletin* 62 (March 1980): 97–112.

23. Londa Schiebinger, *The Mind Has No Sex?* (Cambridge, Mass.: Harvard University Press, 1989), 136.

24. Mary D. Sheriff, "The Naked Truth: The Allegorical Frontispiece and Woman's Ambition in Eighteenth-Century France," in *Early Modern Visual Allegory: Embodying Meaning,* ed. Lisa Rosenthal and Crystell Baskin (London: Ashgate Press, 2007), 243–264.

25. Kathleen Nicholson, "The Ideology of Feminine 'Virtue': The Vestal Virgin in French Eighteenth-Century Allegorical Portraiture," in *Portraiture: Facing the Subject,* ed. Joanna Woodall (Manchester: Manchester University Press, 1997), 56.

26. Marjorie Garber and Nancy J. Vickers, "Introduction," in *The Medusa Reader* (London: Routledge, 2003), 1–7.

27. For a discussion of the latter work and the question of attribution, see Georgia Museum of Art, *Jupiter's Loves and His Children,* ed. Frances Van Keuren, Karl Kilinski, and Michael A. Jacobsen (Athens: Georgia Museum of Art, University of Georgia, 1997), 105–106. Published in conjunction with the exhibition at the Georgia Museum of Art, Feb. 1–Mar. 23, 1997. The subject was engraved in 1782. See David Alexander, "Kauffman and the Print Market in Eighteenth-Century England," in *Angelica Kauffman: A Continental Artist in Georgian England,* ed. Wendy Wassyng Roworth (London: Reaktion Books, 1992), 183. My extended analysis of these works is included in "Reading Jupiter Otherwise."

28. Annibale Carracci, *The Choice of Hercules,* c. 1596. Oil on canvas, 65×93 in. Gallerie Nazionale di Capodimonte, Naples, Italy.

29. The story of the hero's choice had already been used as a model for an artist's portrait. Sir Joshua Reynolds painted the actor David Garrick between comedy and tragedy, two allegorical women who, given the difference in presentation, can still be construed as vice and virtue (*David Garrick Between Tragedy and Comedy,* 1762; oil on canvas, 148×183 cm, private collection). In Reynolds's painting the conceit is that Garrick plays comedy and tragedy equally well, and so does not have to make a choice. For a discussion and illustration of this work, see Martin Postle, *Sir Joshua Reynolds: The Subject Pictures* (Cambridge, UK: Cambridge University Press, 1995), 20–32, color-plate 3. Angelica Kauffman's self portrait is discussed in Roworth, *Angelica Kauffman: A Continental Artist,* 55.

30. For an extended discussion of Kauffman's position as a woman artist, see Wendy Wassyng Roworth, "Kaufmann and the Art of Painting in England," in *Angelica Kauffman: A Continental Artist,* 11–95.

31. The Menacing Cupid was a well-represented figure in eighteenth-century art, and is discussed at length in Gisela Zick, "Amor-Harprokrates; zur Wirkungsgeschichte und ikonographischen Herleitung einer Skulptur von Etienne-Maurice Falconet," *Wallraf-Richartz Jahrbuch* 37 (1975): 215–246. The French sculptor Falconet made a garden statue of Cupid, pulling an arrow from his quiver and holding a finger to his lips, in a gesture that asks the spectator not to warn some hapless victim that he or she is about to be hit by Cupid's arrow. Both the sculpture and the figure of the Menacing

Cupid were also represented in many paintings, for example, in Jean-Honoré Fragonard's *The Swing* of 1767. For a discussion of this figure see Mary D. Sheriff, *Fragonard: Art and Eroticism* (Chicago: University of Chicago Press, 1990), 88–89.

32. For a discussion of Boucher's use of the theme, see Alistair Laing, *François Boucher* (New York: Metropolitan Museum of Art, 1986), 283–284 and Melissa Hyde, *The Agreeable Game of Art: François Boucher and the Worldly Play of Gender,* Ph.D. dissertation, University of California, Berkeley, 1966; 154–203.

33. Sheriff, *Moved by Love,* 12–13.

34. Here I am alluding to Simone de Beauvoir's assessment of Elisabeth Vigée-Lebrun's self-portraits in *The Second Sex,* trans. and ed. H. M. Parshley (New York: Vintage Books, 1989), 707.

CHAPTER EIGHT

Unlikely Couplings

The Gendering of Print Technology in the French Fin-de-Siècle

JANIS BERGMAN-CARTON

I begin this essay with a trope of late–nineteenth-century French print culture—the erotic pictographic coupling of a solo female dancer with the star wheel of a lithographic press. Typically this mechano-sexual hieroglyph is used to distinguish "art prints" pulled by hand from those mechanically produced. But occasionally the pair is enlisted to perform a more elusive, improvisatory dance. I mean "dance" both literally, in terms of pictorial references to actual dances and dancers, and metaphorically, in Mallarmé's terms, where the solo female dancer signifies artistic innovation. It is the latter that interests me here.

The pictograph, born of shifting technologies and systems of valuation in late–nineteenth-century French print culture, appears mostly in watermarks, bookplates, and posters for print collectors and the luxury book trade. Through a close reading of three works, this essay recuperates the pictograph's visual syntax, its distinct signs and variable patterns of interrelation. An address card by Richard Ranft for Auguste Delâtre's *Imprimerie artistique* (fig. 8.1) and a print *cartonnier* carved by François-Rupert Carabin (fig. 8.2) use related versions of the schema's erotic coupling of dancer and printing press to signify the possibility of an "advanced" graphic art. The mechanical and reproducible are recast as a link between transgressive sexuality and a libidinal impulse for repetition grounded in the late–nineteenth-century discourse of hysteria. The third case study, Toulouse-Lautrec's 1893 lithograph *L'estampe originale* (fig. 8.3), utilizes the same primary elements but a very different pictographic logic. The dancer stands remote from the working of the press; she is identifiable—the well-known cancan dancer Jane Avril—rather

Figure 8.1. Richard Ranft (1862–1931), address card for *Imprimerie artistique*.

than generic; and, absent any sexual encounter of figure and machine, there appears to be no radical disjunction or transgression. But I will argue Toulouse-Lautrec's pictographic improvisation does in fact unsettle sexual and social norms by casting Jane Avril as the artist's surrogate in a variant that posits the ideal of a new, self-generative model of artmaking.

Juxtapositions of women and printing presses as related signs of reproduction date back to the origins of the technology. Female personifications of print processes appear continuously in early modern illustrated histories of the technology and in advertisements for nineteenth- and twentieth-century print ateliers. Women were associated with the technology of printing, in part, because it was one of the few trades with a genuinely mixed-sex culture. From the technology's beginnings women worked alongside men and, as Joan Wallach Scott writes, in the nineteenth century the numbers grew exponentially.[1] There is no evidence, however, that women ever were employed by art

FIGURE 8.2. François-Rupert Carabin (1862–1932), carved bookcase, 1890. Wood, wrought iron, glass, 290 × 215 × 83 cm. Musée d'Orsay, Paris, France. *Photo: Réunion des Musées Nationaux / Art Resource, N.Y.*

FIGURE 8.3. Henri de Toulouse-Lautrec (1864–1901), wraparound cover for the portfolio *L'estampe originale* (The original print), 1893. Lithograph, sheet: 22⅞ × 32¾. Publisher: Editions du Journal des Artistes (Andre Marty). Printer: Edward Ancourt, Paris. Edition: 100. Grace M. Mayer Bequest, 1997. The Museum of Modern Art, New York, N.Y. *Photo: Digital Image © The Museum of Modern Art / Licensed by SCALA / Art Resource, N.Y.*

presses, the specific context for the hieroglyph. In fact, the opposite seems to be true. Though important work remains to be done on the relation of this image to the material conditions of actual women in France's print trade, my focus here is the realm of the symbolic.[2]

The earliest couplings of women and printing presses are found in July Monarchy caricatures directed at censorship debates such as J. J. Grandville's *Descente dans les ateliers de la liberté de la presse* (fig. 8.4). Credit for the "birth" of a free press is represented in the lithograph as a power struggle between Marianne, the materfamilias, and Louis Philippe, the usurping paternal authority. Marianne is cast as the press's maternal protector, and the September

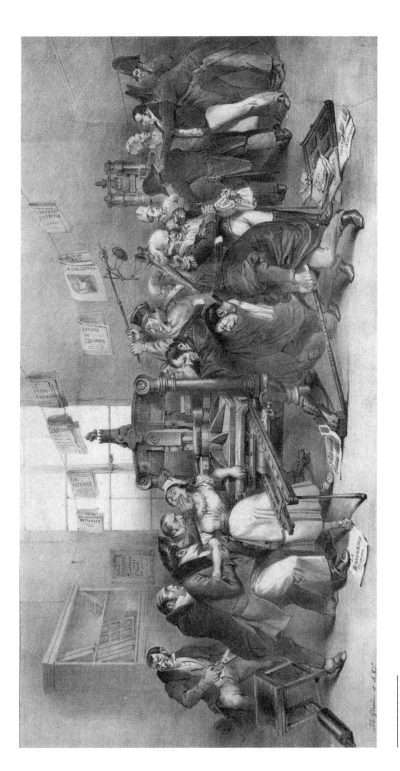

FIGURE 8.4. J. J. Grandville (1803–1847), *Descente dans les ateliers de la liberté de la presse*, 1835. Lithograph, 28.6 × 46.6 cm (sheet). Library of Congress.

Laws (countermanding the press freedoms that ensured Louis-Philippe's ascent to the throne five years earlier) as her silencing by the King and his henchmen, and implicitly her rape.[3]

Late–nineteenth-century versions of the mechano-sexual pictograph operate through a different visual economy, but are linked similarly to censorship, albeit indirectly. Their appearance was triggered by press reform laws in 1881 that relaxed restrictions on printed material and fueled the "Golden Age" of the French illustrated press, the entrepreneurial arena that launched the careers of many visual artists. Richard Ranft, a beneficiary of that vibrant fin-de-siècle print culture, generated one of the pictograph's earliest incarnations for an address card advertising the services of Auguste Delâtre's *Imprimerie artistique* (fig. 8.1). Like Grandville, Ranft riffs on analogies between female biology and graphic reproduction, but the similarity ends there. The Ranft image is not menacing and lacks an obvious "father." Marianne has been replaced by the figure of a dancer, and her sexual encounter, here consensual, is with a machine, not a man.

The dancer's posture and intimate handling of the star wheel tell us this is an imaginary print atelier. As previously mentioned, women generally were not employed by art presses. Moreover, illustrations in histories of the industry of men who did work lithographic presses show them hunched forward, not arched back, to harness the strength needed to turn the wheel. Unlike those illustrations of physical labor in service of art's reproduction, Ranft conjures for the card an image of the art print's miraculous "birth." A visual pun on the phrase "hand-pulled print," the image shows a dancer working the wheel in an act of orgasmic self-pleasuring.

The pictographic trope of Immaculate Conception was part of an evolving strategy of differentiation within the landscape of late–nineteenth-century French print culture in which Delâtre figured prominently. It illuminates infrastructural and technological changes in that period that cast longstanding tensions between creative and reproductive prints into sharp relief.[4] The printer's first shop, opened in 1848, specialized in skillful graphic translations of paintings.[5] Within a decade demand for such work began to decline due to the introduction of photomechanical technologies able to reproduce art cheaper and faster.

In 1862, Delâtre reoriented himself professionally by joining with printer/publisher Alfred Cadart to found *la Société des aquafortistes* in an attempt to revitalize the art of "original" etching. With the exception of graphic work by Goya and Piranesi, etching had seen a decline in Europe since the death of Rembrandt. Its revival in the second half of the nineteenth century was part of a renaissance in French print culture that engendered the need for codified systems of differentiation. The limited edition and practices of cancellation, numbering, and signing original work evolved in the same decade as *la Société des aquafortistes.*[6] It was in the context of systematizing the distinction between graphic "art" and the commercial print that the pictograph emerged.

Ranft was part of a new generation of *peintres-graveurs* mentored in Delâtre's *imprimerie,* a vibrant community that seeded multi-artist collaborations and diverse forms of art production.[7] The address card and its intertextual ties to Paris's bibliophile and entertainment cultures speaks to that diversity, as does the card's foretelling of works like Maurice Denis's *La dépêche de Toulouse* (fig. 8.5) that deploy typological female figures to personify newspapers and print enterprises.[8]

French bibliophile culture, whose most vibrant era dates to this period, provided one of the pictograph's most fertile contexts. For growing numbers of *peintres-graveurs* the illustrated luxury book trade offered creative opportunities and an established audience base. Metaphors like Ranft's of incongruous couplings and miraculous births appear frequently in expensively bound books of the period. One example, the lithographic frontispiece of Octave Uzanne's 1897 *La nouvelle bibliopolis,* pictures the book's supernatural origins as a female nude emerging from a fantastical plant that, in turn, issues from the volume's open pages.[9]

The pairing of dancer and art press is also informed by affinities between Paris's burgeoning entertainment culture and print journalism. French fin-de-siècle illustrated newspapers functioned for Montmartre's dance halls and theatres as the primary site of their advertisement and consecration. The pose and off-the-shoulder dress Ranft used was a familiar feature of the popular press in images of dancers performing the chahut. What is different, of course, is that on Ranft's card she is partnered with a machine. Balanced on one foot, the dancer grasps the arm of the wheel to support her raised right leg as her upper body tilts backward. The anticipation of her leg's extension into the chahut's familiar high kick triggers a visual pun instantiating the interpenetrating forms of dancer and machine into a single, hybrid unit. Like a metal prosthesis, the arm of the star wheel becomes the visual proxy for her lower leg and completes the kick's phallic rise.[10]

Though the pairing of dancer and machine at first seems unlikely, in late–nineteenth-century French literary and visual culture, they are linked regularly. And as Marinetti's "techno-fantasy Futurist choreographies and the machine dances of avant-garde cinema" suggest, in the early twentieth century the pairing was even more common. Analogies between dancers and machines, as Felicia McCarren writes, respond to a shared capacity to balance competing demands of almost superhuman physical strength with agility, speed, and the appearance of effortless movement.[11] In the case of Ranft's pictograph, however, it is less analogy than deflection. Ranft couples the star wheel and dancer, a figure of uncontrollable sexuality, to temper the negative valence of mechanical repetition, the source of printing's value and devaluation. In a clever sleight of hand, the repetition inferred by the star wheel's rotary movement turns to the hypnotic sight of a cancan dancer's libidinal impulse to repeat the same action again and again.

The image of compulsive repetition, the altered state of modern dancing, and the woman's arched back most certainly elicited associations with a related performance arena of the 1880s. On Tuesdays in the amphitheatre of the Salpêtrière Hospital, neurologist Jean-Martin Charcot hypnotized patients for live demonstrations during which they performed the poses of their neurological disorder. Though unsuited to pulling prints, the arched back pose struck by Ranft's dancer is one of the corporeal signs of disorder *tout Paris* turned out to see. Charcot's *leçons du mardi* attracted some of France's best-known writers and artists, some of whom, like Ranft, appropriated the trope of hysteria to signify innovative art.[12]

What is only suggested in Ranft's arched-back dancer—the interconnectedness of dance and hysteria in the modern imaginary as performative expressions of insatiable sexual desire—is explicit in a remarkably odd work of art by François-Rupert Carabin. The elaborately carved bookcase and *cartonnier* (fig. 8.2) that in 1890 launched Carabin's career brackets the shared discourse of fin-de-siècle performance, medical literature, print culture, and bibliophile society that was the pictograph's context.[13]

Carabin became interested in dance in the 1880s. During his apprenticeship, first with an engraver and then an ornamental sculptor, he was a regular at the Chat Noir and Moulin Rouge. The cabarets stimulated a fascination with all kinds of dance and inspired several series of small figurines based on actual dancers. For the 1890 commission by a wealthy engineer and bibliophile named Montandon that made his reputation, the dancer appears within the pictograph adorning the door of a *cartonnier* in the bookcase's lower right quadrant. The pictograph is part of an elaborate decorative program of low and high relief sculptural carving that disorders the bookcase's geometric regularity. Though less fully than Rodin's *Gates of Hell,* the bookcase's organic carvings overwhelm the architectonics, most pronouncedly on top, where three female nudes (personifications of Truth, Intelligence, and Reflection) sit, variously engaged with books and writing tools. Their height makes literal the superiority of the noble qualities books inspire.[14] In contrast to the legible trio, an irregular growth, a piling of carved masques, attaches itself to the lower left corner. These figures of "baseness," relegated to the actual base, are "enemies of knowledge vanquished and rendered powerless by the Book."[15] Max Nordau described the piece as "suited only to the diseased and damned," part of his narrative of modern art's decline.

The *cartonnier's* drop-leaf door, the portal to a protected repository of art prints, is carved in low relief. Befitting its function as print cabinet, the carving reads as graphic more than plastic. Following a *vernissage* Carabin arranged in his studio, the artist's close friend art critic Gustave Geffroy described the piece as a series of oppositional tensions: "the cerebral" and "the incomprehensible," "nobility" and "bestiality," "solidity" and "nervous inversion."[16] Those tensions inform Carabin's alteration of the pictograph's relational schema.

A third figure added to the scene of erotic encounter has the effect of de-centering the composition and rendering it more open-ended. Juxtaposed with the dancer and press is a "calm figure leafing through a portfolio of prints" whom Geffroy calls *l'Estampe*. Her absorbed stillness, seated position, and neatly arranged chignon contrast with the teetering instability of *l'Impression,* the dancer "with wild gestures and windswept hair who turns the flywheel with all the force of her arms and legs."[17] Though there is no clothing that marks *l'Impression* as a dancer, Carabin deploys the same visual pun as Ranft for a figure performing the chahut, a "mechanically assisted kick." Moreover, the trope of hysteria common to visual and literary representations of the dancer in this period, registers loudly in Carabin's carving. The "nervous inversion" to which Geffroy refers goes well beyond the figure's arched back. It is announced in the dancer's now unpinned hair and in the preternatural energy that animates her body.

The contrasting demeanor of the seated and dancing figures makes emphatic the reciprocal ties between arrested movement and implied motion that inform analogies between dancers and machines in this period. It also brackets the so-called "crisis of attentiveness," one of Europe's most cosmopolitan fin-de-siècle preoccupations. As Jonathan Crary writes, in an era of industrialized literary and artistic production, boundaries between entertainment and "authentic" culture were thought to be rapidly eroding. Europeans were said to be suffering from an overload of the senses undermining the capacity to look attentively.[18] The dialectic between prolonged, absorbed looking and dynamic motion that reads as "modern" is inscribed in the conceptual inseparability of the pictograph's two anecdotes. In pose and demeanor the dancer and seated figure could not be more different, but compositionally they are inextricably bound. A circle echoing the wheel's rotary motion inscribes the negative space separating the arcing upper body of the two figures. Like attentive midwife and laboring mother, *L'Estampe* and *L'Impression* form parentheses around the pregnant space between them, the implied space of artistic procreation and its anticipation.

One of the most generative pictographic improvisations with the trope of art's miraculous birth, and perhaps the most elusive, was produced by Carabin's friend and fellow dance enthusiast, Henri de Toulouse-Lautrec. Like Carabin's *cartonnier,* the 1893 lithograph *L'estampe originale* (fig. 8.3) by Lautrec features a figure turning a star wheel, an attentive print connoisseur, and, though not immediately apparent, a dancer. Different, however, is Lautrec's naturalistic setting. It is the shop of Edmond Ancourt, an actual printer, and the inhabitants also are "real." The elderly man, Père Cotelle, a printer for Ancourt, is seen diligently engaged in his work. And though the ample cloak worn by the second figure camouflages all indicators of profession or sex, the absorbed connoisseur is one of the Moulin Rouge's most famous dancers, Jane Avril. Ancourt's firm handled most of Lautrec's printing, so its prominence on the cover of the inaugural issue of *L'estampe originale,* one of the most important print enterprises of the late nineteenth century, is logical. Less clear is why Lautrec selected Avril as the "face" of the enterprise and removed all signs of her primary identity as a dancer.

Published quarterly between 1893 and 1895, *L'estampe originale* consisted of a series of selections of original prints by promising *peintres-graveurs.* The publisher, André Marty, was active in the changing landscape of French visual culture; he was an advocate for vehicles to make art accessible to a broader demographic and new venues to support and nurture young talent. In 1893 Marty secured the rights to the title *L'estampe originale* from an earlier publication that had had promise but little financial success. While the purpose of the first, issued between 1888 and 1891, had been to reverse the devitalizing effects of photomechanical processes on French print culture, Marty brought a different set of priorities. He was interested in more experimental print processes and set prices lower to attract a more diverse clientele. Most provocatively, he emphasized color, which in traditional print circles remained associated with vulgar mercantilism.[19]

Marty's choice of Lautrec for the inaugural cover was strategically clever. Within late–nineteenth-century French print culture, Lautrec had become the color artist par excellence. Moreover, a "crossover" project needed a "crossover" artist. Lautrec was independently wealthy and of aristocratic origin, but best known for his posters of seedy performance venues in Montmartre. His celebrity posters allowed Lautrec to cultivate the persona "artist of the street," but, in fact, many were printed as limited editions intended for the walls of private homes.[20] The immediate chromatic power of Lautrec's cover for *L'estampe originale*'s inaugural issue announced the project's distance from its more traditional namesake, as did the prominence of Jane Avril as its implied ideal audience.

Toulouse-Lautrec met Avril in 1890 while she was performing at the Moulin Rouge, and they remained close personal friends until the artist's death in 1901. The subject of over thirty of his paintings, prints, and drawings, Avril was actually born Jeanne Louise Beaudon. At age fourteen, to ameliorate the effects of her mother's verbal and physical abuse, she apparently was removed from her home by family friends and placed in the care of Jean-Martin Charcot at Salpêtrière. For sixteen months, between 1882 and 1884, Avril lived in the ward of *les Grandes Hystériques*. Her memoir, written five decades later, provides perhaps the only account of life at Salpêtrière from the perspective of a patient. "I lived for two years in this 'Eden,'" she writes, "which it was for me, so much in this world being relative. . . . There were those deranged girls whose ailment named Hysteria consisted above all in simulation of it. . . . For me it was a comic show to see these crazies come away so proud and delighted to have been chosen and pointed to by the 'master.'"[21] According to her origin tale, Avril first came to dancing at Salpêtrière. During a masked ball the hospital sponsored, she claims she had a revelation of her calling while dancing all alone. Not surprisingly, most literary descriptions of Avril allude to this history and leverage hysteria's late–nineteenth-century cachet, as the dancer did herself. In her particular case, however, as Lautrec's disguised portraits suggest, the trope is invoked in relation to Avril to signify the possibility of a new, self-generative art—not art's miraculous birth through a female vessel of transgressive sexuality tightly choreographed behind the scenes by a Ranft or Carabin.

Today Avril is rarely mentioned outside the literature on Toulouse-Lautrec, but she was quite well known in fin-de-siècle dance and literary circles. According to contemporaries, she was more self-directed artist than dance hall performer, a rare female celebrity who retained control of her work and her body. The example of that independence cited most often is her refusal of a lucrative contract with the Moulin Rouge. Despite her small income, apparently she asked to be paid nightly instead to maintain control over hours, costumes, and dances. That decision also freed her from the obligation to dance in the quadrilles and enabled her, most of the time, to dance alone.

She met Lautrec when both were starting out, and their association, socially and artistically, was mutually beneficial. The critical success of posters like the one commissioned in 1893 by the Jardin de Paris at Avril's request helped launch her career as a celebrity who, like Lautrec, "went both ways"— though, in her case, without benefit of an inheritance. Avril was both a staple of Montmartre dance hall culture and a rare valued female member of the elite circle of artists and writers to which Lautrec also belonged. Reminiscences from the period consistently speak of her intelligence and artistic integrity—qualities they emphasize set her apart in the arena of dance.[22]

Arthur Symons, Maurice Barrés, Stéphane Mallarmé, and Téodor de Wyzewa were among the writers and playwrights she met while dancing at the Bal Bullier and Jardin de Paris—public dancing gardens to which she gravitated after leaving Salpêtrière. Symons writes about Avril's striking remoteness on the dance floor, her private withdrawal in this public arena and unusual disengagement with the audience. She was, he writes, unlike any other performer he had seen. Withdrawn and self-absorbed, she was not like the dancers always on display. Avril's dances were improvisatory and her affect disarming, as these passages from Symons's 1892 poem about the dancer conveys:

La Mélinite: Moulin Rouge

Alone, apart, one dancer watches
Her mirrored, morbid grace;
Before the mirror, face to face,
Alone she watches
Her morbid, vague, ambiguous grace.

And, enigmatically smiling,
In the mysterious night,
She dances for her own delight,
A shadow smiling
Back to a shadow in the night.[23]

The poem's title references one of Avril's two nicknames—*l'Étrange* (the strange one) and *la Mélinite* (dynamite). Most dancers of the period cultivated sobriquets in consultation with proprietors of dance venues and poster artists as a strategy of branding. The doubleness of Avril's, *l'Étrange* and *la Mélinite,* recalls the dialectic of prolonged absorption and frenzied movement in Carabin's pictograph for the *cartonnier.* But the quality Carabin conveyed in two distinct figural anecdotes—duality of body and mind—Avril was perceived to both embody and perform. A remarkable painting of the dancer by Lautrec (fig. 8.6) from 1891 makes literal that duality.[24] In the composition's top half, containing Avril's head and upper body, she appears in a state of reverie, unaware of her surroundings and the movement of her own legs below. Her interiority and indifference to audience is punctuated by the drawing's radical cropping and its narrow vertical format. Only two audience members are

FIGURE 8.5. Maurice
Denis (1870–1943), *La
dépêche de Toulouse*, 1892.
Color lithograph
(141.3 × 95.1 cm). Jane
Voorhees Zimmerli Art
Museum, Rutgers, The
State University of New
Jersey. Alvin and Joyce
Glasgold Purchase Fund.
1986.0089. *Photo by Jack
Abraham.*

visible, tiny figures in the upper right, who look like marionettes. And they
are depicted pointedly looking at each other, not at Avril. The top half of
dancer's bifurcated body is *l'Étrange,* the introvert of Symons's poem, and *la
Mélinite* registers in the near illegibility of her leg's gyrations below in her performance of a cancan. Her leg's wobbly rotary movements look like the tor-
tured convulsions of a wounded animal—or the star wheel of an art press
come loose.

Avril's self-reflexive capacity to function simultaneously as art and artist
made her a natural for the artistic surrogates Toulouse-Lautrec regularly channeled in his work.[25] As an 1892 photograph he had made of himself wearing
Avril's boa and hat suggests, for Lautrec the identification with Avril was fertile. The dancer's portrait, disguised and not, shows up regularly in his work.
Like Stéphane Mallarmé with Loïe Fuller, the period's other better-known

FIGURE 8.6. Henri de
Toulouse-Lautrec (1864–
1901), *Jane Avril Dansant,* 1891.
Oil on board, 85.5 × 45 cm.
Musée d'Orsay, Paris, France.
*Photo: Réunion des Musées
Nationaux / Art Resource, N.Y.*

solo dancer, Lautrec was less interested in Avril as a dancer per se, than in her
creative example in the arena of dance.

In the majority of Lautrec's more than thirty depictions, Avril is removed
from the context of dancing, as if to distinguish the sensate visuality of her
performative body from its visual spectacle on stage. In the stunning golds
and blacks of Lautrec's poster for the cabaret *Le Divan Japonais,* for example,
the elegant arabesque of Avril's body is the clear compositional focus. But our
eye is directed formally toward Avril not because she is performing (the performer, in fact, is a secondary figure pointedly cropped so she appears with-

Figure 8.7. Henri de Toulouse-Lautrec (1864–1901), *La danse mauresque ou les almées* (The Moorish dance), 1895. Musée d'Orsay, Paris, France. *Photo: Erich Lessing / Art Resource, N.Y.*

out a head), but because she is the only attentive spectator, the spectator "who actually sees."

Toulouse-Lautrec's 1895 *La danse mauresque* (fig. 8.7) also prioritizes Avril's capacity to see beyond the merely visible. Squeezed between portraits of Oscar Wilde and the artist himself, she figures at the center of Lautrec's intellectual circle. By representing the group from behind, Lautrec distinguishes them from those seated in the audience, who see only with their eyes. Avril is identifiable, as she is in *L'estampe originale,* by her signature feather hat and red hair. And as a small group of initiates would have realized, the narrow taper and puffed shoulders of Avril's jacket is a visual pun for Lautrec's favorite animal self-caricature—the elephant.

It is as artistic surrogate that Lautrec casts Avril as the "face" of *L'estampe originale*. Like the personality Marty crafted for the project, and the persona Lautrec crafted for himself, she was at once "of the street" and a valued member of an artistic elite. But Avril's prominence in the 1893 enterprise that bestowed on Lautrec, the poster artist, a new kind of artistic legitimacy as *peintre-graveur* was more than that. For *L'estampe originale,* his own improvisation, Lautrec extracts from Avril's corporeal stage identity—one he helped create—the quality of unbounded generativity innovated by Avril the artist. In place of the literally missing "cocked, black-stockinged leg"—what Griselda Pollock calls "the graphic sign for Toulouse-Lautrecness"—is a sexless red cloak that flaunts the print's embrace of color.[26] Its brash red shape reads like a miasmic emanation from the freshly pulled print, the newly born, that absorbs Avril.

There is much less caricatural distortion and decorative flourish in *L'estampe originale* than is typical for Lautrec. But that is part of the print's pictographic "charge." Behind its veneer of normalcy that reads as an ordinary day at the *imprimerie* is a variation on the motif of art's miraculous birth. We detect its possibilities in a pulsating energy barely containable by the contours of Avril's sexless red cloak, and the androgyny implied. Avril prods us, as she does in Lautrec's *Le Divan Japonais* and *La danse mauresque,* to look beyond what we think we see, to the mystery of self-generative art Avril the artist conceived, barely veiled by the cloak's fabric.[27]

NOTES

1. See Joan Wallach Scott, "Feminist versus Trade Unionists in the Printing Trades: Guerre des sexes ou lutte de classe?" in *Women in the Printing Trades,* ed. J. Ramsay MacDonald (New York: Garland Publishing, 1980), and Jacques Alary, *Le travail de la femme dans l'imprimerie typographique, ses consequences physiques et morales* (Paris: C. Marpin et E. Flammarion, 1883).

2. Prominent among those who have treated this subject are Elizabeth Eisenstein, *The Printing Press As an Agent of Change: Communications and Cultural Transformations in Early-Modern Europe* (Cambridge, UK: Cambridge University Press, 1983); Susan Broomhall, *Women and the Book Trade in Sixteenth-Century France* (London: Ashgate, 2002); and Marie-Hélène Zylberberg-Hocquard, *Femmes et feminism dans le mouvement ouvrier français* (Paris: Les éditions ouvrières, 1981). The inspiration for this essay actually began with Man Ray's *Érotique voilée,* the striking 1934 photograph of artist Meret Oppenheim pressing her naked body into the flywheel of a hand press. The wheel rim and spokes, like a giant eye through which we can and cannot see, both masks and rivets our attention to her naked body. Oppenheim's left hand, smeared with printer's ink and raised theatrically to her brow, reads multiply as a swooning gesture, a feather hat (like Jane Avril's), the handprint of the artist, and a cock's comb—a signifier of the phallus made

literal by the wheel crank that appears to protrude from Oppenheim's pubis. *Érotique voilée* is one of a group of photographs by Man Ray and Brassai published to accompany André Breton's 1934 exposition on a visual surrealist practice in *Minotaure,* "Beauty Will Be Convulsive." The nineteenth-century pictograph of dancer and printing press presages this image of "convulsive beauty," the paradigmatic aesthetic of Surrealism that works through the defamiliarization and the coupling of incongruous forms.

3. Enacted on September 9, 1835, following an attempt on Louis-Philippe's life, the September Laws effectively eliminated freedom of the press.

4. Those tensions are elaborated in Phillip Dennis Cate, *Prints Abound: Paris in the 1890s* (Washington, D.C.: National Gallery of Art, 2001); Patricia Eckert Boyer and Phillip Dennis Cate, *L'estampe originale: Artistic Printmaking in France 1893–1895* (Amsterdam: Waanders, 1991); and Trevor Fawcett, "Graphic Versus Photographic in the Nineteenth-Century Reproduction," *Art History* 9 (June 1986): 185–212. See also Miriam Levin, "Democratic Vistas—Democratic Media: Defining a Role for Printed Images in Industrializing France," *French Historical Studies* 18 (Spring 1993): 82–108.

5. Auguste Delâtre (1822–1907), a French etcher and printer, was a student of Charles Meryon and Louis Marvy who set up his own studio as an artist's printer in 1848. He pioneered the mobile etching technique, a method of painting ink on the plate so that up to forty unique impressions could be made from the same plate. This technique influenced the monotypes of artists such as Degas and Lepic, and also stimulated debate about the degree to which a printer should influence artistic matters. Delâtre's shop became a meeting place for figures like Whistler, Daubigny, and Ranft. His studio was destroyed in the siege of Paris in 1870 and, like many, he left for London. He came back to Paris in 1876 and set up the new shop, which is probably the one for which the address card was made. Richard Ranft (1862–1931), a Swiss artist, began as a pupil of Sordet in Geneva; he also studied with Courbet near Vervey, Switzerland. Most of his career was spent in Paris, where he began painting landscape and human figure studies. He was a member of the Société Nationale des Beaux-Arts, took part in the exhibitions they organized, and participated in the exhibitions held by the Indépendants. See Leon Maillard, "Richard Ranft," *La Plume* 134 (November 15, 1894:) 468–70.

6. Cadart and Delâtre decided to publish an etching album dedicated to Baudelaire after the poet wrote admiringly about etching. After that they continued issuing an album a year until 1867 when it was replaced by *Le nouveau illustration* (1874–1881). Their efforts contributed to the founding in 1881 of the *Société des peintres-graveurs,* whose first major exhibition was sponsored by the dealer Durand-Ruel in 1889. See Antonia Lant, "Purpose and Practice in French Avant-Garde Print-Making of the 1880s," *Oxford Art Journal* 6, no. 1 (1983): 18–29.

7. Levin, "Democratic Vistas," 101. The waning authority of state-sponsored institutions of art training and display during the Second Empire engendered more entrepreneurial systems of art production, sale, and display. This changing model of art culture fed and benefited from an increasingly vibrant dealer-critic system and the growth of alternative exhibition venues that included Montmartre's burgeoning entertainment culture and illustrated press.

8. Denis was one of the "innovative Paris artists" invited to Toulouse by the paper's publisher to participate in an art exhibition inspired by the success of his poster. Installed in the paper's offices, the exhibition—like the poster—was conceived to advertise the regional paper's urbanity and sophistication. That urbanity registers in the poster's allusion to the so-called crisis of "attentiveness," a by-product of capitalist modernity scrutinized in hundreds of research studies, books, and articles by figures ranging from William James and Georg Simmel to Max Nordau. In an era of industrialized production, unprecedented urban growth, and a thriving culture of entertainment, Europeans were said to be suffering the effects of a plague of "distractibility," an overload of the senses undermining the capacity to look and think attentively. Both Ranft and Denis play on the mystical effect of unlikely couplings. In Denis's poster, a woman is depicted literally "transported" by the sight of the pages she consumes. And we, in turn, are transfixed by, and enticed to consume, the sight of her. In Ranft's design, the magic resides in the trope of miraculous birth.

9. See Willa Z. Silverman, *The New Bibliopolis: French Book Collectors and the Culture of Print 1880–1914* (Toronto: University of Toronto Press, 2008).

10. Among the artists and writers who invoked the image of spiraling, self-propagating motion are Mallarmé, Jarry, and Duchamp.

11. Felicia McCarren, *Dancing Machines: Choreographies of the Age of Mechanical Reproduction* (Stanford, Calif.: Stanford University Press, 2003), 2–3; also see Mary Ann Caws and Elizabeth Coffman, "Women in Motion: Loïe Fuller and the 'Interpenetration' of Art and Science," *Camera Obscura* 49, vol. 17, no. 1 (2002): 73–104. Art historical writing about the dancer in late–nineteenth-century French art tends to focus on Degas' scenes of the corps de ballet and the heterosexual couplings in Renoir's dance hall paintings. With the exception of Salomé, the fin-de-siècle's pathologized and quintessential "fatal woman," the solo female performers who gave birth to modern dance have been almost exclusively the purview of dance historians and literary critics.

12. There is a rich literature about the shared discourse of performance, medical literature, and poetry by Felicia McCarren, Rhonda Garelick, Susan Sidlauskas, and Jan Goldstein.

13. The bookcase was commissioned by a wealthy engineer named Montandon who told Carabin only that he wanted a large piece of furniture; otherwise, he gave him complete creative freedom and advanced him 4,000 francs. Carved furniture was not considered art and therefore could only be shown in commercial expositions, so Carabin organized a showing in his studio and invited amateurs and critics to generate some press.

14. Gustave Geffroy, "A propos d'une bibliothèque du sculpteur Carabin," *La Revue de l'Art Décoratif* 11 (1890–1891): 48–49.

15. Ibid., 48.

16. Ibid., 70, 80.

17. Ibid., 48–49.

18. Jonathan Crary, *Suspensions of Perception: Attention, Spectacle, and Modern Culture* (Cambridge, Mass.: MIT Press, 1999), 397, 492.

19. Sponsored by the *Société de l'Estampe originale,* the albums were issued quarterly in editions of 100 and sold as annual subscriptions for 150 francs. The artists were mostly French but also Belgian and British. See Boyer and Cate, *L'Estampe originale.* Lautrec designed two of the three album covers, and also contributed a third lithograph, *Au café concert,* for the sixth album. Additionally, a portrait of the artist by Charles Maurin was included.

20. They were in fact printed with *rémarques* in small editions of twenty-five. See Frances Carey and Antony Griffiths, *From Manet to Toulouse-Lautrec: French Lithographs: 1860–1900,* catalogue of an exhibition at the Department of Prints and Drawings in the British Museum (London: British Museum Publications, 1978). At the same time rather than shunning the commercial taint of photomechanical technology, he embraced its opportunities both early and later in his career, most notably his work for the popular illustrated weekly *Le courrier français,* with which he continued to work even at the height of his fame.

21. As quoted in Michel Bonduelle and Toby Gelfand, "Hysteria Behind the Scenes: Jane Avril at the Salpêtrière," *Journal of the History of the Neurosciences* 7 (1998), 37.

22. David Sweetman, *Toulouse-Lautrec and the Fin-de-Siecle* (London: Hodder and Stoughton, 1999), 268.

23. Quoted in Frank Kermode, *Romantic Image* (New York: Vintage Books, 1964), 70. Loïe Fuller is the fin-de-siècle dancer who figures more prominently in the poetics of literary Symbolism, particularly the work of Stéphane Mallarmé. The female solo dancer seemed the antithesis of the corps de ballet's mindless regimentation, narrative orientation, codified gestures, and overemphasis on costume. For Mallarmé in particular, the solo dancer offered an appealingly unstable sign for a new kind of modern art.

24. Catherine Pedley-Hindson, "Jane Avril and the Entertainment Lithograph: The Female Celebrity and Fin-de-Siècle Questions of Corporeality and Performance," *Theatre Research International* 30 (2005): 115.

25. Marcus Verhagen, "Whipstrokes," *Representations* 58 (Spring 1997): 129–133. Also see Félix Fénéon, "Henri de Toulouse-Lautrec et Charles Maurin," *L'en dehors* 1 (12 February 1893), 217. Fénéon writes that Toulouse-Lautrec's work is "not a carbon copy of reality but rather an amalgam of signs that suggest it."

26. Griselda Pollock, "Fathers of Modern Art, Mothers of Invention: Cocking a Leg at Toulouse-Lautrec," in her *Differencing the Canon: Feminist Desire and the Writing of Art's Histories* (London: Routledge, 1999), 70–71.

27. That mystery is the subject of a characterization of Avril's solo dancing by a contemporary, Tony Toulet: "Watching her, we see a whirlpool that tunnels into the crystalline surface of a river without disturbing it . . . but then suddenly, she departs from her own rhythm, breaks it, and creates a new one . . . always re-inventing herself." Quoted in Bonduelle and Gelfand, "Hysteria Behind the Scenes," 37.

CHAPTER NINE

Screening the Avant-Garde Face

MARY ANN DOANE

The term "gender" seems to me to harbor dangers and potential pitfalls that are rarely acknowledged in feminist discourse, perhaps because it is a term that is too easily taken for granted as self-evident, both in the social/cultural arena and in theory. The greatest risk has to do with its seemingly unavoidable contract with the notion of identity. Unlike the concept of sexual difference, a primary focus of psychoanalysis, which insists upon processes of differentiation and the work of absence rather than describing fully constituted, coherent, and present entities or concepts, gender always seems to invoke a sense of stability, if not constraint, and identity.

However, as Joan Scott has pointed out in a precise and nuanced analysis of certain historical uses of the word, "gender" is a term that will not simply go away, and must be rethought and reanalyzed in the various contexts in which it is invoked.[1] While it has been the focus of a rallying cry for feminists attempting to demonstrate that gender is socially constructed—a cultural rather than a biological concept—gender has also been appealed to as a form of absolute self-evidence and certainty, a kind of limit to discussion or argumentation, the fundamental bedrock of knowledge about humanness. This was certainly the case in the tautological statement of the U.N.'s Committee on the Status of Women staking out the meaning of the term in preparation for the 1995 World Conference on Women in Beijing.[2] That statement avoided definition or specification by mandating that "gender" should be used as it always had, in some supra-historical realm of complete transparency. Gender was allied with immediate recognizability of meaning.

Nevertheless, Scott argues that gender can be "a useful category of historical analysis" as long as one is attentive to its *lack* of stability and its specific historical instantiations—the necessity of constantly reading and reinterpreting the concept.

> A relativized concept of gender as historically specific knowledge about sexual difference allows feminists to forge a double-edged analytic tool that offers a way to generate new knowledge about women and sexual difference *and* to inspire critical challenges to the politics of history, or for that matter, any other discipline. Feminist history then becomes not just an attempt to correct or supplement an incomplete record of the past but a way of critically understanding how history operates as a site of the production of gender knowledge.[3]

This definition has the advantage of resisting the notion that feminist academics must simply ferret out instances of women who acted "historically," and add them to the history books. It assumes that feminist analysis will interrogate the very basis of our understanding of what history is, and undermine the idea of a firm and solid, unshifting ground of historical knowledge. But it is not clear to me that this approach situates gender as a tool or category of analysis, as on the side of feminist methodology. If gender is "historically specific knowledge about sexual difference," isn't gender on the side of the object rather than the subject of analysis? For if it is precisely the idea that there *is* a stable, generative, even formative knowledge (or perhaps any knowledge at all?) of gender that has caused so much havoc historically, would it be the task of feminists to produce their own form of knowledge, no matter how much it acknowledged its own ephemerality?

Such a knowledge would inevitably raise the specter of recognition and recognizability (and hence identity) that has always been allied with the concept of gender. And because gender has been for so long the buttress of all that is "natural," "universal," and the source of "stable values," it unavoidably drags along with it the premise of immediate recognition ("It's a boy" or "It's a girl" being the first and most formative moment of interpellation of identity). Even multiplying genders will not escape the insistent adherence of recognizability—is it bisexual, transsexual, heterosexual, gay, lesbian, hermaphrodite? What is at stake in this problematic is a positivity, a characteristic that specifies, an identity that unifies and makes coherent and legible a person.

In this respect, it is the concepts of recognition and recognizability as social and cultural processes grounding a sexual politics that demand analysis.

The concept of recognition bears within it the potential of a structuring contradiction—while the preface "re" denotes a repetition of a past event of knowing, in usage, the term is frequently employed to specify an immediate or instantaneous understanding. The Oxford English Dictionary's etymology of the term traces it to the Latin "cognoscere," to know, and the prefix "re," with the general sense of "back" or "again"—hence, "to know again." "To recognize" a person, word, or place means that one has previously experienced or known that entity and hence a comparison is being made between two moments of time, a past and a present, and a continuity between them is posited ("to recall knowledge of: make out as or perceive to be something previously known").[4] Yet, "recognize" also bears the meanings "to perceive clearly: be fully aware of," "to acknowledge formally," and "to admit the fact or existence of"—all of which sanction the negation of the past, of the "re."[5] Recognition of someone in a meeting authorizes that person to speak, acts as a form of pointing, acknowledges an existence and a right, in the present tense.

Hence, the concept of recognition bears within it both a present entitlement or acknowledgment and a temporal doubling, a haunting of present knowledge by the past. The past instance of knowledge stamps and guarantees the present as authentic ("I recognize you"), while the present performative utterance, sanctioning speech, also acts as a form of guarantee or authorization. The dualism is particularly poignant in the case of recognizing a person. For to forget an other is often read as an insult, a de-authorization, a consignment to nonexistence, as well as evidence of a treacherous breach between past and present. And it is the face that combines both recognition's reference to history and a sense of pure presence, a face that in mainstream cinema is insistently sexually specified, gendered. To analyze the work of recognition and recognizability is to probe, warily, the very bases of the category of gender.

The cinema provides a rich and productive arena for the study of processes of recognition, particularly in relation to the human face and its deployment in close-ups and scenes with a certain affective epiphany. The star system itself, with its massive machinery promoting repetition and recognition, hinges on the simultaneous uniqueness and generality of the individual face and its continuity over a multiplicity of roles. However, the cinema that I would like to focus on here is not that of classical Hollywood but of the avant-garde in two historical periods. For it is the avant-garde that feminist film theory has embraced as a radical alternative, precisely because it troubles representation and, in the process, disrupts any immediacy of recognition. An obsession with the female face as screen, as support of representation but also as support of the conundrum of recognition, recognizability, and otherness, conjoins the concerns of the avant-garde with the concerns of mass culture. Both attempt to come to terms with the problem of mediation and loss—the loss, precisely, of an alleged immediacy and knowability seemingly guaranteed by face-to-face communication. What is interesting to me in this respect is the extent to which it is the white female face that acts as the figure of this anxiety about legibility, both in the avant-garde and in classical cinema—two cinemas that historically have been pitted against each other.

In an essay titled "The Sublime and the Avant-Garde," Jean-François Lyotard problematizes the notion "It is happening."[6] He connects the dismantling of the unthought acceptance of the certainty of the event to art—and specifically to the project of the avant-garde. The avant-garde dissects the integrity and homogeneity of the "event"—the "It"—but also the notion of "happening." What can it mean to happen? To take place? And it is precisely this kind of interrogation of an everyday certainty, of a seemingly unquestionable banality, that has drawn various feminisms, historically, to the avant-garde. The avant-garde was a crucial concern in the 1970s and early '80s during the heyday of "theory" within feminist film studies. In "Visual Pleasure and Narrative Cinema," most famously perhaps, Laura Mulvey characterized the avant-garde as a negation of Hollywood cinema's complicity in the patriarchal ordering of sexual difference: "The first blow against the monolithic accumulation of traditional film conventions (already undertaken by radical filmmakers) is to free the look of the camera into its materiality in time and space and the look of the audience into dialectics, passionate detachment."[7] Much of the feminist film practice of the 1970s and '80s embraced a project of negation, a systematic interrogation and undermining of classical codes of sexual looking and imaging; I am thinking here of films like those of Mulvey and Wollen, Sally Potter's *Thriller* (1979), Babette Mangolte's *What Maisie Knew* (1976), and *Sigmund Freud's Dora* (1979, directed by Anthony McCall, Jane Weinstock, Claire Pajaczkowska, Andrew Tyndall). It is this negativity at the heart of an affirmation of feminism that is most intriguing. Yet, it was often a negativity lodged in formal categories, susceptible to the tendency to equate aesthetic radicalism with political radicalism, collapsing politics into aesthetics.[8] As Andrew Hewitt has pointed out, "Once political judgments can be displaced onto formal considerations—once a text can be called 'progressive' by virtue of its formal qualities, and that judgment extended to its political aspects—the political itself becomes superfluous as a critical tool."[9] One of the difficulties of the feminist advocacy of the avant-garde in the 1970s lay, ironically, in its local approach, in its failure to situate these films in the larger theoretical context of a history of the avant-garde.[10]

The theory of the avant-garde and its history are potentially useful to feminism because they have been haunted by the insistent question of the autonomy of art and the desire to forge a link between aesthetics and politics. In other and stronger words, it should not be possible to accept the feminist assumption of an intimate articulation of aesthetics and politics—especially insofar as it has historically privileged the avant-garde as an alternative realm—outside of a thorough examination of the history of debates about aesthetic autonomy.[11] Peter Bürger traces a history whereby art became increasingly autonomous with the breakdown of its connections to religion and court life. The apex of this autonomy was nineteenth century Aestheticism and the "art for art's sake" movement, which involved a rupture of the relation between art and everyday life. Art hence came to constitute a separate realm characterized precisely by its social ineffectivity. The historical avant-garde (movements of the 1920s such as Surrealism and Dada) attacked the institution of art for this insularity and tried to reconnect art and praxis. It failed, but succeeded in revealing the institutional status of art. Nevertheless, institutionalized as art themselves, assimilated within the world of the museum, such movements were stripped of any political valence.[12]

The rationalization characterizing capitalist modernity produced a process of differentiation within the public sphere that, among other effects, separated and distinguished aesthetics and politics. From one point of view, this autonomy isolated art from mass culture and hence from the capitalist circuit of commodity exchange, allowing it to serve as a space of resistance or critique. On the other hand, such autonomy and specialization, deprived of effectivity, are no real escape and can easily be seen as part of the rationalization strategies of capitalism. According to Hewitt, the twentieth century witnessed a shift in modes of legitimating the autonomy of art. The earlier mode, the structural legitimation strategy (which Hewitt associates with the Frankfurt school), described art as an outlet from capitalist reification that allowed it to satisfy "residual needs."[13] The strategy that displaced it was a specifically aesthetic one, a mimetic one by means of which fragmentation in art (in modernism, the avant-garde) was perceived as a true or accurate representation of fragmentation in everyday life. For Hewitt, all of this points to the fact that the problem of modernity is not a crisis or collapse of representation or of the mimetic tradition but rather its retention.[14]

It is not my intention here to work out all the ramifications of this history of thinking about the avant-garde for film feminisms, but I am citing it in order to raise a number of questions. What are the ways in which aesthetics and politics have been figured in relation to each other? What are the grounds of their separation and the resultant attempts to bridge that distance? How has the avant-garde been thought as both site of resistance and the failure of resistance? What are the relations between the avant-garde and mass culture with respect to questions of autonomy? If the division between aesthetics and politics is produced through processes of capitalist rationalization, can we simply force a merger?

The tendency to polarize the avant-garde and mass culture intermittently throughout the twentieth century has had a negative impact on our understanding of the intricate relations and complicities between the two. This situation has been recognized and addressed by a number of theorists, including Andreas Huyssen and Jonathan Crary among others, but I would like to focus here on a particular aspect of this relationship that figures critical intersections between technologies, faces, subjectivities, and knowledges—one that is, of course, inflected by understandings of sexual difference, and one whose reading is also informed by the current interest in archaeologies of technologies (especially of mechanical and electronic reproduction).[15] The technology here is the seemingly basic and simple one of the screen, one that we tend to take for granted as having the minor role of substrate and support of a representation. Yet, we are surrounded by screens today, screens of varying sizes, from the miniature screens of cell phones, iPods, and Palm Pilots, to the medium screens of computers and televisions, to the gigantic screens of IMAX (which is an acronym for "Image Maximum"). The screen haunts both private and public realms and, indeed, challenges their division. Miniaturized, the image it bears can now literally be held in the hand, sustaining the illusion of its possession. Made gigantic in IMAX theaters, the screen presents the spectator with a vision of impossible totality, of modern transcendence. Here, I would like to isolate a certain phenomenon—a tendency exhibited in two widely different types of films, to situate the "modern" female face as a screen, doubling and representing the function of the cinematic screen as support, carrier of the image.

The screen is the largely unthought ground of imagistic representation in both mass culture and the avant-garde (excluding various early experiments with split screen, wide screen, and multiple screen processes, and at least until the advent of the notion of "expanded cinema" in the 1960s and '70s). In the realm of mass culture, the Screen was for a very long time simply a synonym for the Cinema. The Oxford English Dictionary cites a 1915 reference in a film magazine to "screen fever."[16] But the term precedes the emergence of cinema and, as the OED outlines, was used initially to denote a form of concealment or protection: the first definition given is "a contrivance for warding off the heat of a fire or a draught of air" (examples range from 1393 to 1899).[17] In the seventeenth and eighteenth centuries, small handheld screens, often with decoration, were produced to shield ladies' faces from the fire. These screens were also like fans, according to Erkki Huhtamo, and acted as "objects of fashion, aesthetic pleasure, and erotic play. Veiling one's face behind a hand-screen incited desire and curiosity, like a mask; hiding and revealing were indistinguishable aspects of this 'screen play.' "[18] The protection extended to other potentially dangerous or uncomfortable threats, including the gaze.[19] The semantic transformation from barrier/defense to ground or support of images seems to have been consolidated with the projection of images in magic lanterns and phantasmagoria. The OED cites a reference from 1810: "To make Transparent Screens for the Exhibition of the Phantasmagoria." The term screen came to denote a surface or support for the exhibition of images. The etymological trajectory of the word traces a movement from a technology designed to protect a woman's face (from fire or the male gaze) to a technology designed to intercept a beam of light in order to make images visible on a mass scale, enabling an industry that would thrive on the exhibition of the female face.

There is an insistent and recurrent scene in Hollywood narrative cinema that plays out certain permutations of screening, identity, knowledge, and the female face. In it, a male character, constantly on the lookout for a lost object of desire, sees from behind a woman with the same hairdo as that of his lost love and with great anticipation approaches her only to find, when she turns her face toward him, that she is not the one he sought.[20] The intensity of the desire is often marked by a frenetic chase or a tracking shot moving steadily toward the woman. Often this happens in an urban setting, on the street, in the midst of crowds of nameless and unknown passers-by, invoking the uniquely modern cliché of the "faceless crowd." According to Joe Milutis, "The city's relation to the face, the major trope of which is 'the faceless crowd,' is productive of one of the great cliches of the movies."[21] In the midst of overwhelming anonymity, of the faceless crowd, only one face will do, and it is one that is tauntingly suggested but absent. This scene resonates with a crisis of knowledge and knowability and can be found in films as varied as *The Fabulous Baker Boys* (1989), *Funny Face* (1957), *My Fair Lady* (1964), and *Vertigo* (1958). It marks a trauma of recognition, desire, and loss circulating around the face as screen (for the projection of a memory) and screened. But it is a trauma that is not unique to the Hollywood narrative cinema, although it may be here that it finds the terms of its most explicit enunciation as psychological trauma, embedded within the narrative. The avant-garde has also historically struggled with issues of recognition, the vacillation of knowability and unknowability, visibility and invisibility, and the screen as support of the image. And much of this interrogation has, tellingly, circulated around the trope of the female face as screen.

The notion of the screen in cinema is indissociable from conceptions of light, projection, and materiality/immateriality. As Dominique Païni has pointed out, the concept of projection combines spectacle (the action of projecting images on a screen) and geometry (the representation of a volume on a flat surface). According to Païni and from an art historical perspective, the image can be produced in two ways: through its attachment to a material support (he is thinking here of painting, frescos, and the like, but one could also add optical toys) or through the interception of a beam of light by a surface (the screen) that is totally foreign to the image. In the first case, the image is made visible through direct or ambient light; in the second, the image is

> dependent on the light that traverses the transparent veil of its support. . . . In this 'other' history, light no longer encounters an image, nor bathes it, nor illuminates it. Light penetrates it at first, then transports it, duplicates it in dematerializing it, sometimes temporalizing and sublimating it . . . since the projection of an image mixes in a single composite the image and the light necessary for its exhibition, it associates *representing* and *exhibiting*. Vision equals light and light is identified with the sense of sight.[22]

Projection of the illusion of motion collapses representation and exhibition and calls up the notion of spectacle. It magnifies the image, whose scale is no longer dominated by the scale of a body but by that of an architecture, of the abstract authority of spectacle and a collective, public life.

Writing in 1925, Laszlo Moholy-Nagy foregrounded light as the medium of photography and film. Light was not so much dematerializing as a new material, no longer that which simply facilitated access to other, seemingly more material objects. His experiments with photograms (photographic images made without a camera, produced by placing objects directly on a photosensitive material and exposing it to light) made light both agent and mold of the representation. In his short film, *Ein Lichtspiel Schwarz-Weiss-Grau* (Light play: black-white-gray, 1930), recognition of the material object or its parts is completely subordinated to the tracing and recording of the play of projected and reflected light and shadow (fig. 9.1).[23] More radically, perhaps, in his theoretical writings, Moholy-Nagy envisaged a utopian future which would "attach the greatest importance to kinetic, projected composition, probably even with interpenetrating beams and masses of light floating freely in the room without a direct plane of projection; the instruments will continually be improved so that it will be able to embrace far larger fields of tension."[24] He also imagined a projection surface divided into different obliquely positioned planes and a projection screen in the shape of a sphere (or a segment of a sphere), instead of the traditional flat rectangular screen. In this construct, more than one film could be projected simultaneously, and, most intriguingly, these films would not be projected onto a fixed location of the screen but the process of projection itself would be mobile, freed from the rigidity of convention.[25] The historical avant-garde produced a host of other experiments with light and projection, including the films of Richter and Eggeling, Man Ray, and Fernand Léger, as well as Marcel Duchamp's *Anemic Cinema* (1926).

Not infrequently, these experiments deployed the female face or body in a privileged manner as screen, as support of the play of light and image. Man Ray's *Le Retour à la Raison* (Return to reason, 1923) cuts from a suspended geometric mobile spinning and producing a play of shadows on the wall behind to the torso of a woman, itself the receptacle of or screen for the performance of light and shadow (fig. 9.2, 9.3). The cut here marks a significant conjunction, a bleeding of meaning between object and subject, representation and screen, projection and surface. The first shots trace the turn of the mobile, its shadow separate from itself, doubling its movement on the wall behind. Different shots of the turning mobile and its shadow are superimposed. After the cut, the turn (or the trope of the turn) is taken up and reiterated by the naked torso of a woman at a window, her body acting as a screen to support the swirling play of light and shadow. No face, no limbs—just the merger of an eroticized and simultaneous fascination with breasts and with forms. The recognizability of the female body as female is not lost—to the contrary, that body is both support and supplement of representation. *Le Retour à la Raison* as a whole is a film obsessed with form and with the action of light and the impressionability of surfaces (many of the shots are Rayograms, Man Ray's version of the photogram). Heidegger, for whom the dialectic between concealing and revealing is fundamental and whose work is permeated by metaphors of visuality, discusses the concept of the "shadow" in "The Age of the World Picture":

> Everyday opinion sees in the shadow only the lack of light, if not light's complete denial. In truth, however, the shadow is a manifest, though impenetrable, testimony to the concealed emitting of light. In keeping with this concept of shadow, we experience the incalculable as that which, withdrawn from representation, is nevertheless manifest in whatever is, pointing to Being, which remains concealed.[26]

For Heidegger, technology in the age when the world becomes picture is aligned with quantification, measurability, calculability, with the production, in

FIGURE 9.1. *Ein Lichtspiel Schwarz-Weiss-Grau* (Light play: black-white-gray, 1930), Laszlo Moholy-Nagy

FIGURES 9.2 AND 9.3. *Le Retour à la Raison* (Return to reason, 1923), Man Ray

modernity, of the object and objectivity over and against the subject of certainty and knowledge (of, in effect, the subject/object split). The avant-garde purports to interrogate cinema—as the technology of light and shadow and of movement's representation. It interrogates as well "everyday opinion," which "sees in the shadow only the lack of light, if not light's complete denial." The shadows in *Le Retour* mark the body of the woman, producing it as aesthetic artifact. The shadow of the mobile in this film is separate from its object, clearly the object's projection on the wall/screen behind it. The shadows on the body of the woman, on the other hand, merge screen and object, producing that body as aesthetic surface. While it would be hazardous to "apply" Heidegger's categories of light and shadow directly to this film (or any film), it is also possible, indeed necessary, to note that *Le Retour à la Raison* struggles with the concept of the object and its representability, struggles with mimesis and its relation to a dialectic of light and shadow, and, in the course of doing so, produces the female body as screen—screen as both access and defense (defense against capitulation to a vision of the whole.) The trope of the "turn" is crucial here as well, resonating with the turn in the recurrent Hollywood scene of misrecognition discussed earlier. For the turn makes visible that which was concealed—the "other side"—an other side that does not materially exist in the two-dimensional realm of cinema but is continually evoked,

FIGURES 9.4 THROUGH 9.9. *Emak Bakia* (Leave me alone, 1926), Man Ray

imagined, assumed. Just as light reveals what was previously not accessible to vision, the turn is a constant reiteration of otherness and the limits of knowability, a denial of the sufficiency of the surface/screen. Knowledge resides *somewhere else*—behind, on the other side—or *inside,* within the depths signaled by the face.

In Man Ray's *Emak Bakia* (Leave me alone, 1926), it is the face of the woman that becomes the surface of display. Undulating lights and forms, incapable of retaining fixed or legible shapes, precede and overlay the face of the first woman, which is itself, with its prominent makeup, explicitly a painted surface (fig. 9.4, 9.5). The fleeting reflections generated by a revolving cube are projected onto the face of the second woman, who, like the first, stares directly at the camera (fig. 9.6, 9.7). The flower that introduces the image of a third woman (not shown) becomes a shape projected onto a face that unhesitatingly and directly confronts the camera. All these shots foreground the act of opening one's eyes, while the plastic, mannequin-like quality of the fourth female figure is produced by doubling the representation of the eyes, using the eyelid itself as the carrier of the image (fig. 9.8). The essential artificiality is flattened even further when her face becomes the screen for another image of her own face, upside down, now assuming the undulations and malleability of the original lights and forms (fig. 9.9).

A similar treatment of the female face emerges a bit later in the realm of mass culture—albeit in the work of a filmmaker, Busby Berkeley, who was strongly influenced by surrealism. In *Gold Diggers of 1935*, the well-known sequence, "Lullaby of Broadway," opens with a woman's face, surrounded by blackness, gaining in scale as her head grows from a pinpoint on the screen to an extreme close-up (fig. 9.10). As the woman's head rotates and she places a cigarette (a strongly marked signifier of modernity) between her lips, her face and any recognizable features are evacuated from the image and replaced by a highly stylized representation of an urban setting, which the camera gradually penetrates (fig. 9.11, 9.12, 9.13). This gesture brackets a highly disturbing scene involving a woman's fall to her death at the height of the social frenzy of a party. Closure is attained by returning to the representation of the city, which is gradually relinquished as it dissolves into the same, now recognizable face of the woman, who turns and ultimately disappears again into the depths of the image as a point enveloped by blackness. It is not accidental that this, again, is the face of a woman, clearly specified as "modern," whose representation merges with that of a city—becomes, in effect, the screen for a city defined by a claustrophobia, a starkness, and a convoluted navigability. The special trope of cinematic modernity, the faceless crowd, is enacted through the loss of faciality and its supplementation by an urban space never quite knowable in its entirety, filled with unidentifiable strangers. By mapping the city onto the form of the female face, Berkeley intensifies the tropes of unknowability and unrecognizability. The city and the woman are both difficult to navigate, never quite specifiable, confounding the recognition traditionally aligned with the face.

For the historical avant-garde, emerging during the early years of film with an unbridled optimism about its possibilities, it was the very conditions of cinema—light, projection, movement, screen—that were at stake. But the

FIGURES 9.10 THROUGH 9.13. *Gold Diggers of 1935* (1935), Busby Berkeley

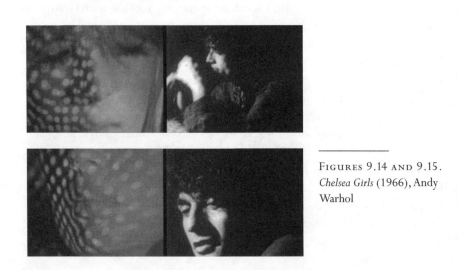

FIGURES 9.14 AND 9.15. *Chelsea Girls* (1966), Andy Warhol

excessively formal nature of these concerns seemed to require for its support a particular conceptualization of the female face, by definition, the *white, Western* female face. It was the face of the "modern woman," open, almost geometric in its clarity, serving to double the capacities of the screen, while signaling a certain historical specificity. For the woman's close affiliation with fashion aligns her with the perpetual production and redefinition of the new, with modernity itself. And as each new "modern" era redefines itself as new, the modern Western woman reemerges as the incarnation of the fashionable moment, whatever it might happen to be (bangs, straight hair, curly hair, short or long hair, thin eyebrows, thick eyebrows, etc.) To see the woman is to recognize most effectively and instantaneously the historical moment. In the 1960s and '70s, this woman materializes most prominently in the avant-garde in the work of Andy Warhol and Jean-Luc Godard.

The fascination of the historical avant-garde—of Moholy-Nagy, of Léger, of Man Ray and Duchamp—with light, reflection, and projection, can be seen as an engagement with the intensive thinking of location, and bodies in relation to location, at the moment of the emergence of a cinematographic modernity. In the 1960s and '70s, the filmic avant-garde, in a return to what it viewed as the Ur-cinema, or the cinema before its rigidification by Hollywood classicism, and in a move deeply influenced by the historical avant-garde, resuscitated an obsession with projection and with light as medium. Andy Warhol's fixed camera stare was reminiscent of Lumière, and he persistently explored the vicissitudes of different modes and manners of projecting his films. The 1966 *Chelsea Girls* makes use of two projectors and of complex lighting schemes, coupled with the insistence upon a scriptless scenario of pure improvisation on the part of the actors. It is made up of twelve scenarios (single shots) of thirty minutes each, two projected simultaneously at all times. The specific configuration of each individual screening of this film is unique given the inevitably different rates of changing reels on the part of the projectionists.[27] The final scenario on the left, beginning with Nico crying, is an extended play with light, projection, and the face as screen.

In the beginning of this scene, Nico plays with a tape measure and a light meter, the tools of focus and lighting whose conventions are violently assaulted by the mode of filming. The coincidence of extreme affect—marked by Nico's tears in excruciatingly close close-up—and an extended and unrepentant camera stare dissolves into the reduction of face and body to a surface, a screen intercepting and displaying the movements of colored lights, textures, and patterns (in the mode of the strobe-lighting so characteristic of the '60s) (fig. 9.14, 9.15). The combination of excessively fast zooms in and out with the projected lights and patterns obscuring the face flattens screen space to the point where the face itself becomes the screen, blank space of reception and reflection of light. Much as in Freud's scenario in "A Case of Paranoia Running Counter to the Psychoanalytic Theory of the Disease,"[28] the contortions of the body become the signs or symptoms of the work of an imaging system or technology, an apparatus of mechanical reproduction. The fragmentation of the projected patterns combined with the extremity of the close-up troubles recognition and knowledge in their relation to the human face.

Jean-Luc Godard, as well, yokes together the female face and a problematics of the screen and knowability. When Nana (Anna Karina) in *Vivre sa vie* (My life to live, 1962) goes to the cinema, her face in close-up echoes the screen on which Dreyer's *La passion de Jeanne d'Arc* (The passion of Joan of Arc, 1928) is playing (fig. 9.16, 9.17). A commentary on/critique of the notions of mimesis and identification (of Karina with Falconetti), the scene nevertheless resonates with the obsessive attention to faces and facing throughout the film, incarnated in the persistent return to scenes that invoke and adamantly avoid the structure of the shot/reverse shot. Yet it is the credit sequence that most explicitly situates Karina's face as both object of investigation and screen, bearer of writing and bearer of light and shadow (fig. 9.18). It is difficult to imagine Godard (or even Warhol, despite his fondness for the transgression of conventional gender identities) assigning the male face a similar function.

In Godard's and Gorin's *Letter to Jane* (1972), Jane Fonda's face becomes the screen for the projection of an entire history of Hollywood facial expressions that express, according to Godard and Gorin, only how much they know. The film consists of an extended semiotic and ideological analysis of a photograph of Jane Fonda listening to the North Vietnamese during a visit to Hanoi in 1972 (fig. 9.19). Godard and Gorin analyze, in their commentary, the focus, framing, and "acting" in the photograph; and the object of their criticism (despite their awareness of a potentially problematic sexual politics) slides between the photograph itself and Jane Fonda as a "militant actress." Fonda's face, here, is isolated and acts as the screen for this masculine deconstruction, and her expression, they claim, reflects a history of similar expressions in Hollywood cinema and in politics—examples include Marlon Brando, Henry Fonda, Claudia Cardinale, and Richard Nixon (fig. 9.20, 9.21). It is a "knowing expression that only says how much it knows." While Jane's face is an "expression of an expression" and a "function reflecting a function," the face of the North Vietnamese man in the background is a "function reflecting reality."[29] Godard and Gorin claim that the choice of Jane Fonda's face (that is, a female face) is contingent—she appeared both in their film *Tout va bien* (Everything's all right, 1972) and in the photo published in *L'Express*. Yet, Fonda's presence in the photograph is, in the words of their commentary, that

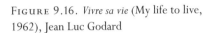

FIGURE 9.16. *Vivre sa vie* (My life to live, 1962), Jean Luc Godard

FIGURE 9.17. Godard uses the image of Joan of Arc, originally from *La passion de Jeanne d'Arc* (The passion of Joan of Arc, 1928), in *Vivre sa vie*

FIGURE 9.18. *Vivre sa vie* (1962), Jean-Luc Godard

FIGURES 9.19 THROUGH 9.21. *Letter to Jane* (1972), Jean-Luc Godard and Jean-Pierre Gorin

of a "star disguised and veiled by the absence of Max Factor." The strategy of using her face as privileged screen (screen as both ground of representation and act of concealment—of American imperialism, of New Deal humanism) also reflects the filmic history of Godard's use of the female face (as in, for instance, *Vivre sa vie*). Why, in the context of an otherwise self-conscious and politically engaged filmmaking practice, does the woman's face take on such a familiar function? Simultaneously revealing in its exemplariness and concealing in its ideological work?

What does it mean that these very different avant-garde practices in two historical periods—the 1920s/'30s and the 1960s/'70s—should persistently situate the woman's face as screen? For Huhtamo, the screen is a "liminal zone between the material and the immaterial, the real and the virtual."[30] Much earlier, E. H. Gombrich, in the essay "Conditions of Illusion," elaborated a concept of "screen" in relation to painting, as an "empty or ill-defined area" onto which the viewer projects his or her "expected image."[31] Far from an insistence upon mimesis or verisimilitude, this is a demand for blankness, illegibility, and absence as the support of illusion. The screen in cinema is a fundamental but almost always unacknowledged basis of representation, intercepting and materializing the image carried by light.

Within the interstices of film movement in the classical era resided what is, perhaps, one of the most telling instances of situating the female face as screen, as technological support of the process of imaging. The leader of a 16mm or 35mm film (blank film at the beginning and end designed to protect the film during storage and threading in the projector) is usually unseen by the audience unless a projectionist makes an error in threading. But often spectators do catch glimpses of this concealed section, which, in addition to protection, has a twofold technical function. On the one hand, it contains a numerical countdown (8-7-6-5 etc.), with a bleep sounding at the moment of the number 2's appearance to guarantee that sound is synchronized with image. Its other technical role has to do with color timing, the process of ensuring that color balance and tonal density remain consistent across shots taken at different times or locations or perhaps with different film stock. This is done by juxtaposing a posing woman, often in close-up, with a color bar. These images are embedded within the leader and often consist of only three or four frames so that, at 24 frames per second, they are barely glimpsable. They exist only as the signal of a technological function. Women's faces were used, allegedly, given their "smooth skin" and the fact that "women's skin was thought to offer a particularly nuanced tonal gauge."[32]

These women were referred to as "China Girls" or "China Dolls," although there is great uncertainty about the origin of this nomenclature. They appeared in every country that had a major film industry (Sweden, Germany, France, China, India, Japan), but in their U.S. incarnations they were always Caucasian. China Doll is a common name for a doll made of porcelain, a material whose clarity, whiteness, resonance, and translucence would have seemed compatible with the requirements of producing subtle color balance. Yet the term China Doll is also a Western stereotype referring to the racist belief that Asian women are docile, submissive, the simple carriers of meaning—the *screen* for its display.

The posing of the women brings to bear all the weighty codification of classical cinema's representation of women in relation to beauty, attractiveness, and "star qualities." The China Dolls enable the incorporation of the female stereotype/icon/image into the technical apparatus to guarantee its verisimilitudinous functioning ("believable" color, matched to skin tone). The term "stereotype" traces its history to yet another technology of reproduction—printing. Originally, a stereotype was a duplicate impression in metal of an original typographical form, used in the actual printing of a text instead of the original. It thus connoted secondariness, nondifferentiation, and invariability—meanings that were displaced onto its colloquial usage as signifying a predictable, stable, over-used, and unnuanced "type." The effectivity of mechanical reproducibility is to a large extent what is at stake in the phenomenon of the China Doll, and the standardization of the female face, its use as a kind of technical measure, reveals a great deal about the historical situation of that visage as ground of representation.

In recent years, artists have revived and reinterrogated the China Doll in a practice that reactivates found footage. An exhibition of photographs by Julie Buck and Karin Segal, titled Girls on Film, consists of seventy images of China Dolls, salvaged from old film leaders and subjected to a process of enlargement, editing, and digital rehabilitation, removing scratches and countering the fading of the film over time.[33] What emerge are glamorous Hollywood style portraits, rescuing the women from their historical oblivion and returning to them the status of star. Much of the critical commentary on the exhibition as well as Buck's and Segal's own discourse locates the pathos of these images in the fact that these women (office and lab assistants, secretaries, as well as some actresses) never attained the celebrity status they mimed so desperately within this concealed realm of the cinema. The artists mourn the fact that the identities of these women will never be known and harbor a desire that one of them will recognize herself in the exhibition and come forward. What we witness in the China Doll phenomenon is the hollowed out form of the star system, its evisceration—the impossible oxymoron of the anonymous star. In these hidden "screen tests," the figure of the star is drained of its most essential traits—recognition and recognizability—and the female face becomes sheer surface. Michelle Silva's short film, *China Girls* (2006, 16mm, 3 min.), on the other hand, does not perform any digital manipulation on the images, preserving the scratches, flaws, and fading that are the marks of the work of time on celluloid and contribute to the historicization of these faces. *China Girls* is a montage of countdowns and glimpses of China Dolls, retaining the bleep at the appearance of the number 2, as well as the sounds of technicians' voices, the scratching of film against the projector's sound head, and frequency signals. The China Dolls here are "left in their natural habitat of countdowns and end-tones."[34] The film does not collaborate or negotiate with the star system's problematic of recognition and glamorous identity but, instead, reveals the intricate entangling of a fundamental female anonymity and crisis of recognition with the substrate of classical cinematic representation.

The face, both inside and outside of the cinema, has been located by certain theorists as the very ground of representation. Jacques Aumont expounds upon the global significance of the face (which is, for him, equivalent to the close-up in the cinema, both producing a surface that is simultaneously sensible and legible). The face is the very origin of representation insofar as it is founded upon resemblance and identity. When we say that someone resembles or does not resemble someone else (or oneself, for that matter), we are referring, above all, to the face. According to Aumont,

> all representation is really inaugurated by the desire of man to figure himself as face. In addition, the phrase "it resembles" is the first experience of representation. . . . What we call representation is nothing other than the more or less complicated history of that resemblance, of its hesitation between two poles, that of appearances, of the visible, of the phenomenon, of representative analogy, and that of interiority, of the invisible or of the beyond-the-visible, of the being, of expressive analogy. The face is the point of departure and the point of anchorage of this entire history. It is not possible to represent without representing the face of man.[35]

The grandiose or totalizing tendencies of these statements are evidenced by the return of the term "man," used in a generic sense. For Béla Balázs, the cinematic close-up compensates for the fact that a technology—the printing press—effectively rendered the faces of "man" illegible, by providing an intense form of mediation. His words document a crisis of legibility, recognition, and knowledge around the face, a crisis that is linked to the proliferation of technologies of representation.[36]

In the twentieth century, hysteria, as the emblematic pathology of the nineteenth century, gives way to prosopagnosia, sometimes referred to as "face blindness." Prosopagnosia is a pathological condition characterized by an impairment in the ability to recognize faces. Although cases of these symptoms were described in the nineteenth century by Hughlings Jackson and Charcot, the condition was first named by Joachim Bodamer, a German neurologist, who in 1947 derived the term from the classical Greek *prosopon,* or "face," and *agnosia,* meaning "non-knowledge." Prosopagnosia is not sexually differentiated in the medical literature, although it is extremely relevant that the facial recognition test produced by the Prosopagnosia Research Center (Harvard and University College London) uses only the faces of women as the testing ground for the level of the pathological condition.[37]

Anxieties about the face and the potential diminishing of its power address a destabilization not only of representation but of intersubjectivity as well. In the work of Emmanuel Levinas, the face is theorized as the very instantiation of the ethical relation and of intersubjectivity. The face is the marker of absolute otherness, infinite and irreducible alterity. It exceeds any possible means of appropriation—including the attempted containments of vision, knowledge, theory, which Levinas associates with an economy of the Same. But what can this mean in relation to the close-up of the face in film? Levinas's interest in the face is ineluctably linked to the extent to which the face "breaks through the form that nevertheless delimits it."[38] It does this through the reversibility of the gaze— not only do I look at it, try to contain it as an image, but it looks back, it speaks to me, and exceeds whatever image I might have of it. According to Levinas, the presentation of the other to the same, which is the definition of the face, is "without the intermediary of any image or sign."[39] His analysis of the face is a philosophical treatment of the originary importance of the face-to-face encounter, of its operation as the ground of sociality and of ethics. In the cinema, there is no such face-to-face encounter—the face in close-up, by definition, cannot respond to me, cannot present itself to me as an obligation or responsibility. It does not inhabit the same time as myself. What are the ethics of the technological reproduction of the face? And why morality, why ethics? Is it coincidental that the philosophical and theoretical obsession with the face emerges in an era of intensified mediation of that face? In an era often seen as characterized by the loss or diminishment of that face-to-face encounter, that direct and unmediated conversation in which the face breaks through form? In an era of the interface?

In Hollywood narrative film, the male character in search of the lost object of desire is subjected over and over again to the trauma of misrecognition, to the literal and metaphorical *turn* whereby the woman he confronts is not the one he knows, wants, or expects. Avant-garde film provides a mirror image of this conundrum, its articulation in the vocabulary of formalism or aesthetics. But here, in place of a missed or aborted recognition, we have the dismantling or putting into crisis of recognizability as such, the imaging of the woman as screen and the screen as site of illegibility—the collapsing together of the fascinating illegibility of the woman and that of the screen. The anxieties surrounding the diminishing power of the face as anchor of representation in a highly mediated society are exhibited differently in narrative cinema and the avant-garde. But we have to question whether, ultimately, the sexual politics of this avant-garde and of mass culture are not dangerously tangential. Whether the female face becomes in both the sign or symptom of the failure of recognition and intersubjectivity. Whether a curiously modern fear of prosopagnosia infiltrates both domains, reducing their difference— producing an affinity any discussion of politics and aesthetics, any politics of reading, must confront.

NOTES

1. Joan Scott, *Gender and the Politics of History,* rev. ed. (New York: Columbia University Press, 1999).

2. Ibid., ix.

3. Ibid., 9–10.

4. *Webster's Third New International Dictionary,* unabridged ed., s.v. "Recognize."

5. Ibid.

6. Jean-François Lyotard, "The Sublime and the Avant-Garde," in *The Inhuman: Reflections on Time,* trans. Geoffrey Bennington and Rachel Bowlby (Stanford, Calif.: Stanford University Press, 1991), 90.

7. Laura Mulvey, "Visual Pleasure and Narrative Cinema," *Narrative, Apparatus, Ideology: A Film Theory Reader,* ed. Philip Rosen (New York: Columbia University Press, 1986), 208.

8. See Renato Poggioli, *The Theory of the Avant-Garde,* trans. Gerald Fitzgerald (Cambridge, Mass.: Harvard University Press, 1968).

9. Andrew Hewitt, *Fascist Modernism: Aesthetics, Politics, and the Avant-Garde* (Stanford, Calif.: Stanford University Press, 1993), 26.

10. There have been a number of important works by feminists exploring the boundaries of the avant-garde in relation to women filmmakers and questions of the canon, e.g., Lauren Rabinovitz, *Points of Resistance: Women, Power & Politics in the New York Avant-garde Cinema, 1943–71* (Urbana: University of Illinois Press, 1991) and Constance Penley and Janet Bergstrom, "The Avant-Garde: Histories and Theories," *Screen* 19, no. 3 (Autumn 1978): 113–127. However, these do not address the broader questions of the general and historical relation between aesthetics and politics, the question of autonomy, and the place of mimesis in feminist film theory.

11. I am neglecting here all the debates about misogyny within the historical avant-garde because my purpose is to emphasize the historical and theoretical vicissitudes of the link between aesthetics and politics more broadly understood. The avant-garde—even the historical avant-garde—is by no means a cure or a utopian moment, but rather a particularly dense and complex instance that brings these issues to a point of crisis.

12. Peter Bürger, *Theory of the Avant-Garde,* trans. Michael Shaw (Minneapolis: University of Minnesota Press, 1984).

13. Hewitt, *Fascist Modernism,* 62.

14. Ibid., 66–67.

15. Andreas Huyssens, *After the Great Divide: Modernism, Mass Culture, Postmodernism* (Bloomington: University of Indiana Press, 1986); Jonathan Crary, *Techniques of the Observer: On Vision and Modernity in the Nineteenth Century* (Cambridge, Mass.: The MIT Press, 1990).

16. *Oxford English Dictionary* online, s. v. "Screen," http://dictionary.oed.com/cgi/ entry/50216741?query_type=word&queryword=screen&first=1&max_to_show=10 &sort_type=alpha&search_id=kGL7-fdUKEB-5799&result_place=2 (accessed May 22, 2010).

17. Ibid.

18. Erkki Huhtamo, "Elements of Screenology: Toward an Archaeology of the Screen," *ICONICS* 7 (2000), 35.

19. In this respect, it is very interesting to note that the term *purdah,* designating the veil worn over a woman's face in Islamic societies, is derived from the Hindi and Urdu *parda,* meaning "screen," "curtain," or "veil." It can refer to the veil over a woman's face, an architectural screen used to divide female and male spaces, or to the entire system of sexual segregation practiced in many Islamic and Hindu cultures. *Purdah* does not experience the semantic slippage from screen as divide or protection to screen as the surface of projection of images that characterizes the English term, but is used primarily to indicate a form of protection, segregation, or isolation. I am indebted to Corey Creekmur for alerting me to the multiple meanings of this term.

20. I am indebted to Joe Milutis for calling my attention to this scenario. See his intriguing website devoted to the representation of the face, "F2F": http://www .hyperrhiz.net/issue01/f2f/ (accessed November 14, 2006).

21. Ibid.

22. Dominique Païni, "Should We Put an End to Projection?" trans. Rosalind Krauss, *October* 110 (Fall 2004): 24, 27.

23. The "object" of the film is ostensibly one of Moholy-Nagy's kinetic sculptures, "Licht-Raum-Modulator" (Light-space modulator), which is overwhelmed by the play of light and shadow it itself generates.

24. Laszlo Moholy-Nagy, *Painting, Photography, and Film* (Cambridge, Mass.: MIT Press, 1969), 26.

25. Ibid., 41.

26. Martin Heidegger, "The Age of the World Picture," in *The Question Concerning Technology and Other Essays,* trans. William Lovitt (New York: Harper and Row, 1977), 154.

27. Unfortunately, the DVD fixes the relation of right screen to left screen, erasing the original appeal to contingency in the screening situation. In addition, the DVD also deviates from the strict projection instructions included whenever the 16mm film is screened. These provide for staggering the timing of the reels on the different projectors so that the final scene ends with only Nico on the left side, outlasting the other reel with the Ondine-as-Pope sketch.

28. In this analysis, Freud claims that the woman's perception of a "click" she associates with a camera photographing her in a compromising position is actually a projection of a "sensation of throbbing in the clitoris. This was what she subsequently projected as a perception of an external object." Sigmund Freud, "A Case of Paranoia Running Counter to the Psychoanalytical Theory of the Disease" (1915), in *The Standard Edition of the Complete Psychological Works of Sigmund Freud,* trans. and ed. James Strachey, vol. 14 (London: Hogarth, 1953–1974), 104.

29. It is interesting to compare Godard and Gorin's analysis here to Barthes' conceptualization of both the woodcutter's and the revolutionary's relation to language as denotative and operational in *Mythologies* (145–146). Because these two types of workers "act" language, their words are closer to the real than those of the myth or the mythologist. Barthes and Godard/Gorin share a semiotic-political fantasy of linguistic transparency. In addition, Godard and Gorin isolate Jane Fonda's face, which, unlike that of the North Vietnamese soldier, is designated by them as eminently separable from its context, the visual insistence of an eternal, ahistorical truth of pity. While the North Vietnamese soldier's face demands a concrete, material, historical context, when confronted with Jane Fonda's look, there is "no reverse shot possible."

30. Huhtamo, "Elements of Screenology," 34.

31. E. H. Gombrich, "Conditions of Illusion," in *Art and Illusion: A Study in the Psychology of Pictorial Representation* (Princeton, N.J.: Princeton University Press, 1969), 208.

32. At artdaily.org, "Artists Reveal and Reinterpret Captivating Imagery," July 16, 2005, http://www.artdaily.com/indexv5.asp?int_sec=2&int_new=14311 (accessed November 9, 2008). I am indebted to Oliver Gaycken for bringing to my attention the relevance of the China Dolls to my work on screening the female face.

33. Girls on Film has been exhibited at the Fogg Art Museum, Harvard; at Anthology Film Archives in New York (2005); and at the Columbus College of Art and Design, Columbus, Ohio (March 2006). See Julie Buck's website for more details: http://juliebuck.com/index.htm (accessed November 9, 2008). Several images can be seen in Ken Gewertz (Harvard News Service), "A bevy of unknown beauties," *Harvard University Gazette,* July 21, 2005, http://www.news.harvard.edu/gazette/2005/07.21/00-girls.html (accessed June 3, 2010).

34. Michelle Silva, *China Girls* (2006), distributed by Canyon Cinema, http://canyoncinema.com/catalog/film/?i=4116.

35. Jacques Aumont, *Du visage au cinéma* (Paris: Editions de l'Etoile/*Cahiers du cinéma,* 1992), 15. My translation.

36. Béla Balázs, *Theory of the Film: Character and Growth of a New Art,* trans. Edith Bone (New York: Dover Publications, Inc., 1970), 39.

37. In the new faces recognition test, not the famous faces recognition test, where both celebrity men and women are used.

38. Emmanuel Levinas, *Totality and Infinity: An Essay on Exteriority,* trans. Alphonso Lingis (Pittsburgh, Pa.: Duquesne University Press, 1969), 198.

39. Ibid., 200.

PART 4
BODY AND SEXUALITY IN QUESTION

CHAPTER TEN

The Sexual Schema

Transposition and Transgenderism in Phenomenology of Perception

GAYLE SALAMON

[The body] is always something other than what it is, always sexuality and at the same time freedom. . . .

　　—Maurice Merleau-Ponty, *Phenomenology of Perception*[1]

What I am all told overflows what I am for myself. . . .

　　—Maurice Merleau-Ponty, *The Visible and the Invisible*[2]

Phenomenology and Ambiguity

In *Phenomenology of Perception,* Maurice Merleau-Ponty makes but a single reference to what might be called mixed-gender embodiment: "A patient feels a second person implanted in his body. He is a man in half his body, a woman in the other half" (*PP,* 77). This remark would not seem to promise much for thinking about non-normative gender configurations. We are introduced to this person of indeterminate gender as a "patient," already marked by some indistinct but defining sign of emotional or mental distress. That patient is doubly confined within a binary system of gender. Even though this patient is, phenomenologically speaking, both a man and a woman, this gender configuration is not thought as some new, third term that might exceed the binary of man and woman, but is conceived by Merleau-Ponty as a man, intact and entire, somehow fused with an also properly gendered woman, with the body divided down the middle neatly between them.[3] Despite this, I want to argue that even given the dearth of attention to non-normative genders in this text, the phenomenological approach to the body that Merleau-Ponty offers in *Phenomenology of Perception* can be uniquely useful for understanding trans embodiment.[4]

Perhaps the most vital aspect of phenomenology is its insistence that the body is crucial for understanding subjectivity, rather than incidental to it or a distraction from it. And one of the most important aspects of the body is its manifestation and apprehension of sexuality. Though Merleau-Ponty has been criticized for his masculinist approach, his insistence that sexuality is vital for understanding both the human body and subjectivity offers at least the promise of new ways of conceptualizing each that would seem to be aligned with feminism and trans studies.[5] That his work has not been much utilized in this way speaks perhaps to the strangely liminal position that sexuality holds within his work: embodied yet not entirely physical, inescapable yet inchoate, both persistently present and impossible to locate.[6] In Merleau-Ponty's work, there is something essentially *ambiguous* in sexuality. I want to suggest that this ambiguity need not be read, as it most often has been, as a phobic or hostile "avoidance" of sexual difference, but rather a more purposeful confounding of that category.[7] There is something enabling in this philosophy of ambiguity; it is precisely the ambiguity attending sexuality that can become the means for understanding bodies, lives, and especially *relationality* outside of the domains of male or female.

Merleau-Ponty describes that ambiguity through his explication of the sexual schema. Like the body schema, the sexual schema is a temporal affair, and like the body schema, the present-ness of the sexual schema is inescapable and spans different temporalities, always pointing both to the past and to the future. This temporality of the sexual schema extends forward, insofar as that which animates my body through desire depends upon those sensations, either compelling or painful, that I have previously experienced—my history shapes my desire. It also extends backward, in that those things I have previously experienced coalesce into a recognizable whole for me, to which I then give a narrative. My sexual desire, located always in this futural mode, thus marries with my sexual history, located in my past, and creates a sexual self. The sexual schema both depends upon my history and makes a history out of my past.

There is a danger of overstating the confluence of sexuality and identity, and this danger is particularly acute in relation to transpeople. Second wave feminist receptions of transsexuality, some recent biological theories about transsexuality, and popular misconceptions of trans all share this conflation of gender expression with sexual expression.[8] Historically, transsexuality has often been fantasized to be—and thus described as—a kind of hypersexualization; some trans writers' effort to *disengage* transgenderism from the realm of sexuality stems from this historical conflation of transgenderism with sexuality. For example, Christine Jorgensen's autobiography, in which she claims to have no sexual feelings at all, can be read as a counterargument to the assertion that transsexuality is really "about" sexual desire rather than gender expression, and that transformation of gender at the level of the body is only undertaken for the purposes of a closed circuit of sexual gratification.[9] The trans body thus becomes something akin to a fetish, and those aspects of bodily transition in particular or transgender experience in general that are motivated by a desire for a specific kind of gender presentation, rather than a specific kind of sexual expression, drop out of the model entirely. But de-emphasizing sexuality to avoid the perils of fetishization would seem to be accompanied by a different set of perils, for it is certainly an impoverished account of subjectivity that cannot make room for desire, and we might ask what sorts of contortions result when trans subjects are required to suppress or deny their sexuality. Might there be a way of avoiding the groundless conflation of transsexuality with sexual fetishism without denying trans subjects a sexuality altogether? Is there room in this picture for desire?

The Sexual Schema

Merleau-Ponty opens his inquiry into the nature and experience of sexuality and its importance to embodiment in a curious way, by offering sexuality as a causal impetus for beloved objects in the world. "Let us try to see how a thing or a being begins to exist for us through desire or love" (*PP*, 137). This is not only a recognition of the difficulty that we have, as embodied subjects, in recognizing other embodied subjects as subjects, the sometimes surprising efforts required, both rational and affective, in order for us to recognize that *this other who stands before me is like-me but not-me.* I only become bound to this other through "desire or love," and through that relation of desire or love, the other comes to exist for me as a thing or being. But through a revisitation of Descartes and a tour through empiricism's correspondence problem, Merleau-Ponty comes to ask after the being of the self, the ontological solidity of *my* body, and not just the body of the other. What he eventually concludes is that I, too, am brought into being through desire or love. The beloved other comes to exist in my phenomenological field as such to the extent that sie comes to exist *for me.* But I, too, come to exist *for myself* in this scenario, and only to the extent that either the other exists *for me* or I exist *for the other,* or perhaps both. Sexuality may be ambiguous, but it has an immensely generative power, a power that refuses to be distributed along familiar lines of heteronormative procreation. Indeed, this power to bring about the self is realized only to the extent that that power refuses lines of procreation that would be either heteronormative on the one hand or autogenetic on the other. The former would require that the other and I are in some sense *for* a third, and the latter would have me only *for myself.*

What might it mean to suggest that the body itself comes to be through desire? This claim underscores the degree to which our embodiment is intersubjective, a project that can only be undertaken in the presence of, and with the recognition of, other embodied beings.[10] Merleau-Ponty's project must then be read as a radical unsettling of the Cartesian tradition that understands me to be a subject only to the extent that I am distinct and separate from others, where physical confirmation of that separateness can be found in the perfect boundedness of my body. These boundaries, Merleau-Ponty will suggest, are dissolved by sexuality. In this way, sexuality is more than just an affective response to a bodily event; there is, he claims "nothing to be said" about affectivity in this regard (*PP,* 137). This can be read as a reaction against aspects of the psychoanalytic model of sexuality, which he understands to be both determinative (bodily morphology determining psychic structures, anatomy is or as destiny) and programmatic (any somatic symptom lends itself to only one interpretation, that of sexual repression). Merleau-Ponty is writing specifically against Freud here, and this section of the *Phenomenology* is offering the least interesting reading possible of Freud's theories of sexuality. For all of his quarrel with psychoanalysis, Merleau-Ponty is in fact not rejecting understandings of either the mind *or* the body that psychoanalysis offers, but merely moving the capacities of the unconscious from the domain of the mind to the domain of the body, and thus reconfiguring the imaginary topography of the subject rather than diminishing its capacity by doing away with the unconscious altogether. Unincorporated traumatic events from a "past that was never a present" (*PP,* 217) thus find both their retention and expression through a bodily, rather than a psychic, unconscious.[11]

Nevertheless, just as proprioception offers us a way of reading and understanding the body beyond the visible surface of its exterior, so too does sexuality make of the body a thing that is internality and externality folded one around the another. Indeed, internality and externality are themselves not perfectly bounded, and sexuality is described in terms that precisely match a psychoanalytic, proprioceptive model of embodiment. The description of sexuality that Merleau-Ponty offers, its suffusion of the body entire and its transformation of the body into something whose erotogenic zones are almost entirely labile, maps almost perfectly onto the topography of sexuality that Freud lays out in *Three Essays on the Theory of Sexuality*.[12]

Sexuality is a matter not of seeing but of *sensing*, which takes place below and beyond the threshold of the visible: "The visible body is subtended by a sexual schema, which is strictly individual, emphasizing the erogenous areas, outlining a sexual physiognomy, and eliciting the gestures of the masculine body which is itself integrated into this emotional totality" (*PP*, 139). In this description, sex is not simply compared to or analogized with proprioception: sexuality *is* proprioceptive (and so, too, is sex—but more on that below). There is the visible body, the for-itself as viewed by others, the material stuff of flesh that is animated and inhabited by a sexual schema. That sexual schema delivers to the subject a sexual physiognomy, just as the body schema delivers to her a bodily morphology. We might even say that the sexual schema in this moment exists prior to the bodily schema: Merleau-Ponty begins with a body, visible but vaguely defined, and then moves to a consideration of the sexual schema beneath it, only after which the physiognomy of the sexual regions of the body become delineated. It is only after that delineation wrought by de- sire that gender appears, first as a bodily fact ("the masculine body") and fi- nally as an emotional one.

Merleau-Ponty's description of the visible body subtended by its sexual schema offers us two different kinds of gender. The presumptive masculinity of the ostensibly universal subject is unremarkably present, as it is through- out Merleau-Ponty's work. But there is a more nuanced and productive ac- count of gender here as well, subtending Merleau-Ponty's more orthodox account of male bodies. Masculinity is specifically described as *gestural* rather than anatomical—and the very purpose of the body's materiality is finally to transmit this inchoate but expressive gesture. There is also a double mimeti- cism at work here, whereby the gesture becomes the property of the body by virtue of being elicited *by the sexual schema itself.* This masculinity is also mi- metic because it is citing, perhaps even soliciting, an other masculine body, a body located in some remote elsewhere, yet proximate enough to function as a structuring ideal. What is perhaps most surprising in this account is its insis- tence that the sexual schema is neither *one,* that which might describe the presumptively masculine, nor *two,* that might encompass the excluded femi- nine and thus might be parsed between masculine and feminine or male and female. The sexual schema is instead, Merleau-Ponty writes, *strictly individual.* This theorization of bodily inhabitation is simultaneously dependent on the "individual," and thus grounded in particularity, but also insisting on relation, and as such cannot be attached to one singular region of physicality or even one singular mode of being. Merleau-Ponty suggests that a systematic and rigid notion of erotogenicity will not do, that it is not my morphology but rather my experiences and mental representations that fundamentally constitute which regions of my body will give me pleasure, and how.

We are offered here a view of sexuality that is fantastically ambiguous, so much so that it should come as little surprise that it has not been taken up as a model by more identitarian conceptions of sexual difference and sexual identity.[13] An insistence that phenomenological experiences of the body and the subject are individual rather than categorical situates the subject differently, temporally and socially. In terms of social organization, this insistence on particularity frustrates categorical summary; it means that neither sexual embodiment, nor situatedness, nor expression, can be predicted by membership in any particular category of gender or sex. The implications of this disarticulation are more profound than the comparatively clearer decoupling of sexed identity (male or female), gendered identity (man or woman, femme, butch, or trans) and sexuality (lesbian, gay, bisexual, or heterosexual). Nor is this an articulation of the now familiar enough notion that feminine desire is by its nature unlocatable, diffuse, ambiguous (we might think of Irigaray again here). I am interested in arguing that an embodied response to desire is, through its radical particularity, unpredictable and impossible to map on the morphology of the body. A woman's experience of sexuality may be tightly and intensely focused on a particular region of the body or it may be distributed throughout the body. So, too, might a man's. That is: we have zones of intensely erotic pleasure, but the relation between a body part and its erotogenic or sexual function is perhaps one of lightly tethered consonance rather than a rigidly shackled indexical mapping. And while a sexual physiognomy might be "outlined" by the erotogenic zones, the body's morphology is neither determinative of the location or behavior of those zones, but is rather determined *by* them. Merleau-Ponty is insisting that sexuality is not located in the genitals, nor even in one specific erotogenic zone, but rather in one's intentionality toward the other, and toward the world.

Desire and Transposition

Merleau-Ponty contends, in *Phenomenology of Perception,* that desire always puts me in relation with the world. Through desire, my body comes alive through being intentionally directed toward another, and I myself come into being through that desire. This does not mean that my desire is always gratified, nor that the existence of my desire alone is sufficient to secure a particular kind of relation to one beloved other or many, or, indeed, any reciprocated relation at all to an other. Desire may be frustrated or unsatisfied, or it may find—for one could hardly call it a *choosing*, since I am often unfree to choose either the inclination or expression of my desire—an object that is unattainable, structurally or otherwise. Desire in these moments may feel only like a constraint or an isolation. But withdrawing from desire, or attempting to stage its death, inevitably involves a truncation of one's own capacities to exist outside of oneself. Desire involves, desire *is,* a being toward the other, and this necessarily conjoins me with, makes me part of, the world.

As we saw above, the organization of desire across different temporal modes and into a narrative coherence is sexuality. Sexuality, Merleau-Ponty writes "is what causes man [*sic*] to have a history" (*PP,* 141). It is embodied and lived, rather than excavated and analyzed. It is not only that which suffuses life; life is not possible without it.

> Sexuality is neither transcended in human life nor shown up at its centre by unconscious representations. It is at all times present there like an atmosphere. . . . From the part of the body which it especially occupies, sexuality spreads forth like an odour or like a sound. Here we encounter once more that general function of unspoken *transposition* which we have already recognized in the body during our investigation of the body image. When I move my hand towards a thing, I know implicitly that my arm unbends. When I move my eyes, I take account of their movement, without being expressly conscious of the fact, and am thereby aware that the upheaval caused in my field of vision is only apparent. Similarly, sexuality, without being the object of any intended act of consciousness, can underlie and guide specified forms of my experience. Taken in this way, as an ambiguous atmosphere, sexuality is coextensive with life. In other words, ambiguity is of the essence of human existence. . . . (*PP,* 149, emphasis added)

What we are asked to consider in this passage is sexuality, taken as a condition not of human *meaning,* as psychoanalysis would have it, nor of *identity,* as some strains of lesbian and gay studies would have it, but of *life itself.* And desire in this most resolutely physical sense is embodied but—importantly—not located. When Merleau-Ponty writes "From the part of the body which it especially occupies, sexuality spreads forth," this may be read as something other than a phallic reference veiled by some coyness that forbids his naming the part. There is an important ambiguity secured with Merleau-Ponty's refusal to name the penis as an encampment of sexuality, an ambiguity that performs an unyoking of bodily parts from bodily pleasures. The join between desire and the body is the location of sexuality, and that join may be a penis, or some other phallus, or some other body part, or a region of the body which is not individuated into a part, or a bodily auxiliary that is not organically attached to the body. This passage asserts that the most important aspect of sexuality is not any particular part, not even the behavior of that part, but the "general function" which causes that part to be animated, the means through which it is brought into my bodily sense of myself and is incorporated into my self-understanding through a reaching out toward the world. Merleau-Ponty designates that function as *transposition*.

The engine of sexuality is transposition; we are offered transposition as a model for understanding what sexuality is for, does with, and brings to me. But what precisely is it? Merleau-Ponty at first makes an analogy between transposition and the ordering and use of the body that is the corporeal schema, suggesting an equivalence, or at least a strong resemblance, between transposition and the function of proprioception. Both are general in the sense that they take place below the level of conscious thought. Both function as conduit between bodily materiality and intention. But there is a difference in that proprioception emphasizes the relation between one part of my body and another part, the assemblage that constitutes my felt sense of my body as a whole. This sense is, of course, gained as I make contact with the world around me, but it is at its core a consciousness that is of and in my body. Transposition describes a slightly different phenomenon, a sense of self that is not additive or cumulative, but a function that emphasizes a shifting from one mode of being or bodily inhabitation to another, involving something like a substitution.

This is a substitution that relates to my material being and is in some sense an intermediary for it, but cannot be reduced to a function of materiality as such. It is assuredly not a linguistic substitution, for Merleau-Ponty designates this transposition as "unspoken," and emphasizes, just as he does in his discussion of proprioception, the unthought and nearly reflexive nature of my relationship to the sexual schema. In the above passage, transposition describes a kind of chiasmic crossing which transforms both body and desire as each comes to stand in the other's place, and with that displacement becomes confused with its other. Transposition describes the process by which the desire that houses itself in my body *becomes* my body itself—not held proximately by thought, but felt and experienced (as opposed to only referred to) through and as the body. If I can be said to have desire, this is only so to the extent that I find it as my body. Simultaneously, my body, in its desire, *becomes* desire itself. The flesh of it is felt only as an animated leaning, intentional in the sense that the desire which animates it has an object—it is desire to the extent that it is desire *of*—but also intentional in that my sense of it coalesces around a purposeful being toward this desired object. My body becomes a leaning or a yearning, a propulsive force that negates any sense of my body as solid or still, or indeed as *mine,* in that this sensation owns me more than I own it.

We are given an eye and a hand in this passage, offered a description of one kind but two expressions of desire, the desiring look and a desire that motivates the reach of a hand. In the desiring look, the eye that comes to rest on an object finds there a still point, an anchor that grounds vision itself and transforms it so that what is, factually speaking, a blurring upheaval in the visual field is sensed as an unremarkable shift of focus through this process of transposition.[14] My look has an object, and I trust that object to ground my look and thus know that the world itself is not turning, that the "upheaval" that occurs when I turn my head and look at something is both occasioned by that desired object and quieted by it. This experience, though entirely mundane and unremarkable, is a de-centering of the self that happens because I turn toward another, and yet that other magically restores me to myself by persisting as the focused and sustained object of my look. The reach, too, is something that is simultaneously disorienting, dizzying, de-centering, *and* consolidating, purposeful, incorporative. When I am thirsty, I move toward the glass on the table, unbend my arm, grasp the glass, move it up to my lips and drink. This is not a matter of cognition, but of changing my comportment, my embodiment, my bodily being so that it encompasses the object of my desire and interacts with it. My body comes into concert not only with those objects in the world toward which my desire is intended but also with itself in that moment—it becomes purposefulness. The transpositional paradox comes when my arm, that which allows me to take hold of the glass, fades from my experience even and only through the act of the reach. In reaching, the arm itself tends to recede from view or disappear as both an object of consciousness and a phenomenological presence. The object of desire supplants the self as center.

Is the scenario different if our body impels us toward another subject rather than an object? What is my experience of my own body if, rather than thirst making me reach for a glass of water, desire causes me to reach toward another person? Instead of reaching toward a *what* that is an object, I am reaching toward a *who,* another subject, and this renders the situation both similar and different. When I reach for the other, I do not feel *my arm* but an intensification of both the proximity and the absence of the one for whom I am reaching. My sensation can in some sense feel itself to be located in that other, and my arm, unbent and reaching out, is no longer the location of my sensation but rather becomes the gesture through which I am toward the other. The arm is the conduit of desire, but not the seat of its sensation. My body is the vehicle that puts me into compelling and sometimes heady proximity to the objects of my desire in this way, and in the case of sexual desire, my body comes alive through being intentionally directed toward another.

This, then, is the substance of the transposition which, according to Merleau-Ponty, animates my body in desire: my sensation becomes more ambiguous and diffuse even as it intensifies because I am suddenly spread out as a sensing subject, located both in my body and that toward which my body bends. The locus of my sensation seems to shift, and my arm, if I reach out, is experienced phenomenologically less in its function as *my arm* and more in its function as *toward you*. This dispersal and transposition need not be read as diminishing either the sensation or the body part in question, but might instead be a way of understanding how in sexuality I am dispossessed of my body and delivered to it at once. A sexual transposition also involves a displacement of the body as a coherent amalgam of conscious thinking, which is surely obvious enough. But this transposition, even as it is the intensification of bodily pleasures, also involves a dissolution of the body as material ground, as phenomenological center of its own world. That center, suddenly, is shared. So self and other together comprise not only the joined unit of my affective life but the phenomenological pivot of sensory apprehension of the world.

But if I am found in the other, so too am I lost there. The "me" that is conjoined with the world in this way is already displaced, disassembled. Phenomenology would suggest, and psychoanalysis would agree, that the object of desire is never a person whole and entire, but a fixation on this particular part or that, or a number of parts in succession. There is already at the heart of sexuality something disassembled about the body as an object of desire, and also *as* the vehicle *of* my desire, to the extent that various areas of my body may be differentially called forth through my desire, that the intensity of my sexual feeling would manifest more intensely in some regions than in others. We unmake the other even as we create hir as an object of our desire.

What significance might this notion of transposition have for transpeople? This phenomenon of transposition is no less true for transpeople than it is for normatively gendered people. Transposition, in the case of transpeople, is also the process through which sensations become animated through the body, and the body becomes animated through sensation. Desire is experienced bodily through a series of substitutions or reconfigurations which are also present, though perhaps less marked, in normatively gendered people.

What happens, in particular if I am a transperson reaching toward that other?

Or if it is a transperson toward whom I reach?

Sex and Transcendence

Existence is indeterminate in itself, by reason of its fundamental structure, and in so far as it is the very process whereby the hitherto meaningless takes on meaning, whereby what had merely a sexual significance assumes a more general one, chance is transformed into reason, in so far as it is the act of taking up a de facto situation. We shall give the name "transcendence" to this act in which existence takes up, to its own account, and transforms such a situation. Precisely because it is transcendence, existence never utterly outruns anything, for in that case the tension which is essential to it would disappear. (*PP*, 151)

When it is misconstrued as pathology, transsexuality has most often been characterized as a mental disturbance in which a person fantasizes hirself to have the genitals of the sex to which sie does not belong. It is on the basis of this fantasy, whereby a misrecognition of one's own body is understood to signal a break from reality, that transsexuality has been characterized as a psychosis rather than a neurosis. As this logic would have it, the materiality of the body is the arbiter of reality; the presence of, say, the transman's phallus is a hallucination if he has not had bottom surgery, and merely "ersatz" if he has.

But phenomenology, as we have seen, is a realm in which one's own perceptions retain pride of place as a means of determining truth. My own phenomenological mode of embodiment—of bodily configuration or comportment—is itself understood as constituting a truth. This does not mean that I construct the truth, whole cloth, from the cloister of my own experience, nor does it provide hallucination with the stamp of legitimacy. What it means is that my experience of my body, my sense of its extension and efficacy, the ways that I endeavor to make a habitable thing of it, and the use I make of it—or in the throes of desire, perhaps the use that it makes of me—are my necessary relation to whatever materiality I am. The sexual schema is rather a way of becoming uncloistered in the body, in that it delivers my own body to me through the movement of my body toward another. Thus through desire, my body is no longer a conglomeration of its various parts in their expressions as "inner phenomena," but is suddenly the vehicle through which I am compelled into relation with the world, where it is finally only that relation that gives me a body.

On the one hand, Merleau-Ponty suggests above that the transformation of sexuality into something of a more "general" significance, and seems then to be suggesting that sexuality itself, or the baser realm which it might occupy, is transcended, and we are delivered into some more rarified realm. The merely sexual is meaningless; it is only once the sexual achieves a more general significance that it achieves meaning. But it is also true that Merleau-Ponty uses sexuality as the exemplar of transcendence; transcendence is the name he gives to the relation between self and world that is sexuality. He wants to claim both that sexuality only means something once it means something greater than itself, and at the same time that sexuality need not point to some more momentous aspect of existence in order to be significant because sexuality is itself coextensive with existence: "There is interfusion between sexuality and existence, which means that existence permeates sexuality and vice versa, so that it is impossible to determine, in a given decision or action, the proportion of sexual to other motivations" (PP, 150). This confusion is not incidental. Merleau-Ponty's paradoxical conclusions regarding the status of sexuality—does it matter, or does it not?—mirrors the status of sexuality itself, which is constantly "interfused" with existence.

Sexuality offers itself as one means by which a transformation from ideality to particularity becomes possible. We might even say that sexuality is the means by which Merleau-Ponty most thoroughly revises our inherited Cartesian presumptions about body and world. It is through sexuality that the body—and thus the *self*—is transformed from a thing that is concerned with itself to a thing that is concerned with others. Sexuality as a mutual project offers another person's body to me as an object of desire, as "not just a body, but a body brought to life by consciousness" (PP, 149), and my body in turn is visible and vulnerable to the other in this same way. Sexuality then becomes relation itself, not in the sense that all relations are at their heart sexual, nor that sexual relations are about the masquerade of one thing for another (as bad readings of Freud would have it), but that sexuality is always offering my embodied existence as held in this inescapable and tensile paradox: I am for me, and I am for the other, and each of these modes of existence realizes itself in my body. Sexuality is perhaps the only way I can experience both of these modes simultaneously. Sex is the means by which the distinction between the for itself and the for others can be broken down, enacting the confusion that will become transcendence.

In the Full Flesh

> Mom,
> I seen him in the full flesh.
> I seen it.
> I know he's a man.
> Problem done. Now let's go to bed.
>
> —Lana Tisdale, *Boys Don't Cry*[15]

The 1999 film *Boys Don't Cry* is based on the story of Brandon Teena, a young Nebraska man who is killed when he is discovered to be transgendered.[16] There is a scene in the film where Lana Tisdale, Brandon Teena's lover, is confronted by two of her friends, John Lotter and Tom Nissen. They have heard rumors that Brandon is not really a man but in fact a woman only pretending to be a man, and have come to Lana's house looking for Brandon, with plans to forcibly strip him and lay bare his "true" identity. This is undertaken to punish and humiliate Brandon, and the wrong that Brandon is being punished for is not just misrepresenting his gender, but misrepresenting it *to Lana*. Thus forcibly stripping Brandon is only part of their aim—it is not enough that they see Brandon's nakedness, what they then want is for Lana to see it. They do not want merely to satisfy their own suspicion that Brandon has no penis and is therefore not male; they also want to force Lana to look at Brandon's naked body in their presence. The nature of the assault sets up Lana as the arbiter of Brandon's gender.

Thus humiliation is conceived by Lotter and Nissen as the way to "protect" Lana from being duped by Brandon and his duplicitous presentation of the "wrong" gender. Lana's response to this is to protect Brandon: she attempts to call off Lotter and Nissen by telling them, "I seen it."

"I seen him in the full flesh. I seen it. I know he's a man. Problem done."

How ought we read that claim, "I seen it?" Is it just an untruth offered by Lana as a form of protection, to spare Brandon the violence that threatens him at this point in the film, a violence that will kill him by its end? I want to ask whether Lana's statement might be understood as something other than an instrumental lie. The "it" that she has never seen is unspecified; Lotter and Nissen and perhaps the audience understand her to be referring to a penis, but she will not name the part as such. In declaring "I know he's a man" she is pointing not only to Brandon's own conviction but also to her understanding of him and his gender; her utterance serves to confirm Brandon's masculinity and his sense of himself as male by asserting that she shares that sense. That knowledge of his masculinity is emphatically bodily but also ambiguous. She knows him to be a man because she has "seen him in the full flesh," a statement of embodiment rather than the naming of a body part, an ambiguity that enables both Brandon's gender identification and Lana's recognition of that gender.

There is a dual ambiguity contained in Lana's statement, situated in the relationship between materiality and "flesh," and also surrounding perception itself. The "full flesh" does more work than simply acting as a veil for the phallic reference, and "flesh" does a great deal of theoretical work. I want to suggest that the work done by that use of the word "flesh" in Lana's utterance can be explicated by considering its meaning in the phenomenological vernacular, and that Lana's description of flesh has useful concordance with "flesh" in the Merleau-Pontian sense of that word, what he calls "my carnal relation with the world" (*VI,* 208). It can name an aspect of embodiment that is not quite the body, or a dimension of the world that is not quite quantifiable.

Merleau-Ponty considers perception to be a relational structure, where those relations do not map neatly onto the relation between subject and object. He attempts to frustrate this distinction between subject and object, between the seer and seen, between inside and outside, by according relation a primacy that had previously been reserved for the object itself. His final, unfinished work, *The Visible and the Invisible,* can be read as an attempt to show the ways in which familiar philosophical distinctions—and even familiar experiential ones—between subject and object, between the hand that touches and the hand that is touched, between our visible, bodily being and those aspects of ourselves that are not visible, are undermined by the importance of the relations between these categories. If the physical body can be thought as a discrete and bounded entity, capable of being distinctly set apart from the ground that is its world, this identification is less a matter of disconnection or differentiation and more a product of relation. A body becomes so by virtue of its interaction with what surrounds it, not because it is composed of a stuff that is radically foreign to its surroundings.

How are we to understand the relation between body and world, and our perceptions of those relations? We are certain of our perceptions of the world, we are sure that they "belong" to us, and we are sure that they show us the world as it "truly" is. And yet, a reliance on perception to confirm our certainty about what we know of the world can be misleading, in that it cannot always account for those nameless structures that are true to experience but foreign to an objective assessment of that experience. If I stand in the middle of the road and survey it as it stretches before me, it differs in width as it approaches the horizon, but "the road close up is not 'more true': the close, the far off, the horizon in their indescribable contrast form a system, and it is their relationship with the total field that is the perceptual truth" (*VI,* 22). In this way, perception points toward a network of relations rather than confirming the material "truth" of any single element in that network or system, and in considering perception in this way, "every distinction between the true and the false, between methodic knowledge and phantasms, between science and the imagination, is ruined" (*VI,* 26).

This conclusion might seem at first to difficult to support, since it is one thing to claim that our perceptions of the world are inescapably perspectival, and another to claim that this collapses distinctions between true and false, between methodic knowledge and phantasms. In the case of the body, the distinction that Merleau-Ponty wishes to challenge would seem to be the very distinction that allows the body to be thought as a bounded and legible entity. Ultimately, the act of perception "ruins" any clean division between the body and the world in which that body is situated, and if my body can still be understood as mine, it cannot be thought as more proximate to me than the world through which my body moves:

> What I "am" I am only at a distance, yonder, in this body, this personage, these thoughts, which I push before myself and which are only my least remote distances; and conversely I adhere to this world which is not me as closely as to myself, in a sense it is only the prolongation of my body. (*VI*, 57)

How is it possible to understand the world as something capable of being as close to me as I am to myself, that the entire world is felt and functions as an extension of my body? This is an account of ontological "truth" that refuses to give primacy to either the perceiver who registers perceptions of the world or the world as a material fact over and against our perceptions of it. The "truth" of being exists somewhere in between these two registers, between what appears (the visible) and that which cannot be captured by flat and factual assertions about the appearances of the world (the invisible). The way in which Merleau-Ponty offers the category of the phantasmatic is significant in its restructuring of the relation between the visible, the invisible, and bodily being. We might expect the phantasmatic to be paired with "materiality," thus presenting an opposition (even if a collapsing one) between the phantasmatic and the invisible and that which is visible, material, and substantive. The phantasmatic is instead paired with "methodic knowledge," suggesting a relation of opposition between the phantasmatic and what we can know, rather than the more familiar opposition between the phantasmatic and what we can see. If the phantasmatic can be described as something (or, more properly, some non-thing) which escapes our attempts to grasp or survey it, it would seem that the aspect of the phantasmatic that retreats from our perception is not the solidity of its materiality, but the solidity of our own knowledge of it. Merleau-Ponty reconfigures the phantasmatic, transforming it from a register characterized by a lack of materiality into a register characterized by an ungraspability. The phantasmatic may or may not be material. It is not necessarily invisible, but it is indefinable, rendering the phantasmatic as that which cannot be encompassed by our knowledge of it, rather than that which cannot be perceptually grasped. There exists a certain borderlessness to the phantasmatic; a methodical attempt to survey it as we would any commonplace object always fails to fully encompass it and cannot give a thorough account of its material dimensions nor translate that material into meaning.

This failure of perception to account for the totality of a thing is, of course, true of any object in the world toward which perception might be intended. Every object is shot through with an infinite number of possible appearances that no single act of perception can encompass, and no series of perceptions can exhaust. Even a perception in which we have all faith, which seems to deliver a truth about the object, cannot encompass the reality of that object, because " 'reality' does not belong definitely to any particular perception . . . in this sense it lies *always further on*" (*VI,* 41). Perceptual faith cannot help us locate the "reality" of the object—it is not even able to finally decide on its *own* location, seeming sometimes to emanate from the presence of the object, and sometimes to be located in the body of the perceiver, and the incompossibility of these two positions (my perception cannot be both in the thing itself and in me) leaves the question of the location of perception undecidable. Yet perception is not impoverished by its inability to deliver the "whole" of any object; perception always gives us something less than this whole, but also gives us something more through the multitude of connections it makes between the perceiver and the thing perceived. For Merleau-Ponty, perception is not a passive activity whose aim is to capture a quantifiable measurement of the world through recording and measuring the qualia of any particular object within it. Perception produces our relations with other objects and subjects, and these relations are, finally, the location of the object's meaning. The perceptual truth of the object becomes the creation of its meaning, a meaning that is produced rather than found.

What consequences might this theory of perceptual truth have for thinking gender variance? First and most obviously, it suggests the possibility of a lack of accord between the object as it is delivered by our perception and the "reality" of the thing perceived, a reality which always lies "further on" than any objective perception. What one might "read" from the contours of the body is something less than the "truth" of that body's sex, which cannot be located in an external observation of the body, but exists instead in that relation between the material and the ideal, between the perceiver and the perceived, between the material particularity of any one body and the network of forces and contexts that shape the material and the meaning of that body. The perceptual truth of the body is not necessarily what we see, and the traditional binary of sexual difference might have less purchase on the body's "truth" than other ways of apprehending its lived reality. Or, to turn again to the film, Brandon's sex "close up" is not more true than Brandon's sex "far away," just as "the road close up is not more true than the road far away."

The category of the "flesh" also offers a way of thinking embodiment that takes seriously the productive capacities of its psychic investments, and understands the phenomenological experience of the body to be as vital as an objective assessment of the body's corporeality. So what is "flesh"? Merleau-Ponty offers a theorization of "flesh" in which it is not reducible to the material, and is a product of relations between myself, the other, and the world. Of course, the term is often employed as if its referent were clear and obvious: flesh is understood as bodily substance.[17] This has been true also in discussions of the transgendered body in particular: Jay Prosser describes the body's "fleshy materiality," making no distinction between these two terms.[18] It is simple, it is visible, it is material, and, in both of these instances, the term is deployed to dispel the cloud of linguistic abstraction that is thought to attend discussions of the body. More colloquially, the term "flesh" is used to describe a mode of being allied with visibility and presence and often indicates a certain relational component to that being. To say that one is present "in the flesh" connotes being present to or for someone else, an observing or other entity differentiated from the self and for whom the flesh becomes a display, a guarantor of the embodied presence of personhood. (The phrases "in the flesh" and "in person" are practically interchangeable—the former acts as a guarantor of the latter.)

Merleau-Ponty's definition of flesh shares with the colloquial, everyday deployment of the term the notion of relation, but is both more restricted (my flesh and my person are not the same thing) and more expansive (my flesh need not be coterminous with my body, but can extend into the world, which itself has a flesh). He asks: "Do we have a body—that is, not a permanent object of thought, but a flesh that suffers when it is wounded, hands that touch?" (VI, 137).

In working to differentiate body from flesh, Merleau-Ponty opposes them, attributing the one the characteristics of object, and to the other the characteristics of a subject. The first distinguishing property of flesh is that it suffers, it is only secondarily important that it has "hands that touch." This is not quite a distinction between passivity and activity—suffering may be as active an engagement with the other as touching. (Recall that the body is active when it "opens itself to others," including opening itself to the possibility of being wounded by the other.) It does, however, draw a distinction between the body as it is seen (as object) and the body as it is felt, as it is phenomenologically experienced. And herein lies the greatest difference between Merleau-Ponty's explication of flesh and flesh thought as merely the material stuff of the body.

Flesh is that which, by virtue of psychic investment and worldly engagement, we form our bodies into, rather than the stuff that forms them.

To become flesh is to enter the world and engage with it so fully that the distinction between one's body and the world ceases to have meaning. It is to inhabit one's body, to "to exist within it, to emigrate into it, to be seduced, captivated, alienated by the phantom, so that the seer and the visible reciprocate one another and we no longer know which sees and which is seen . . ." (*VI*, 139). If the materiality of the body is the simple substance that promises to save us from the seductions of theory, flesh is itself a seduction by which we are led to abandon the distinction between body and world: it is the world's seduction of the body, and the body's incorporation of the world into itself.

Merleau-Ponty continues:

> It is this visibility, this generality of the Sensible in itself, this anonymity innate to itself that we have previously called Flesh and one knows there is no name in traditional philosophy to designate it. . . . The Flesh is not matter, is not mind, is not substance. To designate it, we should need the old term "element," in the sense of a general thing, midway between. . . . Flesh is an ultimate notion, that it is not the union or compound of two substances, but thinkable by itself. (*VI*, 140)

Merleau-Ponty insists that flesh is not a singular substance, but neither is it the "union or compound of two substances, but thinkable by itself" (*VI*, 140). Flesh designates a certain unlocatability of the body, neither the substance of the thing nor a pure ideality, but that which is constructed somewhere between these two. When Merleau-Ponty asks, "Is my body a thing, is it an idea?" he answers that "it is neither, being the measurement of things. We will therefore have to recognize an ideality that is not alien to the flesh, that gives it its axes, its depth, its dimensions" (*VI*, 152). The body itself is, finally, a mixture or amalgam of substance and ideal, located somewhere between its objectively quantifiable materiality and its phantasmatic extensions into the world. Merleau-Ponty suggests a mode of bodily inhabitation through which we allow ourselves to be seduced by the phantasmatic aspects of the body, that we give ourselves over to the world in affirming the flesh that is not-quite-the-body, and thereby find a more deeply rooted and expansive engagement with the other, and the world.

Flesh, then, is a thing that is thinkable, but a thing that has not been thought. Flesh is neither matter nor mind but partakes of both of these things, and yet cannot be described as a mixture of them. It is forged through our relations with others, in all of their phenomenological particularity, yet is itself "a general thing." What, then, might we take from this theorization of the flesh to help us understand transgendered embodiment? Merleau-Ponty's description of flesh sounds, in many ways, like a description of transgenderism or transsexuality: a region of being in which the subject is not quite unitary, and not quite the combination of two different things. An identity that is not secured by the specificity of the materiality of the body, nor by a particular mental quality, but is something involving both of these. It can be thought by itself, yet has been unnamable. Neither a singular substance nor a union of two substances. In both, too, the question of relation is primary. To feel one's own flesh, or to act as witness to another's, is to unsettle the question of subject and object, of material and phantasmatic, in the service of a more livable embodiment.

NOTES

1. Maurice Merleau-Ponty, *Phenomenology of Perception,* trans. Colin Smith (London: Routledge and Kegan Paul, 1962), 178. Hereafter cited as *PP* in parenthetical references.

2. Maurice Merleau-Ponty, *The Visible and the Invisible,* ed. Claude Lefort, trans. Alphonso Lingis (Evanston, Ill.: Northwestern University Press, 1968), 60. Hereafter cited as *VI* in parenthetical references.

3. This fantasy of a magical fusion of sexes, and its production of a body that is cleaved exactly in half, might be understood as the dominant fantasy about nonnormative sexes, inclusive of both hermaphroditism and transsexuality, since the dually sexed creatures of Ovid's *Metamorphoses.* For a history of gendered bodies beyond the binary in classical antiquity, see Luc Brisson, *Sexual Ambivalence: Androgyny and Hermaphroditism in Graeco-Roman Antiquity* (Berkeley: University of California Press, 2002). For a depiction of how such fantasies of bodily division, in which sex cleaves the body into two halves, persist in depictions of hermaphroditism, see Elizabeth Grosz, "Intolerable Ambiguity: Freaks as/at the Limit" in *Freakery: Spectacles of the Extraordinary Body,* ed. Rosemarie Garland Thompson (New York: NYU Press, 1996). See also the critical account of transsexuality offered in the final pages of Elizabeth Grosz, *Volatile Bodies* (Bloomington: Indiana University Press, 1994).

4. Phenomenology has been utilized variously by authors doing trans work. See Henry Rubin, "Phenomenology as Method in Trans Studies," *GLQ: A Journal of Lesbian and Gay Studies* 4, The Transgender Issue (1998): 263–281. Rubin's most recent book is a sociological account of transmen that uses Merleau-Ponty's *Phenomenology of Perception;* he reads phenomenology's insistence on the perspectival situatedness of subjects as shoring up and fortifying both the speaking "I" and the truth claims of that "I." See Henry Rubin, *Self-Made Men: Identity and Embodiment Among Transsexual Men* (Nashville, Tenn.: Vanderbilt University Press, 2002).

5. Luce Irigaray is perhaps Merleau-Ponty's most trenchant critic here. For her engagement with Merleau-Ponty's *The Visible and the Invisible,* see Luce Irigaray, "The Invisible of the Flesh," in *An Ethics of Sexual Difference,* trans. Carolyn Burke and Gillian C. Gill (Ithaca, N.Y.: Cornell University Press, 1993). For a reading of Irigaray's engagement with Merleau-Ponty, see Tina Chanter, "Wild Meaning," in *Ethics of Eros* (New York: Routledge, 1995), and Penelope Deutscher, "Sexed Discourse and the Language of the Philosophers," in *A Politics of Impossible Difference: The Later Work of Luce Irigaray* (Ithaca, N.Y.: Cornell University Press, 2002). Judith Butler suggests that Irigaray's trope of two sets of lips speaking finds its inspiration in Merleau-Ponty's *deux lèvres* in "Merleau-Ponty and the Touch of Malebranche," in *The Cambridge Companion to Merleau-Ponty,* ed. Taylor Carman and Mark B. N. Hansen (Cambridge, UK: Cambridge University Press, 2005). Butler offers a different reading of the intersection of phenomenology and feminism in "Sexual Ideology and Phenomenological Description: A Feminist Critique of Merleau-Ponty's *Phenomenology of Perception,*" in *The Thinking Muse,* ed. Jeffner Allen and Iris Marion Young (Bloomington: Indiana University Press, 1989). See also Linda Martin Alcoff, "Merleau-Ponty and Feminist Theory on Experience," in *Chiasms: Merleau-Ponty's Notion of "Flesh,"* ed. Fred Evans and Leonard Lawlor (Albany: SUNY Press, 2000). For a more optimistic reading, see Roslyn Diprose's reading of Merleau-Pontian embodiment as a site for a transformed ethics in *Corporeal Generosity: On Giving with Nietzsche, Merleau-Ponty and Levinas* (Albany, N.Y.: SUNY Press, 2002).

6. Iris Marion Young's essay "Throwing Like a Girl," her follow-up essay "Throwing Like a Girl, Twenty Years Later," and her piece "Pregnant Embodiment" remain singular as examples of both critiques of the presumptively male body in Merleau-Ponty and positive phenomenologies of specifically female embodiment. There also appears to be a new interest in using phenomenology for queer theory: see Sara Ahmed, *Queer Phenomenologies: Orientations, Objects, Others* (Durham, N.C.: Duke University Press, 2006).

7. For an example of this kind of critique, see Grosz, *Volatile Bodies.*

8. For a feminist critique of transsexuality, see Janice Raymond, *The Transsexual Empire* (Boston, Mass.: Beacon Press, 1979), which reads the motivation for MTF transition to be sexual gratification, and, in particular, the sadistic sexual gratification of "becoming" a woman, a sadistic gratification that is, Raymond suggests, akin to rape.

For biological theories of transsexuality, see J. Michael Bailey, *The Man Who Would Be Queen: The Science of Gender Bending and Transsexualism* (Washington, D.C.: National Academies Press, 2003). In an inversion of Raymond's theory, Bailey asserts that bodily transitions of "transmen" (by which he means MTF transwomen) is a result of their attraction not to the women that they want to become and thus supplant, but to themselves reimagined as women. The theory of "autogynophilia"—the term originates with Ray Blanchard—recasts the theory of a sexual attraction to oneself in a different scientific genre. This fetal androgen bath theory of transsexual development suggests that transpeople are "made" by exposure to the wrong kinds of hormones *in utero,* and is regarded positively by some transpeople (such as Anne Lawrence, a doctor herself) though rejected by most, in the same way that the "gay gene" or "gay brain" research is regarded positively by some homosexuals: a single, and resolutely biological, explanation of the "condition" means that its sufferer cannot be thought as morally culpable for her homosexuality or transsexuality, which is a biological, and thus ostensibly immutable, "fact." This recent discourse, both insisting on the biological basis of trans and asserting that it is fundamentally a sexual obsession with oneself, replicates with surprising faithfulness the concepts of inversion and homosexuality understood as a form of sexual narcissism that once dominated discourses on homosexuality. Though the structural similarities of these two misreadings are noteworthy, I don't want to suggest that transgenderism has replaced homosexuality in this regard, which would risk obscuring the fact that the narcissistic interpretation of homosexuality is still dominant in some circles.

In popular conceptions, the abbreviation LGBT demonstrates this conflation in its inclusion of transgenderism (and sometimes intersexuality in the case of LGBTI), with the other categories that denote sexuality rather than gender. For more on the sometimes uneasy relations in what Dean Spade has called the "LGB fake T" community, see Susan Stryker, "Transgender Theory: Queer Theory's Evil Twin," in *GLQ: A Journal of Lesbian and Gay Studies,* 10 (2004): 212–215.

9. Sandy Stone expresses both sympathy for this disengagement and doubt of its efficacy in "The Empire Strikes Back," in *Body Guards: The Cultural Politics of Gender Ambiguity,* ed. Kristina Straub and Julia Epstein (New York: Routledge, 1991). Joanne Meyerowitz, *How Sex Changed* (Cambridge, Mass.: Harvard University Press, 2002), also explores accounts of early trans autobiographies in which the subject of sexual desire is either politely avoided or entirely disavowed.

10. For an extended consideration of this concept in philosophy and its particular implications for women, see Gail Weiss, *Body Images: Embodiment as Intercorporeality* (New York: Routledge, 1999).

11. Gayle Salamon, "Is There a Phenomenological Unconscious? Time and Embodied Memory in Merleau-Ponty" (unpublished manuscript).

12. Sigmund Freud, *Three Essays on the Theory of Sexuality,* ed. and trans. James Strachey (New York: Basic Books, 1962).

13. Merleau-Ponty's commitment to ambiguity in his discussions of the body has frustrated even his least identitarian critics. This is, for instance, Derrida's chief quarrel with Merleau-Ponty as outlined in *On Touching—Jean-Luc Nancy,* trans. Christine Irizarry (Stanford, Calif.: Stanford University Press, 2005).

14. For a consideration of the eye, the look, and their structuration of perception as well as a challenge to Sartre's theorization of the gaze, see Maurice Merleau-Ponty, *The Primacy of Perception* (Evanston, Ill.: Northwestern University Press, 1964).

15. *Boys Don't Cry* (1999), dir. Kimberly Peirce.

16. For reflections on the iconic place of Brandon Teena within the trans movement, see Judith Halberstam, *In a Queer Time and Place* (New York: NYU Press, 2005).

See also BRANDON (1998–1999), a multimedia collaborative project by Shu Lea Cheang, Jordy Jones, Susan Stryker, and Pat Cadigan, commissioned by the Guggenheim museum and accessible at http://brandon.guggenheim.org.

17. Thomas Laqueur describes flesh as that which "shines through in its simplicity" in *Making Sex: Body and Gender from the Greeks to Freud* (Cambridge, Mass.: Harvard University Press, 1992).

18. Jay Prosser, *Second Skins: The Body Narratives of Transsexuality* (New York: Columbia University Press, 1998).

CHAPTER ELEVEN

Foucault and Feminism's Prodigal Children

LYNNE HUFFER

In her 2006 book, *Split Decisions: How and Why to Take a Break from Feminism,* legal scholar Janet Halley tells a personal, theoretical, and political story about feminism's wayward "offspring," those "prodigal sons and daughters who have wandered off to do other things."[1] She herself is one of those children, though whether son or daughter is not quite clear: "And if I could click my heels and become a 'gay man' or a 'straight white male middle-class radical,' I would do it in an instant—wouldn't you?" (*SD,* 13). As it turns out, those children are more rebellious than wayward, not "wandering off" but running away from a "governance feminism" (*SD,* 32) they regard as unjust. Halley is referring specifically to feminist legal reforms such as sexual harassment legislation when she writes, "any force as powerful as feminism must find itself occasionally looking down at its own bloody hands. . . . Prodigal theory often emerges to represent sexual subjects, sexual possibilities, sexual realities, acts, bodies, relationships onto which feminism has been willing to shift the sometimes very acute costs of feminist victories in governance" (*SD,* 33).

To buttress her argument that "feminism . . . is running things" (*SD,* 20), Halley divides all of feminism into its two legal versions: power feminism, represented by Catherine MacKinnon, and cultural feminism, epitomized by Robin West. And if she continues to be filled "with awe" (*SD,* 60) by the dazzling power analyses of early MacKinnon, such is not the case with regard to the "bad faith" (*SD,* 60) of an "intensely moralistic" (*SD,* 76) Robin West, who tries to combine an ethics of justice with an ethics of care. Halley complains: "The distinctive cultural-feminist character of West's project . . . is the pervasive *moral* character of patriarchy and feminism" (*SD,* 61, original emphasis). Cultural feminists see a male-dominated world in which "female values have been depressed and male values elevated in a profound *moral error* that can be corrected only by feminism" (*SD*, 61, emphasis added). Her own position as a Harvard law professor notwithstanding, Halley asserts that she cannot follow either MacKinnon or West into the corridors of legal and institutional power where their "governance feminism" has taken them. And if she continues to admire MacKinnon and to profess an allegiance to the epistemological focus of her early work, this is not the case with Robin West. The vehemence of Halley's rejection of cultural feminism and, with it, her former self, takes on the force of a religious conversion:

> I was a cultural feminist for years, a fact that I confess with considerable shame. Somehow, now, cultural feminism is a deep embarrassment to me. . . . It was a time of intense misery in my life—misery I then attributed to patriarchy but that I now attribute to my cultural feminism. And it was a wrenching and painful—also liberating and joyful— process to move into a different metaphysics, a different epistemology, a different politics, and *a different ethics*. (*SD*, 59–60, emphasis added)

I begin with this sketch of the opening arguments and confessions of Halley's provocative book in order to situate my own project on queer theory, feminism, and the gendered matrix from which queer sexuality was born.[2] Although it is tempting to engage Halley in the detail of her arguments, that is not my purpose here. Rather, I use her image of prodigal children in their rebellion against an "intensely moralistic" (*SD*, 76) feminist mother to situate my work within a queer feminism that continues to interrogate, long after queer theory's feminist birth, gender's "translations" into ever-new contexts and fields of study. My specific focus is the complex result of a series of divergences— figured by Halley as "split decisions"—within a configuration of terms— specifically, sex, sexuality, and gender—that have now been institutionalized and theoretically established as that inchoate project we call queer theory.

I am especially interested in the ethical dimensions of those split decisions, and view Halley's work as but the latest moment in a string of events that might well be described as a queer resistance to an age-old figure: the scolding feminist prude. In her figuration within queer "prodigal theory," that sex-phobic nag is both overly victimized and overly powerful: always "about to be raped," as MacKinnon puts it, and, at the same time, as Halley complains, always "running things" (*SD*, 20) in order to ensure her own protection.[3] As a result of the feminist movement, the scolding prude now "walk[s] the halls of power" (*SD*, 21), using the state to do violence to sexual "others"—those loving perverts we have come to call "queer"—in the name of feminism's superior moral values.

But how, exactly, did this feminist-queer split come about? In the complex play of translations and interpretations that solidify as theoretical and political positions, no one is more important for the establishment of queer theory as distinct from feminism than Michel Foucault. Most prominently, Gayle Rubin's aegis-creating article "Thinking Sex" (1984) draws heavily on Foucault to make the case for "an autonomous theory and politics specific to sexuality" distinct from a feminist "theory of gender oppression."[4] And if the founding thinkers of the queer come out of feminism—I'm referring specifically to Rubin (1984), Butler (1990), and Sedgwick (1990)—its institutional and theoretical distinctiveness has, to a great extent, been defined in terms of its *difference* from feminism and gender.[5] In that process, Foucault has taken his place as the radically poststructuralist, foreign father of a host of queer children bent on rejecting a feminist, Anglo-American mother whose normative governance projects are threatening to them. This is what Halley has come to call "Taking a Break," and she lists Foucault first in her genealogy of "some classics" (*SD,* 38) in that anti-feminist project.

Significantly, when Halley and other queer theorists—including feminist ones—refer to Foucault, they mean a very limited, specific Foucault: the Foucault of that massively read first volume of *History of Sexuality,* published in French in 1976 and translated into English in 1978. In her brief chapter on Foucault, Halley is typical of queer theorists generally in her attention to Foucault's familiar theories about sexuality as power-knowledge: power appears as relational and productive, subjectivity emerges as subjectivation or *assujettissement,* and sexuality, not gender, becomes the "primum mobile" of modern subjectivation (*SD,* 119–123).

Halley's typical queer privileging of sexuality over gender as the "prime mover" of subjectivation in Foucault exposes a terminological knot worth unraveling, especially with regard to the ethical incommensurabilities outlined above. My critique of Halley's reading here is not directed at her alone, and could be applied to Rubin and others as well. It follows a path already laid out by Butler in "Against Proper Objects" and Elizabeth Weed in "The More Things Change" in *Feminism Meets Queer Theory* (1997).[6] In focusing on Foucault, I want to open a queer-feminist, Franco-American question about some incipient linguistic and conceptual problems that swirl around the terms "sex," "sexuality," and "gender." Most fundamentally, there is a problem of translation: like Rubin before her, Halley imputes to Foucault a semantic distinction between sexuality and gender that cannot be supported by the original French vocabulary that would designate such a difference.[7] Broadly speaking,

The History of Sexuality, Volume 1 (*Sexuality One*) is about sex: *le sexe*. Foucault describes *le sexe* as "a fictitious unity" produced from within the *dispositif* (grid of intelligibility) of sexuality.[8] As its linguistic ambiguity in French suggests, the "dense transfer point of power" (*HS1,* 103) Foucault calls *le sexe* includes within it all of the meanings English speakers differentiate into sex-as-organs, sex-as-biological-reproduction, sex-as-individual-gender-roles, sex-as-gendered-group-affiliation, sex-as-erotic-acts, and sex-as-lust. And if *le sexe* is produced by the *dispositif* of sexuality, this hardly means it supersedes or reverses the primacy of gender, as many queer theorists would like to claim. Sex, sexuality, and gender are inseparable and coextensive.[9]

The queer overreading of sexuality in Foucault through a causal logic that makes gender secondary or "epiphenomenal" (*SD,* 123) produces a messy tangle of problems. To begin, Foucault is not a causal thinker, either historically or conceptually speaking: Foucauldian genealogical events and concepts have no origin, but repeat themselves in complex doublings and feedback loops. Second, the queer emphasis on sexuality's primacy in Foucault reinterprets him within a non-Foucauldian identitarian logic that yields an Anglo-American division between "sexuality" and "gender." This problem is compounded by queer theory's almost exclusive focus on the Foucault of *Sexuality One*. *Sexuality One*'s "archeology of psychoanalysis" (*HS1,* 130) has been read as a critique of sexual "identity" as it emerged in the nineteenth century. In a chiastic twisting of the standard reading of Foucault, where sexuality is primary and gender is secondary, early queer theory used Foucault's critique of "sexuality" to resignify "gender" as non-identitarian and, in so doing, to trouble the stability of sexual identities as well. That radical interrogation of identity itself has been the most salient and distinctive of queer theory's claims.

But for all the value of that identitarian critique, queer theory has been less successful in articulating, beyond morality, an ethics of lived sexual experience. The result has been the kind of ethical split we see in Halley, between feminist moralists and sex-positive queers. And if Foucault has provided queer theory with an arsenal of weapons for unraveling the moralism of governance feminism, his work has been less useful for articulating sexuality within a constructive ethical frame that can actually be used as a map for living. Beyond his vague gestures toward the "resistances" of "bodies and pleasures" at the end of *Sexuality One* or, even less usefully, his descriptions of erotic subjectivities in the ancient world in the final two volumes of *History of Sexuality,* Foucault seemingly gives us little to work with for constructing an ethics that would speak to the political dilemmas of contemporary experiences of *le sexe*.

This is where I hope to reengage Foucault as a theoretical resource for a constructive ethical project that can speak to queers and feminists alike. To read sexuality in Foucault as Halley and so many "prodigal theorists" do—through the lens of sexuality as the *primum mobile* of subjectivation in *Sexuality One*—is to read only the middle of a longer Foucauldian story about sex, sexuality, and gender. And if some queer theorists have turned their attention to the end of that story in the final two volumes on the Greco-Roman world, the beginning of the story has remained virtually unexamined from either a queer or feminist theoretical perspective. I refer, specifically, to the emergence of sexuality in 1961 with Foucault's first major book, *History of Madness*.[10]

In my attention to *Madness*, I take my cue both from Foucault himself—he repeatedly refers to its importance in both published and unpublished interviews—and from Didier Eribon who, in his 1999 book, *Réflexions sur la question gay* [translated into English as *Insult and the Making of the Gay Self* (2004)], insists on the importance of *Madness* as part of Foucault's thinking about the production of non-normative sexualities.[11] Eribon focuses specifically on homosexuality as a category of unreason in the Age of Reason, and interprets Foucault to be laying the groundwork for his later critique of psychoanalysis in *Sexuality One*. As Eribon explains, the seventeenth-century exclusion of homosexuality into the domain of unreason takes place within bourgeois structures of moral exclusion that attach shame and scandal to "abnormality" and thereby silence its expression. This ultimately moral experience of unreason leads to the establishment of scientific and medical knowledge about madness in the form of psychology, psychiatry and, eventually, psychoanalysis.

Despite its obvious relevance to radical thinking about sexuality, *Madness* is seldom, if ever, cited or referred to by the leading lights of queer theory.[12] The reason for this lack of queer theoretical attention is not, as one might think, because *Madness* deals with these sexual issues only tangentially. Indeed, as Eribon notes, *Madness*'s dissection of the structures of reason and unreason in the Age of Reason constitutes an analysis of the consignment of abnormal subjects to the realm of madness, and many of those abnormals are sexually marked. Foucault's archeology of a vast field of unreason uncovers an array of figures of sexual alterity, including not only homosexuals, but also hysterics, onanists, libertines, prostitutes, debauchers, nymphomaniacs, and other sexual "abnormals." *Madness* therefore directly engages the question of sexuality as what we might call a queer experience by incorporating it within the frame of the experience of madness.

A major reason for this lack of queer attention to *Madness* has to do, I think, with the history of its translation. Indeed, translation raises not only conceptual issues, as the ambiguities of *le sexe* attest, but also the practical and institutional matter of a book's reception and impact in the world. Translation is one of those forms of what Foucault calls the "doubling" of a book-event; as he puts it in the 1972 preface to the French reedition of *Madness,* the specific doublings of translation, commentary, interpretation, retranslation, and reinterpretation determine both a book's appearance and its disappearance "into the series of events to which it belongs."[13] In the case of the sexual matters interrogated by queer theory, the non-reading of *Madness* in an English-speaking context is a direct result of its non-translation. Let me briefly recount that history.

The first English translation of *Madness* occurred in 1965, four years after its first appearance in French. Originally published in 1961 as *Folie et déraison: Histoire de la folie à l'âge classique* (Madness and unreason: History of madness in the classical age), the book was soon reissued by Plon in truncated form in an inexpensive French paperback version for "train station waiting rooms," as Foucault puts it.[14] Although pleased with a popular edition of *Madness,* Foucault was disappointed when Plon refused to republish it in its unabridged form. Not only was the French public likely to read an incomplete book but, with the exception of the Italian version, the popular edition became the basis for all the foreign language translations of the book. This explains the severely abridged English translation by Richard Howard, titled *Madness and Civilization: A History of Insanity in the Age of Reason,* that was published in 1965.[15] At 230 pages, the book was about one-third of Foucault's original version. *Madness and Civilization* was widely distributed to an American audience that had, for the most part, never heard Foucault's name before. And although the book had a considerable impact on American readers, it was not subsequently engaged by queer or feminist theorists.[16]

Forty-five years after the book's initial publication in French, a complete English translation of *Madness* finally appeared in 2006. This unabridged translation by Jonathan Murphy and Jean Khalfa includes both the 1961 and 1972 prefaces; a foreword by Ian Hacking; an introduction by Jean Khalfa; two appendices from the 1972 French edition, "Madness, the Absence of an Oeuvre" and "My Body, This Paper, This Fire"; an additional appendix, "Reply to Derrida," from a 1972 Tokyo lecture; and four critical annexes with supporting historical documents and bibliographical material. There is no denying the importance of this translation-event; for the first time, English speakers have access to the arguments that establish the groundwork for Foucault's thinking during the remaining twenty-three years of his life. It is not yet clear, however, whether or not this new translation—still poorly marketed in the United States—will have any impact on queer or feminist theory and the study of sexuality, or on the Anglo-American reception of Foucault's thought more generally. Whatever that impact might be, it is worth highlighting Ian Hacking's astute comments in the foreword that I follow. Describing the difference between the original and its translation, he writes: "Doublings: I suggest that you hold in your hands two distinct books. . . . Despite the words being the same, so much has happened that the meaning is different" (*HM*, xii). I'm interested specifically in how that difference in meaning emerges, post-queer theory, in a doubling return to sexuality in *History of Madness*.

My return to *Madness* opens an ethical interrogation into its non-reading in the English-speaking world. Specifically, I reengage *Madness* in detail through the lens of a queer theoretical project that missed it the first time around. My queer close reading of *Madness* builds on the work begun by Eribon in *Insult* but moves in a slightly different direction. Eribon's attention to homosexuality's exclusion into the world of unreason and his emphasis on Foucault's critique of psychoanalysis in *Madness* clearly make the case for a more sustained engagement with the book, especially in a queer context. My project begins where Eribon ends by looking more closely at the critique of psychoanalysis and asking, more specifically, about the question of ethics as it relates to sexual experience. Providing an alternative to the psychoanalytic language that purportedly allows the madness of sexuality to speak, *Madness* offers an alternative—what I'm calling an ethical language of eros—for articulating the difference of sexual unreason.

In the context of the moral and political issues that have led Halley and others to take a break from feminism, I focus on the ethical work a reengagement with *Madness* can do. Importantly for queer feminism, Butler in particular has engaged Foucault's later work on ethics for a conception of "ethical agency" that "is neither fully determined nor radically free."[17] But *Madness* offers resources for ethical thinking in our historical present that the Greco-Roman and Christian worlds of Foucault's later volumes cannot provide. If we continue not to read *Madness* we will miss an explicitly *modern* historicization of the rationalist moralisms that produce the queer. Foucault's genealogical approach to morality in *Madness* uses Nietzsche to move beyond moralism toward a postmoral ethics of erotic experience that we have yet to realize. This genealogy for a queer ethics is something that we, feminists and queers alike, desperately need, as an alternative both to the kind of moralism that Halley decries and to the thinness of queer ethics as it has been articulated up to the present moment. For if, despite its problems, feminism can lay claim to a robust tradition of ethical thinking, this is not the case for queer theory, which generally relies either on psychoanalytic rupture (Bersani, Edelman) or Enlightenment autonomy (Rubin, Warner) for its ethical models.[18] Foucault's *Madness* gives us a different frame for thinking about sexuality in the context of ethics that remains consistent with his life-long critique of Enlightenment humanism, his sustained problematization of psychoanalysis, and his rejection of governance politics.

Specifically, *Madness* allows us to contextualize ethics within a conception of sexuality that links the apotheosis of reason and the objectifying gaze of science with bourgeois structures of moral exclusion. This conceptual frame resituates ethics within Foucault's critique of psychoanalysis, his attention to lyricism and literary discourse, and his insistence on the category of experience as a crucial dimension of sexuality. If we ignore *Madness,* we miss a moral critique of rationalism that 1) challenges Freud's despotic "patriarchal" Oedipal model as the culmination of positivist science, 2) draws on literary devices to highlight sensibility and affect as aspects of sexuality, and 3) articulates a concept of sexual experience that both deepens and complicates Foucault's later work on ethics in *The History of Sexuality, Volume 2* and *Volume 3* (*Sexuality Two* and *Sexuality Three*).[19] All of these dimensions of ethics in *Madness* can be linked to the more explicitly ethical and political language of Foucault's middle and later work, in what Michel Feher calls Foucault's focus on "the potential for moral innovation and a politics of resistance."[20]

I want to focus here on the familiar Foucauldian theme of experience as a concept that bridges his early and late work on ethics.[21] As I mentioned above, toward the end of his life Foucault returned to his early interest in the problem of sexuality as a problem of experience. He did this, primarily, in his minute dissection of the technologies of the self that, in the Greco-Roman world, constituted sexuality as an ethical experience whose condition of possibility was freedom. That project was his attempt to release sexuality as an ethical experience from its suturing to bourgeois categories of morality— precisely the kind of moral values that Halley objects to in cultural feminism. And if in his later work Foucault explores, as Butler points out, experiences of self-making according to ancient codes of conduct that are not, like modern moral codes, codes of punishment, Foucault's ethical genealogy of an ancient world leaves open the question of how to engage the modern suturing of sexuality with morality.[22] In that context, *Madness* both explores how that suturing occurred, and forges an opening toward alternative ethical perspectives for living in the present, whether we live that present as feminists, queers or, like me, as a sometimes uncomfortable but always generative combination of the two. Remembering Foucault's final work on an ethics of experience, we can thus return to ethics in *Madness* through the back door, as it were, by asking the question Foucault posed in 1984 not long before his death: "Why [have] we made sexuality into a moral experience?"[23]

There are a number of possible responses to that question. Some might answer: it was Christianity that turned the erotic relation into something to be judged according to a rigid system of moral norms. This is, in fact, what Foucault saw after writing the still unpublished fourth volume of "History of Sexuality:

Confessions of the Flesh," about the Christian period, the practices of confession, and the beginnings of the discursive proliferation of sexuality that culminated in the modern production of perversions. If Christianity was at least partially responsible for turning sexuality into a moral experience in the Western world, how do we get out from under it? Faced with that question, it is tempting to turn, along with Foucault, toward a Greco-Roman world and an ethics of the self as self-fashioning. Such an unearthing of pre-Christian corporeal practices not coded according to a modern conception of the body and desire offers one way "out" of *assujettissement* and, specifically, the Western rationalist moralisms of Enlightenment thinking. Not a utopia, this pre-Christian Petri dish delineates a limited experimental field of forces where ethical self-fashioning in relation to others can take place within a context Foucault calls freedom.

This familiar reading of a Foucauldian ethics of self-fashioning is not a false story about Foucault. But I propose reading Foucault somewhat differently, from a different angle and under a different light. Specifically, in order to grapple with that difficult question—why have we made sexuality into a moral experience?—we must also return to *Madness* and the great division between reason and unreason. If returning to the Greeks was Foucault's way of getting out from under Christian morality, returning to the moment of splitting in the Age of Reason was Foucault's way of getting out from under philosophy's despotic moralizing power. This is not to deny either the value of Foucault's pre-Christian approach to ethics in *Sexuality Two* and *Three* or the suggestive uses that have been made of that work for ethical thinking beyond morality. Rather, it is to offer a different way of proceeding. This way of proceeding takes seriously the secular, rationalist production of a normative ethics through which the erotic bonds of modern bodies continue to be coded as moral experience. This approach to Foucault teases out, in the *Madness* book, his ethical alternative to the philosophical production of moral norms by a sovereign secular reason. That ethical alternative to rationalist morality—something we might imagine as sexual experience released from its moral frame—is what I call Foucault's ethics of eros.

That ethics is situated in a trajectory of thought that confronts the Cartesian mind-body dualism with an insistence on the role the body plays in intersubjective relations. As a site of pleasure but also of death, of erotic connection but also of pain, the body reactivates the tragic dimension of subjectivity, the fact of our life and our annihilation in the body's eventual death. In its premodern form, madness as unreason stood in for that bodily dimension of human experience: the cosmic, tragic presence of life and death—Eros and Thanatos—at the heart of all subjectivity. By the late eighteenth century, that tragic subjectivity had been masked by science in the capture of madness as mental illness.

Within that conception of modern subjectivity as a mask that hides our tragic corporeality, Foucault celebrates an erotic subjectivity that embraces the body in its experience of life and death. Paradoxically, however, to reclaim that tragic erotic experience is also to negate it as already captured by the gaze of scientific reason. As Foucault puts it in the 1961 preface to *History of Madness:* "Any perception that aims to apprehend [those insane words] in their wild state necessarily belongs to a world that has captured them already."[24] Thus the historical objectification by the Age of Reason of our bodily selves as a repudiated madness makes Foucault's reclamation of erotic experience not only tragic but also ironic, since it can only be grasped through the hindsight of its undoing.

Let me emphasize here Foucault's professed aim in writing *Madness* to describe an "experience" of madness that includes within it the "experience" of sexuality. *Madness*'s exposure of the historical split between reason and unreason traces, more than anything, an experience of alienation in the modern world. But as a description of experience, Foucault's story is odd. Philosophically speaking, *Madness* does not, as John Caputo claims, "perfectly parallel the phenomenological goal of finding a realm of pure 'prepredicative' experience, prior to its being carved out by the categories of logical grammar."[25] Indeed, there is more going on in *Madness* than the simple uncovering of a hermeneutic depth within which we will find the (mad) truth of a subject.

Neither does Foucault's history of experience make sense in traditional historiographical terms. Unlike the personal testimonies, private journals, letters, or other documents historians tend to use to get at the "truth" of an experience in the past, Foucault's materials—artistic and literary representations, individual cases documented by doctors, anonymous brochures, royal edicts, hospital regulations and rules of order, medical treatises, architectural plans, statistical inventories, and proposals for reform—are strangely impersonal. And yet he insists, over and over, that his book recounts the experience of madness.

The oddness of the relationship between the experiential claim and the lack of documents or philosophical approach that would support that claim in traditional terms suggests something about the difficulty of accessing experiences in history. Indeed, as Joan Scott argues in "The Evidence of Experience" (1991), the difficulty of that access might lead us to think differently about experience itself. Quoting Gayatri Spivak, Scott writes: "It ought to be possible . . . to 'make visible the assignment of subject-positions,' not in the sense of capturing the reality of the objects seen, but of trying to understand the operations of the complex and changing discursive processes by which identities are ascribed, resisted, or embraced, and which processes themselves are unremarked and indeed achieve their effect because they are not noticed."[26]

This astute comment by a feminist historian about the complexity of using "experience" to get at the truth of the past is especially germane to what Foucault is doing in describing the "experience" of madness and, by extension, what it means to be queer. To "captur[e] the reality of the objects seen," as Scott puts it, would be to repeat the despotic gesture of a positivist science that pins down and names sexual deviants ("EE," 408). That gesture of capture not only turns the subject into an object, but also misses the experience of sexuality altogether. In addition, because the voices of the mad have, for the most part, been lost to us—we have very few documents in which they speak for themselves and in their own words—the problem of accessing the "reality" of their experience is compounded.

As the project of a traditional historian or philosopher, then, the task of rendering the "experience" of madness, including its specifically sexual forms, is, as Foucault puts it, "doubly impossible" (*HM,* xxxii), both because the rendering captures and objectifies the subject, and because "those insane words that nothing anchors in time" (*HM,* xxxii) are lost to us. But in another, antihistorical or antiphilosophical sense, Foucault does render something like the experience of madness and sexual deviance. He does so by uncovering the "structure" and the "rudimentary *movements* of an experience . . . before it is captured by knowledge" (*HM,* xxxii, emphasis added). This is not a move, as Caputo claims, to find a pure truth that would precede knowledge—Foucault is hardly as naïve as that, as his nonlinear conception of the interdependence of history and knowledge demonstrates. Rather, Foucault is working from the perspective of the present, from *within* a knowledge that knows too much and therefore misses experience itself: "In our time," Foucault writes, "the experience of madness is made in the calm of a knowledge which, through *knowing it too much, passes it over*" (*HM,* xxxiv, emphasis added). He is thus, as Scott puts it in a different context, both "trying to understand the operations of the complex and changing discursive processes" by which mad sexuality is formed, and trying to get at those processes which are "unremarked and indeed achieve their effect because they are not noticed" ("EE," 408). In the *Madness* project, Foucault tries "to allow these words and texts"—the documented cases that form his corpus and "which came from beneath the surface of language"—"to speak of themselves" so that those words and texts might "find their place without being betrayed" (*HM,* xxxiv–xxxv).

One might be tempted to linger here, as so many Foucault critics have done, over the language of depth that figures madness "beneath [a] surface." But the images of depth are only part of the picture. Foucault knows better than anyone that if the project to bring words from beneath a surface is the attempt to avoid a betrayal, that project is doomed from the moment of its inception. For of course the betrayal is there, from the start, as the constitutive irony of the project itself: the experience of madness cannot be captured, and even if we could capture it, to do so would be to betray it. Foucault knows this well, as he states repeatedly in the pages of *Madness*. Given the irony of this inevitable betrayal, "it is tempting," as Scott puts it, "to abandon [experience] altogether" ("EE," 412). And yet, as Scott asserts, and as surely Foucault would concur: "Experience is not a word we can do without" ("EE," 412). Nowhere does this hold more true than in Foucault's project to trace the "rudimentary movements of an experience" (*HM*, xxxii) of madness. Especially with madness, "what counts as an experience is neither self-evident nor straight-forward; it is always contested, and always therefore political" ("EE," 412). The documents are thin, written most often with the words of others and never those of the mad subjects themselves. Indeed, as Foucault's 1964 essay "Madness, the Absence of an Oeuvre" makes abundantly clear, when the mad actually "speak"—as in the empirical cases of Nerval, Nietzsche, and Roussel—their "work" disappears. Their experience becomes, then, the opening of a question, an approach that "interrogates the processes of [a subject's] creation" and, in so doing, "refigures history . . . and opens new ways for thinking about change" ("EE," 412).

I emphasize this problem of experience in order to contrast Foucault's project in *Madness* with the project he undertakes in *Sexuality One*. Specifically, one of the queer sexual experiences *Madness* describes is the disappearance of a Renaissance "homosexual lyricism" in the Age of Reason, a kind of closeting of the queer through the suppression of its expression. This suppression corresponds to the historical cessation of the physical execution of sodomites. So as the last sodomitical body burns in the eighteenth century, a fire begins to rage that will engulf in its flames an entire lyrical world of queer sentiment and sensation. We can see in this example from *Madness* that Foucault is tracing "the rudimentary movements of an experience" (*HM*, xxxii) by, paradoxically, describing its disappearance. Neither the lyricism nor its silencing captures the experience of homosexuality itself, either as a historical truth or as the result of a phenomenological *epoché* (bracketing). But this hardly means that sexual experience has no relevance for the story Foucault wants to tell. The image of a disappearance—as the shadow of "homosexual lyricism" sinking over the edge of the horizon of reason—ultimately renders something that had not been noticed before. And that something is what Foucault describes as a world of expression, sensation, and sensibility "whose wild state," like madness, "can never be reconstituted," but that we can, nonetheless, "strain our ears" to hear (*HM*, xxxii–xxxiii).

The result is a certain thickness and stylistic flourish in the written qualities of *Madness* itself: a descriptive density, rhetorical texture, imagistic play and—why not say it?—a certain lyricism that produces not only a cognitive effect, but also, importantly, translates as affect in the manner of a "literary" text. Indeed, Foucault's rendering of a movement of alienation—the experience of being queer—that stretches from the age of lepers to the age of Freud is not only conceptually antiphilosophical, but also stylistically so. And this signals not only a writerly quality apparent to all who read Foucault, but also, as Deleuze puts it, "a style of life, not at all something personal, but the invention of a possibility of life, of a mode of existence."[27] Nowhere is this stylistic quality as a style of life—what we might call a writerly eros—more visible than in *Madness*. Again Deleuze, in his comments on Foucault, must surely have been thinking of *Madness* when he described Foucault as "a great stylist. Concepts take on with him the rhythmic quality, or, as in the strange dialogues with himself with which he closes some of his books, a contrapuntal one. His syntax builds up the shimmerings and scintillations of the visible but also twists like a whip, folding and unfolding, or cracking in time to the rhythm of its utterances" (*Neg,* 101).

But if *Madness* is marked by the lyrical thickness of a stylistic flair that uses the texture of writing to transmit the erotic qualities of sexual experience— what Deleuze calls "style . . . [as] a way of existing"—that sense of a "possibility of life" (*Neg,* 100) is entirely missing from Foucault's rendering of sexuality in the first volume of *History of Sexuality* fifteen years later. In *Sexuality One,* sexuality is thin—as Nietzsche might put it: "as thin as if it were stretched between two membranes."[28] No longer articulated in terms of the "rudimentary movements" of a subject's experience as "scintillations of the visible" (*Neg,* 101) or twists of a whip, sexuality in *Sexuality One* reflects Foucault's turn in the early 1970s toward what he calls a microphysics of power and away from the rhetoric and imagery of "representations"—precisely those aspects of *Madness* that make it thick. As the French title of *Sexuality One* (*La Volonté de savoir*) insists, modern sexuality in that volume is the discursive and nondiscursive result of an objectifying "will to knowledge" that has developed over time to specify sexual "individuals" (*HS1,* 43) as a tantalizing array of perversions within a *dispositif* or cultural grid of intelligibility. And if the *dispositif* is complex, it is also thin: "a great surface network" (*HS1,* 105). It is a skeleton that has no flesh, no passion, no eros. And if it has style—which I think it does—the style is as thin as the sexuality it describes. As a "style of life" (*HS1,* 100), *Sexuality One* offers us the aporetic rhetoric and anorectic imagery of an erotic experience whose possibility is no longer even a shadow.

Even its ghost, it seems, has disappeared altogether under the objectifying gaze of science.

I insist on the thinness of the *dispositif* not only to contrast an experiential *Madness* with a discursive *Sexuality One,* but also to demonstrate what will be missed when readers engage Foucauldian sexuality only through the lens of his middle and later work. Reencountering Foucault in *Sexuality One,* through the lens of a *Madness* that most of his queer and feminist readers have missed altogether, allows me to resituate his thinking about sexuality as a consistent engagement, from start to finish, with the problem of ethics. The concepts and frames for thinking about sex that emerge out of that process of reengagement and revision challenge some of the most dogmatically reiterated *idées reçues* about sexuality in Foucault. More constructively, they point toward the project of a queer ethics that would release queer feminists from an agonizing moral split.

Specifically, in highlighting sexuality as an ethics of experience, I want to contest the ubiquitous readings of Foucault that interpret him primarily as a historian who rearranges sexual acts and identities on a linear timeline. This is important for the feminist-queer split, because the queer position explicitly constructs itself as a non-identitarian intervention into the petrifying logic of normative identities associated with categories like "woman." It would be easy to fill a book with the numerous examples, from historians and nonhistorians alike, of scholarship that captures sexuality in Foucault as primarily a denaturalization of sexual identity through its precise localization in history. Especially problematic are those introductions that present Foucault to an uninitiated audience of virgin readers. Let me give just a few examples.

Tamsin Spargo asserts, in *Foucault and Queer Theory* (1999), that Foucault "insisted that the category of the homosexual grew out of a particular context in the 1870s."[29] Along the same lines, in *Queer Theory: An Introduction* (1996), Annamarie Jagose is impressed by a Foucault who is "confident" enough to furnish "an exact date for the invention of homosexuality."[30] More recently, in their introduction to the interdisciplinary anthology, *Queer Studies* (2003), Robert Corber and Steven Valocchi state that "Foucault traced the transformation of sexuality in modern societies from a set of *practices* and relations governed by religious and secular law into a set of *identities* regulated by norms."[31] The examples of these assertions about Foucault's purported specification of the invention of homosexual identity in the nineteenth century are as pervasive as they are repetitive. Virtually every reader of Foucault with an interest in queer sexuality begins with *Sexuality One,* and often with two preconceptions already, like perversions, implanted in their heads: first, that Foucault contrasts earlier sexual *acts* with later sexual *identities;* and second, that Foucault locates the moment of the shift from one to the other at a precise point in the nineteenth century.

In order to buttress and build on those assertions, queer Foucauldians typically cite the following passage, which I quote at length both in French and English. I will spend some time on the passage in order to tease out the larger conceptual assertions I want to make, countering what I view as queer theory's repeated misreadings of Foucault. I also linger on the passage as another acknowledgement of the concept of "translation" in our collective thinking about sex, sexuality, and gender. For reasons that will become clear, I italicize those words and phrases, in both the French and English versions, where the English translation will produce a significant distortion of the French meaning. After citing the passage in French, I include in brackets within the English translation a more precise rendering of the terms in question:

> Cette chasse nouvelle aux sexualités périphériques entraîne une incorporation des perversions et une spécification nouvelle des individus. La sodomie—celle des anciens droits civil ou canonique—était un type d'actes interdits; *leur auteur* n'en était que le sujet juridique. L'homosexuel du XIXe siècle est devenu *un personnage:* un passé, une histoire et une enfance, un caractère, une forme de vie; une morphologie aussi, avec une anatomie indiscrète et peut-être une physiologie mystérieuse. Rien de ce qu'il *est* au total n'*échappe* à sa sexualité. Partout en lui, elle *est* présente: sous-jacente à toutes ses conduites parce qu'elle en *est* le principe insidieux et indéfiniment actif; inscrite sans pudeur sur son visage et sur son corps parce qu'elle *est* un secret qui se trahit toujours. Elle lui *est* consubstantielle, moins comme un péché d'habitude que comme une nature singulière. Il ne faut pas oublier que la catégorie psychologique, psychiatrique, médicale de l'homosexualité s'est constituée du jour où on l'a caractérisée—le *fameux* article de Westphal en 1870, sur les "sensations sexuelles contraires" peut valoir comme date de naissance—moins par un type de relations sexuelles que par une certaine qualité de la sensibilité sexuelle, une certaine manière d'intervertir en soi-même le masculin et le féminin. L'homosexualité est apparue comme une des *figures* de la sexualité lorsqu'elle *a été rabattue* de la pratique de la sodomie sur une sorte d'androgynie intérieure, un hermaphrodisme de l'âme. Le sodomite *était un relaps,* l'homosexuel *est* maintenant une espèce.[32]

This new persecution of the peripheral sexualities entailed an incorporation of perversions and a new specification of individuals. As defined by the ancient civil or canonical codes, sodomy was a category of forbidden acts; *their perpetrator* [their author] was nothing more than the juridical subject of them. The nineteenth-century homosexual became *a personage* [a character]: a past, a case history, and a childhood, in addition to being a type of life, a life form, and a morphology, with an indiscreet anatomy and possibly a mysterious physiology. *Nothing that went into his total composition was unaffected by* [Nothing of what he is, in total, escapes] his sexuality. It *was* [is] everywhere present in him: at the root of all his actions because it *was* [is] their insidious and indefinitely active principle; written immodestly on his face and body because it *was* [is] a secret that always *gave itself away* [gives itself away]. It *was* [is] consubstantial with him, less as a habitual sin than as a singular nature. We must not forget that the psychological, psychiatric, medical category of homosexuality was constituted from the moment it was characterized—Westphal's *famous* [notorious (with strong irony)] article of 1870 on "contrary sexual sensations" can stand as its date of birth—less by a type of sexual relations than by a certain quality of sexual sensibility, a certain way of inverting the masculine and feminine in oneself. Homosexuality appeared as one of the *forms* [figures] of sexuality when it was *transposed* [cut away] from the practice of sodomy [and reattached] onto a kind of interior androgyny, a hermaphrodism of the soul. The sodomite *had been* [was] a *temporary aberration* [a fall back into heresy]; the homosexual *was* [is] now a species.[33]

This passage from *Sexuality One* is undoubtedly one of the most frequently quoted passages of Foucault's corpus. It has been quoted and requoted—not only by queer theorists and feminists, but also by historians, literary critics, and legal scholars—to fashion arguments about the relative merits, or lack thereof, of conceptualizing sexuality as either acts or identities in particular contexts or historical moments. This proliferation of citations, often from a not-quite-precise English translation, has had a number of consequences, not least of which is a drastic simplification of what Foucault is actually saying in the paragraph. My intent is not to be pedantic by indulging in obscure etymologies or hair-splitting differences of definition. Rather, because of the considerable importance of the passage in question for an entire generation of thinking about sexuality, I linger on what I see as some key distortions of interpretation in order to challenge what have long been considered to be some basic Foucauldian queer "truths." Indeed, since Foucault insisted on the instability of what he called the "games of truth," it seems appropriate to question those truths that have somehow solidified into a kind of queer dogma.

When one reads the passage closely, both with *Madness* in mind and with an attention to the nuances of Foucault's French terminology, one may be surprised that the passage has been so widely read as a definitive statement about sodomitical acts becoming homosexual identity in the nineteenth century. That commonly accepted reading of Foucault is questionable for a number of reasons. First, from the start we see quite clearly that nowhere in the passage does the word "identity" appear. In fact, it is a word that Foucault uses infrequently, usually ironically or in its arithmetical meaning: identity as equality.[34] Like most of his French compatriots, Foucault saw identity, in its personal and political meanings, as a specifically American obsession. In the passage, he uses the words *individus* (individuals), *personnage* (character), and *figure* (figure) to name a phenomenon of emergence that Anglo-American readers have interpreted, again and again, as identity. And while an "individual"—a single human being—could have the personality or specific traits that, together, we sometimes call an identity, this is not necessarily the case. Particularly in queer and feminist theory, "identity" means not only a general sense of identification or sameness (from the Latin *idem*) in one's relation to oneself or to others. It also includes, more importantly, the connotations of group belonging or affiliation associated with American identity politics. Identity in this political sense is what the French tend to call the *communautarisme* of American politics, as opposed to a French *universalisme* that grows out of their republican political tradition. In fact, more often than not, from a French perspective the "individual" is viewed as exemplifying the free choices and freedoms of a French republicanism that stands *in opposition* to an "identity" that grows out of an American *communautarisme*. Indeed, as Éric Fassin points out, since the 1990s French philosophers like Alain Finkelkraut and Frédéric Martel have reclaimed, "recycled," and repatriated Foucault—"as a titular figure of French republicanism"—a philosophical force of "individual" French resistance against what is viewed, sometimes homophobically, as the scourge of American "identity" politics: the "communitarian wind that blows in the U.S.," as sociologist Irène Théry so derisively puts it.[35]

This initial suspicion about an assumed equivalence between Foucault's "individual" and an Americanized "identity," in either the political or personal sense of the word, is confirmed by the other terms. Both *personnage* and *figure* (officially translated as "personage" and "form," respectively) highlight an understanding of sexuality as the fictive or metaphorical product of a representational order, like a character in a play or the protagonist of a novel or even the "face" acquired through a rhetorical troping. In addition, the seemingly minor matter of punctuation becomes important here. In the French version, *personnage* is not one of a long series of attributes separated by commas—"a personage, a past, a case history, a childhood," and so forth—thus constituting, as "personage," one of the elements that, taken together, might form an identity. In fact, a colon separates the "character" from the attributes with which it is endowed; those attributes are deposited within the character that simply provides a container for them. In that sense, the *personnage* is not so different from the social types one might find in a medieval morality play or a Renaissance allegory like the Bosch paintings or Brandt's narrative verses about the *Ship of Fools* that Foucault invokes at the beginning of *Madness*.

However, a familiarity with *Madness* provides a clue to one important difference between the Renaissance *personnage* and its modern version. It is *not* the distinction between acts and identities that matters, as so many readers have asserted, but rather the difference between the ethical universes each set of characters represents. The Renaissance figure of the ship of fools in *Madness*'s opening chapter, "*Stultifera Navis*," symbolizes a moving social microcosm in its struggle with complex ethical questions about love and the body, one's relations with others, life's destiny in death, and how reason and unreason determine the limits of subjectivity. The individual "character" who emerges in *Sexuality One*, by contrast, is an isolated, objectified puppet-like figure whose insides—its past, its childhood, its inner life—is merely the reversal of what the gaze of science sees on the outside: "written immodestly," as Foucault puts it, "on his face and body." This structure of reversal is only an identity to the extent that identity names a subject deprived of the complexity of lived experience. It is not an identity in either the political or personal sense—in the fullness of its lived, experiential meanings—but rather the draining away of erotic life into a thin shadow Foucault calls "sexuality."

Read through the lens of the moral reorganization that *Madness* describes, this ethical shift from the ship of fools to a modern scientific morality play provides a key for reinterpreting the relationship between acts and the characters who perform them. In *Sexuality One*, modern "characters" act, but only as the medicalized, psychiatric doubles of premodern juridical subjects; as specifically "homosexual" characters, they are what Foucault calls in *Abnormal* the "ethico-moral doubles" of premodern sodomites.[36] In the passage I have cited from *Sexuality One*, this psychiatric doubling and objectification of the modern homosexual "character" is reinforced by its opposition, lost in the English translation, to the earlier term that is its binary complement: the "author" of sodomitical acts. Further, the "character" in question is not "socially constructed" by some interchangeable, generalizable array of juridical, pedagogical, literary, or political *dispositifs*, as many have implied. Rather, he is specifically constructed by psychological science. The combined structures of rationalist exclusion and bourgeois morality which led to the apotheosis of that science is precisely what the six hundred pages of *History of Madness* so meticulously describes. Here in *Sexuality One*, Foucault insists on the fictional construction of the ontological essence that results from the apotheosis of the psyche as sexual:

"what he *is, in total*" is the creation of a "*psychological, psychiatric, medical category*" (*HS1,* 43, emphasis added).

So if the ancient "juridical" subject was still the "author" or agent of the acts for which he was then judged according to a moral code, here the modern medical subject faces a different kind of moral control with the depositing of guilt and shame into the heart of his inner life: an alienated, monstrous sexual interiority. *Madness* describes how that internalization of bourgeois morality occurs, from the moment of the great confinement to its culmination in the creation of the Freudian unconscious. With the rise of positivism, that inner life has been frozen into the attributes of a character to be viewed under a microscope and dissected into the elements that constitute a "case history." This ethical alteration describes not so much the constitution of a modern "identity"—again, Foucault does not use the word here—than it does a process of rationalist, positivist objectification. The premodern juridical subject who was the "author" of his acts comes out of the Age of Reason as the object, puppet, or character of the psychiatric author or agent who created him.

In that sense he is not simply neutrally "transposed," as the English translation of *rabattue* suggests at the end of the passage. Rather, psychological knowledge cuts out or abstracts "homosexuality" from a thicker set of experiences called sodomitical practice that involve not only the singular body of a sodomite but also a form of social organization that Foucault calls "a type of sexual relations." Knowledge diminishes that complex, subjective, relational experience of sexuality by capturing it and pinning it down as a "figure" it can use. The verb *rabattre,* from the Latin *abattere* ("to beat," "to fell"), insists on this sense of a weakening, a diminishment, or even a fall from what came before: the practice of sodomy within a perhaps brutal system of moral codes, but within which the juridical subject was the "author" of his acts. The diminishment of *rabattre* also reinforces a sense of the repetition of an earlier "fall" back into a condition designated by the specifically religious meaning of the word *relaps* in the final sentence. Not a "temporary aberration," as the English translation would have it, "the sodomite was a *relaps*": a fall back into a *heresy* that had been previously abjured.

But if the fall into heresy—produced as the repeated, iterative acts of "habitual sin"—marks a position of resistance, however tenuous or unsuccessful, to the dogma of the age, such is not the case for the modern equivalent of that religious fall. With the fall of modern homosexuality into "a singular nature" that cannot be changed, the possibilities contained in the agency and resistance of the heretical sodomite disappear. As science rises, the homosexual falls into his modern condition as object: "the homosexual is now a species" (*HS1,* 59). Thus an ethical experience—the judgment, choices, acts, feelings, sensations, sensibilities, and forms of relation of resisting, heretical subjects together—is degraded and reversed as a singular essence or "sensibility" within. The subject-turned-object can have no experience—resistant or otherwise, relational or not—that would constitute an ethical life of freedom. Although as a "character" he acts *like* a subject engaged in practices of freedom, as a medicalized double he can only act as a puppet. The condition of possibility of an ethics of experience—the freedom to be the author of one's acts, to form relationships, to make judgments, and to resist—have been taken away from the now fully subjugated (*assujetti*) subject-as-object captured by the rationalizing gaze of science.

I insist on this detailed attention to the French and English versions of *Sexuality One* in order to make a larger point about queer theoretical readings of Foucault, of which Halley's reading is but one example. Reengaging *Sexuality One* through the ethical lens of *Madness* both challenges and complicates categorical interpretations of a taxonomic Foucault who would simply slot sexualities into acts or identities at a precise moment in history. As *Madness* demonstrates, the objectifying act of the rationalist puppeteer does not occur only once, or as a singular event in time; it happens over and over, taking different shapes during different periods. Indeed, even in *Sexuality One,* which lacks the detail and nuance of *Madness,* one can see that the objectification of sexual alterity is ongoing, as the repeated French verbs in the historical present tense insist: "It *is* everywhere present in him," "it *is* a secret that always betrays itself," "it *is* consubstantial with him," and "the homosexual *is* now a species." This sense of the ongoing nature of subjectivation also marks sexuality in the past, reinforced here by the imperfect tense of the verb *être* in the final sentence: "The sodomite was a fall back into heresy." Oddly rendered as "had been" in the English version, the better translation of *était* as "was" conveys a past whose beginning and end cannot be specified; the *imparfait* verb form signals the past as a condition or state of being that not only happens again and again, but cannot be definitively separated from the time of the present. Thus the time of the sodomite and the time of the homosexual are coextensive. And yet, if we take seriously the historic breach between reason and unreason after the Renaissance, they are also radically incommensurable with each other. In that sense, the historical, epistemic movement that links the ancient sodomite to the modern homosexual makes them, paradoxically, both temporally coextensive and conceptually untranslatable.

As *Madness* shows, the modern epistemic breach that divides the sodomite from the homosexual "begins" with the Cartesian coup of the *cogito* and the great confinement of the mad in hospitals during the seventeenth century; this coup will be repeated by different actors over the course of the centuries—by

Tuke and Pinel in the eighteenth century, by Charcot in the nineteenth, and by Freud in the twentieth. Those with a taste for the acclaim and career-making precision of a positivist discovery will proclaim, as Foucault parodically does in the famous passage from *Sexuality One,* that we can objectively pin down the exact date of birth of a new scientifically designated "species." And so, the story goes, Foucault declares the birth of homosexual identity in 1870.

But given all that we know about genealogy, rupture, and a Foucauldian conception of the past that refuses to posit an origin of *anything,* these "straight" readings of Foucault seem naïve. We can only read this inaccurate declaration—the actual date of Westphal's article is 1869—of the "notorious" scientific birthday of "the homosexual" as highly ironic, in the same way that "identity" can only be ironically American from a French perspective.[37] We can only hear Foucault's "confident dating," as Jagose puts it, of homosexuality's birth, as the parodic repetition of what a serious scientist might confidently assert.[38] And in case we didn't get it, that irony is underscored by the French "*fameux*" which describes the scientific paper where the birthday declaration is so notoriously made; unlike *célèbre,* which carries the "straight" meaning of famous, *fameux* is usually tinged—again, like "identity"—with a slightly derisive irony. Indeed, to read the date 1870 as other than ironic is to buy into the psychological, psychiatric, and medical authority that Foucault goes to great pains to dismantle.

Thus rather than opposing acts and identities along the linear timeline of history, as so many identity-obsessed readers are wont to do, Foucault describes here an ethical shift with regard to sexuality that is perfectly clear if we read the passage through the lens of *Madness.* "Juridical" morality before the advent of modern psychology translates certain "acts" into a mode of subjectivity we might describe as practices or ways of living. Another form of morality—what we might call, following Nietzsche, the morality of interiority—creates a "character" (*personage*) and the illusion of an inner life: the modern soul. That new subjectivity is the product of a rationalism that creates a psyche and, along with it, psychology, psychiatry, and psychoanalysis. Not only that, with the advent of the psyche, exteriority is transformed and captured: science manages the horizontal complexity of "sexual relations" and "the masculine and the feminine" by "inverting" that complexity through a play of mirrors that makes it appear as an inner depth (*HS1,* 43). And if the psychic management of sexual alterity is no less despotic than the ancient juridical codes through which sodomitical acts were judged, it masks that despotism through the inverting process.

If we haven't read *Madness* in its unabridged form, we will miss the nuances of those ethical meanings that flicker across the surface of *Sexuality One;*

we will read it, instead, as so many have, as a categorical claim about acts and identities in history. For indeed, what we don't get here in *Sexuality One* is the complex scaffolding that explains how those shifts occur in relation to rationalist structures of exclusion, the shifts Foucault describes in *Madness* as the ethical reorganization of love and unreason. Over the course of *Madness*, a Nietzschean genealogy of those rationalist structures emerges in Foucault's critique of the bourgeois production of morality as interiority. Although Nietzsche's *Genealogy of Morals* is never directly cited in *Madness*, Foucault's repeated descriptions of the institutional and conceptual structures that link reason and unreason to the historical emergence of a moral subject make clear his indebtedness to Nietzsche's conception of a self-negating "bad conscience" that grounds the modern humanist subject. *Madness* shows us that Foucault's story is not about an absolute historical shift from acts to identities; rather, it is about the internalization of bourgeois morality that produces, eventually, the "fable" (*HS1*, 35) of an inner psyche, soul, or conscience. Only in this way does the "thin" homosexual "thing" of modern science acquire the illusory "thickness"—a self-doubling trick of mirrors—of what so many have called an "identity." It may be more accurate, like Foucault with his "fable," to call that thickness the fiction of the psyche. That psyche is a "character" that inverts the magnificent exterior diversity of the world—the proliferating gender trouble of homosexuals, androgynes, hermaphrodites, and all they will become as modern gender-queers—and stuffs it "inside." That "inside," of course, doesn't really exist in what is merely the flat space of a scientific fiction. But if the inner "secret" of sexuality is ultimately no secret at all, it is nonetheless "indispensable" as the "fable" that is "written immodestly" (*HS1*, 43) all over a queer object, which rationalism and morality want to contain.

Generally speaking, then, the interest of sexuality in Foucault is not to plot acts versus identities on a historical timeline. Foucault reminds us, again and again, that he is not a historian. Rather, he "uses" history in a particular way, to locate those moments of rupture that Deleuze would describe, along with Blanchot, as the confinement of the outside.[39] The seventeenth century is one of those moments for several reasons, including, most pertinently in the case of *Madness*, the advent of Cartesian rationalism and the great confinement of the mad in the hospitals of Paris. The classical age is obviously not the only moment of rupture in the story of sexuality; neither is it the first. There is nothing in Foucault's analysis that excludes the possibility of medieval sodomites as "personages" or Renaissance tribades as "characters." But as Foucault insists numerous times in *Madness*, the historical "geography" within which those characters appear is "half-real, half-imaginary" (*HM*, 11, translation modified). They are spatiotemporal Deleuzian "diagrams" or "assemblages," continual processes of folding and unfolding that describe Foucault's histories as repeated but changing stories. In that conception, acts and identities cannot emerge just once, because history itself is an ongoing process of emergence. As Deleuze puts it: "That everything is always said in every age is perhaps Foucault's greatest historical principle."[40]

If we understand this strongly anti-Historical (with a capital H) dimension of Foucault's histories, we can make some headway into the endless debates about acts versus identities and how they emerge in history. It would be difficult to overstate how strongly Foucault rejects a Sartrean "totalizing" sense of history that would pin *anything* down—sexual or otherwise—as an object of knowledge fully available to "human consciousness," as he puts it in an unpublished interview with Roger-Pol Droit.[41] Even more important, the insistent focus on a binary choice between acts and identities—a choice that effaces Foucault's reference to "sexual sensibility" (*HS1*, 43) in *Sexuality One* as the inverted thing pinned down by science—disregards entirely the affective dimension of erotic experience. We are more than the fables we tell about ourselves—that aspect of sexuality that readers of Foucault have called our modern Western identities. We are also more than the juridical interpretation of what our bodies do—that dimension of subjectivity that the famous passage from *Sexuality One* calls our acts. To miss the nuance of what Foucault is saying, and limit ourselves merely to a choice between acts and identities, in fact reinscribes the Cartesian coup—splitting the mind from the body—that was so effective in rationalizing the great confinement.

My purpose in challenging a pervasive understanding of identity in Foucault is ultimately not negative but constructive: to expand Foucauldian conceptions of sexuality to encompass the problems of lived experience in relation to our historical and political present. Such an expansion can occur on the far side of a critique that challenges acts versus identities in *Sexuality One* through the retrospective lens of *Madness*. So what specifically does the acts versus identities critique bring us, constructively speaking?

First, it allows us to shift the terms of historical scholarship on sexuality, displacing arguments about acts versus identities toward other, more interesting questions about the specific configurations of bodies, sensibilities, sensations, feelings, acts, and relations in different times and places, without being trapped in a rigid binary frame for thinking about those configurations. Second, within Foucault scholarship itself, we can resolve what Eribon sees as the "contradictory presentations" of the historical "invention" of homosexuality in *Madness* and *Sexuality One,* in the seventeenth and nineteenth centuries, respectively.[42] As we have seen, a linear timeline is beside the point, and contradiction doesn't end with the seventeenth century, as we can clearly see with the disappearance of a specifically "homosexual" lyricism Foucault associates with the European Renaissance. Third, in conceptual terms, we can alter our focus away from the Anglo-American concept of identity toward a more capacious understanding of gendered, sexual experience—as lyrical or silenced, relational or confined—that includes, beyond acts and identities, the thick residue of sensations and sensibilities that constitutes an ever-expanding "archive of feelings," to borrow Ann Cvetkovich's evocative title.[43] This shift toward experience promises to be a more fruitful approach to sexuality and gender in Foucault than the search for an "identity" that Foucault himself does not directly invoke. It will allow us to open up new questions for queer and feminist scholarship, moving our inquiry away from the "identity" versus "non-identity" binarism on which, to a large extent, the concept of queerness was founded—with the "queer" constituting the non-identitarian, slightly Frenchified alternative to a flat-footed American feminist (or LGBTQI) identitarian position. Reading the passage through the lens of *Madness* as I have done turns the queer toward the question of sexuality and ethics, where it has needed to turn for far too long. We can let go of the need to pin Foucault down on a historical timeline and turn to ethical questions about sexuality that can speak to our political present.

In more general terms, this close reading of *Sexuality One* in the light of *Madness* shows more clearly the salient conceptual figures in Foucault that have worked to define what we mean by queer theory. The thin, de-eroticized model of sexuality we find in *Sexuality One* has significantly shaped the discursive terms within which queer theory has been framed. Put simply, it has produced a queer theory that, in many of its manifestations, is drained of the experience of life and love, of eros. *Madness,* by contrast, engages sexuality as a field of sensibility, sensation, and forms of relation that cannot be reduced to a binary choice between acts and identities or the "singular nature" (*HS1,* 43) of modern science described in *Sexuality One.* Further, *Madness*'s coding of sexuality as "lyrical" links this repressed sensibility to a literary history of sexuality that Foucault will swerve away from in his later work. The loss of the affective, literary expression of sexual experience produces, in *Sexuality One,* a theory of sexuality that, in pinning down "sexual sensibility" (*HS1,* 43) as simple inversion, actually cuts sexuality off from the world of sensibility and lived experience from which to shape an ethics.

So what ultimately is at stake for queer and feminist theories in this reading of *Madness* as a story about sexuality? In *Madness,* what is now sexuality emerges out of an experience of love as eros, but only to be targeted as the site of ethical condemnation in the Age of Reason. This perspective on love provides a piece of the answer to Foucault's 1984 riddle—why have we made sexuality into a moral experience? We have done so, we might say, because eros was repudiated by the Cartesian splitting of the mind from the body and forced underground in the great confinement. The object of this repudiation and confinement was not simply a set of bodily acts or identities at a specific moment in history, although acts, identities, and history constitute a few of the elements of a more complex movement of confinement Foucault describes in *Madness*. That complexity shows that confinement cannot be reduced to acts and identities in a linear history. Blanchot saw this complexity in Foucault better than anyone, as Deleuze reminds us in *Foucault:* "Confinement refers to an outside, and what is confined is precisely the outside. It is by excluding or placing outside that the assemblages confine something."[44]

From that perspective, what I'm calling erotic love might describe an ethical attitude or sensibility that remains unconfined and unexcluded; its condition of possibility is figured as freedom. Diagrammatic examples of this freedom can be found, historically, not only in the Renaissance figure of the ship of fools or the tragic lyricism of its poets, but also in the Platonic eros of ancient Greece. Even after its containment in the great confinement, eros emerges as glimmers of freedom in the amorous literary experimentation of the *précieuses* (*HS1,* 89); in the libertine writings of Sade (*HS1,* 104, 532–35); and throughout *Madness,* in the mad rebirth of lyricism in Nietzsche, Nerval, Artaud, Hölderlin, and Roussel. In this way the diagram is always becoming something other. It both speaks to the specificity of an event in history and, at the same time, signals the ongoing possibility of transformation in a conception of history as nonlinear. "The diagram," Deleuze writes, "stems from the outside but the outside does not merge with any diagram, and continues instead to 'draw' new ones. In this way the outside is always an opening on to a future; nothing ends, since nothing has begun, but everything is transformed."[45]

This conception of an open future traces the outline of an erotic alterity whose presence is crucial in Foucault. The glimmers of eros that episodically burst through the pages of *History of Madness* and other Foucault writings point to what I call an erotic other as the figure for an ethical love conceived as freedom. She corresponds to what Caputo calls, in the later Foucault, "the murmurings of a capacity to be otherwise."[46] I argue here that this murmuring of otherness is there, from the start, as a consistent presence in all of Foucault's writing, as "scintillations of the visible" and a "style of life." For if that otherness is silenced in the great confinement, that closeting is never total. If it were, we would never know that the erotic other had ever been there at all. In her emergence as ghost—as the persistent shadow of something leaving—she is both there and not there, as images and murmurings that both reactivate the monstrous imaginary of earlier ages and transform themselves into new forms of monstrosity. Ironically, because she is closeted, eros is as muted in Foucault as she is in the philosophical and historical discourses he contests. Nonetheless, her stuttering voice is not only *Madness*'s most important one, but a voice that signals, over and over in Foucault's writings, interviews, and lectures, the persistence of an ethical resistance to "the great confiscation of sexual ethics by family morality" (*HM*, 89).

The voice of that resistance is one that can be claimed by queers and feminists alike. It is a lyrical and ironic voice that both ruptures and amplifies the still dominant voices of rationalism and moralizing family values. It is easy to mishear it, emerging as it does in the gaps of the pervert's silence or the hysteric's delirious babble. As the result of an erotic *assujettissement*, the voice is both old and new, trapped and free: both "all that is strange in man . . . suffocated and reduced to silence" (*HS1*, 431, translation modified) and a defiant, living strangeness. Like the heretic closeted in the word *relaps* in *Sexuality One*, she never disappears altogether. If we had to give her a modern name, we would have to call her queer.

Let me return, like the prodigal son, to the place where I began, with Janet Halley's image of queers as rebellious children who, unlike the Biblical character, seem unlikely to come back to the fold from which they emerged. I want to "put my cards on the table," to use one of Halley's favorite phrases. As a queer feminist, I object to the "Taking a Break project" (*SD*, 38) and would make a bid to disqualify Foucault as one of its progenitors. To be sure, Foucault's capacity to raise feminist eyebrows is undeniable, as is demonstrated by the famous Jouys passage in *Sexuality One* or his 1977 comments to David Cooper about rape and penal reform, to offer but two examples.[47] Nonetheless, I want to argue for a Foucault who provides us, in *Madness,* with a valuable, still untapped store of conceptual resources for dealing with the sexual dilemmas that continue to fracture us into "split decisions."

I recognize that in my desire to remain a "queer feminist" and, more generally, to keep feminists and queers together, Halley would see me as a "convergentist," a position that she, as a clear "divergentist," ultimately eschews. She doubts that the "convergentist ambitions of feminism" will "bring the prodigals back home" (*SD*, 34). And even though she admits that "prodigal theories . . . have their own will to power" and are, like feminists, likely to "get blood on their hands," in Halley's view they will only do so if they become convergentist, a political position she equates with being "prescriptive" and threatening "to wield power while denying it" (*SD*, 34–35). But the divergentist Halley—"a sex-positive postmodernist, only rarely and intermittently feminist" (*SD*, 15)—could herself be accused of convergentism in her prescriptive performance of a judicial decision to "Take a Break" from a feminism she repudiates. And if the "rarely and intermittently feminist" quotation vitiates that accusation, the phrase rings false in the context of a book whose rhetorical force is that of a "how to" manual designed to teach its readers "how and why" to split up with feminism completely. Given how generative even intermittent queer-feminist affinities can be, I wish Halley's "break" were less categorical. What are the ethical terms within which the rare or not-so-rare conjunctions between sex-positivism and feminism might—do, in fact—occur? What are the conditions of possibility for a more constructive and more visible realization of that intriguing conjunction? Or should the terms themselves be subjected to scrutiny—not just "feminism," as a limiting form of personal and political self-positioning, but also "sex-positivism," as a term that epitomizes the modern, scientistic, positivist "sex" project that Foucault spent his life critiquing?

Foucault's story about sexuality in *History of Madness* uses the great split between reason and unreason to reframe the binary oppositions that function, like Halley's, to split sexuality across an ethical divide. For if *Madness* brings together, along convergentist lines, all those categories of otherness labeled as unreason, it also, divergently, speaks to those differences that Halley cele-brates as the specifically queer—and *not feminist*—"revelations of the strange-ness and unknowability of social and sexual life" (*SD,* 15). But as Foucault, Irigaray, and other thinkers of difference have been arguing since the 1960s, the divergentist move is the move of alterity: both the result of exclusion and the reclaiming of one's otherness as a stance of resistance to the processes of othering through which the exclusion occurred. To remain stuck in that stance—what Halley calls convergentism—is hardly the sin of feminists alone, nor does it define all feminism. As just one example, a queer Irigaray—whom Halley unfairly recuperates under the cultural feminist banner—powerfully demonstrates that processes of othering endlessly reproduce a he-gemonic structure of the Other of the Same. It is not unlike the structure that Foucault calls the great split between reason and unreason. Stuckness is the problem, and that can be true for queers as well as feminists, for a project about sexuality as well as one that focuses on gender.

So let me end by retelling this story about queerness not as Halley tells it, but in a madly Foucauldian rewriting. The story of queerness—as a story about madness—begins with the story of a split: the great division between reason and unreason. That split organizes Foucault's *histoire*—his history and his story—about forms of subjectivity tossed into a dustbin called madness. Queer is a name we have given to one of those forms. In recent years, since the early 1990s, we—queer feminists and loving perverts—have tried to rescue the queer from the dustbin of madness and make her our own. Theory calls this gesture resignification: we have dusted her off, turned her around, and made her into something beautiful.

But somehow, over the years, the queer has become a figure who has lost her generative promise. She has turned in on herself and become frozen into an Anglo-American, often white, masculine identity. And if the transformation itself is to be celebrated, the final stuckness is not. Getting stuck in identities that are often politically or medically engineered, the queer is drained of her transformative, contestatory power. This is where *History of Madness* can help us, as the story of a split that produced the queer not as a break away from feminism, but as one of *reason's* prodigal children.

The queer prodigal child is not "going out in this world"—as the Rolling Stones sing it in "Prodigal Son" (1968)—only to return to reason.[48] For if we tend to think of "prodigal" within a lost-and-found Biblical family structure, the word's actual "extravagant" meanings point to an excess that reorganizes love into new forms of relation. Both feminists and queers are to be counted among those extravagant prodigals of reason who can't or don't want to go home again; we are the ever-changing subjects of the exclusions of rationalism and family morality. Pinned down, as we are, as reason's others, we have resignified ourselves as forces of resistance. The danger of resignification is that we can get stuck in ourselves, to our own detriment: we can be recaptured and pinned down again, like dead butterflies, in our perversions and our genders. So if resignification threatens to bring us right back, like the prodigal son, to that place of patriarchy where we started, the trick is to keep things turning into something other. *History of Madness* has much to teach us about that resistant, transformative turning: about turning the adversity of "split decisions" into new ways of thinking, feeling, and acting in the world.

NOTES

1. Janet Halley, *Split Decisions: How and Why to Take a Break from Feminism* (Princeton, N.J.: Princeton University Press, 2006), 5, 31. Hereafter cited as *SD* in parenthetical references. In one of the early, article-length versions of the "Taking a Break" project, first delivered as the Brainerd Currie Lecture at Duke Law School in November 2002, Halley takes on a masculine subject position as "Ian Halley." See Ian Halley, "Queer Theory by Men," *Duke Journal of Gender, Law & Policy* 11 (2004): 7–53. Also see Robyn Wiegman's remarks in "Dear Ian," *Duke Journal of Gender, Law & Policy* 11 (2004): 93–120, on Halley's increasing identification "with and as a gay man" and her implicit rejection of lesbian feminism.

2. William Turner, *A Genealogy of Queer Theory* (Philadelphia, Penn.: Temple University Press, 2000) argues that "the originators of queer theory are all feminist schol-

ars" (34), and gives Teresa de Lauretis pride of place as the theorist to first use the term "queer" in 1991 (5). See Teresa de Lauretis, "Queer Theory, Lesbian and Gay Studies: An Introduction," *differences: A Journal of Feminist Cultural Studies* 3 (Summer 1991): iii–xviii. For an interesting argument on the specifically poetic lesbian-feminist roots of queer theory, see Linda Garber, *Identity Poetics: Race, Class, and the Lesbian-Feminist Roots of Queer Theory* (New York: Columbia University Press, 2001).

3. Catherine MacKinnon, *Feminism Unmodified: Discourses on Life and Law* (Cambridge, Mass.: Harvard University Press, 1987), 7.

4. Gayle Rubin, "Thinking Sex: Notes for a Radical Theory of the Politics of Sexuality," in *The Lesbian and Gay Studies Reader,* ed. Henry Abelove, Michèle Aina Barale, and David M. Halperin (New York: Routledge, 1993), 34, 32.

5. For the founding thinkers of the queer, see Rubin, "Thinking Sex"; Judith Butler, *Gender Trouble: Feminism and the Subversion of Identity* (New York: Routledge, 1990); and Eve Kosofsky Sedgwick, *Epistemology of the Closet* (Berkeley: University of California Press, 1990).

Robyn Wiegman, "Heteronormativity and the Desire for Gender," *Feminist Theory* 7 (2006): 97, notes the reversal of this opposition. The association between queer studies and sexuality specifically has been complicated by the proliferation of queer work on transgender issues and what Wiegman calls the "transitivity of gender": "feminist, queer, and trans-ed studies, along with heterosexuality itself, share a desire for gender."

6. See Judith Butler, "Against Proper Objects," in *Feminism Meets Queer Theory,* ed. Elizabeth Weed and Naomi Schor (Bloomington: Indiana University Press, 1997), 1–30; and Elizabeth Weed, "The More Things Change," in *Feminism Meets Queer Theory,* 266–291.

7. Since the *History of Sexuality, Volume 1: An Introduction,* and as a direct result of Anglo-American gender studies, the paired French terms *genre* and *sexualité* have begun to find their way into the vocabulary of a growing minority of French writers who work in this field. See especially Éric Fassin, "Le genre aux Etats-Unis," in *Quand les femmes s'en mêlent: Genre et pouvoir,* ed. Christine Bard, Christian Baudelot, and Janine Mossuz-Lavau (Paris: La Martinière, 2004), 23–43. Also see Fassin's preface to the 2005 French translation of Butler's *Gender Trouble,* "Trouble-genre," in Judith Butler, *Trouble dans le genre: Pour un féminisme de la subversion,* trans. Cynthia Kraus (Paris: Editions de la découverte, 2005), 5–19.

8. Michel Foucault, *History of Sexuality, Volume 1: An Introduction,* trans. Robert Hurley (New York: Vintage, 1978), 154. Hereafter cited as *Sexuality One* in the text proper, and as *HS1* in parenthetical references.

9. In this sense, Foucault's "sexuality" is conceptually indistinguishable from MacKinnon's collapsing of sex, sexuality, and gender. Along the same lines, when I use the term "sexuality" in my discussion of Foucault, the multiple meanings of what English speakers call "sex" and "gender" should be understood to be included within it.

10. Michel Foucault, *History of Madness,* ed. Jean Khalfa, trans. Jonathan Murphy and Jean Khalfa (London: Routledge, 2006); translation of the French original *Folie et*

déraison: Histoire de la folie à l'âge classique (Paris: Plon, 1961); reedited as *Histoire de la folie à l'âge classique* (Paris: Gallimard, 1972). Hereafter cited as *Madness* in the text proper, and as *HM* in parenthetical references.

11. Didier Eribon, *Réflexions sur la question gay* (Paris: Fayard, 1999); Eribon, *Insult and the Making of the Gay Self,* trans. Michael Lucey (Durham, N.C.: Duke University Press, 2004).

12. David Halperin, *Saint Foucault: Towards a Gay Hagiography* (New York: Oxford University Press, 1995), makes two brief mentions of *Madness:* he compares "sexuality" to "madness" (40) and critiques James Miller's distorting use of *Madness* to create a sensationalist portrait of Foucault as bent on death (166).

13. Michel Foucault, *Histoire de la folie à l'âge classique,* xxxviii, translation mine.

14. Michel Foucault, *Dits et écrits I, 1954–1975,* ed. François Ewald and Daniel Defert, 2 vols. (Paris: Gallimard, 2001), 133, translation mine.

15. Michel Foucault, *Madness and Civilization: A History of Insanity in the Age of Reason,* trans. Richard Howard (New York: Random House, 1965).

16. One important feminist reader of Foucault, Lois McNay, does treat *Madness* at length. And although her account of governmentality through a feminist lens has been important for gendered scholarship on Foucault, I find her interpretation of a *Madness* stuck in a phenomenological model of hermeneutic depth to be unpersuasive. McNay ultimately dismisses *Madness* as a resource for feminists because of its reliance on what she calls Foucault's romantic quest "to recover an authentic experience of madness" (40) and to celebrate the mad "as the bearers of an ineffable source of otherness" (46). For reasons too involved to elaborate here, I differ with McNay in this reading of *Madness.* See Lois McNay, *Foucault: A Critical Introduction* (New York: Continuum, 1994).

17. Judith Butler, *Giving an Account of Oneself* (New York: Fordham University Press, 2005), 19.

18. See Leo Bersani, "Is the Rectum a Grave?" *October* 43 (1987): 197–222; Lee Edelman, *No Future: Queer Theory and the Death Drive* (Durham, N.C.: Duke University Press, 2004); Rubin, "Thinking Sex"; and Michael Warner, *The Trouble with Normal: Sex, Politics, and the Ethics of Queer Life* (New York: Free Press, 1999).

19. Michel Foucault, *The History of Sexuality, Volume 2: The Use of Pleasure,* trans. Robert Hurley (New York: Vintage, 1990), hereafter cited as *Sexuality Two;* Michel Foucault, *The History of Sexuality, Volume 3: The Care of the Self,* trans. Robert Hurley (New York: Vintage, 1988), hereafter cited as *Sexuality Three.*

20. Michel Feher, "Les interrègnes de Michel Foucault," in *Penser avec Michel Foucault: Théorie critique et pratiques politiques,* ed. Marie-Christine Granjon (Paris: Karthala, 2005), 262.

21. For a useful overview of "experience" in Foucault, see Timothy O'Leary, "Foucault, Literature, Experience," *Foucault Studies* 5 (2008): 5–25.

22. Butler, *Giving an Account,* 16.

23. Michel Foucault, "Final Interview," *Raritan* 5, no. 1 (1985): 10.

24. Foucault, *Folie et déraison: Histoire de la folie à l'âge classique,* xxxii, translation mine.

25. John Caputo, "On Not Knowing Who We Are: Madness, Hermeneutics, and the Night of Truth in Foucault," in *Foucault and the Critique of Institutions,* ed. John Caputo and Mark Yount (University Park: Pennsylvania State Press, 1993), 243.

26. Joan Scott, "The Evidence of Experience," in *Lesbian and Gay Studies Reader,* 408. Hereafter cited as "EE" in parenthetical references.

27. Gilles Deleuze, *Negotiations, 1972–1990,* trans. Martin Joughin (New York: Columbia University Press, 1995), 100. Hereafter cited as *Neg* in parenthetical references.

28. Friedrich Nietzsche, *On the Genealogy of Morals,* trans. Walter Kaufmann (New York: Vintage, 1969), 84.

29. Tamsin Spargo, *Foucault and Queer Theory* (Cambridge, UK: Icon, 1999), 17.

30. Annamarie Jagose, *Queer Theory: An Introduction* (New York: NYU Press, 1996), 10–11.

31. Robert J. Corber and Stephen Valocchi, "Introduction," in *Queer Studies: An Interdisciplinary Reader,* ed. Robert J. Corber and Stephen Valocchi (Oxford: Blackwell, 2003), 10, emphasis added.

32. Michel Foucault, *Histoire de la sexualité 1: La volonté de savoir* (Paris: Gallimard, 1976), 59.

33. Foucault, *Sexuality One,* 42–43.

34. We find examples of this use of "identity" in Foucault in *The Order of Things* (especially chapter 2, "The Prose of the World") and at the end of *Sexuality One* (as that aspect of an individual that "gives the force of a drive to the singularity of history" [156]).

35. Éric Fassin, "Genre et sexualité: Politique de la critique historique," in *Penser avec Michel Foucault: Théorie critique et pratiques politiques,* ed. Marie-Christine Granjon (Paris: Karthala, 2005), 226, 227, translation mine.

36. Michel Foucault, *Abnormal: Lectures at the Collège de France, 1974–1975,* trans. Graham Burchell (New York: Picador, 2003). Many thanks to Mark Jordan for helping me to see this parallel between *Sexuality One* and *Abnormal,* especially in his presentation, "Are There Still Sodomites?" at the Remember Foucault symposium, Emory University, November 2007.

37. Rictor Norton describes Foucault's declaration of the birth of "the queer moment" as "slovenly": "Foucault got it wrong!" Norton gleefully asserts, in a typical irony-deaf reading. See Rictor Norton, "A False 'Birth,' " in *A Critique of Constructionism and Postmodern Queer Theory,* http://www.rictornorton.co.uk/social15.htm (accessed August 27, 2008).

38. Jagose, *Queer Theory,* 11.

39. This critique in Foucault of the "confinement of the outside" corresponds to what Peter Hallward calls his contestation of "the limits of our specification" (101), in contrast to the Deleuzian singularities that "create their own medium of extension or existence" (93). See Peter Hallward, "The Limits of Individuation, or How to Distinguish Deleuze and Foucault," *Angelaki: Journal of the Theoretical Humanities* 5 (August 2000): 93–111. Also see Gilles Deleuze, *Foucault,* trans. Seán Hand (Minneapolis: University of Minnesota Press, 1988).

40. Deleuze, *Foucault,* 54.

41. The interview was conducted in 1975 over the course of fifteen hours. Foucault was dissatisfied with the results and, with the exception of brief excerpts published in the *Le Monde* in 1986 and *Le Point* in 2004, the interview remains unedited and unpublished. See "Entretien avec Roger-Pol Droit," June 1975, nine cassettes, available for consultation at the Foucault archives at the Institut Mémoires de l'Edition Contemporaine (IMEC) in Normandy. For the two excerpts from *Le Monde* and *Le Point,* see Roger-Pol Droit, *Michel Foucault, entretiens* (Paris: Odile Jacob, 2004).

42. Eribon, *Insult,* 9.

43. See Ann Cvetkovich, *An Archive of Feelings: Trauma, Sexuality, and Lesbian Public Cultures* (Durham, N.C.: Duke University Press, 2003).

44. Deleuze, *Foucault,* 43.

45. Ibid., 89.

46. Caputo, "On Not Knowing," 257.

47. See *Sexuality One* (31–32) for the Jouys passage that feminists have criticized for ignoring rape. See Monique Plaza, "Our Damages and Their Compensation: Rape: The Will Not to Know of Michel Foucault," *Feminist Issues* 1, no. 3 (1981): 25–35, for an angry critique of Foucault's comments regarding rape in the context of the 1977 French Commission for the Reform of the Penal Code. In a conversation with David Cooper and others recounting a phone exchange with the commission, Foucault says: "Whether one punches his fist in someone's face, or his penis in the sexual organ (*le sexe*) makes no difference" (in Plaza 28). For the original context of Foucault's 1977 comments see David Cooper and Michel Foucault, "Dialogue sur l'enfermement et la répression psychiatrique," *Collectif Change* 32–33, *La Folie encerclée* (October 1977): 76–110. For a more detailed description of the Jouys case, see Foucault's March 19, 1975, course at the Collège de France in *Abnormal.* For a more balanced assessment of Foucault and the problem of sexual violence, see Éric Fassin, "Somnolence de Foucault: Violence sexuelle, consentement, et pouvoir," *Prochoix* 21 (Summer 2002): 106–119.

48. "Prodigal Son," from the Rolling Stones' 1968 album *Beggar's Banquet,* is a remake of the 1929 song by Reverend Robert Wilkins, "That's No Way To Get Along."

CHAPTER TWELVE

From the "Useful" to the "Impossible" in the Work of Joan W. Scott

ELIZABETH WEED

Continuous history is the indispensable correlative of the founding function of the subject: the guarantee that everything that has eluded him may be restored to him; the certainty that time will disperse nothing without restoring it in a reconstituted unity; the promise that one day the subject in the form of historical consciousness will once again be able to appropriate, to bring back under his sway, all those things that are kept at a distance by difference, and find in them what might be called his abode.

—Michel Foucault, *The Archaeology of Knowledge*[1]

The Dull Edge of Gender

The Daumier lithograph on the cover of the 1999 revised edition of *Gender and the Politics of History* is printed in a cool grey-green, quite different from the warm rust color of the 1988 first edition.[2] Indeed, in the 1999 version, a new preface and a new final essay cast a harsh *fin-de-siècle* light on the category of "gender," finding it drained of critical vitality, exhausted. Once a crucial tool intended, in Scott's words, "to separate biology from culture and to justify change as an aspect not of radical social engineering, but of history" (*GPHR,* xi), gender no longer destabilizes the familiar:

> As the 1990s draw to a close, "gender" seems to have lost its ability to startle and provoke us. It has, in the United States, become an aspect of "ordinary usage," routinely offered as a synonym for women, for the

differences between the sexes, for sex. Sometimes it denotes the social rules imposed on men and women, but it rarely refers to the knowledge that organizes our perceptions of "nature." Books that purport to offer a "gender analysis" are often quite predictable studies of women, or . . . of differences in the status, experience, and possibilities open to women and men. But they rarely examine how the meanings of "women" and "men" are discursively established, what contradictions inhere in these meanings, what the terms exclude, what variations of subjectively experienced "womanhood" have been evident in diverse "regimes of truth." Indeed, many feminist scholars who use the term "gender" do so while explicitly rejecting the premise that "men" and "women" are historically variable categories. This has the effect of denying "gender" its radical academic and political agency. It is, these days, a term that has lost its critical edge. (*GPHR*, xiii)

"Gender" may have lost its vitality, but judging from what Scott says, the problem does not stem from simple overexposure. As banal as the term may have become, it has also become increasingly confused. To illustrate this, Scott opens her new preface with a discussion of the by-now familiar controversies that attended the 1995 United Nations Conference on Women in Beijing. Anxieties about the term "gender" were high (did it mean biology or culture, and if the latter, to what possibly perverted ends?), and those expressing anxiety were far-ranging, from conference participants and their international constituents, to the United States House of Representatives, to the Vatican. In an effort to manage the controversy, the United Nations Commission on the Status of Women appointed a contact group to draft a resolution of clarification that was appended to the conference's Program of Action. Scott cites the following excerpts from that statement:

> Having considered the issue thoroughly, the contact group notes that (1) the word "gender" had been commonly used and understood in its ordinary, generally accepted usage in numerous other United Nations forums and conferences; (2) there was no indication that any new meaning or connotation of the term, different from accepted prior usage, was intended in the Platform for Action. . . . Accordingly, the contact group reaffirmed that the word "gender" as used in the Platform for Action was intended to be interpreted and understood as it was in ordinary, generally accepted usage.[3]

This seemingly unexceptional, if disingenuous, appeal to customary usage is striking in that *no definition* of this "ordinary, generally accepted usage" is given. However agile the group's efforts to defend gender against Papal criticism, the strategy depends entirely on the possibility of asserting a common knowledge. We are simply invited to assume, as Scott says, that the meaning is self-evident and unproblematically available to all. Of course, the statement can't possibly achieve its ends; it can't, in Scott's words, "settle controversy by denying that it exists" (*GPHR,* x). It can only ever be the failed attempt of strategic doublespeak to damp down the many and complex worries about perceived threats the term "gender" poses to dominant patriarchal and heterosexual orders.[4] Viewed from another theoretical register, however, what the statement also does is offer a stunningly candid glimpse at the *aporia* that is gender. Ideally, the contact group's statement would like to be able to appeal to some kind of apodictic truth. That not being available, it appeals to "ordinary, generally accepted usage," a usage that is, according to item (1), validated by past custom (no matter that "gender" as something other than a grammatical term has existed scarcely more than several decades). In short, all the statement can offer is a language that *stands in* for a referent that can't be named. And whatever that unnamed referent is, it must always depend on the power of customary usage and the meanings it evokes. In other words, in lieu of demonstrable truth, language does its work.

In the new, final essay of the 1999 edition, "Some More Reflections on Gender and Politics," Scott continues her discussion of the limits of gender. Rather than try to pin gender down, to impose some discipline on the term, it is better, she argues, to read its incoherencies symptomatically. For Scott, such a reading demands a deconstruction of the very nature/culture opposition that had for so long grounded feminist criticism:

> As long as the two realms are conceived as antithetical, bodies (and sex) will seem inadequately accounted for by reference to social construction alone. "Gender" will not replace "sex" in discussions of sexual difference; instead, "gender" will always refer to sex as the ultimate ground of its meaning. When sex resides within gender in this way, nothing can prevent its being identified with (or as) gender itself. (*GPHR,* 200)

Scott remarks further that the feminist project of splitting the physical off from the social and cultural has had the effect of elevating rationality and conscious agency at the expense of the workings of the body and the unconscious. Such a split is reflected, for example, in the notion of "gender roles":

> These kinds of analyses of gender roles and the politics of their production lent support to the enterprise of the human sciences as Michel

Foucault critically described them: dedicated to denying the operations of the unconscious by producing man as a rational subject and installing the "sovereignty of [his] consciousness," those very qualities that had "increasingly eluded him for over a hundred years." These analyses, in other words, were an aspect of the ideological production of "man" as an entirely rational being and of politics as the activity of fully rational agents. (*GPHR*, 205)[5]

Scott goes on to propose ways in which psychoanalytic insights might move feminist critical work beyond the impasses of gender. What she doesn't mention is that she herself had recently published a book that offers a striking example of a move beyond these impasses. The 1996 *Only Paradoxes to Offer* does not leave gender behind; that is something one cannot do.[6] The very reading of "paradox," however, turns on something other than gender, and that something other can be grasped by an appeal to the theoretical insights afforded by the psychoanalytic notion of "sexual difference."

I am interested in the ways theories of gender and theories of sexual difference operate differently in Scott's work, the ways they play on usefulness and impossibility, and how that play allows Scott to produce critical readings that are grounded in different if complementary theoretical formulations. To explore these differences, I want to revisit briefly Scott's well-known theory of gender in order to see how its *usefulness* might bring the impossibility of sexual difference into relief.

Gender as a Useful Category

Although feminists used the term "gender" in the 1970s to serve a number of purposes, it wasn't until Scott's essay on "Gender: A Useful Category of Historical Analysis" that it became a dominant critical term.[7] Prepared for the American Historical Association meetings in December 1985 and published in the *American Historical Review* the following December, the essay addresses the challenges "gender" posed at that time to the practice of feminist history. Of course, the specificity of the address in no way limited the essay's reception, and with its publication in *Gender and the Politics of History* in 1988, Scott's formulations of gender were eagerly taken up by feminists across the disciplines. This was no surprise given the interdisciplinary breadth of the essay, which brings the problematic of history into conversation with a number of other fields—literature, philosophy, anthropology, sociology—all within the context of poststructuralist thinking. Despite some lively criticism (largely disciplinary), the essay and the book transformed feminist scholarship and criticism by opening up a field of analysis to subsequent elaboration and debate. "Gender" proved to be an enormously generative term. Indeed, we can only remark in retrospect at the understated restraint of the "usefulness" of the title.

The "Gender" essay emerged, as have Scott's other major interventions, from a sense of needing to move on, to see differently. Just as the preface to the revised 1999 edition of *Gender and the Politics of History* expresses frustration with the limitations of gender, so did the 1988 edition express Scott's response to the limitations that were beginning to become apparent in various branches of women's history. For all of the achievements of "her-story" (which aims to look at women as historical subjects) or feminist social history (which looks at social systems through the lens of women's experience), for all of the crucial new knowledge such work had achieved, Scott worries about what is occluded by the two approaches. By incorporating gender within existing frames of explanation (largely economic), social history is too integrationist; whereas "her-story," aiming to explain how women's histories differ from men's, fails to theorize gender historically and is more often than not too separatist in both a political and epistemological sense.

"Gender: A Useful Category of Historical Analysis" is the effort to study the register of *gender itself* and to look at how it operates historically. What enables that effort is Scott's reading of the particular intellectual moment:

> It seems to me significant that the use of the word "gender" has emerged at a moment of great epistemological turmoil that takes the form, in some cases, of a shift from scientific to literary paradigms among social scientists (from an emphasis on cause to one on meaning, blurring genres in inquiry, in anthropologist Clifford Geertz's phrase) and, in other cases, the form of debates about theory between those who assert the transparency of facts and those who insist that all reality is construed or constructed, between those who defend and those who question the idea that "man" is the rational master of his own destiny. ("GUC," 41)[8]

It is the space opened up by these epistemological debates that Scott claims for the articulation of the category of gender. But it can't escape notice that this same space—between cause and meaning, between fact as transparent and fact as constructed—presents big challenges to the practice of history. Indeed, for some historians, Scott's "gender" was received not as the serviceable category suggested by the anodyne adjective "useful," but as something much more dangerous, something like a Trojan horse. And yet the "Gender" essay, like the book, leaves no doubt as to Scott's commitment to her discipline. For her, the epistemological turmoil in question is not a call for retrenchment but an opportunity for historians to see things differently:

> What should be done by historians who, after all, have seen their discipline dismissed by some recent theorists as a relic of humanist thought? I do not think we should quit the archives or abandon the study of the past, but we do have to change some of the ways we've gone about working, some of the questions we've asked. ("GUC," 42)

What Scott suggests is that there are different ways to answer the discipline's fundamental question as to why historical change occurs:

> Instead of a search for single origins, we have to conceive of processes so interconnected that they cannot be disentangled. . . . We must ask more often how things happened in order to find out why they happened; in anthropologist Michelle Rosaldo's formulation, we must pursue not universal, general causality, but meaningful explanation. ("GUC," 42)

"Gender: A Useful Category of Historical Analysis" is, in fact, as much about the mandate to move from cause to meaning as it is about the need for a more adequate theory of gender, as much about the practice of history as it is about gender. Or rather, gender is seen as at once a *stage for* and a *staging of* historical meaning. Scott's careful and detailed formulation outlines how one might think about this double operation. There are two integrally connected propositions: gender as "a constitutive element of social relationships based on perceived differences between the sexes" and gender as "a primary way of signifying relationships of power" ("GUC," 42). To study the first, Scott looks to cultural symbols that evoke multiple and contradictory representations (like light and dark, purification and pollution); normative concepts that aim to fix representations of masculinity and femininity into meanings that don't allow for slippage and assert themselves as self-evident (such as those found in religious, educational, legal, scientific, or political doctrines); institutional instantiations of gendered meanings that include not only kinship systems but also the labor market, education, the polity, etc.; and subjective identity.

The challenge is to understand how these four aspects are related first to one another and then to the second proposition: gender as a primary way of signifying relationships of power. Here, Scott appeals to Foucault's notion of

power as "dispersed constellations of unequal relationships, discursively constituted in social 'fields of force'" ("GUC," 42).[9] Unlike Foucault, she points
to gender as one of the primary fields for this articulation of power, an articulation that does not, of course, have to have any explicit connection to the
differences between the sexes but can serve to structure and legitimate all
aspects of social organization. Scott offers numerous analyses in the essay and
in the book of the workings of gender—in formulations of class, the politics
of labor, the development of statistical representation, and in contemporary
debates such as the Sears Case. In each instance, her analysis seeks not to distill lines of historical causality but to understand how gender becomes entangled with various discourses so as to produce meanings that take on a force of
truth. The usefulness of gender as a category of analysis indeed turns out to be
the power of these processes of signification. It is the stage for and the staging
of prolific productions of meaning through "processes so interconnected that
they can't be disentangled." There seem to be no limits to the meanings generated; contained by neither reason nor rhetoric, gender works though processes that turn on multiple registers of signification—symbolic, normative,
institutional, subjective—all mobilized as force fields in which and by which
power is constituted.

Gender and the Politics of History accomplishes a great deal: it reconceptual-
izes gender from a descriptive category to a complex of processes that generate meaning, and it offers dynamic and insightful ways of reading historical
and cultural texts. With this new, useful category, both gender and history
are opened to change.

Gendered Paradoxes

Scott's 1996 book, *Only Paradoxes to Offer,* does nothing to undercut her argument for the efficacy of gender as a tool of historical analysis. To the contrary,
the analysis she presents would not be possible without a keen attunement to
the manifold meanings that gender takes on in the historical periods ranging
from 1789 through 1944: extravagant, dogmatic, contradictory, and fantasmatic meanings that change from one historical moment to the next, all the
while retaining their discursive force. The four feminists Scott studies—
Olympe de Gouges at the time of the French Revolution, Jeanne Deroin in the
Revolution of 1848, Hubertine Auclert during the Third Republic, and Mad-
eleine Pelletier from the turn of the century through her death in 1939—are
by the nature of their political engagements thoroughly entangled in the
gendered meanings of their times. What particularly interests Scott is the
way each of the four identifies crucial contradictions in the political and

epistemological discourses with which she engages, contradictions that go on to shape her own formulations. These contradictions are the "paradoxes" that are the focus of Scott's study, borrowed from a comment of Olympe de Gouge's that she should temper a particular argument she was making lest people see her "as a woman who has only paradoxes to offer and not problems easy to resolve" (*OPO*, 4). Although the political and epistemological contexts of the four feminist are quite different, Scott agues that the fundamental contradiction they all face is the need to argue simultaneously the relevance and irrelevance of their sex. Rather than seeing this—as many other feminist historians do—as a strategic question of the relative efficacy of "equality" versus "difference," Scott sees the conundrum as constitutive of feminism itself. And instead of contributing to the story of feminism's progress, she follows the tenacious twists and turns of feminism's fundamental paradox and its many enabling contradictions. Like the soldiers in Joseph Heller's *Catch 22*, the feminists Scott examines are trapped in a world of doublethink. The soldier who wants to be dismissed from the nightmare of combat on the grounds of insanity has to request an examination from his superiors, but the very request for an examination is seen in turn to demonstrate rationality rather than insanity. When Hubertine Auclert argues that women's interests aren't particular, that they are part of the general social interest, she can only make the argument from the position of the woman, which is by definition particular. If the contradictions in question are so effective in keeping women in their place—the women's suffrage Olympe de Gouge agitates for in 1790 isn't granted until 1944, and even today, post-*parité,* the percentage of women in the National Assembly is only 12 percent—this effectiveness, in Scott's view, is due to the gendered conundrum being constitutive not only of feminism but of French republicanism itself. On the one hand, the revolutionary discourse promised universal liberty and equality; on the other hand, women were consistently denied the rights of men. And however much the terms of republicanism—notions of the individual, citizenship, and rights—change in subsequent republics, the foundational contradictions remain operative. Scott argues, moreover, that today's feminism with its conundrum of "equality versus difference" is a product of this contradiction: "Feminism is not a reaction to republicanism, but one of its effects" (*OPO*, 168).

Viewed strictly from the perspective of political theory, the feminist problem might be seen as one rooted not in contradiction but in a necessary tension between formal and concrete rights. The notion of an abstract disembodied individual is, after all, precisely what enables the conceptualization of universal rights, permitting, in revolutionary thinking, a movement away from concepts of feudal bondage. The relationship between the abstract and the concrete is thus one of *incommensurability,* a gap to be negotiated. More-over, abstract rights form feminism's ground of possibility; indeed, as Scott points out, the feminists are all in one way or another empowered by them. In order to grasp what turns *formal incommensurability* into a chronic experience of *contradiction and paradox,* Scott looks closely at the ways the various histori-cal negotiations between the formal and the concrete are repeatedly short-circuited by political and epistemological investments in gendered meanings.

In the century separating Olympe de Gouges and Herbertine Auclert, for example, much had changed. The state was seen no longer as expressing the will of the people but as managing and balancing conflicting interests; and the citizen, no longer modeled on the abstract individual, was seen as having a collective social identity (*OPO,* 92–95). Yet, in spite of the changes, and in spite of continued feminist efforts, the exclusion of women persisted. Univer-sal manhood suffrage had been granted in 1848, but women continued to oc-cupy the space of exclusion. How to understand this seemingly necessary ex-clusion of women? What are those political and epistemological investments in gender that seem always to short circuit change? Are they to be attributed to some transhistorical understanding of male domination? Surely not. In all of her work, Scott demonstrates that the value of gender lies precisely in its ability to expose the historically *specific* circumstances that underlie the im-pression of timeless domination of women by men. Gender, for Scott, is never the answer; it is the question that opens up inquiry, showing the utter useless-ness for historians of a notion such as that of an ahistorical "patriarchy."

And yet, in *Paradoxes,* the usefulness of gender seems to find its limit. For all the historically particular struggles illuminated by the paradoxical play of gendered meanings, there are impasses that can't be accounted for by such analyses. One of those impasses is revealed by asking what the failures of the four feminists have in common. In spite of the historical dissimilarities that separate them, the feminists all elicit the same response on the part of their opponents: *to allow women to be like men would be to risk men becoming like women.* However complicated and convoluted the arguments between the feminists and their adversaries, this protest, so banal as to seem natural, has the last word. To have a sense of what this insistent repetitive response has to do with the historical specificity of modernity, like Scott we must turn to the work-ings of "sexual difference."

The Impossibility of Sexual Difference

It is noteworthy that "gender" is not the term Scott uses in *Paradoxes;* the term is "sexual difference," printed most often with quotation marks. The quotation marks do a good deal of theoretical work. They, of course, indicate a skeptical stance to referential truth, the truth, let us say, of biology. If none of the historical debates denies the existence of biological difference (though Pelletier looks to the withering away of sex), the feminists argue in various ways that "sexual difference" in no way grounds the exclusion of women from political rights. For all of their differences, they are in agreement that it is not nature that gives birth to law but law that essentializes nature. In other words, the feminists understand the performative nature of law, that law "recognizes the things that correspond to the definitions it constructs."[10] The quotation marks, however, do more than trouble the foundational truth of "sexual difference." In Scott's readings of the various historical texts, they can also put into question the term's referential truth *tout court*. "Sexual difference" can appear as something fantasmatic, or more, as something that cannot be finally known.

The theoretical underpinnings of Scott's use of "sexual difference" are embedded in her study. Although indispensable for feminist theorists, *Paradoxes* makes its arguments more through historical readings than theoretical exposition. My interest in looking more closely at those underpinnings has to do not with a desire to provide a theoretical gloss of the book, which is in no way necessary, but with a belief that reading psychoanalytic notions of sexual difference along with *Paradoxes* can be productive in both directions. It can underscore how powerful Scott's insights are, and it can perhaps bring to light the usefulness of the psychoanalytic theory. What makes the conjunction potentially so rich is that both *Paradoxes* and psychoanalysis have to do with the enormous anxiety sexual difference presents for modernity. Luce Irigaray calls sexual difference "one of the major philosophical issues, if not the issue, of our age."[11] The *psychoanalyst* Irigaray knows that whereas philosophy might not recognize the relevance of sexual difference, for psychoanalysis, that science of modernity, there is nothing more important.

"Sexual difference" is, of course, not a technical psychoanalytic term; the technical term is sexuality. It is primarily through the work of feminist theorists that sexual difference came to designate a crucial problematic, and largely through readings of the late work of Jacques Lacan. Like Freud, Lacan returned to the woman problem in his later years, particularly in his Seminar XX, conducted in 1972–1973, the full title of which is *Encore: The Seminar of Jacques Lacan: On Feminine Sexuality, the Limits of Love and Knowledge*.[12] The old knot of sexuality and knowledge, of questions of knowing and not knowing, are foundational to psychoanalysis. Indeed, Freud was particularly concerned with the nature of psychoanalytic knowledge itself. Insisting that psychoanalysis is a science, he was equally insistent that science's conception of knowledge as the "intellectual working-over of carefully scrutinized observations" is limited by forces that are not available to scientific delimitation or knowledge.[13] Taking the human mind itself as its object of study, he argues, psychoanalysis demonstrates that the carefully limited and fully conscious intellect is not the center of man's mental life.

What Lacan laments in Seminar XX is that this revolutionary insight of Freud's has so little lasting impact on thinking in general and psychoanalysis in particular.[14] Freud's decentering of consciousness, Lacan says, is not unlike Copernicus's great decentering of the earth centuries before: "Man . . . was far from ever having been shaken by the discovery that the earth is not at the center. He had no problem substituting the sun for it" (*Enc,* 42). What is crucial is to have a center; any center will do. In *Encore,* Lacan visits the ways dominant systems of Western thought secure the center, and particularly how Enlightenment thought works to consolidate reason as its center. At stake is not just conscious reason versus unconscious forces, but the very question of the wholeness of being. For Lacan, the fantasized center guarantees being-in-its-wholeness, as the center guarantees the existence of the circle (hence Lacan's predilection for ellipses, the Moebius strip and other such figures). One of the Enlightenment fantasies Lacan derides in *Encore* is that of the "individual." For him, the word is just a way of presuming being: "I am going to say once again . . . 'There's no such thing as a metalanguage.' . . . When I say that, it apparently means—no language of being." And a little further on: "Being is merely presumed in certain words—'individual,' for instance, and 'substance' . . ." (*Enc,* 118).

For Lacan, the "individual" smacks of the fantasy of the fullness of being, a fantasy that, for all of its long philosophical history, is subjected to special pressures in modernity. Eager to disturb Enlightenment dreams, Lacan borrows Heidegger's notion of *ek-sistence,* which draws on a Greek word, the root of which means "standing outside of," or "standing apart from," which is closely connected to the word in Greek for "existence." From this, he develops the neologism "extimate." Rather than something intimate and contained, existence is seen as extimate, "as if from the outside" (*Enc,* 22, n. 24).

With Lacan's view of the individual in mind, let us look again at the role of the individual in *Paradoxes.* The term is, of course, central to Scott's examination of the feminist conundrums. She discusses the complexities of the word in the eighteenth century and looks at the uses to which it is put in revolutionary rhetoric:

> The word "individual" has ambiguous meanings that are present in its various usages. One the one hand, the individual is the abstract prototype

for the human; on the other, the individual is a unique being, a distinct person, different from all others of its species. (*OPO*, 5)

To illustrate the second individual, the unique being of its species, Scott cites the following entry on the "individual" from Diderot's *Encyclopédie:*

> Peter is a man, Paul is a man. They belong to the same species; but they are distinguishable from one another by numerable differences. One is handsome, the other ugly; one learned, the other ignorant. Each is etymologically an individual because he cannot be divided into another subject who has an existence that is really separate from him [*un tel sujet est un individu suivant l'étymologie, parce qu'on ne peut plus le diviser en nouveaux sujets qui aient une existence réellement indépendante de lui*]. His assembled traits are such that, taken together, they cannot apply to anyone but him.[15]

This is the individual that Lacan both sustains and disturbs. The psychoanalytic subject is unique; no other subject has its psychic formation. But this is not a uniqueness produced by assembled traits that the individual contains like a container of being impervious to division. The psychoanalytic subject is unique in its division; Diderot's individual defies division. If, as Scott shows, women seem definitively excluded from the category of the individual, it is in no small part because of the very etymological meaning to which Diderot points: the individual is indivisible, a being that one cannot divide into new subjects who would have an existence really independent of him. As we shall see presently, it is in the psychoanalytic theory of sexual difference that this indivisibility proves to be most consequential.[16]

The first individual—the abstract prototype of the human—also finds its full flowering when viewed through the psychoanalytic notion of sexual difference. As Scott says, it was the abstract individual that French Enlightenment philosophers and politicians used as the basis for claims of natural and universal human rights, and that served as the rhetorical basis of the French republic, a more inclusive notion than those on which republics were based historically. And yet, as *Paradoxes* demonstrates so well, women could not gain access to the inclusivity of the universal. Citing a vignette from the record of the National Convention in 1794, Scott shows how the universal is buttressed by a (barely) unconscious appeal to the difference of the sexes. Having just conferred citizenship on former male slaves, the revolutionaries single out a woman of color who, having fainted with joy at the action, is recognized for her civic virtue by their cheers and applause. Scott comments that the woman's "virtue" consisted in her gratitude to the legislators for allowing men of color to represent her:

> It was no accident that [deputy] Chambon seized on this moment of fra-
> ternal inclusion to make a black woman the sign of the entry of black
> men into the ranks of citizenship. The men's difference from women
> served to eradicate differences of skin color and race among men; the
> universality of the abstract individual was in this way and at this mo-
> ment established as a common maleness. (*OPO,* 9)

Throughout *Paradoxes,* Scott shows that what has come to be a commonplace of feminist theory—the maleness of universality—was not installed and is not maintained without a great deal of unconscious and conscious work. The paradoxes the feminists face only mirror that work in the form of the rhetori-cal contortions of their opponents. What the formulation of sexual difference affords is a look at the energy that fuels that work.

Suzanne Barnard offers an entry into sexual difference "itself" in this con-cise description of Lacan's project: "Arguing that the subject of psychoanalysis is a consequence of the Enlightenment's rejection of reality in pursuit of the real, Lacan sets out in Seminar XX to articulate how a psychoanalytic science of the real might transform accepted ideas about sexual difference, being, and knowledge."[17] Seen in terms of this description, the work referred to above would be everything entailed in the "rejection of reality in pursuit of the real," and the energy driving that work would have to do with the insistent draw of the real. To grasp more fully Lacan's use of the term "real"—one that is noto-riously and deliberately difficult—it is helpful to return briefly to Freud's theory of sexuality, from which the term is derived.

It is, after all, Freud who exposes the cleft or the split in the human psyche.

In order to assert that sexuality is both infantile in its origins and not instinctual—that is, not a natural function like hunger that proceeds from innate need to ultimate satisfaction in hetero-sexual union—Freud theorizes the relationship between instinct and the drive. In this relationship, Jean Laplanche reminds us, the drive is not the simple other of instinct. Rather, it is propped upon or supported by instinct, from which it is derived and from which it differs.[18] The classic example, evoked by Laplanche in *Life and Death in Psychoanalysis,* is the nursing infant:

> Now the crucial point is that simultaneous with the feeding function's
> achievement of satisfaction in nourishment, a sexual process begins to

appear. Parallel with feeding there is a stimulation of lips and tongue by the nipple and the flow of warm milk. This stimulation is initially modeled on the function, so between the two, it is at first barely possible to distinguish a difference. The object? It would appear to be furnished at the level of the function. Can we be sure whether it is still the milk or already the breast? . . . [A]t the level of the source, we find the same duplicity: the mouth is simultaneously a sexual organ and an organ of the feeding function.[19]

Freud goes on to theorize a second stage or "moment" of "sexual sucking" in the absence of the (partial) object. Again, Laplanche:

It should be understood that the real object, milk was the object of the function, which is virtually preordained to the world of satisfaction. Such is the real object which has been lost, but the object linked to the autoerotic turn, the breast—become a fantasmatic breast—is, for its part, the object of the sexual drive. Thus the sexual object is not identical to the object of the function, but is displaced in relation to it. . . ." (*LDP*, 20)

In other words, this means "*that on the one hand there is from the beginning an object, but that on the other hand sexuality does not have, from the beginning, a real object*" (*LDP*, 19, emphasis added).[20] What the sexual drive does have is the lost object that has become the fantasmatic breast. In this way, for Freud, "a local biological stimulus finds its delegation, its 'representation' in psychical life as a drive" (*LDP*, 13).

Psychical life is thus inaugurated in a rupture that Freud is able to theorize, not through pure speculation, but by listening to his patients, and by listening, moreover, not to what they know but to what they don't know they know. And it is the rupture of this psychical representation that allows Lacan to say that the unconscious is structured like a language, like a structure of signifiers always circling an unsymbolizable real. We are far from the intact indivisible individual. Here, rather, a subject of language, of signifiers, for which the loss of the object functions fantasmatically as a loss of the fullness of being. For the psychical life of the subject, the life of unconscious and conscious desires, there is a hole in being. And there is castration, understood as the fantasized loss of integral being through the loss of the breast, the feces, the penis, and more.[21]

For psychoanalytic theory, sexual difference comes into play as consequence of the Oedipal complex and the castration threat. Of course, very small children can recognize gender differences and align themselves with others of their perceived gender. But it is not until the Oedipal drama that the child enters into sexual difference.[22] In the language of psychology, one might say that at the point of entering into sexual difference the child "realizes" that one cannot *be* both male and female, that human beings are split by the fact that human reproduction is sexed reproduction. In psychoanalytic thinking, however, the assumption of sexual difference occurs not in the register of cognitive realization but in the scene of what Freud calls love, played out in the triangulation of the maternal dyad by the paternal function. This is the scene of the fantasy of genital castration.

Long before psychoanalysis or the Enlightenment, the castrating woman had become a cultural convention, a convention that is certainly evidenced in *Paradoxes*. Jeanne Deroin's campaign for a seat on the legislature in 1849 was met with exuberant cartoons evoking outlandish role reversals and grotesque emasculation (*OPO*, 31). And an official who witnessed Auclert's 1908 demonstration at a polling place (she knocked over a voting urn), testified that "witnessing this scene had produced in him an awful stillness, as if he had gazed on the Medusa" (*OPO*, 118). In Seminar XX, Lacan helps us see something of what is involved when such an automatic and clichéd response is uttered in the context of modernity.

For Lacan, the triangulation of the maternal dyad by the paternal function entails a castration for both male and female subjects. For him, Oedipal castration takes the form of the entry into the "I" of language (as against the "me" of the imaginary), of entry into the symbolic order of Law and culture. Whether a subject assumes a feminine or a masculine position in this process is not determined by biology. It is not that biology has no role whatsoever; it is that it is not deterministic. What matters are the subjects' fundamental fantasies that emerge in their drives and desire. Even as the entry into the realm of sexually divided beings represents for Lacan a castration for all subjects, not all subjects are positioned in the same way with regard to this castration. The difference has to do with the subjects' relationship to the phallus, that signifier of desire that draws its force from the paternal fantasy in the triangulation of sexual differentiation. The feminine subject is taken to be already castrated in the mother's displacement by the paternal function (as Lacan says, all feminine subjects are mothers in fantasy). The masculine subject is castrated by the paternal prohibition against sexual relations with the mother. (Again, the bearers of the paternal and maternal functions need not be biologically male or female.) Thus far, the story is familiar.[23] It is Lacan's further treatment of the subject in Seminar XX that provides special insight into male anxieties.[24]

In his thinking, the feminine subject is in the symbolic order "without exception." By this perplexing notion, he indicates something more about the difference between feminine and masculine castration. Unlike the feminine subject, the masculine subject is in the symbolic order by virtue of a fantasized exception. As Suzanne Bernard explains, masculine *jouissance* or psychic enjoyment "is produced within the structure of a finite logic—as a closed set determined by a fixed limit that remains outside of or 'extimate' to the set itself."[25] That outside is the fantasmatic figure who can't be castrated—the primal father, for example. If the masculine subject can be castrated, it is only because there is some one figure who cannot be. In other words, the masculine subject has the fantasy of one who is exempt from the law of castration:

> Thus, while man is "whole" [or wholly] within the symbolic, the exception that delimits him precludes him from fully identifying with castration. One could say that while man is wholly subject "to" and hence "in" the symbolic, he is "in it with exception," that is, he "takes exception" to it in some way. As a result, the fantasy of a subject not subject to Law— the fantasy of no limit—determines masculine structure in an essential way. The point here is that the masculine subject is "caught" in the phallic function, ironically because he does not fully identity with it but maintains a kind of distance toward it through believing in an exception to the symbolic Law. ("TA," 177)

The feminine subject, who is in the Symbolic without exception, " 'knows' that the signifier of phallic power merely lends a certain mysterious presence to the Law that veils its real impotence" ("TA," 178). But from the point of view of the masculine subject, the woman, having no access to phallic exception, is positioned as what Lacan calls the not-all. Positioned in an infinite logic (of no exception), she cannot be seen as existing. Indeed, Lacan's infamous *la femme n'existe pas* takes its meaning from the *la*, the definite article that can indicate the general as well as the specific. In psychical life, *la femme,* in her infinite lack, cannot be generalized; only *l'homme* can be taken for the universal. As Lacan says, women "do not lend themselves to generalization, even to phallocentric generalization." Woman thus takes on the hole in being. She is, as Lacan tells us, "man's symptom."[26]

Man's fantasy of negating castration is the fantasy of full presence, of the plenitude of being. The fantasy is doomed, of course, because the phallus as signifier of desire can only ever be the phallus of the "phallic function," or castration:

Paradoxically then, the figure that lends the symbolic its seeming integrity, its automatic and "Law-like" functioning, is only an illusion. Thus the deterministic, repetitive character of desire as it plays out in and through the symbolic functions only within the frame of a certain finite logic, one fixed by a constitutive exception. Moreover, it is an illusion that Woman as man's symptom (e.g., the Lady, the Virgin Mother, etc.) is put to work in support of. ("TA," 177)

Psychoanalytic theory thus shows us that men have their paradoxes, too. Caught in the phallic function ("because he does not fully identity with it but maintains a kind of distance toward it through believing in an exception to the symbolic Law"), pinning his fantasy of escape on a phallus that can only fail, man has a great deal at stake in managing these paradoxes ("TA," 177). Scott's reading of the struggles waged by the four French feminists shows in fascinating specificity the ways men actually do the managing. The individual who "cannot be divided into another individual who has an existence that is really separate from him" betrays his pursuit of the real not only by keeping his distance from the mother as Other, but through his fantasy of exception to the phallic function of castration. And man *must* occupy the position of the universal because woman, as already castrated, as having no possibility of phallic exception, cannot. This "universal," this crucial term of French modernity, is, in Lacan's thinking, a grand symptom of the Enlightenment's turn away from reality in pursuit of the real. In this pursuit, to posit women as universal is simply unthinkable.[27]

For all of the historical differences among the four sets of debates Scott examines in *Paradoxes,* the opponents to the feminist arguments manage to express in one way or another an urgent warning: *to allow women to be like men would be to risk men becoming like women.* Scott shows us the warning in its many historical permutations; Lacan helps us appreciate the psychical energy involved.[28]

The Future of the Impossible

If theories of gender lead necessarily to the exploration of meaning, as Scott indicates in "Gender: A Useful Category of Historical Analysis," theories of sexual difference take us, as in *Paradoxes,* to the impossibility of meaning. The psychical rupture constitutive of Freud's and Lacan's theories of sexuality, what Lacan calls the real, what cannot be known, cannot be symbolized, is this impossibility. This is not to say that the impossibility of knowing doesn't produce enormous amounts of knowledge. To the contrary, the unknowability of sexuality is what makes theorists of us all. Tracy McNulty, in her essay "Demanding the Impossible: Desire and Social Change," calls attention to Freud's own epistemophilia:

> In an interview given shortly before his death, Freud spoke of the "desire to know" that guided him for his entire life, a desire to know what causes the human subject that led him away from the empirical sphere of science and toward an object that could not be verified empirically, but only witnessed in speech. The subject is itself an "impossible object" in this sense, a pure hypothesis that cannot be observed scientifically or explained as a product of culture.[29]

In its clinical mode, psychoanalysis engages with the subject's desire, or the anxiety produced by the psychical rupture of castration. The analyst's desire to know represents for the patient the place of the Other's desire (the Other that cannot be assimilated by identification). The patient supposes that the analyst knows; what she is confronted with is the analyst's desire to know, a desire that the patient doesn't understand, that she can't contain in her fantasies of seduction, and to which she doesn't know how to respond. If the anxiety is maintained and not covered over by fantasies of fulfillment by the analyst, the analyst's desire will call forth responses from the patient's unconscious. Here is where the possibility of psychical change resides, in the very gap, the psychical rupture that produces a desire that can only be known in its effects. When Lacan bemoans the Enlightenment's rejection of reality in pursuit of the real, he is speaking of a pursuit that is just the opposite of the analytic project. While the Enlightenment aims to sustain fantasies of escaping castration, analysis works in the gap of the real to effect change.

Of course, critical thinking's engagement with the "impossible" is quite different from that of analysis. Psychoanalytic time—the time of the encounter with the unconscious—is not that of conventional time or historical time. And while the symbolic order is not ahistorical, neither can it be assimilated to what we might call a cultural text. However, psychoanalysis does bring lessons to critical thinking, and those are in the form of *reading* lessons. One example is Louis Althusser's theory of symptomatic reading, a notion inspired by Lacan. Althusser proposes "an account of reading," in Ellen Rooney's words, "as a guilty, dynamic, flawed, open-ended, historically contingent, and wholly political practice of displacements."[30] When Scott seeks to disrupt the consolations afforded by continuous historical narratives, she is working in the Althusserian tradition. Indeed, in her 2007 essay, "History-writing as Critique," Scott argues vigorously that history-writing needs to be uncomfortable, disturbing, destabilizing; in other words, in Althusser's terms, history-writing needs to expose itself as the *reading* that it is.[31]

Scott's appeal for a destabilizing history echoes Foucault's words in the passage that serves as an epigraph to this essay, a passage that Scott cites in her essay, "The Evidence of Experience."[32] For Foucault, unbroken history is a compensatory phenomenon: "Continuous history is the indispensable correlative of the founding function of the subject: the guarantee that everything that has eluded him may be restored to him." Continuous history provides the promise, Foucault writes, "that one day the subject—in the form of historical consciousness—will once again be able to appropriate, to bring back under his sway, all those things that are kept at a distance by difference, and find in them what he calls his abode."[33]

The "difference" Foucault evokes is not that of the decentered subject as theorized by Lacan, but neither is it unrelated. I want to look briefly at the ways Foucault's and Lacan's registers of analyses are connected in order to think more concretely about the critical future of the impossible. The connection between the two lies in the "analytic of finitude" that Foucault elaborates in *The Order of Things,* and the relationships among finitude, "man," and the sciences of man. "Man," a complex formation that appears at the end of the eighteenth century, is the other side of the end of metaphysics, Foucault says, and the beginning of modernity:

> Modernity begins when the human being begins to exist within his organism, inside the shell of his head, inside the armature of his limbs, and in the whole structure of his physiology; when he begins to exist at the center of a labor by whose principles he is governed and whose product eludes him; when he lodges his thought in the folds of a language so much older than himself that he cannot master its significations, even though they have been called back to life by the insistence of his words. But, more fundamentally, our culture crossed the threshold beyond which we recognize our modernity when finitude was conceived in interminable cross-reference with itself.[34]

Man is the figure caught in this cross-referencing, the famous "empirico-transcendental doublet," who is both the condition of possibility for empirical positivities and himself an object of empirical knowledge, that is, a mode of being in which subject and object are mutually constituted. It is on this figure of Man that the sciences of man—the sciences of labor, life, and language—turn:

> It was the involution of labour, life, and language upon themselves that determined the appearance of this new domain of knowledge . . . and it was the appearance of that empirico-transcendental being, of that being whose thought is constantly interwoven with the unthought, of that being always cut off from an origin which is promised to him in the immediacy of the return—it was this appearance that gave the human sciences their particular form. (*OT*, 350)

Man is the being who "by one and the same interplay of reasons, must be a positive domain of knowledge and cannot be an object of science" (*OT*, 366–7). The human sciences are the site where that impossibility can be seen at work, and the space of the impossibility, for Foucault, is the unconscious: "By unveiling the unconscious as their most fundamental object, the human sciences showed that there was always something still to be thought in what had already been thought on a manifest level" (*OT*, 406).[35] In this sense, Foucault sees psychoanalysis as being closest to the critical function that is found in all the human sciences. Psychoanalysis points "not towards that which must be rendered gradually more explicit by the progressive illumination of the implicit, but toward what is there and yet is hidden, towards what exists with the mute solidity of a thing, of a text closed in upon itself, or of a blank space in a visible text, and uses that quality to defend itself" (*OT*, 374). What is involved, Foucault says, is not a simple combination of the interpretation of meaning and of the modes of resistance to it, but rather something more radical. Psychoanalysis "moves towards the moment—by definition inaccessible to any theoretical knowledge of man . . . at which the contents of consciousness articulate themselves, or rather stand gaping, upon man's finitude" (*OT*, 374).

When Luce Irigaray argues that sexual difference is the most crucial question of our time, she does so within a Lacanian context.[36] One might argue as well in a Foucauldian context that the scene of man's finitude finds a powerful staging in the psychoanalytic theory of sexual difference. There the subject is caught both in life and language through the unconscious assumption of the division of sexed reproduction. There is the site of the fold that cannot be known, the effects of which are everywhere to be recognized but nowhere recuperated.

As Foucault sees it, there is a critical struggle in the thinking of modernity that takes the form of a confrontation between historicism and the ana-

lytic of finitude. Historicism is the mode of knowledge limited by the positivity of the knowing subject; it is the domain of "living comprehension (in the
element of the *Lebenswelt*), of interhuman communication (against a background
of social structures), and of hermeneutics . . ." (*OT,* 373). In this mode of
knowledge, the analytic of finitude disappears: "The positive knowledge of
man is limited by the historical positivity of the knowing subject so that the
moment of finitude is dissolved in the play of a relativity from which it cannot
escape" (*OT,* 372). What historicism fails to see is that what makes all these
positivities possible is, indeed, *finitude.* In a Foucauldian register, then, those
who celebrate the demise of poststructuralist theory or psychoanalysis or
feminist theory, or who believe that postmodernism has resolved the challenges of modernity, might be called on to account for finitude. There are
reasons to argue that contemporary thinking has far to go in such an account-
ing, and reasons to insist that the reading of sexual difference, in particular,
has barely begun.

Indeed, sexual difference, finitude, the unconscious, and reading can
all be seen as related theoretical notions. If we bring a psychoanalytic understanding to the *reading* of a text, we see what Jean-Luc Nancy and Philippe
Lacoue-Labarthe call "the double law by which th[e] 'text' offers itself to be
read while constantly derailing or deferring the conditions of its reading."[37]
It is, as they say, "actually impossible to avoid the detour of reading . . .
reading itself becoming that very overflowing of the text read in (or by) the
reading text." And it is in the texts of sexual difference, in their various
modes, that Man, finitude's doublet—the mutually constituted subject and
object—is displayed, disguised, hidden, and brought to crisis. The knot of
sexual difference, the riddle of being and knowing, *is* the knot of the
unconscious.[38]

To return finally to the distinction between gender and sexual difference, the challenge for feminist critical work is not a choice between theories of gender that turn on meaning and theories of sexual difference that
engage the impossible. What is gender, after all, but one of the most telling
texts of sexual difference? If, as Scott says, "gender" has come to be a term
that consolidates the known, then her own work, like the work of Butler
and others, demonstrates that gender's presumption of a ground can never
hold. Is not the rush to *know* gender a particularly anxious move to shut
down the very overflowing of the text that gender opens up? It is, in fact,
the impossibility of sexual difference that guarantees that gender will never
be fully knowable or semantically stable. What matters, finally, for the
feminist critic, is not gender versus sexual difference, but what side of the
real one is on.

NOTES

1. Michel Foucault, *The Archaeology of Knowledge*, trans. A. M. Sheridan Smith (New York: Harper and Row, 1972), 12.

2. Joan W. Scott, *Gender and the Politics of History*, rev. ed. (New York: Columbia University Press, 1999). Hereafter cited as *GPHR* in parenthetical references.

3. United Nations Conference on Human Settlements (Habitat II), "Annex V: Statement on the Commonly Understood Meaning of the Term 'Gender,'" in *Report of the United Nations Conference on Human Settlements (Habitat II)*, Istanbul, Turkey, June 3–14, 1996 (New York: United Nations, Secretary of the Publications Board), 229, http://ods-dds-ny.un.org/doc/UNDOC/GEN/G96/025/00/PDF/G9602500.pdf ?OpenElement (accessed May 11, 2010). Quoted in Scott, *Politics of History*, iv–v. Scott cites an earlier instance of "Annex V."

4. There is no domesticating gender. See Judith Butler, *Undoing Gender* (New York: Routledge, 2004), 183. Butler observes that while for the Vatican "gender" seems to stand for homosexuality, for queer theorists it seems to mean the opposite.

5. Scott cites Foucault, *Archaeology*, 14.

6. Joan W. Scott, *Only Paradoxes to Offer: French Feminists and the Rights of Man* (Cambridge, Mass.: Harvard University Press, 1996). Hereafter cited as *OPO* in parenthetical references.

7. Joan W. Scott, "Gender: A Useful Category of Historical Analysis," *The American Historical Review* 91 (December, 1986): 1053–1075. Hereafter cited as "GUC" in parenthetical references.

8. Scott cites Clifford Geertz, "Blurred Genres," *American Scholar* 49 (1980): 165–179.

9. Scott cites Michel Foucault, *The History of Sexuality, Vol. I, An Introduction* (New York: Vintage, 1980) and *Power/Knowledge: Selected Interviews and Other Writings, 1972–1977* (New York: Pantheon, 1980).

10. Parveen Adams and Jeff Minson, "The 'Subject' of Feminism," in *The Woman in Question: m/f*, ed. Parveen Adams and Elizabeth Cowie (Cambridge, Mass.: MIT Press, 1990), 81–101, quoted in Scott, *Politics of History*, 215. The Adams and Minson text reads as follows: "Legal recognition is a real and circular process. It recognizes the things that correspond to the definitions it constructs."

11. "Sexual difference is probably the issue in our time which could be our 'salvation' if we thought it through." Luce Irigaray, *An Ethics of Sexual Difference*, trans. Carolyn Burke and Gillian C. Gill (Ithaca, N.Y.: Cornell University Press, 1993), 5.

12. Jacques Lacan, *Encore: The Seminar of Jacques Lacan; On Feminine Sexuality, the Limits of Love and Knowledge*, trans. with notes by Bruce Fink (New York: W. W. Norton, 1998). Hereafter cited as *Enc* in parenthetical references.

13. Sigmund Freud, "The Question of a *Weltanschauung*," *The Standard Edition of the Complete Psychological Works of Sigmund Freud*, vol. 22 (1932–1936), trans. James Strachey (London: The Hogarth Press, 1953–1974), 159.

14. It is the former that concerns us here. Lacan's scathing criticisms of ego-centered analysis and any form of psychoanalysis that focuses on integration and adaptation rather than the unconscious are well known.

15. Denis Diderot, *Encyclopédie, ou dictionnaire raisonné des sciences, des arts et des métiers,* vol. 8 (Neufchâtel, 1751–1765), 684–85, quoted in Scott, *Paradoxes,* 5.

16. One must acknowledge that the *Encyclopédie* definition itself strains in its erudite appeal to etymology. Making an argument for uniqueness dependent on etymologically correct individuality produces this oddly ambiguous phrase—translating literally: "Such a subject is an individual according to etymology because one can no longer divide him into new subjects who would have an existence truly [*réellement*] independent of him." It is the "truly" that troubles our assurance.

17. Suzanne Bernard, "Introduction," in *Reading Seminar XX,* ed. Suzanne Bernard and Bruce Fink (Albany: State University of New York Press, 2002), 1.

18. Laplanche finds the term "anaclitic," normally used in French and English translations of *Anlehnung,* to be pseudoscientific and unsatisfactory.

19. Jean Laplanche, *Life and Death in Psychoanalysis,* trans. Jeffrey Mehlman (Baltimore: The Johns Hopkins University Press, 1976), 17. Hereafter cited as *LDP* in parenthetical references.

20. Laplanche is addressing here "aberrations" in psychoanalytic thinking that led to debates as to whether the sexual object is generated ex nihilo (a notion of inconceivable biological idealism, he says), or whether sexuality per se has an object from the beginning, as in the theories of Balint. Laplanche regards the debate as a false and unfortunate impasse.

21. "All of which," Laplanche comments, "have in common the fundamental characteristic of being, in fact or in fantasy, detached or detachable" (*LDP,* 12).

22. As is evident, there are fundamental differences between feminist formulations of sex/gender and the psychoanalytic understanding of those terms. Laplanche offers a psychoanalytic definition: "Above all, it is unacceptable to assign one of the terms to the side of anatomy and the other to the side of psychology. It is proper to designate by *sex* the ensemble of physical or psychical determining factors, behaviors, fantasies, etc. directly connected with the sexual function and sexual pleasure. And by *gender,* the ensemble of physical or psychical determining factors, behaviors, fantasies, etc. connected to the distinction: masculine–feminine. Gender distinctions range from 'secondary' somatic differences all the way to grammatical 'gender,' passing through the habitus, clothing, social role, etc." Jean Laplanche, *Problématiques II: Castrations-Symbolisations* (Paris: Quadrige/PUF, 1998), 33.

23. Less familiar is Lacan's theory of the fundamental fantasies of masculine and feminine subjects. In very schematic terms, the fundamental fantasy of the masculine (obsessive) subject has to do with the relationship between the lost object and the Other, Lacan's term for the otherness the subject cannot take into himself through identification. The masculine subject refuses to acknowledge that the lost object has anything to do with the Other. The feminine subject (a hysteric) has the very different

fantasy that the lost object has to do with the Other's loss. So, while the obsessive refuses to recognize the Other's desire, the hysteric has the fantasy of being the missing object that causes the Other's desire. See Bruce Fink, chapter 8, "Neurosis," in *A Clinical Introduction to Lacanian Analysis: Theory and Technique* (Cambridge, Mass.: Harvard University Press, 1997).

24. Lacan's greater interest in this seminar is with the feminine subject and her drives. In other words, what do women want? For the purposes of this essay, I focus on the masculine subject.

25. Suzanne Bernard, "Tongues of Angels: Feminine Structure and the Other Jouissance," in *Reading Seminar XX,* 177. Hereafter cited as "TA" in parenthetical references.

26. Something that feminists have always known, though not precisely in these terms.

27. The fantasy of masculine universality is one mode of pursuing the real. Another, Lacan says, is the fantasy that the male and the female together form a totality. Lacan's declaration of the "impossibility of the sexual relation" is one of his ways of casting derision on the Platonic myth of the androgyne. The inevitability of heterosexuality is another such fantasy. Heterosexuality, far from being "authorized" by sexual difference, serves to cover over the anxiety sexual difference produces.

28. There is nothing to be gained by viewing the relationship between history and psychoanalysis in terms of causality, by asking which drives the other. Since the two disciplines produce their objects of knowledge in radically different ways, those objects cannot be seen as commensurable. Rather, it is the historical and psychoanalytic *readings* that can inform one another.

29. Tracy McNulty, "Demanding the Impossible: Desire and Social Change," *differences: A Journal of Feminist Cultural Studies* 20 (2009): 4.

30. Ellen Rooney, "Better Read than Dead: Althusser and the Fetish of Ideology," *Yale French Studies* 88 (1995): 185.

31. Joan W. Scott, "History-writing as Critique," in *Manifestos for History,* ed. Keith Jenkins, Sue Morgan, and Alun Munslow (New York: Routledge, 2007), 19–38.

32. Joan W. Scott, "The Evidence of Experience," *Critical Inquiry* 17 (1991): 789–790, footnote 31. The citation is from Foucault, *Archaeology,* 12.

33. Foucault, *Archaeology,* 13.

34. Michel Foucault, *The Order of Things: An Archaeology of the Human Sciences* (New York: Random House, 1994), 318. Hereafter cited as *OT* in parenthetical references.

35. The past tense here is rhetorical. The sentence continues: "by revealing the law of time as the external boundary of the human sciences, History shows that everything that has been thought will be thought again by a thought that does not yet exist."

36. Irigaray argues, with Lacan, that woman does not exist in the symbolic order. Where she differs from him is in her conviction that there must be change in the symbolic order, that change being, in itself, in the register of the impossible.

37. Jean-Luc Nancy and Philippe Lacoue-Labarthe, *The Title of the Letter: A Reading of Lacan,* trans. François Raffoul and David Pettigrew (Albany: State University of New York Press, 1992), 5.

38. See Nancy and Lacoue-Labarthe, *Title of the Letter,* xxix–xxx: "Under the name of the 'unconscious' . . . the question for Lacan is presumably to reassume, in his own way, that constant and more or less hidden movement that takes philosophy to its limits: to the point where the system of the constitution of an object for a subject, the system of representation and certainty, yields to the 'arch-constitution' of 'being,' whose representation can only be made possible, secondarily by existence. Essentially, there is no existence 'beyond' the world of representation, except in the difference-to-itself of presence in general."

Thinking in Time

An Epilogue on Ethics and Politics

WENDY BROWN

This rich, erudite and imaginative collection of essays is testimony to the continued fecundity of gender studies and of Joan Wallach Scott's work. Particularly striking is the authors' reflexivity about gender analysis itself, as they continuously redraw and rethink analytic arcs and categories. This reflexive impulse, of course, is contoured by Scott's own explicit commitment to critique as the intellectual trace of what was once widely promulgated on the left as "permanent revolution"—a practice perhaps better suited to the needs and possibilities of theoretical than political life. Striking as well is the extent to which these papers move toward and are moved by realms, problems, and fields of knowledge exceeding gender analytics. These include but are not limited to new lines of inquiry in phenomenology, new readings of Foucault, considerations of liberalism in postcolonial spaces, revisions of art historiography, projective identificatory readings of classical and contemporary humanisms, the problem of NGOification of gender reforms, questions about the mutability of Islam, concern with democratic imperialism, lurid melodramas of failed agency, the problem of imitative reification, eccentricity in the service of an economy of erotic normalcy, isolation of the aesthetic, reproducibility of the screen, and a dozen different angles on ethics. Especially exciting is the ease with which the papers traverse from gender and sexuality to these other thematics and fields of inquiry, passing through borders once gated and policed by the keepers both of gender studies and of other fields and disciplines, but now merrily unguarded, sometimes even unmarked.

One particularly strong current in this collection is the matter of "thinking in time"—a phrase comprising the importance both of allowing historical time to do the work of dissolving certain seeming impossibilities or contradictions and of apprehending the specificity of problematics constructed by particular historical discourses and times. It is within this current that I want to place two other recurring concerns in the volume—the strong preoccupation with ethics, and the anxiety about the co-optability of gender and sexual equality projects by forces that disingenuously appropriate them for nefarious ends, such as racism or empire. Briefly, I want to reflect on each in turn.

Perhaps the turn to ethics by humanists, especially literary scholars, is only one long overdue. If, as Lionel Trilling famously declared, "Literature is the human activity that takes the fullest and most precise account of variousness, possibility, complexity, and difficulty," what more verdant pasture could there be for the development of ethics?[1] And yet, it is telling that fifteen years ago, at an academic conference on gender, each moment of identity configuration, knowledge production, reading, critique, interpretation, and contestation would have been identified with the "political" rather than the "ethical." Politics carried the same ubiquitous, overreaching, and underspecified place in humanities work now held by ethics. Then, the de-naturalizing, de-essentializing and antifoundational moves of poststructuralism were mobilized to politicize everything: language, subjects, identities, readings, performances, and all social relations. Indeed, the governing assumption of critical work in the humanities was that anything not natural—and nothing was—was political. One might have worried then that such a relentless reach of the political produced at once its dilution and imperialism, and that this reach was perhaps also inattentive to constitutive features of the distinctive scene of powers binding and organizing human collectivities. Now, however, as the political has given way to the ethical in humanities discourse, it is the political that seems to have gone missing. Or, perhaps more precisely, what is often missing is the necessary connection between ethics and politics that thinkers as diverse as Aristotle, Spinoza, and Foucault taught us to sustain.

There is much to be said for concerns with ethics, of course. More than the attitudinal demeanor or set of moral ideals to which it is sometimes reduced today, the ethical is fundamentally centered on action: it signals modes of conduct toward others and hence modes of being with others. Aristotle formulated ethics simply as good men acting in the pursuit of happiness in the rich Greek sense of *eudamonia* (a simplicity that evaporates, of course, as soon as action, goodness, humanness, and happiness are plumbed for their respective complexities). Moreover, given the capacity of ethics to reckon with distinctly human affective and expressive qualities that purely political logics frequently elide, ethics is an important partner to politically animated intellectual work. However, the virtues and importance of the ethical domain do not explain the heightened concern with ethics across the humanities today. Even if, *pace* Nietzsche, developing an ethics and acting ethically seems an incontestable good, we still might ask: What could this concern be holding or holding off, displacing or replacing, symptomizing or reacting to? I want to suggest that its ubiquity in our work today is overdetermined, spurred at the very least from the following sources:

First, we are living in dark times, by which I mean not only that the world is full of troubles and foreboding—the specters of planetary ecological collapse, economic collapse, terror, imperial wars, and more localized violence, along with the quotidian devastations wrought by global capitalism—but that many of our greatest ills have no obvious antidotes or solutions. There are no evident counters or alternatives to the present order of things, and we have ceased to rely upon either progressive or redemptive narratives to carry us forward. "Hope" may be a winning campaign slogan but, as has become painfully apparent, it is neither a program nor a strategy; nor is it, I think, a deeply felt political affect among critical intellectuals. Historically, eras of despair, especially those following on intensely politicized eras, are notable for provoking an ethical turn. The post-Socratic schools of the Stoics, Epicurians, and Cynics represented just such a turn, one that openly entailed a withdrawal from politics. Similarly, Habermas and Foucault could both be understood to have made something of an ethical withdrawal after the ferments of the 1960s and 1970s; Habermas turned to communicative ethics and Foucault to the arts of the self. Max Weber performs this turn in the very narrative structure of "Politics as a Vocation," a darkly pessimistic meditation that nearly paints political action into a corner before resolving into a discussion of a distinctly political ethics.

But dark times are only one condition spurring the turn to ethics. For humanists shaped by postfoundational thought, and from those opposed to (and often ignorant of the substance) of such thought, we have for several decades faced the charge that postfoundational thought is without ethics or even unethical. Feminist poststructuralists who, in their deconstruction of gendered subjects and insistence on the sliding meaning of gender, have been tarred by critics with indifference to the plight of "real women"; antimarriage queers are charged with a lack of sexual ethics; poststructuralists generally are said to be unable to distinguish good and evil and more generally to reject the foundations and limits upon which ethical life depends. Something called postmodernism, it will be recalled, was declared dead after the events of 9/11, events said to clearly enunciate a category of evil that "postmodernism" was imagined to dilute. And when not accused of ethical relativism, we are accused of displacing ethical with political concerns, politicizing everything, seeing power everywhere, attending too little to matters of soul and suffering. We are either hapless relativists or hapless politicizers—all politics, no ethics.

But responding to charges of being unethical or antiethical with a hyper-investment in ethics was not a simple matter of refutation or reclaiming ground. To the contrary, even while drawing on Spinoza, Hegel, Heidegger, or Kant, a poststructuralist ethics would have to be fashioned from elements quite different from those of the past. Thus a third force overdetermining the turn to ethics pertains to the effort to elaborate a responsible and responsive subject after the Kantian one. If the Kantian inheritance of an autonomous moral subject and transcendental notion of the good were an important part of what poststructuralism challenged, then this challenge redounds back to poststructuralism itself. For poststructuralists, the problem was this one: How might a historically constructed, disunified, non-self-consistent and non-self-constituting subject stand ethically for itself as an "I" and respond ethically to another "I"? This difficult question is yet another incitement to the consideration of ethics in a postfoundational vein.

Fourth, responding to the relentlessly moralizing left discourses of the 1980s, many of us yearned not only for a post-Enlightenment ethical subject but for an ethics beyond moralism. This desire also picks up a different thread of the post-Kantian ethics problem, one that aims to adumbrate possibilities for a nonregulatory ethics, and one that also varies from bourgeois morality, libertinism, or solipsism. This is what some have also called a "radical ethics," one that is wary of the political contouring or instrumentalization of ethics for extant normative regimes.

Fifth, the ethical turn would seem to respond to two overextensions of what were important and useful critiques of conventional formulations of power. On the one hand, there are Foucault's critique of power understood as rule, repression, or sovereignty in favor of an appreciation of power's normativizing work and Derrida's insights into normative operations of power in language. However important these critiques, when normativity comes to occupy the entire field of power and comprises the whole vocabulary of power, we appear left with nothing other than a politics of counternormative conduct, that is, with an incisive politics of critique or resistance but one lacking a positive project. A well-known risk here is a paralysis of action itself born from a fear of normativity in any claim or action, precisely the fear that allowed critics of poststructuralism to claim that it had no ethical *yes,* only a *no.* On the other hand, the deep attunement to power in normativity may have carried us to a point of exhaustion with power and its negotiations . . . a certain over-politicization of every field of activity and existence. Perhaps this constitutes the affective delight generated by Lynne Huffer's return to love and lyricism in her rereading of Foucault's theory of sexuality and *Madness and Civilization* in this volume. And, again, perhaps it also signals our own exhaustion from decades of a left moralizing politics: ethics becomes our lyrical form of "awayness" amid relentless demands for political knowingness and positioning.

Here, even Derrida's and Foucault's ethical turns appear a bit different from the earlier framing of rejoinders to charges against them as nihilists or ethical relativists. The ethical turn in each was surely spurred in part by a desire for an awayness from French Marxism. Indeed, perhaps the turn to the ethical paradoxically waged an assertion of freedom from these discourses as well as from a more generally closed political universe. This reminds us again that an ethical turn can be, rather than the supplement to political life it was conceived to be by Aristotle, a reaction to or even a rejection of politics, or at least of a certain kind of politics. Today the loss of common worlds heretofore marked by the nation-state or even by the West might also be occasioning this turn, as would be the fear of the heavy normativity of a "common good" implicated by or in the political.

If the turn to ethics on the part of left humanists is both overdetermined and reactive, occurring at the site of an undertheorized displacement, this does not make it thoroughly wrongheaded. Rather it suggests the need for cognizance of this contextualization and practices of caution and critique, practices themselves in keeping with Joan Scott's argument for permanent revolution in thought, for upturning and calling into question assumed categories of analysis and value. Or, to borrow from one of the most incisive sentences in Scott's "The Evidence of Experience" ("Experience is . . . not the origin of our explanation but that which we want to explain"), we might say: "A turn to ethics is not only the substance of our work but also that which we want to explain."[2] This means doing something particularly difficult, though not impossible, in discussions of ethics, namely grasping the forces of history producing the constellation of our contemporary intellectual concerns and concepts, our projects, our passions. It requires, in short, a deep commitment to thinking in time. Such a contextualization also suggests the importance of reconnecting the concerns with ethics to politics, with express attention to the historically specific powers organizing collective human arrangements and the predicaments and affects generated by these powers.

I want to conclude here by turning from the discussion of ethics to another problem of thinking in historical time, one that also emerged frequently across these papers. This is the problem of discourses of gender equality and sexual democracy mobilized for imperialist or racist projects—Sarkozy's use of them to distinguish progressive French republican values from those of new immigrants, American neoconservatives' use of them to distinguish a Western "us" from an Islamic "them" and their use in building "moderate Muslim networks" and the figure of the "moderate Muslim." In each case, we often stand aghast before the appropriation of feminist and queer terms and aims by conservative projects at odds with our own yet which make use of ours to legitimize racially exclusionary, openly imperialist, or more subtle Western supremacist endeavors. Thus, for example, neoconservatives identified the liberation of Afghan women as a pretext for the United States projects of regime change in the Middle East, just as some Europeans use orthodox Muslim sexual and gender *mores* as a pretext for excluding Muslims from entry or citizenship, and Israel casts gender equality and tolerance of homosexuality as indexical of its status as the "lone democracy" of the Middle East and as the civilized outpost among its barbaric neighbors. Such deployments of gender and sexual equality are neither new nor always calculated instrumentalizations. The putatively freer and more egalitarian status of Western women is an old theme in colonial discourse about nativism and the orient. It gains contemporary standing in Western feminisms ranging from those of Susan Okin to Catharine MacKinnon to Laura Bush; it is right under the surface of much international human rights discourse and at the heart of many well-intended NGOs working on behalf of women in the global South.

Here we are reminded of an especially important, albeit frustrating, political feature of thinking and living in time: there is no party monopoly on any concept, value, or even ideal, let alone on any tactic or strategy, all of which live in time and are activated in historically specific circuits of power that condition their content and ramifications. Co-optation is not the right word for this; it fails to capture the extent to which, by virtue of temporally shifting discourses and contexts, what was at one point a critical, progressive, or even revolutionary cause can, over time, be transposed into an order of domination or a strategy of exploitation. Hard-won rights or radical bids for tolerance can become regulatory regimes of biopower, the extraordinary achievement of democracy can transmute into free market savagery and liberal empire, revolutionary slogans can become institutionalized nodes of despotism or bourgeois privilege. Contemporary elder inhabitants of former Soviet republics know well how policies of state feminism operated to double the duties of women rather than emancipate them—gender equality as an instrument of state regulation and repression is not news to them. Similarly the language of civil rights and universal equality was easily deployed in the 1990s to dismantle affirmative action for racial minorities and women. The language of "revolutionary" was taken up by neoconservatives to hail a new form of

American governance, and the language of "sexual difference" has recently emerged in screeds opposing gay marriage in the United States, as it has also been used to oppose same-sex parenting in France. On the other side, it would seem that the ascendency of the picture-perfect Obama family has successfully shorn the American right of its monopoly on "family values," that economic "nationalization" and state ownership have been fully detached from socialism or even public welfare, and that "centrism" and "moderation" have become a liberal retort to the right.

Our ability to navigate such appropriations and inversions depends upon political perspicacity and artful strategies—neither moral outrage nor a radical ethics are likely to be much help. It depends in particular on the recognition that political life features fantastic temporal shifts and that, aided by technology and the media, its tempo is ever quickening. Thus while enduring commitments have a place in politics, these cannot be codified in unified and unchanging discourses, nor inflected by a consistent context. Here, one only need consider the historically shifting fates of "republicanism" over the course of modernity or consider today the disorientation for liberalism produced today by the coinage of "neoliberalism" to describe the saturation of every human sphere with entrepreneurial rationality. So of course feminism will be taken up for purposes that will gall, and "gender" can become a reactionary category of analysis (and politics!), but these turns of events are not well met by howling indignation or reproach, two strikingly nonpolitical responses. Rather, they are occasions to apprentice ourselves to Joan W. Scott's incisive appreciation of paradoxical political discourse and to enlist her deep commitment to critique, to "thinking in time," to "permanent revolution," and to "speaking back . . . to instate the new and to open a different future."[3]

NOTES

1. Lionel Trilling, *The Liberal Imagination: Essays on Literature and Society* (New York: Viking Press, 1950), xv.

2. Joan W. Scott, "Experience," *Feminists Theorize the Political,* ed. Judith Butler and Joan W. Scott (New York: Routledge, 1992), 38.

3. Judith Butler, in this volume, p. 18.

CONTRIBUTORS

Janis Bergman-Carton is Associate Professor of Art History at Southern Methodist University and author of *The Woman of Ideas in French Art, 1830–1848*.

Wendy Brown is the Heller Professor of Political Science at the University of California, Berkeley. She is the author of *Manhood and Politics: A Feminist Reading in Political Theory; States of Injury: Power and Freedom in Late Modernity; Politics Out of History; Edgework: Critical Essays in Knowledge and Politics; Regulating Aversion: Tolerance in the Age of Identity and Empire;* and *Walled States, Waning Sovereignty*.

Judith Butler is the Maxine Elliot Professor in the Departments of Rhetoric and Comparative Literature and the Co-director of the Program of Critical Theory at the University of California, Berkeley. She is the author of *Gender Trouble: Feminism and the Subversion of Identity; Bodies That Matter: On the Discursive Limits of "Sex"; The Psychic Life of Power: Theories of Subjection; Excitable Speech; Undoing Gender;* (with Gayatri Spivak) *Who Sings the Nation-State?: Language, Politics, Belonging; Frames of War: When Is Life Grievable?;* and (with Talal Asad, Wendy Brown, and Saba Mahmood) *Is Critique Secular?*.

Miguel A. Cabrera is Professor of Modern History at the University of La Laguna, Spain, and is the author of *Historia, lenguaje y teoría de la sociedad* (History, language and theory of society) and *Postsocial History: An Introduction*.

Mary Ann Doane is the George Hazard Crooker Professor of Modern Culture and Media at Brown University. She is the author of *The Desire to Desire: The Woman's Film of the 1940s* (IUP, 1987); *Femmes Fatales: Feminism, Film Theory, Psychoanalysis,* and *The Emergence of Cinematic Time: Modernity, Contingency, the Archive*.

Éric Fassin is Professor agrégé in the Department of Social Sciences at École normale supérieure in Paris and a researcher at IRIS (Institut de recherche interdisciplinaire sur les enjeux sociaux, CNRS / EHESS). He is the author, with Clarisse Fabre, of *Liberté, égalité, sexualités: Actualité politique des questions sexuelles* (Liberty, equality, sexualities: the current politicization of sexual issues); *L'inversion de la question homosexuelle* (The inversion of the homosexual question); *Le sexe politique* (The political sex); and, with Didier Fassin, *De la question sociale à la question raciale?* (From the social question to the racial question?).

Lynne Huffer is Professor of Women's Studies at Emory University and author of *Another Colette: The Question of Gendered Writing; Maternal Pasts, Feminist Futures: Nostalgia and the Question of Difference;* and *Mad for Foucault: Rethinking the Foundations of Queer Theory.*

Mary Louise Roberts is Professor of History at the University of Wisconsin–Madison and is the author of *Civilization without Sexes: Reconstructing Gender in Post-War France, 1918–1928* and *Disruptive Acts: The New Woman in Fin-de-Siècle France.*

Gayle Salamon is Assistant Professor of English at Princeton and the author of *Assuming a Body: Transgender and Rhetorics of Materiality.*

Elora Shehabuddin is Associate Professor of Humanities and Political Science at Rice University, and is the author of *Reshaping the Holy: Development, Democracy, and Muslim Women in Bangladesh.*

Mary D. Sheriff is the W.R. Kenan, Jr. Distinguished Professor of Art History at the University of North Carolina at Chapel Hill. She is the author of *The Exceptional Woman: Elisabeth Vigée-Lebrun and the Cultural Politics of Art* and *Moved by Love: Inspired Artists and Deviant Women in Eighteenth-Century France.*

Mrinalini Sinha, the Alice Freeman Palmer Professor of History at the University of Michigan, is the author of *Specters of Mother India: The Global Restructuring of an Empire* and *Colonial Masculinity: The "Manly" Englishman and the "Effeminate Bengali" in the Later Nineteenth Century.*

Elizabeth Weed is Director of the Pembroke Center for Teaching and Research on Women and Professor of Modern Culture and Media at Brown University. She is the editor of *Coming to Terms: Feminism/Theory/Politics;* with Naomi Schor, *The Essential Difference* (IUP, 1994); *Feminism Meets Queer Theory* (IUP, 1997); and is the founding co-editor of *differences: A Journal of Feminist Cultural Studies.*

INDEX

Gogh, Theo (Theodoor) van, 127, 153
Goldberg, Harvey, 22
Gombrich, E. H., 222
Gorin, Pierre, 220, *221,* 228n29
Gouges, Olympes de, 22, 24, 293–295
Government of India Act. *See under* India
Grainger, Judith, 57
Grandville, J. J., 190, *191,* 192
Great Depression, the, 85
Greece, 127, 263, 279; Greek language, 58, 297, 313
Grosz, Elizabeth, 163

Habermas, Jurgen, 314
Halley, Janet, 255–259, 261–262, 274, 280–281, 282n1; *Split Decisions,* 255–258, 280–281
Hamlet; the play, 50, 155; the role, 60
Hegel, G. F., 16, 22, 315
hegemony, 18, 85
Heidegger, Martin, 214, 215, 297, 315
Heloise, *172,* 174–175
Hewitt, Andrew, 209–210
Hinduism, 81, 85–87, 89, 91, 93–94, 100n33; Hindu-Muslim riots, 86; Hindu women, 89, 105, 108, 227n19
historical reproduction, 21
historiography, 6, 31, 80; new historiography, 6, 31–32
history: discipline of, 80; of feminism, 40, 47, 92; of the Left, 26, 165, 312; the problem of, 11; social, 6, 11, 15–16, 18, 31–32, 34, 291; subject of, 12
homosexuality, 36–39, 42, 67, 147, 153, 268–279, 308n4, 317; biological basis of, 252n8; category of unreason, 259, 261; a lyricism of, 266, 278; Zacarias Moussaoui on, 154–156
Horowitz, David, 112; David Horowitz Freedom Center, 112, 113
Horowitz Academic Bill of Rights, 25, 27
Hossain, Rokeya, 107–110
Howard, John, 127
human rights, 44, 115, 298, 317
humanism, 124, 222, 261
Husain, Sarah, 129

Hussein, Saddam, 116
Huyssen, Andreas, 211

identity, 6, 7, 19, 31–34, 41–47, 58–59, 61, 65, 83–96; class, 34; collective, 87, 90; feminist, 44, 47, 49n20; gender, 61, 88, 90; homosexual, 271, 275; national, 151; politics, 271; sexual, 168, 268; theory of identity formation, 41, 168; women's, 38–40, 42–45, 53, 83–96
imaginary, the, 301; modern, 194; neoconservative, 104; topography, 236
immigration, 4, 110, 150–151, 154
imperialism, 4, 80, 103, 117, 155–156, 222, 312–313
inclusion, 2, 16, 18, 19, 299
India, 6, 43, 80–96, 105–108, 123–124; All-India Women's Conference, 89, 92; caste system, 81–82, 86–87, 93–94; Government of India Act, 91, 94; Non-Cooperation movement, 86, 89; Self-Respect Movement, 89
individualism, 6, 16, 45, 55–56, 94
inequality, 12, 144
intelligibility, 7, 14, 18, 32, 51, 58–59, 68, 90, 258, 267
International Alliance of Women for Suffrage and Equal Citizenship (IAW), 110
Iran, 113
Iraq, 104, 111, 113, 116
Irigaray, Luce, 163, 238, 252n5, 281, 296, 306, 310n36
"Is Gender a Useful Category of Historical Analysis?" (unpublished title, Scott), 1
Islam, 6, 103–106, 109–150, 152, 155, 312, 317; Islamic Reformation, 103; Islamic veil, 145, 148–149, 152; *The Violent Oppression of Women in Islam,* 113, 117
Islamo-Fascism Awareness Week (IFAW), 112–113
Israel, 26, 115, 117–120, 125–126, 132, 317

Jackson, Michael, 58
Jagose, Annamarie, 268, 275

power, 2–3, 13–14, 20, 67, 81, 84, 91, 105, 170, 257–258, 263, 267, 280, 282, 289, 292–293, 315–317; and feminism, 255–256; generative power of sexuality, 235–236; and knowledge, 39, 257; operations of, 8, 315; phallic, 302; signifying, 3–4; struggle, 190; of truth, 170; will to, 280

Prakash, Gyan, 82

prodigal theory, 255–256. *See also* Halley, Janet

production: of art, 166–167, 193, 195, 203n7, 204n8; of difference, 21; of gender, 3, 207, 251n3; knowledge production, 2–4, 25, 27, 32, 35, 37, 39, 43, 207, 212, 222, 288, 293, 303, 306, 313; of meanings, 32, 290; of modernity, 219; of morality, 263, 276; of non-normative sexuality, 251n3, 259, 263; of power, 3; of rational agents, 290; relations of, 32, 33, 47; of sexual difference, 21; of social life 4, 20–21, 23

projection: of history of cinema, 220; of images, 212, 213, 214–215, 217, 219, 222; of a memory, 212

prosopagnosia, 225–226

psychoanalysis, 149, 172, 220, 236, 239, 242; and Foucault, 258–259, 261–262, 275; and sexual difference, 7, 163, 206, 290, 296–307, 310n27

purdah, 108, 227n19

queer theory, 7, 256–261, 268–269, 278

race, 125, 151–152, 157, 299; and art history, 161–162, 165, 182; as category of identification, 41–42, 47, 58

racialization, 150–151, 156

Radical History Review, 27

radicalism, 22, 25, 26, 209

Ranft, Richard, 187, *188,* 192–195, 197, 204n8

rationalism, 262, 275–276, 280, 282

Ray, Bharati, 108

Ray, Man, 202n2, 214, *215,* 216, *216,* 219

recognition, 7, 207–208, 212, 224, 226, 236; facial, 217, 220, 225, 227n37; of

Islamic culture, 120, 132; legal, 308n10; misrecognition, 215, 243; of women, 87, 91, 95–96

Renaissance, the, 127, 266, 272, 274, 276, 278, 279

revolution, 5, 16, 22–24, 27, 45, 85, 294, 298, 312, 316–318; Bolshevik, 85; French, 293; Iranian, 111; permanent, *see under* Scott, Joan W.; sexual, 153

Revolutionary Association of Women of Afghanistan (RAWA), 121–122

rhetoric, 36, 47, 170, 267, 271, 281; of gender, 7, 88–90, 125, 136n36, 293; paradoxical, 23; political, 22, 86, 88–90, 95, 125, 136n36, 150–151; revolutionary, 297, 298; of sexual democracy, 151, 153–156

Riley, Denise, 88

Rokeya, Begum, 108

Romantics, the, 64

Rome Conference of 1923, 109–110

Rosenburg, Rosalind, 15. *See also* equality vs. difference debate

Rosenthal, Lisa, 163

Roy, Arundhati, 116

Royal, Ségolène, 145

Rubin, Gayle, 257, 261

Rushdie, Salman, 123, 127, 130

Said, Edward, 27, 58, 111, 115; *Orientalism,* 74n38, 111, 115

Sand, George, 55; *Journal de ma vie,* 55

Sappho, 175

Sarcey, Francisque, 50

Sarda Act, 86–91, 95, 96, 100n32

Sarkar, Tanika, 84

Sarkozy, Nicolas, 150–151, 156, 316

Saslow, James, 60, 67

sati (satidaha), 89,105

Schiebinger, Londa, 175

Scott, Joan W., 1–8, 11–27, 31–48, 95, 104, 162, 188, 206–207, 264–266, 287–299, 303–305, 307, 312, 316, 318; permanent revolution, 5, 27, 312, 316, 318; the Sears case, 12, 14, 19, 22–23, 293; thinking in time, 8, 312, 316, 318

Scott, Joan W., works of: "Academic Freedom as an Ethical Practice," 25; "Deconstructing Equality vs. Difference: or, the Uses of Post-Structuralist Theory for Feminism," 32–34; "The Evidence of Experience," 37–39, 42, 48, 264–266, 305, 316; "Fantasy Echo: History and the Construction of Identity," 5, 40–42, 49n20; "Feminist versus Trade Unionists in the Printing Trades: Guerre des sexes ou lutte de classe?," 188; "Gender: A Useful Category of Historical Analysis," 1, 5, 43, 104, 290–293, 303; *Gender and the Politics of History* (1988), 12, 15, 16, 18, 20, 35–36, 39, 41, 43, 287–291, 293; *Gender and the Politics of History* (rev. ed., 1999), 15–16, 44, 104, 206, 287, 289, 291; *The Glassworkers of Carmaux,* 11, 12, 16; "History-writing as Critique," 304–305; "Introduction," *Feminism and History,* 40–41, 43; "Is Gender a Useful Category of Historical Analysis?" (unpublished title), 1; "On Language, Gender, and Working-Class History," 32–34; *Only Paradoxes to Offer,* 12, 15, 22–23, 45–47, 95, 100n44, 290, 293–299, 301, 303; *Parité!: Sexual Equality and the Crisis of French Universalism,* 12, 22, 24; *The Politics of the Veil,* 15; "A Reply to Criticism," 34–36, 39; review of *Heroes of Their Own Lives* (Linda Gordon), 46–47; "Some More Reflections on Gender and Politics," 289; "A Statistical Representation of Work: *La Statistique de l'industrie à Paris, 1847–1848,*" 35; "'The Tip of the Volcano'," 48; "Vive la différence!," 157n2
Sears case, the. *See under* Scott, Joan W.
Sedgwick, Eve, 257
Seigel, Jerrold, 56
Self-Respect Movement. *See under* India
Servan-Schreiber, Claude 24
sex-positivity, 250, 280–281
sexual difference, 5–6, 17–20, 43–46, 144, 156, 180, 211, 248, 308n11, 318; and ambiguity, 234; and feminism, 11–15, 21–23, 81, 92, 95, 162–163, 206–207,

295–296; and Hollywood, 209; and identity, 41, 238; as psychoanalytic notion, 7, 163, 206, 290, 296, 298–307, 310n27; as transcendent, 148–149; as viewed by the Vatican, 147–148. *See also* equality vs. difference debate
sexual politics, 150, 153
Shaarawi, Huda, 108–110
Skinner, Cornelia Otis, 62, 65
slavery, 4
"Some More Reflections on Gender and Politics" (Scott), 289
Sommers, Christina Hoff, 114, 147
South Asia, 81, 125
sovereignty, 89, 290, 315
Soviet Bloc, 111, 112, 133
Spargo, Tamsin, 268
speech, 14, 15, 18, 23–26; hate speech, 174; speech acts, 24
Spencer, Robert, 113
spheres (variety of): domestic sphere 84; economic sphere 33; political sphere 33, 82, 84, 91–93; private sphere 81, 152; public sphere, 4, 45, 152, 210; social sphere 82
Spinoza, Baruch, 313, 315
Spivak, Gayatri, 117, 138n67, 264
St. Simonianism, 59
Staël, Germaine de, 55
Stanton, Theodore, 60, 72n2
state, the, 4, 82–84, 86–88, 146, 256, 295
Stedman Jones, Gareth, 33
Stillwell, Cinnamon, 114, 116
Sultan, Wafa, 118
Surrealism, 203n2, 210, 217
symbolic order, 149, 301–302, 304, 310n36

Taliban, the, 111, 113, 115–116, 121
technology, 318; of mechanical reproduction, 220, 223; print, 188, 224; representational, 211, 214–215
Teena, Brandon, 245, 253n16
temporality, 14, 23, 163, 203, 213, 234, 238–239, 274, 317–318; temporal subjects, 40–41
therianthropy, 59, 75n42